S0-BDG-978

GOVERNMENT OF THE ATOM

The Integration of Powers

A STUDY SPONSORED BY THE NATIONAL LAW CENTER

OF THE GEORGE WASHINGTON UNIVERSITY

PUBLISHED SIMULTANEOUSLY IN GREAT BRITAIN

BY PRENTICE-HALL INTERNATIONAL, LONDON

GOVERNMENT OF THE ATOM

The Integration of Powers

HAROLD P. GREEN AND ALAN ROSENTHAL

ATHERTON PRESS

70 FIFTH AVENUE, NEW YORK 1963

A DIVISION OF PRENTICE-HALL, INC.

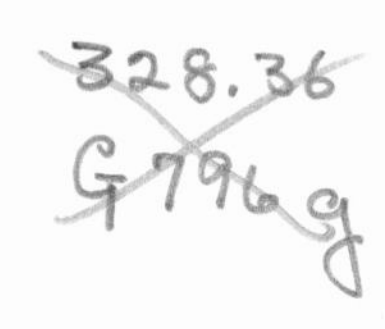

GOVERNMENT OF THE ATOM
The Integration of Powers

Harold P. Green and Alan Rosenthal

Published simultaneously in Great Britain by
Prentice-Hall International, Inc.
28 Welbeck Street, London W.1, England

Atherton Press, A Division of Prentice-Hall, Inc.
70 Fifth Avenue, New York 11, New York

Library of Congress Catalog Card Number 63-8916
Printed in the United States of America 36163

THE ATHERTON PRESS POLITICAL SCIENCE SERIES

General Editor for American Government and Politics

CORNELIUS P. COTTER

Assistant Staff Director
United States Commission on Civil Rights

Preface

Contemporary politics are marked by the limited ability of legislative institutions to formulate national policies. The United States Congress, locus of governmental power in the late nineteenth century, has, particularly in the fields of foreign and defense affairs, become almost entirely dependent on the Executive for development of national policy.

Even the use of standing committees, possessing considerable authority within their respective areas of jurisdiction, has failed to redress the balance of creative power that has swung to the Executive. With few exceptions, the committees of the House and Senate have only mirrored the disabilities of their parent chambers. They, too, react rather than initiate.

Perhaps the ascendancy of the Executive is necessary in a complex and rapidly changing world. But it may not be inevitable. In the field of atomic energy, Congress, or at least its surrogate committee, acts with distinctive vigor and notable success as watchdog, gadfly, partner, and policymaker.

The Joint Committee on Atomic Energy, since its creation in 1946, has played an unusually influential role in the conduct of the nation's atomic enterprise. Although organically a part of the legislature, the Joint Committee's behavior uniquely resembles that of the higher echelons of the executive branch. In this respect, the JCAE represents a significant innovation in a governmental system of separated powers.

Members of the Committee itself, other congressmen, and officials of the executive branch have long recognized the JCAE as an extraordinary Congressional institution. Despite its unique structure as the only joint committee with legislative powers, its broad statutory authority, and its unprecedented role in the formulation of national policy, the Committee has largely escaped the attention of scholars. Those who have observed the JCAE, seemingly in awe of its accomplishments, have been content to describe its achievements rather than analyze the exercise of its power.

Our major interest is the use of power as exhibited by the Joint Committee in its relations with the executive branch and Congress as a whole. One purpose of this study is to examine the sources of the Committee's authority and to describe its particular techniques as legislator and policy-maker. Another is to ascertain the qualities which set the JCAE apart as an unusual governmental mechanism. Finally, we attempt to assess the significance of these dynamic components from the standpoint of accepted concepts of American government.

Although the JCAE has, beyond question, contributed greatly to the present status of the national atomic-energy program, we have not undertaken to evaluate its contribution. Of concern here are the mechanics of government, rather than its results.

Government of the Atom explores the role of a specific committee, but we hope that it also illuminates problems of broader scope. Issues involving executive-legislative relationships and the performance of Congressional committees deserve further attention in an age that promises increasing departures from tradition. The problem of maintaining an appropriate degree of Congressional influence on national policies, especially those at the core of national security, promises to become more pressing, and the JCAE model will continue to be advocated for adoption in other areas of government.

With much information, even that pertaining to the early years, not yet declassified or otherwise unobtainable, any study must be incomplete. We believe, however, that the extensive public record, supplemented by interviews with many present and former officials of the executive branch and members and staff of the Committee, has provided an adequate basis for our evaluations and conclusions.

. . . .

This book was written as part of a one-year study of the JCAE financed by a generous grant from the Edgar Stern Family Fund to the National Law Center of The George Washington University. Throughout, we have had the benefit of the wholehearted cooperation of the university and, in particular, the support of Charles G. Nutting, dean of its National Law Center; Louis H. Mayo, dean of the Graduate School of Public Law; and B.D. Van Evera, dean for Sponsored Research. We are also indebted to Prof. J. Forrester Davison, who served as a consultant on Congressional authorization procedures.

We were also greatly assisted by an able staff. Richard A. Schwarz and Daniel Lewin had chief responsibility for Chapter VII. Mr. Lewin was also responsible for much of the research underlying the study. Laurence Pearl, who encapsulated the entire history of the JCAE in Chapter I, lent considerable perspective to the over-all analysis. Daniel Sachs functioned principally as editor and watchdog over form and style. Finally, Mrs. Penelope Wright proved indispensable in research, editing, and typing.

Despite this valuable assistance, the responsibility for the statements and conclusions of the book remains, of course, solely that of the authors. An earlier version of this study was distributed late in 1961 to government officials and scholars, particularly those with a special interest in the subject. As a result, we have profited from many constructive suggestions offered by persons too numerous to mention. Some errors have been called to our attention and, we hope, eliminated. We are grateful for this interest, which has enabled us to make considerable improvements in the final product.

Harold P. Green
Alan Rosenthal

January 1963

Contents

Fig. A
Senate Members of
The JCAE by Years

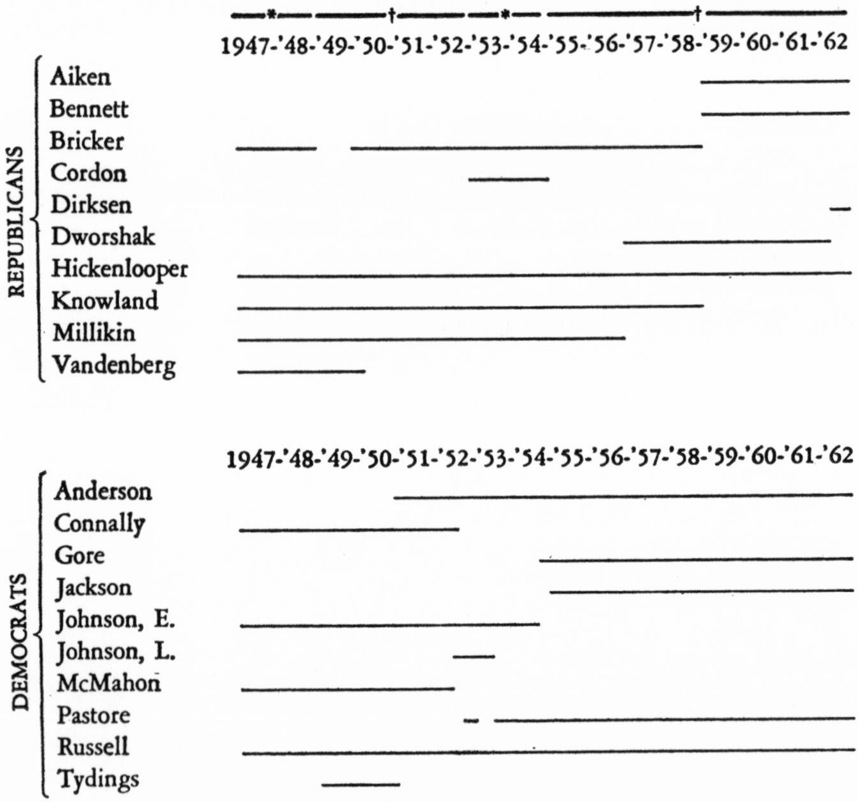

1947-'48-'49-'50-'51-'52-'53-'54-'55-'56-'57-'58-'59-'60-'61-'62

REPUBLICANS

Aiken
Bennett
Bricker
Cordon
Dirksen
Dworshak
Hickenlooper
Knowland
Millikin
Vandenberg

1947-'48-'49-'50-'51-'52-'53-'54-'55-'56-'57-'58-'59-'60-'61-'62

DEMOCRATS

Anderson
Connally
Gore
Jackson
Johnson, E.
Johnson, L.
McMahon
Pastore
Russell
Tydings

*=*Republican majority;* †=*Democratic majority*

Total membership—9

Source: Adapted from Morgan Thomas, *Atomic Energy and Congress* (Ann Arbor: The University of Michigan Press, 1956), pp. 246-247.

Fig. B
House Members of The JCAE by Years

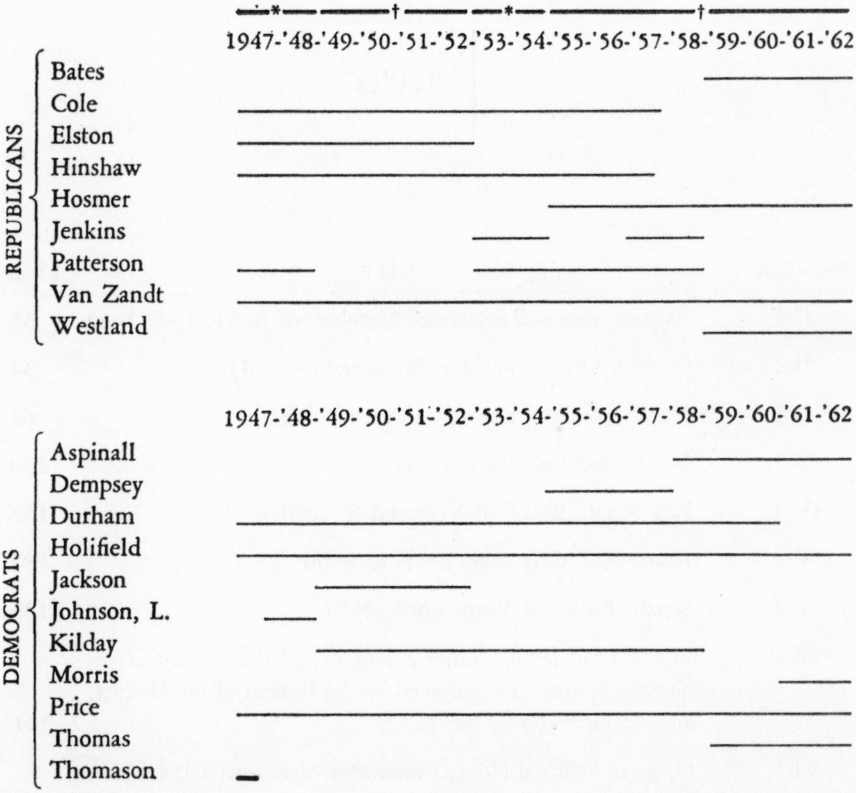

*   †   *   †

1947-'48-'49-'50-'51-'52-'53-'54-'55-'56-'57-'58-'59-'60-'61-'62

REPUBLICANS

Bates
Cole
Elston
Hinshaw
Hosmer
Jenkins
Patterson
Van Zandt
Westland

1947-'48-'49-'50-'51-'52-'53-'54-'55-'56-'57-'58-'59-'60-'61-'62

DEMOCRATS

Aspinall
Dempsey
Durham
Holifield
Jackson
Johnson, L.
Kilday
Morris
Price
Thomas
Thomason

***=Republican majority; †=Democratic majority**

Total membership—9

Source: Adapted from Morgan Thomas, *Atomic Energy and Congress* (Ann Arbor: The University of Michigan Press, 1956), pp. 246-247.

Tables

Figures "A" and "B," showing JCAE membership by years, are located on pages *xiv-xv*.

Short-Title Index

FULL TITLE	SHORT TITLE
Joint Committee on Atomic Energy (JCAE) Hearings	
Hearings before the JCAE, *Development, Growth, and State of the Atomic Energy Industry,* 84th Cong., 1st Sess. (1955)	*"Sec. 202" Hearings* (1955)
Hearings before the JCAE, *Development, Growth, and State of the Atomic Energy Industry,* 84th Cong., 2d Sess. (1956)	*"Sec. 202" Hearings* (1956)
Hearings before the JCAE, *Development, Growth, and State of the Atomic Energy Industry,* 85th Cong., 1st Sess. (1957)	*"Sec. 202" Hearings* (1957)
Hearings before the JCAE, *Development, Growth, and State of the Atomic Energy Industry,* 85th Cong., 2d Sess. (1958)	*"Sec. 202" Hearings* (1958)
Hearings before the JCAE, *Development, Growth, and State of the Atomic Energy Industry,* 86th Cong., 1st Sess. (1959)	*"Sec. 202" Hearings* (1959)
Hearings before the JCAE, *Development, Growth, and State of the Atomic Energy Industry,* 86th Cong., 2d Sess. (1960)	*"Sec. 202" Hearings* (1960)

Hearings before the JCAE, *Development, Growth, and State of the Atomic Energy Industry,* 87th Cong., 1st Sess. (1961)	*"Sec. 202" Hearings* (1961)
Hearings before the Subcommittee on Authorizing Legislation of the JCAE, *Authorizing Legislation,* 84th Cong., 1st Sess. (1955)	*FY 1956 Authorization Hearings* (1955)
Hearings before the Subcommittee on Legislation of the JCAE, *Authorizing Legislation,* 84th Cong., 2d Sess. (1956)	*FY 1957 Authorization Hearings* (1956)
Hearings before the Subcommittee on Legislation of the JCAE, *Authorizing Legislation for AEC's Fiscal Year 1958 Construction Budget,* 85th Cong., 1st Sess. (1957)	*FY 1958 Authorization Hearings* (1957)
Hearings before the Subcommittee on Legislation of the JCAE, *AEC Authorizing Legislation,* 85th Cong., 2d Sess. (1958)	*FY 1959 Authorization Hearings* (1958)
Hearings before the Subcommittee on Legislation of the JCAE, *AEC Authorizing Legislation Fiscal Year 1960,* 86th Cong., 1st Sess. (1959)	*FY 1960 Authorization Hearings* (1959)
Hearings before the Subcommittee on Legislation of the JCAE, *AEC Authorizing Legislation Fiscal Year 1961,* 86th Cong., 2d Sess. (1960)	*FY 1961 Authorization Hearings* (1960)
Hearings before the Subcommittee on Legislation of the JCAE, *AEC Authorizing Legislation Fiscal Year 1962,* 87th Cong., 1st Sess. (1961)	*FY 1962 Authorization Hearings* (1961)
Hearings before the Senate Section of the JCAE, *Confirmation of the Atomic Energy Commission and the General Manager,* 80th Cong., 1st Sess. (1947)	*AEC Confirmation Hearings* (1947)
Hearings before the JCAE, *Labor Policy in Atomic Energy Plants,* 80th Cong., 2d Sess. (1948)	*Labor Policy Hearings* (1948)
Hearings before the JCAE, *Atomic Energy Report to Congress,* 81st Cong., 1st Sess. (1949)	*Atomic Energy Report to Congress Hearings* (1949)
Hearings before a Special Subcommittee of the JCAE, *Natural Gas Pipe Line at Oak Ridge,* 81st Cong., 1st Sess. (1949)	*Natural Gas Pipe Line Hearings* (1949)

Hearings before the JCAE, *Civil Defense Against Atomic Attack,* 81st Cong., 2d Sess. (1950)	*Civil Defense Hearings* (1950)
Hearings before the JCAE, *Community Policy,* Parts 1 and 2, 81st Cong., 2d Sess. (1950)	*Community Policy Hearings,* 2 parts (1950)
Hearings before the JCAE, *Amending the Atomic Energy Act,* 82d Cong., 2d Sess. (1952)	*Amending the Atomic Energy Act Hearings* (1952)
Hearings before the JCAE, *Atomic Power Development and Private Enterprise,* 83rd Cong., 1st Sess. (1953)	*Atomic Power Development Hearings* (1953)
Hearings before the JCAE, *Legislation Concerning Long-Term Utility Contracts,* 83rd Cong., 1st Sess. (1953)	*Long-Term Utility Contracts Hearings* (1953)
Hearings before the JCAE, *Accelerating the Civilian Reactor Program,* 84th Cong., 2d Sess. (1956)	*"Gore-Holifield" Civilian Power Hearings,* pt. 1 (1956)
Hearings before the JCAE, *Civilian Atomic Power Acceleration Program,* 84th Cong., 2d Sess. (1956)	*"Gore-Holifield" Civilian Power Hearings,* pt. 2 (1956)
Hearings before the JCAE, *Governmental Indemnity and Reactor Safety,* 84th Cong., 2d Sess. (1956)	*Indemnity Hearings* (1956)
Hearings before the Subcommittee on Legislation of the JCAE, *Congressional Review of the Atomic Power Program,* 85th Cong., 1st Sess. (1957)	*Congressional Review Hearings* (1957)
Hearings before the Subcommittee on Legislation of the JCAE, *AEC Omnibus Bill,* 85th Cong., 2d Sess. (1958)	*AEC Omnibus Bill Hearings* (1958)
Hearings before the Subcommittee on Agreements for Cooperation of the JCAE, *Amending the Atomic Energy Act of 1954—Exchange of Military Information and Material with Allies,* 85th Cong., 2d Sess. (1958)	*Military Exchange Hearings* (1958)
Hearings before a Subcommittee of the JCAE, *Outer Space Propulsion by Nuclear Energy,* 85th Cong., 2d Sess. (1958)	*Outer Space Propulsion Hearings* (1958)
Hearings before the JCAE, *Proposed Euratom Agreements,* 85th Cong., 2d Sess. (1958)	*Proposed Euratom Agreements Hearings* (1958)

Hearings before the JCAE, *Proposals Under Power Demonstration Program,* 85th Cong., 2d Sess. (1958)	*PDRP Propōsal Hearings* (1958)
Hearings before the Subcommittee on Research and Development of the JCAE, *Aircraft Nuclear Propulsion Program,* 86th Cong., 1st Sess. (1959)	*ANP Hearings* (1959)
Hearings before the JCAE, *Federal-State Relationships in the Atomic Energy Field,* 86th Cong., 1st Sess. (1959)	*Federal-State Hearings* (1959)
Hearings before the Subcommittee on Legislation of the JCAE, *Patents,* 86th Cong., 1st Sess. (1959)	*Patent Hearings* (1959)
Hearings before the JCAE, *Review of Naval Reactor Program,* 85th Cong., 1st Sess. (1959)	*Review of Naval Reactor Program Hearings* (1959)
Hearings before the Special Subcommittee on Radiation and the Subcommittee on Research and Development of the JCAE, *Technical Aspects of Detection and Inspection Controls of a Nuclear Weapons Test Ban,* 86th Cong., 2d Sess. (1960)	*Test Ban Hearings* (1960)
Hearings before the JCAE, *Utility Proposal for Powerplant Addition to Hanford New Production Reactor,* 87th Cong., 2d Sess. (1962)	*Utility Proposal for Hanford Powerplant Hearings* (1962)

Joint Committee on Atomic Energy Prints

Staff of the JCAE, *Atomic Power and Private Enterprise,* 82d Cong., 2d Sess. (1952)	*Staff Study of Atomic Power and Private Enterprise* (1952)
Staff of the JCAE, *Five-Year Power Reactor Program,* 83rd Cong., 2d Sess. (1954)	*Staff Study of Five-Year Power Reactor Program* (1954)
JCAE Committee Print, *Current Statement of the Atomic Energy Commission on the Five-Year Reactor Development Program,* 84th Cong., 1st Sess. (1955)	*Statement of AEC on Five-Year Reactor Program* (1955)
Staff of the JCAE, *A Study of AEC Procedures and Organization in the Licensing of Reactor Facilities,* 85th Cong., 1st Sess. (1957)	*Staff Study of AEC Procedures and Organization in Licensing* (1957)
Staff of the JCAE, *Proposed Expanded Civilian Nuclear Power Program,* 85th Cong., 2d Sess. (1958)	*Staff Study on Expanded Civilian Power Program* (1958)

Staff of the JCAE, *Report of the Joint Committee on Atomic Energy on the Aircraft Nuclear Propulsion Program,* 86th Cong., 1st Sess. (1959) — *Staff Report on ANP* (1959)

Staff of the JCAE, *Technical Aspects of Detection and Inspection Controls of a Nuclear Weapons Test Ban: Summary-Analysis of Hearings,* 86th Cong., 2d Sess. (1960) — *Staff Summary-Analysis of Test Ban Hearings* (1960)

Staff of the JCAE, *Improving the AEC Regulatory Process,* 87th Cong., 1st Sess. (1961) — *Staff Report on AEC Regulatory Process* (1961)

Other Government Documents

Legislative History of the Atomic Energy Act of 1954 (Public Law 703, 83rd Congress), compiled by Madeline W. Losee (3 vols.; Washington: U.S. Atomic Energy Commission, 1955) — *Leg. Hist. 1954 Act,* 3 volumes

Hearings before the Senate Committee on Interstate and Foreign Commerce, *On the Nomination of Lewis L. Strauss,* 86th Cong., 1st Sess. (1959) — *Strauss Confirmation Hearings* (1959)

I | Evolution of the Joint Committee on Atomic Energy

When the atomic bomb exploded over Hiroshima on August 6, 1945, there was general recognition that the United States and the entire world were entering a new era. This recognition was based not only on the awesome nature of atomic energy as a weapon of destruction, but also on its tremendous potential for human welfare. President Truman, in his initial announcement of the atomic bomb, explicitly emphasized these considerations and stated that he would shortly request Congress to enact legislation which would ensure proper public control of this new force.

During the months following Hiroshima, the atom and its significance became almost a national obsession. Uppermost in the public mind was the vast power of the atom and the fact that this was a power possessed only by the United States. Although the necessity for achieving effective international control was generally regarded as a principal factor in national atomic-energy policy, it was also believed that the United States had to continue rapid development of both military and civilian applications as well. Superimposed on these considerations was the further belief, not universally held, that, at least until effective international control was achieved, the United States had to guard the secrets of nuclear technology jealously.

On September 6, 1945, Sen. Brien McMahon (D., Conn.) introduced a bill proposing a governmental framework for dealing with atomic energy. On the same day, Sen. Arthur H. Vandenberg (R., Mich.) introduced a concurrent resolution establishing a joint committee of six Senate and six House members to make a complete study and report to Congress with respect to "the development and control of the atomic bomb." The Vandenberg resolution was favorably reported by the Foreign Relations Committee on September 26, 1945, and was passed by the Senate the following day, but the House took no action.

A week later, October 3, President Truman sent a special message to Congress urgently requesting enactment of legislation establishing a national policy for the control, use, and development of atomic energy in the United States and spelling out the general principles which he believed should be embodied in this legislation. On the same day the May-Johnson bill (H.R. 4280), which had been drafted within the War Department, was introduced in the House of Representatives and referred to the House Committee on Military Affairs, chaired by Rep. Andrew J. May (D., Ky.), one of the bill's cosponsors. When the May-Johnson bill was introduced in the Senate, however, a jurisdictional squabble developed, and Vandenberg prevented its referral to any committee pending action on his concurrent resolution.

A few days later, with Vandenberg's proposal stalled in the House, McMahon introduced a new resolution (S. Res. 179), calling for creation of a special Senate committee with full jurisdiction over all matters pertaining to atomic energy.[1] The resolution was referred to the Committee on Interstate and Foreign Commerce, which reported it favorably on October 15. The Senate adopted it about one week later, and, with the support of Vandenberg and Majority Leader Alben W. Barkley (D., Ky.), McMahon was appointed chairman of the eleven-man special committee.

The basic issue in Congressional consideration of atomic-energy legislation was the extent to which the military should play a role in administering the national atomic-energy program. The House Military Affairs Committee began hearings on the May-Johnson bill on October 9 and reported it favorably early in November, despite charges by critics that the speed of the hearings was intended to prevent opponents of military control from marshaling their forces. On the other hand, the Special Senate Committee, chaired by McMahon, delved into "the entire question of the atomic bomb and atomic energy," without reference to any particular bill. These general hearings began on November 27, 1945, and continued for several weeks. Meanwhile, McMahon and his staff had drafted a new atomic-energy bill (S. 1717) which was the basis for the legislation ulti-

---

[1] *Cong. Rec.*, 91 (Oct. 22, 1945), 9888.

mately enacted as the Atomic Energy Act of 1946. Hearings on this bill began on January 22, 1946, and continued through April 19. The bill was passed by the Senate on June 1, 1946, and emerged substantially intact after extensive House floor debate and a Senate-House conference.[2]

The Atomic Energy Act of 1946 provided in essence for an almost total government monopoly of atomic energy. This monopoly was based upon the generally accepted necessity for exclusive government ownership of fissionable material and of all facilities capable of either producing or using such material. The normal operation of the patent system was largely suspended in the atomic-energy field. Stringent restrictions were imposed on dissemination of atomic-energy information within the United States and on cooperation in atomic-energy matters with other nations, even the closest allies. Management of the entire atomic-energy program was vested in a five-man Atomic Energy Commission, totally civilian, which was given extraordinary and unprecedented power. The act also provided for a Military Liaison Committee and a General Advisory Committee of scientists to assist the Commission in its deliberations.

Members of Congress were completely cognizant of the vast powers which they were bestowing on the executive branch of the government in the 1946 act, and they were clearly concerned. But they were also concerned with the role Congress would assume in dealing with atomic energy. One attempt to solve both problems was a proposal that members of Congress serve on the commission that would administer the program. Although this extreme suggestion generated no support, there was a feeling that an extraordinary legislative device was essential.

The solution provided by the Atomic Energy Act of 1946 was a Joint Committee on Atomic Energy, to consist of eighteen members, nine from the Senate and nine from the House. The Joint Committee was vested with full jurisdiction over "all bills, resolutions, and other matters in the Senate or the House of Representatives relating primarily to the Commission or to the development, use, and control of atomic energy." The Atomic Energy Commission was explicitly required to keep the Joint Committee "fully and currently informed with respect to the Commission's activities." The Committee was authorized to appoint such staff personnel as it deemed necessary and advisable and also to "utilize the services, information, facilities, and personnel" of the executive branch.

The legislative history of the 1946 act does not provide a clear picture of the origin of this uniquely armed committee. The idea of a joint

---

[2] An excellent account of the legislative history of the first atomic-energy act is contained in the official history of the Atomic Energy Commission; Richard G. Hewlett and Oscar E. Anderson, Jr., *The New World, 1939/1946* (University Park: Pennsylvania State University Press, 1962), chaps. 12-14.

committee probably derived from Vandenberg's resolution. A possible precedent may also be found in the informal practice that prevailed during World War II. During that time, the entire atomic program developed by the Manhattan Engineer District was kept from general Congressional scrutiny. Requests for appropriations were hidden in the budgets of a number of executive agencies and were passed on by the chairmen of the Senate and House Appropriations and Military Affairs committees, who constituted an informal joint committee. The proven feasibility of this arrangement and its success in preserving security during the war may have influenced the draftsmen of the 1946 act in suggesting a joint committee.

There were few explicit references to the Joint Committee in the Senate hearings on McMahon's bill. These references dealt with the potential role of the Joint Committee in controlling the Commission's exercise of licensing authority (which was virtually nonexistent until 1955), in safeguarding the position of the military, and in keeping Congress informed of atomic-energy developments. The Senate committee's report on the legislation described the provision relating to the Joint Committee primarily in terms of keeping Congress "fully acquainted at all times with the work of the Commission." The report also suggested that the Joint Committee would "be in a position to give substantial aid to the Appropriations Committee" and could consider supplementary and amendatory atomic-energy legislation as the need might arise. The floor debates in the Senate and House provide equally vague indications as to the origins of the Joint Committee on Atomic Energy. The creation of a joint committee was discussed rather superficially, with emphasis on the facts that it would provide Congress with the means for intimate contact with the Commission's activities, that it would be an instrument for flexibility and change, and that it would play a watchdog role.

There is no indication, however, that Congress considered potentially difficult mechanical problems, such as the technique to be employed in consideration of presidential appointments to the Commission requiring Senate confirmation and the question of whether a senator or representative would chair the Committee. Even the basic question of how bills would be reported out to the House and Senate seems to have been unresolved. On the other side of the coin, neither President Truman and his advisors nor Congress seem to have been aware of the potentially enormous inroads on traditional concepts of executive prerogative which were implicit in the requirement that the Commission keep the Joint Committee "fully and currently informed" and in the Committee's authority to utilize the services, information, facilities, and personnel of the executive branch.

On August 1, 1946, President Truman signed the Atomic Energy

Act of 1946. On the next day, just before the adjournment of Congress, the first members of the Joint Committee were appointed. They held an organizational meeting, elected McMahon chairman, and then left Washington to take part in the first postwar Congressional elections. A sense of urgency was completely lacking, despite the unsettled world situation. This was the year that Winston Churchill warned of the "iron curtain" in Europe, and George Kennan cabled from Moscow that United States policy toward the Soviet Union was characterized by "wishful thinking." But members of the Joint Committee, Congress, and the public were more concerned about food and housing shortages and inflation. The election, reflecting these postwar frustrations, swept in the first Republican Congress since the days of Herbert Hoover.

When the Joint Committee reassembled in January, 1947, it selected Sen. Bourke B. Hickenlooper (R., Iowa) as its chairman and Rep. W. Sterling Cole (R., N.Y.) as its vice-chairman. The first order of business was the confirmation of the five AEC commissioners and the general manager who had been named by President Truman to interim appointments.

In considering the role of the JCAE during its fifteen-year existence, one is impressed by the manner in which its activities fell neatly into separate eras. The years 1947, 1948, and 1949 may be aptly characterized as a period in which the Joint Committee played a relatively passive role, functioning primarily in a "watchdog," or overseer, capacity. Commencing late in 1949, the Committee's role appears to have changed markedly. Though it continued to function as a watchdog to the same extent, it also assumed vigorous leadership in the national atomic-energy program. In this role, it generally encouraged and exhorted the willing but cautious AEC to expand programs which the JCAE regarded as important and functioned as a "big brother," cooperating with and protecting the AEC against its critics and those who favored curtailment of its program. This period extended through the end of the Truman administration and through the first year of the Eisenhower administration. Then, in 1955, largely as a result of the Dixon-Yates controversy and the atomic-power policies of the Republican administration, a Democratic-controlled Joint Committee sought to accelerate the nation's civilian power program. The years 1955 to 1958 were marked by sharp controversy with the executive branch. During this period, the JCAE became a policy-making institution, greatly expanding the exercise of its statutory authority and exerting influence the Executive deemed unwarranted. Finally, 1958 through 1962 were years of relative calm during which the JCAE, having won a position of leadership in the national atomic-energy program, entrenched and consolidated its position with little opposition from the Executive.

■ SCRUTINY

> The Joint Committee does not at this time recommend to the Congress any major legislation affecting the policies or the philosophy of the act. As a legislative committee it does not feel that it should at this time draw any final conclusions respecting the operation of this program or the administrative policies in effect. Sufficient time has not elapsed to warrant conclusions of this kind. This is not to be construed either as an attitude of hostility or an attitude of approval, but on the contrary expresses an attitude on the part of the committee to objectively evaluate the various phases of the program as a result of more mature opportunity.
>
> —First Report of the JCAE to Congress, 1948 [3]

During their first years on the JCAE, members, awed by the magnitude and unfamiliarity of their responsibilities, consciously adopted a policy of caution and self-restraint. Throughout this early period, for example, the Committee never requested information from the AEC concerning the number of atomic weapons in stockpile. As a legislative body, the Committee was relatively inactive. It received few bills and resolutions, since there was at the time little desire to evaluate or improve the 1946 act. In its investigative role, the Committee studied the scope of the atomic-energy program and the operations of the various agencies involved. Thus, the Committee's role was limited; it had not yet assumed substantial responsibility for development of the atom.

Since the period was marked by extreme secrecy, few of the Committee's hearings were open to the public. However, in the first three months of 1947 the Senate section of the JCAE held thirty-two open sessions on the nomination of the original AEC commissioners and general manager. President Truman had appointed four Republicans and an independent to the Commission, but the "independent" was David E. Lilienthal, whose association with the Tennessee Valley Authority tainted his record in the eyes of many congressmen. Lilienthal was particularly unfortunate in facing senators emboldened by the conservative victory in the 1946 Congressional elections. Nevertheless, he and his fellow appointees finally succeeded in winning approval, although Congressional distrust persisted throughout Lilienthal's tenure as chairman of the AEC.

After the confirmation hearings, the JCAE began the task of informing itself on all phases of the atomic-energy program. This included a series of hearings with testimony by the AEC and Defense Department officials, tours of atomic-energy installations, and maintenance of a staff observer at the United Nations. The JCAE's first report to Congress, in

[3] S. Rep. No. 850, 80th Cong., 2d Sess. (1948).

1948, emphasized these aspects of its work. In fact, the Committee was rather self-effacing, pointing out that it was "not equipped to be an authority in highly specialized fields of research or technology." It added that it had "not assumed the responsibilities for administrative policies that are clearly vested in the Atomic Energy Commission" but rather was merely

> . . . attempting to gain as much information and knowledge from an overall standpoint as will enable the committee to recommend, from time to time, any legislation that may be desirable and to keep abreast of the potentially changing needs and requirements of a tremendous program, that, without doubt is still in its infancy.

As the Committee gained more information, problems of security became paramount in its view of the atomic-energy program.[4] Of course, the forerunner of the AEC, the Manhattan District, was one of the most highly secret, security-conscious operations of World War II. One would have expected this attitude to persist after the war, if only because of the orientation of the security staff and the force of habits followed throughout the war. Moreover, the steady deterioration of the international situation reinforced the necessity for security. In 1947, emergency aid was sent to Greece and Turkey to prevent their falling to the Communists. In February, 1948, a Communist coup overthrew the government of Czechoslovakia; shortly afterward, the Berlin blockade began. In 1949, Chiang Kai-shek fled to Formosa, and China fell to the Communists. At the United Nations, Russian intransigence blocked all efforts to achieve international arms control. The exposure of a Canadian espionage ring provided persuasive evidence of unceasing Russian intelligence efforts. These events alarmed all Americans, and protection of atomic "secrets" became a major obsession. The JCAE's predominant concern with secrecy and security was therefore a natural reaction to contemporary world events.

The heightened tension of the early years emboldened those who had lost the battle over military control of atomic energy. In 1948, during the Berlin airlift, the Defense Department formally requested President Truman to shift the custody of atomic weapons from the AEC to the Defense Department. The President's initial reaction was that he could not agree with a proposal "to have some dashing lieutenant colonel decide when would be the proper time to drop [an atomic bomb]." Even though the Defense Department explained that it was concerned only with custody

---

[4] In its 1948 report, the JCAE noted that it had reviewed the personnel files of the AEC and its contractors, that it would continue to do so, and that "the Joint Committee has been assured by the Atomic Energy Commission that it is vitally concerned with the problem of personnel security." The AEC was indeed concerned; according to one estimate, personnel-security matters took up one-third of the Commission's meeting time from January, 1947, to April, 1949. S. Rep. No. 1169, 81st Cong., 1st Sess. (1949), p. 85.

and not with the decision to use the bomb, Truman announced several days later that custody would remain with the civilian authorities. Another proposal along these lines was the suggestion in 1949 that the AEC be replaced by a board of eight military men and one scientist, but this proposal died in the Joint Committee.

Notwithstanding some disagreements between the AEC and the Joint Committee, the JCAE, during the early years, generally defended the Commission and its programs against Congressional criticism, particularly from the House Committee on Appropriations. Because the 1946 act had provided blanket authorization for appropriations, the Joint Committee was unable to provide a sympathetic forum and statutory blessing for the presentation of the AEC's program prior to its transmission to the Appropriations Committee. Consequently, the Appropriations Committee had the difficult task of reviewing a massive, vital defense program subject to stringent security inhibitions. Not unexpectedly, the Appropriations Committee had great difficulty in understanding the atomic-energy program, and this resulted in criticism and suspicion. The AEC, on various occasions, was charged with failing to present an "intelligent financial picture," operating "on a basis of lavish expenditures," and taking advantage of its strategic position to avoid facing "practical realities" on less important budgetary items. Despite these harsh words aimed at the AEC's administrative practices, the House Appropriations Committee treated its budget rather gingerly. The unquestioned importance of the program for national defense led the committee to appropriate all essential funds, except for minor, if annoying, cuts.

The year 1949 was a fateful one for the atomic-energy program and the JCAE. The newly elected Democratic Eighty-first Congress restored McMahon to the chairmanship of the JCAE. During the spring, several incidents occurred which alarmed those who were concerned with the Commission's security policies. The Committee was engaged in investigating charges that Communists were beneficiaries of the AEC's fellowship program and the disappearance of several grams of uranium when former Chairman Hickenlooper issued a broadside to the press charging the Commission and particularly Chairman Lilienthal with "incredible mismanagement." The result was a series of forty-five hearings (only twenty-four of them public) which came to be known as the "Hickenlooper investigation." The inquiry bounded over a vast number of topics: the lack of continuity of administrative personnel, the large number of emergency security clearances, personnel-security procedures generally, the shipment of isotopes to Norway, increases in costs on a number of construction projects, and extravagant and faulty construction practices. Because the Commission often had very short notice of what was to be discussed, it was essential to have a variety of administrative personnel (as many as twenty-nine) in attendance at the hearings. The effect of such an investigation on the AEC's day-to-day management of the atomic program can be readily imagined. No less important was its effect on the subsequent behavior of AEC personnel. The Commission had come of age overnight, and the novelty of the agency and of the atomic-energy program would no longer be accepted as an excuse for imperfect administrative practices.

Before the JCAE could draft its report on the Hickenlooper investigation, President Truman announced the first Soviet atomic explosion. Despite administration attempts to play down the Russian achievement, the public was aware of previous predictions that Russia would not succeed in detonating an atomic bomb until 1952 or later. The sense of shock in the country, particularly since China had just fallen to the Communists and the Hiss trial was making headlines in New York, was immense. By the time the Committee had issued its reports, with a majority rejecting the Hickenlooper charges, the attention to administrative detail which the investigation had stressed belonged to a past era. Now the JCAE and the AEC could get down to the business at hand: mapping an expansion of the country's atomic program to counter Soviet achievements.

■ PARTNERSHIP

> If the Committee has a single general comment to offer, it is this: Greater boldness and more scientific and technical daring should be brought to bear upon the [atomic] program.
>
> —JCAE Report, 1951 [5]

The activities of the Joint Committee from 1950 to 1953 present a sharp contrast to its limited activities from 1947 to 1949. Although the legislative agenda was still minimal and the investigative program proceeded substantially as before, the JCAE played a more active role by prodding the executive branch to adopt a policy of swift, vast atomic expansion. The Committee also stepped up its defense of the AEC budget against the House Appropriations Committee, which frequently threatened the expanding program with budget cuts and restrictive riders.

Shortly after the JCAE had filed its report on the Hickenlooper investigation, David Lilienthal resigned as AEC chairman. Commissioner Sumner T. Pike served as acting chairman from February through June, 1950, when Gordon Dean (who had served on the Commission since May, 1949) became the AEC's second chairman. Within a month, AEC General Manager Carroll Wilson resigned, saying that he lacked confidence in Dean. Wilson received no support from Congress; on the contrary, the selection of Dean met with the complete approval of the JCAE,

---

[5] S. Rep. No. 1041, 82d Cong., 1st Sess. (1951), p. 7.

which issued a statement unanimously supporting the new chairman. Despite this vote of confidence, Dean was acutely conscious of the controversies boiling up around the Commission. He had first been appointed during the Hickenlooper investigation and now had to contend with the Wilson resignation. To effect a closer and more cooperative AEC-JCAE relationship, Dean proposed to "do some selling . . . , not by asserting our perfection, but by demonstrating our skill and our sincerity."

In the three months before Lilienthal stepped down, the decision was made to adopt an all-out crash program for the development of a hydrogen bomb. Although it is difficult to assess the relative contributions of the various governmental bodies and officials participating in these deliberations, it is certain that the JCAE contributed substantially to the final decision. McMahon, on behalf of the Committee, sent several letters to President Truman and spoke with him personally, urging adoption of a crash program.

During the first months after the decision to proceed with the H-bomb, the JCAE was instrumental in encouraging the executive branch to provide increased funds for the atomic program. In August, 1950 (two months after the Korean War started), McMahon called for "expansion of the expanding atomic program," thus proposing an expansion over and above that which resulted from the initial H-bomb decision. Such a program took time to develop, but, by September, 1951, McMahon and the Committee were ready to launch their campaign. In mid-September, McMahon urged mass production of A-bombs so that they could be built at the cost of a tank. After hearing testimony from the armed services and their civilian secretaries, the JCAE unanimously adopted a resolution requesting the AEC and Defense Department to transmit to the Committee by January 3, 1952, a detailed program for maximizing the role of atomic energy in the over-all defense structure.

At the same time, the Committee filed a report to Congress reflecting the aggressive, prodding role that it had adopted.[6] With respect to weapons, the JCAE claimed that it had made "strenuous efforts" to accelerate the hydrogen-bomb program even before President Truman announced his decision. "Since that time the hydrogen program has gone forward, and the Committee renews its urgings that no stone be left unturned to attain necessary objectives in the shortest space of time."

With respect to raw materials, the report noted that the Committee had "attempted to encourage the discovery and development of new uranium sources" and that the Committee had played an "active role" in the international arrangements leading to increased imports. The Committee recommended a "further intensification" of the AEC's raw-materials pro-

---

[6] *Loc. cit.*

gram. In the all-important area of fissionable materials production, ". . . the Committee saw opportunities to step up plutonium production rapidly and at a minimum cost, and it exerted continuous pressure resulting in seizure of these opportunities." The conclusion of the report presaged more aggressive expansion, stating that ". . . there are areas in our atomic program which need to be shored up, and there are opportunities for faster advancement which need to be vigorously exploited."

Through the first weeks of January, 1952, the JCAE pressed the Defense Department and the AEC for their reports. On January 13, Chairman Dean said that the AEC would be ready to report soon on plans for a new, expanded program. Bridling at the JCAE's preoccupation with expansion, Dean said that the Commission welcomed challenges, ". . . but I think we should always remember that the line between boldness and foolhardiness is a thin one and in advance it is not always possible to be bold without being foolhardy. . . . So far, the boldness has been balanced by a sense of responsibility." [7]

Nevertheless, the administration's budget requests for the AEC reflected the success of the JCAE's expansion campaign. The regular appropriation for fiscal 1953 called for more than $1,000,000,000. Later, a supplemental request submitted to Congress in June, 1952, called for more than $3,000,000,000. These requests for substantial increases in appropriations brought to a climax the battle between the JCAE and the Appropriations committees, particularly that of the House, which had been simmering since 1947 and boiling since 1950. When the House Appropriations Committee halved the $3,000,000,000 request and added a restrictive rider, the battle was on. With McMahon hospitalized, former Chairman Hickenlooper led the fight for the JCAE-AEC requests. The Joint Committee enlisted the support of President Truman, who wrote letters to the chairmen of the House and Senate Appropriations committees urging restoration of the cuts and deletion of the rider. After extended debate, which delayed the adjournment of Congress until almost the hour that the Republican national convention convened, the JCAE succeeded in achieving a favorable compromise.

Republican Senator Hickenlooper's leadership in the fight for the Democratic administration is indicative of the bipartisanship that prevailed throughout the expansion period. Not only was there harmony within the JCAE, but the Committee's relations with the AEC were generally cordial. Dean was careful to keep the JCAE fully informed about the Commission's actions, often in advance of their execution. Whether this was a continuing reaction to the Hickenlooper investigation or whether it was merely Gordon Dean's *modus operandi,* the effect was to enhance the joint power of the

[7] *N.Y. Times,* Jan. 14, 1952.

JCAE and the AEC in working for the crucial growth of American atomic strength during the expansion years.

After winning its biggest Congressional battle, the JCAE entered a period of relative inactivity, which extended from July, 1952, to April, 1953. McMahon's death on July 28, 1952, and the Congressional adjournment for the coming presidential nominations and election further discouraged formal Committee activity. The smashing victory of Dwight D. Eisenhower in the 1952 election swept in a Republican Congress, necessitating a reorganization of the Joint Committee when the Eighty-third Congress convened in January, 1953. A lengthy struggle between the House and Senate members over the JCAE chairmanship ended in April with the selection of Representative Cole as chairman and Senator Hickenlooper as vice-chairman.

▪ PREDOMINANCE

> Sometimes we feel that maybe the Congress should set some of the policy in this Nation, and the administrative agencies should help to carry it out. We feel like we have a little bit of responsibility when we have to put up hundreds of millions of dollars and we feel that we might have a little bit to say as to the wisdom of how it is spent and the general direction of it. We do not see the clear-cut line. It is up to us to go back and get elected and it is up to us to come here and vote the appropriations for the work you are doing, and sometimes we think that our judgment of 10 or 12 years in this committee might be just about as good as some other people's.
>
> —Rep. Chet Holifield [8]

The years 1953-1958 were a crucial period for the Joint Committee on Atomic Energy. During the first two years of this period, while both the Committee and the executive branch were under Republican control, the JCAE developed legislation to replace the Atomic Energy Act of 1946. After the Atomic Energy Act of 1954 was approved, the Committee, under Democratic control beginning in 1955, became increasingly critical of the slow speed with which the executive branch was developing the domestic atomic-power program. When the Executive continued to balk at providing the kind of program that the JCAE thought essential, the Committee proceeded to take matters into its own hands. The resulting struggle for leadership of the program led to controversy which continued unabated until 1958.

The Republican election victory in 1952 resulted in personnel changes not only on the JCAE but in the executive branch as well. Shortly after he took office in 1953, President Eisenhower appointed Lewis L.

---

[8] *FY 1958 Authorization Hearings* (1957), p. 672.

Strauss as his special assistant for atomic-energy matters.[9] Subsequently, in April, Strauss' nomination as chairman of the AEC was sent to the Senate, and he was confirmed at the end of June without controversy and with bipartisan plaudits. At the same time, Strauss retained his presidential advisory position, thus assuming dual roles which were soon to become troublesome.

Meanwhile, the JCAE was giving increasing consideration to possible revisions of the Atomic Energy Act of 1946. The chief issue was what role private industry could play in the development of atomic power. For several years, the AEC had explored this problem in cooperation with several industrial groups. By 1953, the Commission, in conjunction with other interested officials of the executive branch, was preparing legislation intended to open the atomic-energy field to private enterprise. In addition, the Commission was drafting proposals for increasing cooperation between the United States and friendly nations in connection with both civilian and military applications of atomic energy, as well as for liberalization of the information-control provisions of the act.

Early in 1954, the AEC submitted two draft bills amending some provisions of the McMahon Act. But Chairman Cole objected strongly to the tenor of the AEC proposals and refused to even introduce the draft bills. Instead, Cole and Vice-Chairman Hickenlooper laboriously produced a single bill designed to accomplish the administration's objectives as well as completely rewrite the earlier law.

The Cole-Hickenlooper bill provided for abandonment of the domestic governmental monopoly established by the McMahon Act. The Commission was authorized to license private possession and use of "special nuclear materials" (plutonium and uranium enriched in the isotopes U-233 or U-235), although the United States would retain title to such materials. Another provision permitted private ownership, under AEC license, of nuclear reactors. These features were similar to those proposed by the AEC, except that the AEC favored private ownership of special nuclear materials.

With respect to cooperation with foreign nations, the bill retained much of the approach of the 1946 act, but was modified to provide for a new concept, an "agreement for cooperation." Under such an agreement, special nuclear materials, reactors, and restricted data could be transferred to another nation, subject to safeguards and guarantees provided by the receiving country. The bill also allowed more liberal declassification of restricted data and greater flexibility in security clearances.

The new bill contained a number of provisions which indicated a

[9] Strauss had been one of the original AEC commissioners, serving from 1947 until his resignation in 1950. Although he had often been the lone dissenter on the Commission, his support of the crash program for the H-bomb won him the confidence of the Joint Committee, which retained him as a consultant several times between 1950 and 1953.

JCAE intent to improve its position in the area of atomic policy-making. Foremost among these was the long-sought power to authorize appropriations, although only for plant construction and real-property acquisition. Provision was also made for JCAE review of several types of executive policy decisions by requiring that the decisions adopted lie before the JCAE for a thirty-day period before going into effect.

While the drafting process was nearing completion in June, 1954, President Eisenhower, through the Budget Bureau, ordered the AEC to proceed with negotiations with the Mississippi Valley Generating Company to provide power for the Tennessee Valley Authority, replacing TVA power used in the AEC plant at Paducah, Kentucky. This proposal, which came to be known as Dixon-Yates, aroused a storm of opposition, particularly among Congressional Democrats. The situation was politically explosive because three of the five AEC commissioners (those appointed by Truman) were dissatisfied with the President's directive, whereas Chairman Strauss and Commissioner Campbell (both Eisenhower appointees) supported the proposed contract.

Moreover, Strauss was in a delicate position. All three commissioners opposed to the directive had described to the JCAE their problems with Strauss. Commissioner Thomas E. Murray was concerned about centralization of authority in the chairman. He said that there had been occasions when he did not have access to pertinent information and that important policy decisions had been made by the chairman without consulting his colleagues. Commissioner Henry DeWolf Smyth said that he had had fewer informal discussions with Strauss than he had had with other chairmen. He also noted a greater tension within the AEC than had existed in the past. Strauss himself testified that there was some "conflict of a psychological nature" between his dual roles as chairman of the Commission and adviser to the president. He noted with exceeding regret that this conflict had been a matter of discomfort to his colleagues.[10]

Strauss' dual roles were also affecting his relations with the JCAE. His frequent attendance at National Security Council meetings and at international conferences as the president's atomic adviser was shifting the atomic focal point away from the AEC. Such a shift made it more difficult for the JCAE to influence atomic policy or, what was equally significant, to be kept informed about it. When Rep. Chet Holifield (D., Calif.) attempted to query Strauss about certain conversations with the President, Strauss replied: "I must not testify on the subject of consultation by the President, however important or trivial the item." [11] This was not the only information which the JCAE had difficulty in obtaining. Cole noted pub-

---

[10] *Leg. Hist. 1954 Act,* v. 2, p. 2463.
[11] *Ibid.,* p. 2460.

licly that the JCAE found it necessary to adopt a formal resolution in order to get certain information from the Commission. To the Committee, fully conscious of its statutory authority to be fully and currently informed, this was a matter of grave concern.

When the Cole-Hickenlooper bill finally came to the Senate floor, debate was dominated by an extended discussion of the Dixon-Yates contract. The bill itself passed largely as proposed. But Dixon-Yates was a bitter legacy, for the controversy resulted in stripping the AEC of its previous nonpolitical cast and making it thereafter vulnerable to political vagaries.

The Democrats regained control of Congress in the 1954 elections, but the JCAE, under "lame-duck" Republican leadership, voted on November 13 to waive a thirty-day waiting period and allow the Dixon-Yates contract to become effective immediately. The vote was a straight party vote of ten Republicans to eight Democrats and was taken despite Democratic threats to reverse the action as soon as the Democratic Eighty-fourth Congress was convened. In January, the Democrats, true to their word, adopted a resolution recommending that the AEC "take appropriate steps to cancel the Dixon-Yates contract"; the contract was soon cancelled,[12] although not in response to the JCAE resolution.

Meanwhile, the AEC had embarked on a "power-demonstration-reactor program" (PDRP). The first round of this program was announced in January, 1955, when the Commission invited competitive proposals for cooperation and assistance from applicants who would "assume the risks of construction, ownership, and operation of reactors designed to demonstrate the practical value of such facilities for industrial or commercial purposes." In September, 1955, the AEC proceeded with a second round, aimed at encouraging construction of relatively small reactors by municipally owned utilities and rural electrical cooperatives, with the AEC financing construction of the reactors and retaining title to any portion financed.

JCAE Democrats were impatient with the rate of progress of nuclear-power development and demanded government construction and operation of power reactors. Public-power representatives urged a vigorous AEC program, and Commissioner Murray, the only remaining Truman appointee, presented a strong plea for a program to ensure 2,000,000 kilowatts of power by 1960 and 10,000,000 by 1965. In order to accelerate the civilian power program, Sen. Albert Gore (D., Tenn.) and Representative Holifield introduced a bill authorizing and directing the AEC

---

[12] The government subsequently refused to reimburse the Mississippi Valley Generating Company for its expenses on the ground that a conflict of interest on the part of one of the company's negotiators had tainted the contract. This position was upheld by the Supreme Court, 81 S. Ct. 294 (1961).

to construct a number of nuclear-power demonstration facilities at a cost of $400,000,000. The AEC (with the exception of Murray) opposed the bill as unnecessary, saying that the existing program was adequate and that there was no need to undertake a "kilowatt race" with other countries. Most galling to the AEC was the phrase "authorized *and directed*" which Strauss thought to be "the kind of an expression you use to your valet." Nevertheless, the JCAE reported the bill with its mandatory language, and the bill passed the Senate, only to be defeated in the House.

The defeat of the Gore-Holifield bill did not signal the end of the struggle for control of civilian reactor development. A Democratic Congress was returned in the 1956 election, despite the re-election of Eisenhower. Partly to forestall a new Gore-Holifield fight, the AEC announced a third round of the power-demonstration-reactor program in January, 1957. The AEC indicated that it would consider proposals for research-and-development assistance (although not for construction) for any reactors that would make a "significant contribution toward achieving commercial utilization of nuclear power." The Commission threatened to initiate government construction of certain types of reactors if private industry did not submit acceptable proposals. This partial accommodation did not satisfy the JCAE, which took advantage of a surprise attack on the AEC to wrest away control of the power program. The attack came from Rep. Clarence Cannon (D., Mo.), chairman of the House Appropriations Committee, who criticized the existing authorization system and stated that no further appropriations would be warranted unless the JCAE "put to searching scrutiny every program of the Commission." The Joint Committee, quick to take the hint, halted its authorization hearings long enough to unanimously recommend legislation requiring statutory authorization for all "cooperative" projects, that is, power-demonstration-reactor projects for which the AEC contributed financial support, directly or indirectly. The bill passed Congress quickly and without objection. Then, returning to consideration of the fiscal year 1958 authorization, the JCAE added a requirement that all proposed power-demonstration-reactor program arrangements be submitted to the JCAE and lie before it for forty-five days before becoming effective (unless this period were waived by the Committee). In addition, the JCAE recommended several atomic projects to be constructed by the government and a complete reversal of the terms of the second round of the power-demonstration-reactor program. The majority report which accompanied the authorization bill was replete with observations, conclusions, and recommendations embroidering on the bill itself and included not only specific projects, but advice on how and by whom they should be carried out. Whether this was "the high-water mark of legislative encroachment on the executive function," as one commentator has stated,[13] it was clear that the Committee majority had abandoned hope of obtaining from the AEC voluntarily the kind of program which it considered essential to America's atomic leadership.

The authorization bill and report drew a bitter dissent from the four House Republicans on the JCAE. They said that it would result in "expensive and unnecessary government reactor construction," that it represented "public-power advocacy run rampant," and that its approach smacked of "improper favoritism and rank discrimination by legislative fiat." Nevertheless, the bill was approved, though in greatly modified form, and the JCAE had proved its power to shape the atomic-power program to its liking.

With his term on the Commission due to expire in June, 1958, Strauss announced his resignation at the end of May. In view of the opposition of JCAE Democrats to his renomination, he recognized the difficulties that might be caused Eisenhower by a confirmation fight on the Senate floor. In fact, the reception given Strauss' nomination for secretary of commerce one year later,[14] when tempers might have been expected to have cooled, indicates that July, 1958, would have been even hotter than usual on Capitol Hill if Strauss had sought to retain his AEC chairmanship.

▪ CONSOLIDATION

> I sometimes feel that as between members of the Joint Committee and members of the Atomic Energy Commission, there exists only a shadowy and blurred understanding of which policy matters are to be decided by the committee and which by the Commission, even sometimes as to what are matters of policy and what are matters of administration. This needs clarification by force of law rather than force of personalities and customs.
>
> —Rep. Craig Hosmer, 1960 [15]

Since the departure of Strauss in mid-1958, the JCAE has led a more placid existence than at any time since 1949. With its influence over the entire atomic program, including the civilian power program, fully recognized by the AEC, the conflict that had characterized the preceding

---

[13] James L. Morrison, "Federal Support of Domestic Power Development: The Policy Issues," *Vanderbilt Law Review,* XII (December 1958), 195, 221.

[14] The nomination was rejected, after protracted debate, by a vote of 49 to 46. For his reasons for not accepting Eisenhower's proffered reappointment as chairman of the AEC, see Lewis L. Strauss, *Men and Decisions* (Garden City, New York: Doubleday, 1962), p. 378.

[15] *Cong. Rec.,* 106 (Jan. 13, 1960), 473.

five years abated. Nor was there any single issue which has captured the Committee's attention as had weapons expansion from 1950 to 1952 or civilian power from 1955 to 1957. The field of atomic energy was becoming more complex, and the JCAE's attention had to be given no less to the everyday problems of the infant atomic-energy industry than to the possibilities of nuclear-powered flight.

Strauss' successor was John A. McCone, a Los Angeles industrialist, whose nomination was well received by the Joint Committee. The confirmation hearings show that the JCAE's chief concern was that McCone would not become another Strauss. McCone was asked whether he would be a presidential adviser and whether he would keep the JCAE fully and currently informed. He gave the correct answers and was confirmed without controversy. Unquestionably, the Committee's treatment of Strauss influenced McCone's view of the AEC-JCAE relationship, and he went to great lengths to seek accommodation with the Committee.

During the McCone chairmanship, the JCAE divided its attention primarily among three general areas—power-reactor development, nuclear propulsion of rockets and aircraft, and problems of nuclear testing.

With respect to power reactors, the JCAE continued its sponsorship of projects by means of authorization legislation. Nevertheless, the advent of McCone so lowered AEC-JCAE friction that the JCAE was able to achieve unanimity on new projects to be added to the Executive's budget request for fiscal year 1960, and the new authorizations were acceptable to the AEC (although not to the Bureau of the Budget and the President). However, as the 1961 and 1962 battles over the Hanford dual-purpose reactor demonstrated, the public–versus–private-power controversy continues to plague the Committee and Congress.

During this period, the Joint Committee also included in authorizing legislation a number of physical-research projects which had not been approved by the Bureau of the Budget, or in some cases by the AEC. Rep. Melvin Price (D., Ill.) dryly remarked that the JCAE had received "testimony after testimony from the top people in our scientific program of the crying need for a step-up of basic research . . . , and yet we are unable to convince the Bureau of the Budget of the importance of basic research."

The Committee's continuing influence in the reactor and physical-research program was not matched by success in the area of nuclear-powered rockets and aircraft. After the Soviet Union orbited the first earth satellites in 1957, the Joint Committee attempted to use the AEC's nuclear-powered rocket project (ROVER) as an argument for adding "outer space" to the AEC's (and hence the Joint Committee's) jurisdiction. This effort was unsuccessful, and project ROVER is now under the joint jurisdiction of the AEC and the National Aeronautics and Space Administration.

Even less success was achieved in the case of ANP, the nuclear-powered airplane which has never left the ground. ANP has been a favorite project of the JCAE, and particularly of Representative Price, since 1948, when the Committee held the first of thirty-six closed sessions on the program. It is ironic that the Committee, which did so much in such a short time for atomic expansion and for power reactors, could not get sustained executive action on ANP. A Committee report issued in September, 1959, after the JCAE held its first open hearings on the program, stated: "Over the years the ANP has been marked by a series of ups and downs in terms of objectives, financing and program guidance. The program has been characterized by changes in policy direction and lack of firm objectives." [16] This bleak truth was not due to any lack of action on the part of the Joint Committee, which repeatedly prodded the executive branch. Rather, it is attributable in large part to the fact that the ANP program was primarily within the province of the Department of Defense, which has been less amenable to JCAE political leverage than has the AEC.[17]

The JCAE continued during McCone's AEC chairmanship to expand its role in the development of an international atomic-energy program. In 1958, the Committee reported legislation which led to the European Atomic Energy Community (EURATOM) Cooperation Act. However, the JCAE was somewhat suspicious of the plan recommended by the Executive, fearing that preoccupation with the international development of atomic energy might divert resources from the domestic power program. In this case, the JCAE was instrumental in drastically revising and curtailing the scope of the administration's proposal. The Committee also concentrated attention on the nuclear-test moratorium, which the United States and the Soviet Union had been observing voluntarily since 1958. In 1960, the JCAE held hearings on the technical aspects of detection and inspection controls of a nuclear-weapons test ban. From these hearings, it appeared that Committee members felt that detection of small underground explosions was uncertain and that a test-ban agreement without stringent controls was therefore ill-advised. Members of the Committee have taken in the past years an increasingly active role in urging the resumption of atmospheric tests, and there is little doubt that JCAE views influenced President Kennedy's decision to resume nuclear tests above the earth's surface in 1962.

---

[16] *Staff Report on ANP* (1959), p. 1.

[17] The Kennedy administration cancelled the ANP project in March, 1961, stating that "the possibility of achieving a militarily useful aircraft in the foreseeable future is still very remote." *Forum Memo,* April 1961, p. 10.

Although it is still too early to properly assess the Joint Committee's relationships with the Kennedy administration, it appears that there have been few significant departures from the McCone era of AEC-JCAE collaboration. The new Democratic administration and AEC Chairman Glenn T. Seaborg have in effect carried forward the nuclear policies of their predecessors. The Committee has continued to initiate ideas and prod the Executive, exercising undiminished influence in the formulation of nuclear policies. Whether in the field of national defense, where it successfully advocated the installation of electronic locks on nuclear weapons as a safeguard against accidental or unauthorized firings, or in the field of domestic reactor development, where it induced the administration to budget more funds for nuclear-power projects and studies, the JCAE has maintained coordinate authority with the executive branch.

Reviewing this short history of the Joint Committee on Atomic Energy, one is struck by the sustained influence of this Congressional institution. Although its early years were spent passively absorbing the atomic environment, after 1949 the JCAE grew vigorously with the expanding atomic program. By 1955, the Committee had become an aggressive claimant for the right to participate on an equal basis in the formulation of atomic-energy policy. Finally, during the latter years of the Eisenhower administration and into the first years of the Kennedy presidency, the Committee's decisive influence was fully recognized and accepted by the executive branch. Clearly, the Joint Committee's powers are not immutable, but accrued influence and habits of leadership ensure that it will continue to play an important role in atomic-energy policy-making.

II | Anatomy of a Political Institution

During this century, the role of Congress as creator of public policy, both domestic and international, has declined sharply. Once supreme, Congress, through circumstances beyond its wishes and control, has delegated broad legislative discretion to the president and executive branch of government. Formerly, Congress initiated and formulated legislation, and the president approved or vetoed it. Today, major measures are nearly always initiated and formulated by the executive branch; Congress now approves, modifies, or vetoes. In the past, the status and power of one branch or the other fluctuated periodically, depending in great part on the tenor of the times and the personalities and leadership qualities of the man in the White House or the men in Congress. Recently, no matter what the qualities or attitudes of the president—be he aggressive, like Roosevelt or Truman, or passive, like Eisenhower—Congress has been no match for the executive branch. As national policy-maker, the legislature has come to play a secondary role.

As the powers of Congress declined in relation to those of the Executive, the powers of Congressional committees increased. Of course, committees and the key roles delegated them by their parent bodies were no new phenomena. Originally *ad hoc* groups to assist Congress with special problems, standing committees soon came to be landmarks of the legislative scene. By the late nineteenth century, committees exercised substantial control of Congress. The prerogatives and powers of the standing committees were unchallenged, and "the principle that the Committees shall rule without let or hindrance" was not contravened.[1] Pressures of time necessitated conduct of legislative business by the process of Congressional fragmentation. Even during that period, bills introduced numbered thousands at each session, and Congress as a whole could not consider each one fully. Thus, the House—and the Senate to some extent as well—was forced to deliberate and legislate in small groups. Time was not the only factor inimical to action by the larger bodies. Even had time permitted, floor debate would not have served to "sift the chaff from the wheat in the bushels of bills every week piled upon the clerk's desk."[2] Congress had to rely on committees for the most important of all decisions—which measures should reach the floor of Senate and House for debate and possible enactment.

The role of committees has by no means diminished; quite to the contrary, it has expanded. Time is still a pressing problem which effectively precludes close scrutiny by Congress of every issue before it. So great is the volume of legislative business today that, in most cases, the actions of Congress are really those of the smaller legislative bodies. Added to this time factor are the complexities of issues which face the legislature in an age of unlimited technological developments, international affairs fraught with dangers to national security and world peace, and innumerable problems connected with an industrial economy and an urban nation. A world fashioned for the application of specialized knowledge and skills is indeed a demanding one for the lay politician, with his small-town experience and legal or business training. Thus, the need for specialization is felt as strongly in Congress as in the nation as a whole. There is even greater justification for fragmentation or decentralization in the national legislature. By delegating complex problems to smaller groups, Congress can take advantage of the specially developed skills of its members. If they serve on the same committee and deal with similar subject matter for a number of years, members are presumed to have acquired a degree of expertness not shared by their Congressional colleagues. On the basis of their recommendations, theoretically, Congress should be able to decide as intelligently as possible.

Another factor which explains the present-day ascendancy of Congressional committees is Congress' collective feeling of frustration, even impotence, in a period which seems to favor centralized leadership at the

---

[1] Woodrow Wilson, *Congressional Government* (New York: Meridian, 1956), p. 66.
[2] *Ibid.*, p. 62.

expense of representative government. In contemporary America, the Executive both proposes and disposes, while Congress doggedly, yet futilely, seeks a means of exercising coordinate authority. One method, which Congress in 1946 tried to improve through internal reorganization, is the committee system. Only by division into standing committees—each with its own tasks and jurisdiction, each with one or several executive departments or agencies accountable to it—could Congress hope to supervise and control the burgeoning executive branch. The Legislative Reorganization Act of 1946, coming after a period of Congressional introspection, provided instruments thought suitable for greater legislative control. The La Follette-Monroney committee, in considering proposals for legislative reorganization, observed that, "without effective legislative oversight of the activities of the vast executive branch, the line of democracy wears thin. . . ." As a result of the committee's deliberations, an act was passed which provided that each standing committee "shall exercise continuous watchfulness" over agencies and the execution of laws within its area of delegated jurisdiction. Partially as a result of this provision, committees which had once been mainly concerned with digesting legislation, have come to function more as "watchdogs" than as legislators. Today, "legislative oversight" has become *a,* if not *the,* principal activity of the standing committees of both houses.[3]

Oversight, however enthusiastically performed, is still only one of the several functions of the Congressional committee. A second function is that of policy-making, or at least policy advice. In practice, if not in theory, committees have yet to exercise their policy-making functions with outstanding success. Certainly, committees have been known to initiate policies, to refuse approval to those initiated by the Executive, and to give a proposal a different direction and momentum than those who framed it intended. By and large, however, committees seldom play a creative role; they usually control by modifications which bring extravagant administrative ideas into conformity with a conservative Congressional temper.[4] It is perhaps because they neither originate nor execute policies that committees have generally paid great attention to spelling them out in statute. They have devoted their energies, their talents, and their staffs to examining the minutiae of executive proposals. But grand designs, initiative, and impetus come from outside Congress.

The third function of committees is to report back to Congress their

---

[3] George B. Galloway, "Congressional Reorganization: Unfinished Business," in Earl Latham, ed., *The Philosophy and Policies of Woodrow Wilson* (Chicago: University of Chicago Press, 1958), p. 221.

[4] Cf. Holbert N. Carroll, *The House of Representatives and Foreign Affairs* (Pittsburgh: University of Pittsburgh Press, 1958), pp. 110-111, and James A. Robinson, *Congress and Foreign Policy-Making* (Homewood, Ill.: Dorsey Press, 1962), *passim.*

findings and recommendations so that Congress is adequately informed and can make its own decisions. Yet, this function is seldom fully performed, for the legislature is unable to make decisions based on the independent judgments of its members. Woodrow Wilson's observation that the House and Senate sit not for serious discussion but to sanction the conclusions of their committees is still true. In general, Congress acts as a body only to legitimize recommendations or actions of its committees. This does not mean that floor debate and action are negligible, only that the bulk of Congressional decisions are made in committee rooms. Even when changes, whether mild or radical, are made on committee proposals, decisions of Congress are usually the outgrowth of views formulated in committee by a minority group of members.[5]

The standing committee, then, is the focal point of the legislative process. Legislative oversight enables the committee not only to keep itself informed about the goings-on of its executive "constituents," but it provides the committee with information useful in any policy struggle. Not every committee has time or personnel to ride herd on a large administrative department, but, if diligently performed, such oversight serves to keep the executive branch constantly attuned to committee desires. Despite the advantages which derive from their watchdog powers, Congressional committees have been only rarely able to mold public policy. The translation of critical prodding, sporadic harassment, and constant advice into positive programs which bear a clear committee stamp is not easily achieved. The most obvious example is foreign relations. Here, the Executive has an overwhelming advantage in policy-making. Although Congress can criticize, modify, or block executive action, it can seldom develop and adopt an alternative policy of its own.[6]

Even the committee's ability to lead Congress is not without qualification. The influence of committees within their parent houses varies considerably, depending primarily on three factors: the issue at hand, the degree of committee consensus, and the attitude of the administration. If the issue is of a type which does not provoke political or partisan sensibilities, the committee's leadership is generally accepted; but, if it is one

[5] The report accompanying the LaFollette-Monroney bill made the points that the content of enacted legislation is largely determined in committees and that most bills recommended by committees become law. Report of the Joint Committee on the Organization of Congress, 79th Cong., 2d Sess. (1946), p. 2. For a statistical analysis, see Donald R. Matthews, *U.S. Senators and Their World* (Chapel Hill: University of North Carolina Press, 1960), pp. 168-170.

[6] In consequence, one observer notes, Congress is suspicious and distrustful, constantly trying to guard its prerogatives and continually frustrated in its attempts to exercise detailed surveillance over executive action in foreign policy. Roger Hilsman, "Congressional-Executive Relations and the Foreign Policy Consensus," *American Political Science Review,* LII (September 1958), p. 729.

relating, for example, to tax policy, labor legislation, or social welfare, the recommendation of the committee is unlikely to be conclusive. If an issue is controversial, and especially if the political parties have differing views on it, the committee itself will likely split into majority and minority factions, usually, but not always, along party lines. Since a committee's cohesion on a particular measure—the amount of agreement it can reach, the compromises that can be worked out—has much to do with the measure's ultimate fate, a divided committee surrenders powers of decision to the whole Congress. When the administration feels strongly and its views do not parallel those of the committee or committee majority, the power of the committee in Congress is further reduced. Party lines are apt to harden, with some members supporting the president as party leader; others following the recommendations of the committee; and a few "swing" members, who take into account constituency, interest group, or other considerations. Here, too, the final decision is no longer that of the committee.

■ THE APOTHEOSIS OF THE CONGRESSIONAL COMMITTEE

When Congress created the Joint Committee on Atomic Energy through an apparently minor and little-discussed provision in the 1946 act, it applied the maxim that Congress delegated its most important work to its committees. The JCAE appears to be the apotheosis of the Congressional committee, with more abilities and fewer liabilities than other committees. It was clearly *designed* to be more powerful within its particular jurisdictional area—the then-limited but potentially immense field of atomic energy—than other committees were in theirs. Unlike the regular standing committees, the JCAE was established, not by rules of the two houses as spelled out in the Legislative Reorganization Act, but by a separate law. Whether or not exemption from the provisions of the Legislative Reorganization Act has made substantial difference in the Joint Committee's performance, the very fact that the JCAE was the only committee with legislative powers established by law attests that the framers of the basic atomic-energy act had a special type of Congressional institution in mind.[7]

If there have been doubts about the intent of the framers, Joint

[7] Unlike committees specified in the Reorganization Act, the JCAE is not required to file semiannual reports and accounts of staff personnel and payroll for publication in the *Congressional Record;* nevertheless, the Joint Committee does make comparable information available to Congress, whereas other committees have been known to keep from view data they did not wish made public. According to one former member of the JCAE staff, the distinction between the legislative basis of the JCAE and other Congressional committees is too subtle to make any operational difference.

Committee members have repeatedly tried to resolve them. In explaining that the JCAE had a relationship quite different from that of other committees with executive departments, Sen. Clinton P. Anderson (D., N.M.) cited an opinion of the Joint Committee counsel to the effect that the JCAE was not a standing committee of either house, but rather one which was established by the Atomic Energy Act of 1946 and continued under the act of 1954. It was, unlike others, a statutory committee, which derived its powers directly from the law establishing it. Anderson's opposite number, the ranking Republican senator, Bourke Hickenlooper, took the same approach and went still further: the JCAE was not a standing committee, created by one house or the other; it was a committee created by "the National Legislature of Congress . . . established by law, with its rights defined by law. . . . The Committee has unique power." [8]

Whereas the statutory basis for the JCAE's authority was precedent-setting, the establishment of a *joint* committee represented no radical departure from tradition. Joint committees had long been used by Congress.[9] In 1946, there were nine joint committees—either select or standing—in existence, ranging in significance from the Joint Committee on Internal Revenue Taxation to the Joint Committee for the Arrangement of Appropriate Exercises in Commemoration of the Life, Character, and Public Services of the Late President Franklin D. Roosevelt. Some had permanent housekeeping functions, others were study groups, and others were single-purpose investigating bodies. None had legislative authority, that is, the power to have bills referred to it by either house of Congress for hearings, reports, and recommendations. It was therefore a milestone in Congressional history when the Joint Committee on Atomic Energy was given legislative authority. All bills or other matters pertaining to atomic energy were to be referred to the JCAE by both chambers. It was thus structurally unique; it was the only joint committee with other than investigative or study prerogatives and the only legislative committee composed of members of both houses. Its legislative powers, however, were not unusually broad. In fact, until 1954, it lacked an authority possessed by most other committees, the power to authorize construction or acquisition of new facilities as a condition precedent to the appropriation of funds for them.

That it was a "joint" committee also seemed to increase its in-

---

[8] *Cong. Rec.,* 101 (July 21, 1955), 11124; *Cong. Rec.,* 100 (July 16, 1954), 10695.

[9] The First Congress set up a select joint committee for internal housekeeping functions. Since then, joint committees have been created for a wide variety of purposes; for example: to oversee the Library of Congress (1843); to dispose of executive papers (1889); to investigate the Ballinger-Pinchot controversy (1910); short-term rural credits (1920); veterans' benefits (1932); governmental reorganization (1937); and federal expenditures (1941). See George B. Galloway, "The Joint Committee Device: History, Pattern, Rationale" (Library of Congress, Legislative Reference Service, June 23, 1960); *idem., History of the House of Representatives* (New York: Crowell, 1961), pp. 228-231.

fluence vis-à-vis Congress, since it made possible an unusual degree of intercameral coordination and provided a forum for continuous mediation between the two chambers. Unlike normal standing committees, the JCAE was believed to possess the advantage of "institutional unity" which prevented wide disagreements between Senate and House. A recommendation by a joint committee, identically reported to both chambers, would be expected to emerge from floor consideration with few and minor differences between the upper and lower houses. At least, both houses would begin consideration with similar proposals, whereas committees of one body often report out measures substantively different from those recommended by their counterparts in the other chamber. Even if changes were made on the floor and, as a result, different versions passed in the two houses, a conference committee composed of members of the JCAE could have the last word. In conference, the JCAE members would probably reflect less the views of their respective houses than the Committee consensus. In this sense, the joint-committee mechanism might be expected to further decrease the powers of the whole Congress.

The JCAE's peculiar structure tended to strengthen its position with respect to the executive branch and the AEC especially. On the one hand, executive officials could be overjoyed that they had to spend less time repeating testimony before twin committees of the two houses. A friendly Joint Committee, furthermore, could be a most effective ally and protector. There would be no need to satisfy two chairmen who might well have conflicting policy preferences; instead, there would be the relatively simple matter of concentrating inducements and blandishments on one chairman alone. But the institution was also fraught with dangers to the Executive. If an amicable Joint Committee could be a more convenient and effective defender, a hostile Joint Committee could presumably be a more powerful opponent. The Executive would not be able to play off the committee of one house against the committee of another. If an AEC proposal were defeated by the Joint Committee, it could not be resurrected by another committee. Alternatively, if a JCAE proposal were unpalatable to the Executive, there was no possibility of having it buried in a committee of the other house. Any battle the Executive lost within the Joint Committee would have to be fought on the floor of each house, and here, on familiar terrain, the JCAE would have considerable advantages.

In setting up the JCAE, Congress not only established a structurally unique legislative committee, it also gave it unusual authority for supervision of the AEC. The Legislative Reorganization Act had delegated to standing committees the power to review the operations of their constituent agencies. The McMahon Act gave the JCAE an even stronger mandate. The standard of "continuous watchfulness" found in the Legislative Reorganization Act was spelled out to direct the Joint Committee to "make continuing studies of the activities of the Atomic Energy Commission and of problems relating to the development, use, and control of atomic energy." "Continuing studies" might in practice mean anything from superficial and hasty reports to intensive and unhurried investigations, depending on the Committee's aggressiveness and competence.

Lest the securing of qualified personnel pose a problem, the McMahon Act set no limits on the number of staff members and consultants the Joint Committee might employ on either a permanent or *ad hoc* basis. By contrast, the Legislative Reorganization Act had limited professional staffs of standing committees (other than the Appropriations committees) to four members and clerical staffs to six. In addition, the JCAE was given more leeway than regular standing committees in setting staff salaries. As revised in 1954, the new section on staff and assistance granted even broader authority to the JCAE by specifying that the Committee "is empowered to appoint and fix the compensation of such experts, consultants, technicians, and staff employees *as it deems necessary and advisable*" (emphasis added). To assure the Committee of an adequate supply of professional assistance, Congress authorized the JCAE to use the personnel of the executive branch whenever occasion warranted. Other Congressional committees might also request personnel from the executive branch, but without similar statutory right. Although these statutory distinctions in the personnel authority granted the JCAE and other Congressional committees had little relevance to the differences in operations among the various committees, what is important is that the Joint Committee was initially given more than usual discretion along these lines.

In setting up the AEC, Congress had placed a large trust in the hands of the five commissioners and the general manager, whose appointment by the president was subject to confirmation by the Senate. Far from trusting blindly, Congress created the JCAE as a watchdog to serve as its eyes. But vision without clear focus was scarcely better than no vision at all. One problem had perplexed Congressional committees for years: how to obtain from the executive branch information the committee deemed necessary to legislate wisely and in the public interest. Congress had long argued that, since the executive branch is coordinate with, but not superior to, the legislative branch, the latter was entitled to all information possessed by the former. In the atomic-energy field, Congress tried to ensure that its watchdog would be as well informed as the AEC commissioners themselves. A key provision of the McMahon Act directed: "The Commission shall keep the joint committee fully and currently informed with respect to the Commission's activities." With this language, Congress again broke new ground; it clearly intended to give the JCAE a unique capacity for legislative surveillance. Since its origins, the Joint Committee has gone further than mere implementation of its original authority; it has enlarged its statutory basis for legislative oversight. In 1954, the Committee obtained an expanded "fully-and-currently-informed" mandate under Section 202 of the revised statute by the addition of a provision requiring the Department of Defense to keep the JCAE apprised of all atomic-energy matters under its jurisdiction. All other government agencies were required to furnish "any information requested by the Joint Committee with respect to the activities or responsibilities of that agency in the field of atomic energy."

Certainly not the least significant function of the JCAE, according to its members, is the positive or creative function by which the Committee recommends policies and programs to both the Commission and Congress. It takes pride in providing encouragement and not infrequently an extra push to the Commission's atomic-energy program. It lists to its credit nearly every advance made since 1947: the crash program on development of the H-bomb, the increase in the Commission's raw-materials program, the expansion of plutonium production facilities, development of the nuclear submarine, and the few accomplishments of the civilian power program. The Committee has done more than prod; it has, according to one member, made crucial decisions. Fundamental policy, though normally originating within the Commission, is usually made with the advice and consent of the Committee. "And in the case of certain vital policy decisions," Sen. Henry M. Jackson (D., Wash.) wrote, "the urging from the Joint Committee has played so powerful a role that it can be said the Committee made the decisions, with the advice and consent of the executive branch." [10] Perhaps more than any other committee, the JCAE has *tried* to implement the general Congressional policy: Congress, or rather the committee as its delegate, should make the basic decisions, and the administrative agencies should carry them out. Accordingly, the Joint Committee has for at least the past ten years made vigorous efforts to act as a coequal policy-maker with the executive branch.

If the JCAE has appeared to both its supporters and critics to perform its oversight and policy-making functions rather more energetically than most Congressional committees, in its relations with Congress it has likewise attempted to carve out a special place for itself. Created as an agent of Congress for the purpose of keeping the House and Senate in touch with the developments of atomic energy and the actions of the AEC, the Joint Committee has become more than a mere agent charged with the conduct of executive-legislative liaison. Today it stands, as Senator Anderson noted, "rather, as a board of guarantors, saying to the Congress and the American people that all is well, even if many transactions are behind

---

[10] "Congress and the Atom," *Annals of the American Academy of Political and Social Science,* 290 (November 1953), 77.

closed doors." In this respect, it is analogous to other committees of Congress which attempt to dominate in their particular areas of jurisdiction and generally succeed. But, at least in the early years of its life, the Joint Committee *was* Congress as far as atomic-energy matters were concerned. At that time, several factors gave it an ascendancy not enjoyed by other Congressional committees. Secrecy, national security, and complex technology made atomic-energy affairs less appropriate for free and open consideration by the entire Congress than other matters. Since the early 1950's, however, atomic energy has become more mundane. The American monopoly was broken, new weapons overshadowed the atomic bomb, and civilian applications of atomic power became an issue. As America grew accustomed to living in the atomic age, Congress became increasingly involved in certain aspects of atomic-energy policy. Still, in many matters and in some of the most important ones, the Joint Committee makes decisions for Congress itself.[11]

■ MEMBERS AND THEIR SELECTION

The major part of the individual legislator's personal attention, effort, and time is generally devoted to his committee assignments. In view of the great concern of each member with his committee work, it is hardly surprising, as one close observer of Congress has noted, that each committee "tends to develop a life of its own, in which members hold individual, rather than strictly party, attitudes and where the influence of strong and set characters is great." [12] Certainly, a committee's life is never immune to outside influences—party leadership, presidential requests and commands, interest-group pressures, and constituency desires—but each member, whatever the forces at work, has some discretion in choosing a path for the committee to follow. Some members, especially the chairman and the active ones, have more to say than others, and they usually have different things to say. Therefore, a Congressional committee, over a period of time or even at any point in time, is far from a monolithic body. Members vary in the characteristics they bring to the committee and in their behavior and decisions while on the committee.

Because of the transcendent importance of atomic weapons and secrets, exceptional care was taken by the political leaders of the House and Senate in making the original appointments to the JCAE. The object

[11] As the then-chairman of the JCAE and its executive director wrote in 1960, Congress has applied in full measure to the Joint Committee on Atomic Energy Woodrow Wilson's maxim that it does much of its work through committees. Clinton P. Anderson and James T. Ramey, "Congress and Research: Experience in Atomic Research and Development," *Annals of the American Academy of Political and Social Science,* 327 (January 1960), 85-86.

[12] Dean Acheson, *A Citizen Looks at Congress* (New York: Harper, 1956), pp. 24-25.

of the leadership in each House was to appoint men who were proven "statesmen," who were old hands in Congress and therefore accustomed to its traditions and mores, who were judicious and restrained and therefore unlikely to jeopardize atomic secrets, and who were serving on other committees which might be presumed to have an interest in the newly discovered atom. Consequently, original appointees to the Committee were men with considerable seniority,[13] drawn largely from the foreign relations and military affairs committees.[14] This preponderance of members with considerable experience in military and foreign affairs was especially appropriate at a time when the Committee's predominant concern was with atomic weapons. Even more important in an institution where seniority and influence often go hand in hand, the new Committee was blessed with members who had been in Congress long enough to have won the trust of their colleagues. In this complex and secrecy-shrouded area, the trust of their colleagues would be crucial in the years ahead.

The newly appointed Committee met and organized on August 2, 1946, but transacted no other business during the Seventy-ninth Congress. For all practical purposes, the Joint Committee as a working Congressional institution made its debut in 1947, with the opening of the Eightieth Congress, and the members who served then and subsequently will be given attention below.

As Congressional committees go, the JCAE has been remarkably stable in its membership. During the fourteen years from 1947 through

---

[13] The average length of Senate service of Senate members of the new committee was nine years, even though four members—Brien McMahon, Bourke Hickenlooper, Eugene Millikin, and William Knowland—were in their first terms. The seniority of Arthur Vandenberg, Tom Connally, Richard Russell, Harry Byrd, and Edwin Johnson easily compensated for the others' short length of service. The average length of nine years compared favorably with the figure for the Senate committee with the most prestige, Foreign Relations, which was only 11.71 years for the period from the Seventieth through the Eighty-first Congress. See Robert A. Dahl, *Congress and Foreign Policy* (New York: Harcourt, Brace, 1950), p. 288.

Owing to the higher rate of turnover in the lower chamber, House members of the original JCAE were junior to their Senate colleagues. Nevertheless, compared to members of other House committees, they could not be considered mere novices. None were freshmen, and, because of the long experience of the few senior members, their average length of service in the House was a respectable 7.5 years. The comparable figure for the House Foreign Affairs Committee for the period from the Seventieth through the Eighty-first Congress was 7.58 years. *Ibid.*, p. 289.

[14] On the Senate side, Edwin Johnson, cosponsor of the unsuccessful May-Johnson atomic-energy bill, was a ranking member of the Military Affairs Committee; Russell and Byrd were key men on Naval Affairs; and Connally, as chairman, and Vandenberg, as leading Republican spokesman, were the most important members of Foreign Relations. Since the House Committee on Military Affairs, under Chairman Andrew May—the other sponsor of the defeated atomic-energy bill—had been responsible for reporting the basic legislation in the field, all but two of the House members on the original JCAE came from May's committee.

the conclusion of the Eighty-sixth Congress in 1960, a total of thirty-seven men have served on the eighteen-member committee—eighteen Republicans and nineteen Democrats, seventeen senators and eighteen congressmen, and two men, Lyndon Johnson and Henry Jackson, who reacquired their Committee positions after they had left the House and come to the Senate. The comparatively slight turnover in total membership, as well as the balanced turnover of Republicans and Democrats, senators and representatives, has given the JCAE a high degree of continuity, a valuable asset for any Congressional committee. (See figures "A" and "B," pages *xiv-xv*, for Joint Committee membership by years. Included on the chart, but not considered in the composite view of the Committee which follows, are the most recently named members: Rep. Thomas G. Morris (D., N.M.), appointed in early 1961, and Sen. Everett McKinley Dirksen (R., Ill.), appointed in mid-1962.) Because six men—Holifield, Price, Hickenlooper, Sen. Richard B. Russell (D., Ga.), Rep. Carl T. Durham (D., N.C.), and Rep. James E. Van Zandt (R., Pa.)—have served from the Eightieth through the Eighty-sixth Congress, the average length of service of members on the Committee has been increasing. (See Table II-1.)

Over the years, criteria for selection to the JCAE have varied, but the great stress put on relative seniority has endured. Only rarely has a freshman senator and never has a freshman congressman been named to the Committee. Nor has there been a decrease in average seniority since the beginning. In 1947, the average length of a member's service in the House or Senate prior to appointment to the JCAE was about 7.8 years. In 1960, the comparable figure was about the same. (See Table II-1.)

Another continuing criterion for appointment to the Committee has been the individual's membership on other committees. As we have seen, the JCAE as originally constituted was overweighted with members of the committees on military (and naval) affairs. The importance of membership on one of the armed services committees [15] has persisted, but the base has broadened to include members of many other committees. By 1959, the only relevant committees not represented by JCAE members—or, perhaps, the only committees involved in closely related affairs where the JCAE had no emissary—were House Science and Astronautics and House Foreign Affairs.[16] Overlapping memberships of JCAE senators and congressmen in 1959, as an example, are given in Table II-2.

Geography has also played an important part in selection of JCAE members. From the beginning, there seemed to be a purposeful attempt

---

[15] As a result of the Legislative Reorganization Act of 1946, the Military and Naval Affairs committees were consolidated into the Senate and House Armed Services committees.

[16] It should be noted, however, that the House Science and Astronautics Committee just came into being in 1959. At the beginning of the Eighty-seventh Congress, Rep. Thomas G. Morris (D., N.M.), a member of that committee, was appointed to the JCAE as well.

TABLE II-1

AVERAGE AGE AND SERVICE OF MEMBERS OF THE JCAE, 1947-1960

Congress	Year	Average age of committee members (years)	Average length of service in House or Senate prior to membership on the JCAE (years)	Average length of service on the JCAE (years)	Average length of service in House or Senate (years)
Eightieth	1947	51	7.8	—	7.8
	1948	51	7.3	0.9	8.3
Eighty-first	1949	52	9.0	1.6	10.5
	1950	53	8.0	2.6	10.6
Eighty-second	1951	54	6.9	3.5	10.4
	1952	55	6.9	4.5	11.4
Eighty-third	1953	56	7.8	3.9	11.9
	1954	57	7.7	3.7	11.8
Eighty-fourth	1955	56	6.4	5.7	12.1
	1956	57	6.4	6.7	13.1
Eighty-fifth	1957	58	7.7	6.8	14.5
	1958	57	7.3	7.0	13.8
Eighty-sixth	1959	57	7.7	5.5	13.2
	1960	58	7.7	6.5	14.2
Average		55	7.5	4.2	11.7

TABLE II-2

OVERLAPPING COMMITTEE MEMBERSHIPS 1959

Senate committees	*Joint Committee members*
Aeronautical and Space Sciences	Anderson, Russell
Armed Services	Russell (c), Jackson
Foreign Relations	Gore, Hickenlooper, Aiken
Appropriations	Russell, Pastore, Dworshak
Agriculture and Forestry	Hickenlooper, Aiken
Finance	Anderson, Gore, Bennett
Government Operations	Jackson
Interstate and Foreign Commerce	Pastore
Interior and Insular Affairs	Anderson, Jackson, Dworshak
Banking and Currency	Bennett
House committees	*Joint Committee members*
Armed Services	Durham, Price, Van Zandt, Bates
Appropriations	Thomas
Government Operations	Holifield
Interior and Insular Affairs	Aspinall (c), Hosmer, Westland
Post Office and Civil Service	Holifield

(c) = chairman

to make the Committee regionally representative of the entire nation.[17] On the first working committee, a regional balance was obtained—four members from the Northeast, five from the Midwest, four from the South, two from the Rocky Mountain area, and three from the Pacific states. Since then, the balance has remained about the same, with only minor alterations. The only real change has been that the Mountain states have increased their representation at the expense of the Midwestern states. During the period from 1947 through 1960, there has been an almost perfect regional balance of individuals who have served: eight from the Northeast, six from the Midwest, eight from the South, seven from the Mountain region, and eight from the Pacific states.

State, as well as regional, background has usually been considered in making appointments. Colorado has never gone unrepresented on the Committee. Neither has Texas, an interesting example. Texas Democrats Rep. R. Ewing Thomason and Sen. Tom Connally were on the original Committee. Late in 1947, when Thomason resigned from Congress, another Texas Democrat, Rep. Lyndon B. Johnson, was named to take his

[17] In 1947, for example, Senator Millikin, then chairman of the Republican Conference, asked Sen. John Bricker (R., Ohio) if he would go on the JCAE in order to give the Midwest its proper number of members. *Strauss Confirmation Hearings* (1959), p. 631.

place. Then, when Johnson left the House to run for the Senate, another Texas Democrat, Rep. Paul J. Kilday, was appointed to succeed him. In July, 1952, Connally left, and Johnson, now in the Senate, was named to the Committee. (When Johnson resigned in 1953 to devote more of his time to his job as Democratic leader, a New Englander filled the vacancy, and Texas membership was reduced to one man.) Finally, when Kilday left the Committee at the end of the Eighty-fifth Congress, another Texan, Rep. Albert Thomas (D.), replaced him. Obviously, being from Texas is an asset when a slot previously filled by a Texan becomes vacant.

Another criterion has been that of interest representation. Although not every state which boasts an atomic-energy production facility, a national research laboratory, or a public or private atomic industrial group has someone on the Committee, some do—namely Illinois (Argonne), New Mexico (Los Alamos), Washington (Hanford), and Tennessee (Oak Ridge). More noticeably, the uranium-extracting and -processing industries, clustered in the Mountain region, have had several spokesmen on the Committee. Perhaps the most obvious instance of interest representation —in this case that of the Tennessee Valley and TVA complex—resulted from the Dixon-Yates dispute in 1954. Reportedly, one stipulation in the compromise eventually reached between Democratic liberals and Republicans was that Albert Gore of Tennessee be given a seat on the JCAE so that he could express TVA's interests. Since the atom was opened to exploitation by private enterprise in 1954, an important consideration for appointment to the Committee has been an individual's views on electric power. Because Republicans are generally hostile to government intervention in the power field and less than friendly to public-power activities by municipalities and cooperatives, Republican appointees have tended to be proponents of private power. JCAE Democrats, on the other hand, have tended to favor public power.

Since 1947, there has been no difficulty finding members to serve on the Joint Committee. Several factors have made the JCAE attractive to able and ambitious legislators. Not least significant has been the strong appeal of the Committee's work, which involves a combination of military, foreign, and domestic affairs. The legislator—an amalgam of politician, constituency delegate, and national statesman—views membership as a means of exercising leadership on matters of utmost consequence to the nation. He sees Joint Committee service also as a method of advancing his own Congressional career.[18]

---

[18] William S. White, "McMahon—Senator and Atomic Specialist," *N.Y. Times Magazine,* Feb. 12, 1950. White raises the question whether personal ambition played a part in motivating the Connecticut senator to campaign for a spot on the JCAE. His answer: Certainly, but there was also a sense of mission apart from motives of personal advancement.

During the early years, not only the atom itself, with its seemingly bright potentialities, but also the secrecy and classification surrounding it, tended to whet the appetite of members of Congress. On the one hand, they were frightened by the security implications of atomic energy. On the other hand, they desired to be privy to secrets shared by a select number. The restrictions imposed on the free flow of atomic information to members of Congress and the aura that attached to those few who were insiders constituted additional attraction. Members of the new Committee were immediately set apart from their colleagues, if only because of their access to information so sensitive it could not be shared among many. Since the early 1950's the esoteric quality of the atom has diminished. Concurrently, a disillusionment with the real usefulness—whether for unilateral military advantage, competitive nuclear power, or the curing of disease through application of radioactive isotopes—of the atom has set in. Still, the number of legislators seeking membership on the Committee has remained high, and there has usually been keen competition for vacancies.

Perhaps a critical advantage the JCAE possesses in recruiting members, one which assures it a buyer's market, is that it is an "extra committee." In other words, in taking on a JCAE assignment, members have to give up no other committee position in return. If a senator or representative desires to take a new committee post, he usually must resign from one of his other committees.[19] Even if a legislator would be far happier on his new committee, he must carefully consider the seniority he has built up on the one he plans to leave. On the new committee, his chances of becoming a committee chairman are also considerably reduced. Therefore, the legislator customarily does his shopping and moving from committee to committee early in his Congressional career, before he has too much seniority at stake in his first assignment. Of the ten senators who came onto the JCAE since 1947, only one quit another committee, and in that case the committee—District of Columbia—was minor and without prestige. Of the nine House members who have become JCAE members since 1947, none has resigned from committees on which he was serving at the time of appointment. All took the Joint Committee as a second assignment.

Once an individual decides that he would like a place on the JCAE, he has wide scope for initiative. It is up to him to make his desire known to ranking Committee members of his own party and to his party's leadership in the House or Senate. Usually a member expresses his interest in a letter to the speaker or minority leader of the House or the majority

[19] By the rules of the House and Senate, members are limited in the number of major and minor committees on which they may serve. The JCAE, however, is exempt from these rules.

or minority leader of the Senate or by personal conversations when possible. At the same time, it is important for the aspirant to round up support from "his bunch" on the Joint Committee. Some members campaign long and arduously for a seat on the coveted committee. Rep. Craig Hosmer (R., Calif.), for example, spent several years trying to obtain appointment to the Joint Committee. After quitting a job with one of the AEC's field offices in 1948, Hosmer decided to run for Congress primarily to become appointed to the JCAE. But, on his arrival in Washington, he found that another California Republican, Rep. Carl Hinshaw, was already on the Committee. Hinshaw's death in 1956 created a vacancy, but it automatically went to Rep. Thomas A. Jenkins (R., Ohio), who had lost his committee seat when the Democrats gained control of the Eighty-fourth Congress. With Sterling Cole's resignation at the end of the 1957 session, the way appeared clear for Hosmer, but even then he had to compete against many aspirants who had served in Congress much longer than he had. In order to overcome his relative lack of seniority, the Californian buttonholed his Republican colleagues with as many arguments as he could muster that it was to their and the GOP's advantage to appoint him to the JCAE. Nor did his campaign stop with his fellow-congressmen; it was also aimed at administration officials and private citizens known to be influential in atomic-energy affairs. Finally, some rivals withdrew their candidacies in his favor, and many of his Republican colleagues gave him written commitments of support to show Minority Leader Joe Martin.[20] On January 15, 1958, Hosmer was finally appointed to the Joint Committee.

Under the Atomic Energy Act (Section 201), House members of the JCAE are appointed by the speaker and Senate members by the president of the Senate. The chief difference in assignments to the JCAE is that the party committees for organizing standing committees—in the House, the Republican Committee on Committees and the Democratic membership of the Ways and Means Committee and, in the Senate, the Republican Committee on Committees and the Democratic Steering Committee—take no part. In practice, assignments to the JCAE are made by the party leaders in each chamber.[21] In the House, for instance, members

---

[20] From a press release issued by Representative Hosmer's office. *Washington Post and Times Herald,* Jan. 19, 1958.

[21] Actually, the party leadership exercises great influence on appointments to all important committees. On the Democratic side of the Senate, for example, the majority leader prepares a slate of appointments which he presents to the Steering Committee. He also sits as chairman of the Steering Committee. Only on rare occasions is he overruled on an appointment by the committee members. In the House, the leadership of both parties is directly involved in assignments to the major committees, although the leaders do not usually review applicants to lesser ones. On appointments to House committees, see Nicholas A. Masters, "House Committee Assignments," *American Political Science Review,* LV (June 1961), 345-357.

of the Republican Committee on Committees or Democrats on the Ways and Means Committee do not even review candidates for the JCAE. The decision is made by the speaker or minority leader, depending on the applicant's party, usually after consultation with ranking members of the Joint Committee. Rep. William H. Bates (R., Mass.), a member of the Republican Committee on Committees, wanted to fill a vacancy on the JCAE in 1953. He approached Joe Martin, then speaker of the House, but was turned down. Martin, however, promised Bates the next vacancy. With Martin's ouster as Republican leader in 1959, Bates informed the new leader, Charles Halleck, of Martin's promise. That year, with two vacancies for Republicans, including one from New England, Halleck redeemed his predecessor's promise, and, after Van Zandt and other JCAE Republicans agreed, Bates was put on the Committee.

In the Senate, as well, the nominating role of the party leaders is crucial. In 1954, Albert Gore and Democratic Leader Johnson, a JCAE alumnus, worked out an arrangement whereby Gore would go on the Committee in return for aid in halting the liberal filibuster against the 1954 act. Instrumental in the appointment of George D. Aiken (R., Vt.) in 1959 was his friendship, not with the ranking Republican member of the JCAE, but rather with the Democratic chairman, Clinton Anderson. Aiken and Anderson had worked closely on agricultural problems, and Anderson was delighted to have the senator from Vermont come on the Committee. Because of Aiken's high seniority in the Republican Party, he had no difficulty having Republican Leader Dirksen name him. Thus, if a seeker of a JCAE membership is a senior man in his party's delegation to Congress and his relations with members of the Committee and with his party leadership are good, his chances of appointment are excellent. If he is junior, much depends on the number and comparative qualifications of his competitors.

■ THE PROCESS OF EDUCATION

When new men take their places on the Joint Committee, they are generally unprepared to make immediate sense of the variety and complexity of problems which they face.[22] Their training and background in foreign and military affairs are helpful, but not sufficient to give them quick grasp of the intricacies of atomic technology. They must on their own initiative exploit the available resources, since there is no formal

---

[22] Some, of course, are better prepared than others, and for them the learning process may be more rapid. Sen. Albert Gore and Rep. Albert Thomas, for example, came to the Committee after experience on the House Appropriations Independent Offices Subcommittee, where they were responsible for reviewing the AEC budget. But budget review on House Appropriations is vastly different from the broad review given AEC programs by the Joint Committee.

routine for teaching them. They must read on their own, depend on explanations of witnesses and the discussions of their colleagues at hearings, and enlist aid from JCAE staff members. Most important to their education are informal conversations—in Capitol corridors on the way to and from hearings, in the Senate and House cloak rooms, or at lunch—with the more experienced members of the Joint Committee.

A JCAE member was not always expected to be thoroughly familiar with the atom. In the early years of the Committee, complete mastery of the field appeared so impossible that members were modest in their expectations of what they could actually learn. Chairman Brien McMahon pointed out in 1947 that the JCAE would make continuing studies, but, when asked if this meant that members were obliged to "fully understand" the subject, he replied without hesitation: "Thank heavens, no." [23] Under the Hickenlooper and McMahon chairmanships, the members of the JCAE were certainly able men, but they were unprepared to examine the whole complex of problems associated with atomic energy. Some of the ablest members were necessarily preoccupied with responsibilities on other committees and could not devote sufficient time and study to matters before the JCAE. The Commission's attempts to educate the Committee were largely failures, and, according to one former commissioner: "Joint meetings, public hearings, and private hearings became infrequent and limited to specific subjects, usually controversies and fears of the moment. . . . The greater part of communication became 'paper work.' It centered increasingly on security matters. It tended to take the form of time-consuming replies to letters apparently designed to make a written record." [24]

Learning a bewildering new field at any time would have been slow, and, during a period defined and characterized by an obsession to achieve "security through secrecy," the Committee's own education was at best a rather minor concern. Nevertheless, during the early 1950's, a gradual transformation took place, and the JCAE began taking the job of self-education seriously. Little by little, the Committee became a vast repository of information and through practice worked out techniques of acquiring additional knowledge. By 1954, active members of the Joint Committee had become almost as well informed as specialists within the AEC. Even the less conscientious members had absorbed information just by occasional attendance at expert briefings and by the reading of Committee hearings, reports, and prints. The mass of informative material was not to be ignored. By 1954, for example, the JCAE had held 112 public hearings and published twenty-eight reports and Committee prints,

---

[23] *AEC Confirmation Hearings* (1947), p. 182.

[24] W. W. Waymack, "Four Years Under Law," *Bulletin of the Atomic Scientists,* VII (February 1951), 54.

which represented an accumulation of information from thousands of books, articles, reports, documents, and pieces of correspondence. There had also been 283 full or subcommittee meetings in executive session.

Since then, the Committee has been especially energetic in educating its members. Obviously, individual members have been free to go about learning atomic energy in their own ways. But the information has always been made available, and, according to one member, it "came in so fast you couldn't read all of it. If you read all of it, you wouldn't have time to do all the rest of your duties. . . ." [25] In addition to hearings on specific legislation and *ad hoc* investigations by the full Committee and subcommittees, the annual "Section 202 hearings" have kept members attuned to the development, growth, and state of the atomic-energy industry. Special hearings have also been held on extremely technical subjects in order to familiarize Committee members and other interested parties with the numerous applications of the atom.[26] Of particular consequence in the education of JCAE members have been the hearings on the nature and effects of radioactive fallout (1957, 1959, and 1962) and on the technical aspects of detection and inspection controls of a nuclear-test ban (1960 and 1961) and the excellent summary analyses prepared by the Committee staff. The 1957 fallout hearings presented a scene which appeared strange in a Congressional committee room:

> As the Joint Committee on Atomic Energy subcommittee assembled in the huge marble-pillared Senate caucus room . . . , the committee members, like enrollees in a high school night course, were given a 9-page glossary explaining such terms as *alleles, keloid, neiosis* and *polidy,* and then told to listen as professors . . . standing before blackboards lectured them on nuclear physics.[27]

Thus, the Joint Committee, responsible for informing Congress and the public, used its investigative powers to inform itself as well.

Committee members have not relied on formal hearings alone for information deemed useful in performance of their duties. They have required the AEC to submit frequent reports on a variety of subjects. They have also learned much as a result of the focused probings and day-to-day surveillance by staff members who have freely roamed the halls of AEC headquarters, traveled on a regular basis to AEC field offices, and

---

[25] Testimony of Senator Bricker, *Strauss Confirmation Hearings* (1959), p. 636.

[26] For example, the 1954 hearings on the contribution of atomic energy to agriculture and medicine; the 1955 hearings on radiation sterilization of foods; the 1956 hearings on research in medicine, biology, agriculture, and food preservation; the 1959 hearings on industrial radioactive waste disposal; and the 1960 hearings on frontiers in atomic-energy research.

[27] *The Nation,* June 8, 1957, p. 490.

inspected national nuclear laboratories—armed by delegation with the Committee's formidable "fully-and-currently-informed" powers. Their knowledge has increased by means of information transmitted informally through carefully cultivated leaks in the executive branch's chain of command. Perhaps the most convincing example of the Committee's ability to develop "informal" channels is provided by the close and constant relationship of the JCAE with Admiral Hyman Rickover. Although in the employ of the Executive in a dual capacity with the AEC and Defense, Rickover, according to Senator Gore, not only reported directly to the AEC and the secretary of defense, "but he also *reported* and *responded* to the Joint Committee on Atomic Energy." [28] Rickover is the most prominent, but by no means the only, executive official who provides the Committee with reports on the activities of the executive branch.

In addition to formal and informal information from the executive branch, the JCAE has used several other means of accumulating necessary facts and opinions. Probably more than any other Congressional committee, the JCAE has made effective use of consultants, advisory panels, and industry-government seminars to develop information and explore outstanding problems. Advisory panels have succeeded in bringing together into a coherent whole elusive strands of unorganized data. Starting with the 1952 Atomic Plant Expansion Advisory Panel, under Lewis Strauss, the JCAE has assembled *ad hoc* "brain trusts" to help it in its huge job of processing relevant information. Notable have been the 1956 McKinney panel, which reported on the peaceful uses of atomic energy, and the Advisory Panel on Military Applications, established in 1958 as a standing body to consider nuclear weapons systems.[29]

The several consultants hired by the Committee since 1956 have been of crucial educational value. During consideration of a civilian reactor acceleration program (Gore-Holifield bill) that year, the Committee, in need of expert technical assistance, employed Walter Zinn, former director of the AEC's Argonne National Laboratory and one of the leading reactor experts in the country. Zinn's briefings on alternative reactor concepts were of inestimable value to Committee members, and his advice was closely followed. In 1957, after President Eisenhower refused to reappoint Thomas E. Murray to the Commission, the JCAE used his services on an intermittent basis. Probably the largest-scale study undertaken by any consultant

---

[28] *Cong. Rec.*, 102 (Feb. 1, 1956), 1768-1769. Emphasis added. Rickover has kept the Joint Committee "currently" as well as "fully" informed. After his July, 1959, trip to the Soviet Union with Vice-President Nixon, the admiral in early August reported to the JCAE on the expedition in general and on Soviet nuclear installations in particular. See *Forum Memo,* August 1959, pp. 35-36.

[29] Panels have also served in extraeducational ways, namely, to give impartial and highly respected support to policy views already formulated by a majority of the Joint Committee.

was that of Robert McKinney, in 1959 and 1960, on international policies and programs associated with atomic energy. Given full cooperation and staff aid by the Committee, the AEC, and other government agencies, McKinney's five-volume study provided a wealth of information. Although individual members did not accept all his conclusions and therefore wished to have the JCAE dissociated from the final report, the Committee as a whole benefited from the assembled data.[30] Recently, the Committee has made use of special technical consultants primarily to refute the conclusions suggested by highly technical studies made by the AEC. In October, 1958, and February, 1960, for instance, two studies of the economic aspects of the proposed Hanford plutonium production reactor were made for the AEC by the Stone and Webster Engineering Company and the Federal Power Commission, respectively. Members of the Committee majority disputed the assumptions on which the Commission's reports rested and therefore retained R. W. Beck and Associates as the JCAE's own consultant to study the economics of generating by-product electrical energy, using the Committee's assumptions as a starting point.[31]

Another informational device exploited by the Committee is the joint industry-government seminar. On the question of government indemnification in 1956, the Committee invited AEC officials, representatives of reactor manufacturers and operators, suppliers, insurance companies, and the legal profession to an executive session seminar to discuss proposed legislation. In 1957, when Chairman Durham's "Ten-Year Demonstration Power Reactor Program" was under consideration, a two-day seminar was held with reactor experts, utility representatives, atomic-equipment manufacturers, architect-engineers, and reactor consultants. Brief examination of the civilian reactor acceleration issue illustrates the educational resources used by the Committee. Study on the problem began with the McKinney panel report and the Gore-Holifield hearings and JCAE report in 1956. The next year, reports of the American Assembly and the National Planning Association were given attention by the JCAE staff

[30] The Committee discussed the report on August 24, 1960, and, by a vote of ten to seven, adopted Chairman Anderson's resolution to publish it. It was cited as a study prepared *for* the Committee and not a Committee report. The Democrats did not agree with McKinney's de-emphasis of the need for building power reactors and prototypes; the Republicans were unhappy about the consultant's criticism of the handling of the "Atoms for Peace" program of the Eisenhower administration. See *Forum Memo,* September 1960, pp. 3-4.

[31] Utilization of consultants is by no means unusual among Congressional committees. During consideration of the 1959 labor bill, both the Senate and House Labor committees employed outside labor experts. House Science and Astronautics has also used technical experts on a temporary consulting basis. Most extensive recent use of consultant services was made by the Senate Foreign Relations Committee in 1959, when it employed several research organizations to conduct fourteen studies of various phases of American foreign policy.

and members. In 1958, there were the reports of the Edison Electric Institute, the AEC, and the JCAE staff report and industry's comments thereon. Extensive informal seminars with all segments of the atomic industry and hearings with the commissioners were held in 1959 on the basis of the report of the Ad Hoc Advisory Committee on Reactor Policies and Programs established by the AEC. Nearly every Committee member attended one or several of the meetings and consequently received thorough briefing on the civilian reactor program.

The Committee has not been content with oral testimony, questioning, and written reports; members have had the opportunity "to get the feel" of the subject of their inquiries. Trips by members to AEC field offices and national laboratories are not unusual.[32] More spectacular trips also take place—for instance, the 1955 overnight cruise of members aboard the nuclear submarine "Nautilus" and the hearing held during the course of a weekend cruise aboard the "Skipjack" several years later. Trips abroad have been less frequent, but in 1954 members of the Raw Materials Subcommittee traveled to Asia, the Middle East, Greece, and Spain to get on-the-spot information on sources of special nuclear fuels. In 1957, Representatives Price and Van Zandt journeyed to the Soviet Union to investigate that country's physical-research programs and facilities. It should be noted that the Joint Committee's foreign trips are much less frequent than those made by some other committees, particularly the foreign-relations groups of both houses.

Like other committees, the JCAE has at its disposal two useful Congressional informational facilities, the General Accounting Office and the Legislative Reference Service of the Library of Congress. The first has served less as an educational device than as a legal critic of executive operations and contracts. The second, because of the research abilities of the JCAE's own staff and consultants as well as its reservoir of talent available within the executive departments, has only occasionally been called on to provide the Committee with comprehensive studies.

The fact that the Joint Committee has devised efficient methods of obtaining and organizing policy and technical information does not necessarily mean that individual members will absorb and make effective use of it. Much depends on the role of subcommittees as study groups, the screening and processing of data by the staff, and, of course, the interests and absorptive powers of individual members. But, over the years, a dominating ethic of the Committee has been an intense concentration on learn-

---

[32] The Committee justified frequent inspection trips in its first report to Congress: "The sheer size and complexity of the plants and the diversity of the laboratory activities cannot be comprehended without personal observation. . . . Such personal observation and inquiry provide an important means for independent judgment which the committee feels is essential." S. Rep. No. 850, 80th Cong., 2d Sess. (1948).

ing. This has been so pervasive that even the least-involved members, those whose attentions have been largely devoted to their roles on other committees, have accumulated a relatively high degree of sophistication in atomic-energy affairs. And those who have been on the JCAE for any length of time and who have worked assiduously at their atomic education have acquired expertise unmatched by their opposite numbers on the Commission.

■ COMMITTEE COHESION

One of the chief powers of the Joint Committee on Atomic Energy is not formally derived from statute; it can be best described as informal and best labeled "moral suasion." The Committee has not been able to say to the executive branch either "You must do this" or "You cannot do this" with certainty its command would be followed. Yet, where its position has been strong, it has usually prevailed. Almost without exception, a strong position has been related to Committee unanimity or near-unanimity in favor of or against a particular policy.[33] As a following chapter will show, a key to the JCAE's influence is its cohesiveness—the consistency with which members reach similar conclusions, though perhaps starting with different preferences and values. Clearly, if the forces which tend to produce cohesion are greater than those working in the opposite direction, the JCAE will be in a better position to face both Congress and the Executive with its proposals.[34]

• Unifying Influences

Since the unity of the JCAE appears to be one of the principal determinants of its influence on any given policy, it is necessary to consider those forces which promote and those which impede Committee cohesion. Some of the centripetal pulls have already been mentioned in another context. Members of Congress often refer to themselves as "we" and

---

[33] During debate on the 1954 act, Senator Hickenlooper mentioned that, when the Committee was unanimous, its opinion was accepted by the AEC. On two or three occasions, he pointed out, the Joint Committee had been unanimous or almost unanimous and, in the end, the Commission had accepted its policy. *Leg. Hist. 1954 Act,* v. 3, p. 3182.

[34] Committees tend to agree on what should be done in their areas of policy to a greater extent than the full House or Senate. Some committees are more united than others, although obviously none presents a solid phalanx on every issue. In the Senate, for instance, Foreign Relations is the most united committee; then come Interior and Armed Services. At the other end of the unity-disunity continuum are the Agriculture and Labor committees, which often divide along partisan lines. Committee cohesion in the House appears to follow a similar pattern. An excellent analysis of committee integration—the degree to which the group is able to resolve internal conflict—is Richard F. Fenno, Jr., "The House Appropriations Committee as a Political System," *American Political Science Review,* LVI (June 1962), 310-324.

executive officials as "the people downtown." The distinction is more than semantic, conveying as it does a sense of solidarity in face of a hostile and encroaching bureaucracy. This traditional rivalry between the executive and legislative branches of government tends to promote Committee unity, particularly on issues which plainly affect the relative powers of the two branches.

A second factor is the peculiar nature of the subject matter with which the Joint Committee deals. All members share the great responsibility imposed by the secrecy requirements and security aspects of atomic-energy affairs. This in itself does not mean that their outlooks are identical or even similar, only that the highly classified nature of their work has brought members closer together. The overriding importance of the atom, especially in the early years, has made the eighteen-man Committee an elite group. As with any elite, differences between it and outsiders are considerably greater than dissimilarities within the group. In this case, at least, cohesiveness and prestige go hand in hand. This separateness from other committees has been enhanced by the JCAE's novel structure, its legislative parenthood, and its unusual statutory powers. In addition, there is the unity which institutional jointness promotes, when there is no other committee coequal in atomic-energy matters. In a bicameral legislature, a unicameral committee of substantive powers is an oddity which sets members apart from colleagues with more routine assignments. Members share the feeling that the JCAE is unique, and this sharing of a difference from outsiders tends to produce *esprit de corps* and committee harmony.

In the Joint Committee, as in any committee of the House or Senate, social pressures engender more conformity to majority and traditional views than might otherwise prevail. The facts that members spend so much time together, have to work together, and have to reach agreements if they wish to get anything done produce pressures for consensus. So does the possibility of achieving compromises, reaching understandings, and making deals behind the closed doors of committee conference rooms. Selective recruitment of new members works along the same lines. If it is thought that a candidate will not fit into the group, one or several older members will likely persuade the leadership not to appoint him.

Ironically, the very representativeness of the Joint Committee's membership has tended to promote unity more often than divisiveness. State and regional balance has reduced the chances of strong, contesting constituency blocs. Because of this fragmentation, instead of conflict between opposing blocs, members indulge one another's regional or state interests in return for like indulgences. Committee members have comparatively little concern about pressures from back home. An individual will, of course, try to ensure that his state or district is not discriminated against when contracts are let by the AEC. Thus, when the AEC installation at Oak Ridge is under discussion, Senator Gore of Tennessee listens attentively; when Los Alamos is the topic, Senator Anderson of New Mexico may act as spokesman for his state. Despite these obvious state concerns, however, internal divisions on the Committee are seldom provoked by geographical factors. There is no visible evidence of internal bickering over fair shares for the state or district.

More likely to divide the Committee are economic interests—coal, uranium, private utilities, or public-power groups. But here, too, the membership's broad base has resulted, more often than not, in consensus. Perhaps an important explanation of the Committee's ability to remain cohesive is simply the fact that there have been comparatively few pressure groups active in the field of atomic energy. Certainly no groups comparing in organizational efficiency or membership base with the farm, labor, business, veterans', or military lobbies which pressure other Congressional committees have as consistently and as effectively prodded the JCAE. The reason for this is that atomic-energy policy has conferred few direct benefits and inflicted few direct deprivations, since few people stood to gain much or lose much—except in some vague and distant future.[35]

This is not to say that group interest never plays a role in Joint Committee decisions. Rather, with the significant exception of the post-1954 running controversy between public- and private-power groups, it has not succeeded in substantially reducing Committee consensus.[36] In 1949, for example, when the AEC decided to substitute gas for coal as fuel for an Oak Ridge power plant, the response of private groups was tremendous. Coal companies, the National Coal Association, the United Mine Workers, and the Railway Executives Association objected to members of Congress and to Chairman McMahon. A special subcommittee of the JCAE held hearings. Representatives Charles H. Elston (R., Ohio) and Van Zandt protested vigorously, the Ohioan on the grounds that the supply of natural gas going to municipalities in his state would be reduced and the Pennsylvanian because of the economic effects on coal mines and railroads if Oak Ridge switched to natural gas.[37] The subcommittee sub-

---

[35] Robert A. Dahl and Ralph S. Brown, Jr., *Domestic Control of Atomic Energy* (New York: Social Science Research Council, 1951), p. 8.

[36] A comparison might be made to interest-group activity in foreign affairs. Outside pressure groups usually play a small role in swaying members of the foreign affairs committees, although in certain areas, as in the tariff, their influence is somewhat greater. As a result, issues like the tariff produce the greatest strains on committee unity. James P. Richards, "The House of Representatives in Foreign Affairs," *Annals of the American Academy of Political and Social Science,* 289 (September 1953), 72. But even on tariffs, interest groups have only a limited influence. See Raymond A. Bauer, Ithiel de Sola Pool, and Lewis A. Dexter, *American Business and Public Policy,* "The Politics of Foreign Trade" (New York: Atherton Press, 1963), Part IV.

[37] *Natural Gas Pipe Line Hearing* (1949), pp. 9, 20.

mitted a report taking issue with the Commission's decision. The full Committee adopted the report unanimously; if several members felt strongly enough about coal and oil, their colleagues were willing to go along.

A similar accommodation was reached with respect to uranium-mining. Several Committee members have looked after the interests of the uranium industry. The late Rep. John J. Dempsey (D., N.M.) paid special attention to AEC's uranium prices and purchases. Senator Anderson has been particularly interested in protecting domestic uranium producers and processors against foreign competitors. Rep. Wayne N. Aspinall (D., Colo.) serves in a dual capacity, as chairman of the House Interior Committee and on the Joint Committee as spokesman for the mining industry. In late 1957, when the AEC announced that it would not extend the guaranteed incentive price for domestic uranium it set in 1956 to new uranium-ore reserves developed after November, 1958, there was an instantaneous outcry from the Mountain states. After appeals to the AEC had failed, the governors of the concerned states protested to their senators and congressmen, who in turn spoke to members of the JCAE. The Committee responded quickly, held hearings, and united behind the uranium industry. As a result, the AEC soon modified its proposed policy. Here, too, a majority of members who did not have strong feelings on the matter were willing to support the minority that did.[38]

Stability of Committee membership has also promoted cohesiveness. Its membership has changed, but the seniority principle, as well as members' satisfaction with their work, has encouraged them to stay on the Committee. The fact that few left the JCAE by choice suggests that members felt service was rewarding, both in terms of career enhancement and program accomplishments. Excluding the original appointees who were dropped when the JCAE reorganized at the start of the Eightieth Congress, only ten senators and nine congressmen have left the Committee. Few have left voluntarily. Three died while serving. Several were dropped when the opposition party took control of Congress and increased its own Committee membership, but they returned at the first opportunity. The

---

[38] When issues become complicated and motives are mixed, it is likely that divergent interest pressures will help to split the Committee. In 1950, for instance, the Senate section of the Committee split 5-4 against the confirmation of Sumner Pike to the Commission. Pike was considered an adherent of Lilienthal policies and had therefore become discredited in the eyes of Republican members of the Joint Committee. Another factor in his rejection, however, was the welfare of the domestic uranium industry. Colorado uranium influenced the attitudes of two Colorado members, Johnson and Millikin, who said that they opposed Pike because of his hostility to their state's mining industry and his support of uranium imports. In arguing against the confirmation, Millikin said on the floor of the Senate that he "was not sent to the Senate to liquidate Colorado." *Cong. Rec.*, 96 (May 25, 1950), 9766.

majority simply retired from Congress for one reason or another.[39] Four members—Senators John W. Bricker (R., Ohio), Guy R. Cordon (R., Ore.), and Millard E. Tydings (D., Md.) and Rep. James T. Patterson (R., Conn.)—were involuntarily retired after suffering defeats in their races for re-election. One member lost a primary campaign. Of the nineteen who left the Committee, only three remained in Congress after their departure. Senator Vandenberg, whose health was failing, quit the Committee to devote all his energies to Foreign Relations. Representative Kilday left so that he could spend full time on House Armed Services, where he was heir-apparent to Chairman Carl Vinson (D., Ga.). And Lyndon Johnson, shortly after his election as Democratic leader, resigned from the JCAE to devote his full energies to leadership activities.

When changes did occur, they were never complete and seldom drastic. In 1957, Holifield stressed this point, noting that most members had been serving for eight or ten years. "The Congressional members . . . ," the Californian said, "have by far the greatest individual and collective continuity of government experience in the atomic-energy field."[40] Compared to their JCAE counterparts, the commissioners and their staff appear to be mere transitory figures on the atomic-energy scene. In 1957, Chairman Strauss had served a total of seven years, Willard F. Libby three years, and Harold S. Vance only fourteen months, and there were two vacancies on the Commission. By contrast, nine members of the Committee had ten years' experience and three others more than six years.[41] Continuity of membership has also contributed to the unity of behavior on the Committee. The JCAE has suffered neither from the potentially disruptive consequences of rapid turnover nor from sudden impositions of new sets of standards governing internal Committee behavior.[42] A tradition of conscientiousness and responsibility has developed, and nearly every member shares it, some more than others. Under leadership provided by the old hands, newer members, whatever their politics or backgrounds, take their jobs seriously, work hard, and show deep concern. Unlike many other

---

[39] The retirees included Carl Durham, Eugene Millikin, Ewing Thomason, Edwin Johnson, Charles Elston, Tom Connally, William Knowland, and Sterling Cole. Johnson left to run for governor of Colorado, Knowland to run for governor of California, and Cole to accept appointment as director-general of the newly created International Atomic Energy Agency (IAEA).

[40] *Cong. Rec.*, 103 (Aug. 5, 1957), 13685.

[41] This is not unusual. Most committees have members with greater experience than top people in comparable departments and agencies. William S. White notes that, when Charles Wilson of General Motors became secretary of defense in 1953, there were men on the Senate Armed Services Committee who had served since long before World War II. Its chairman, Senator Russell, had been a member many years before Wilson himself or even a single one of his military advisers had held any significant position in the defense establishment. William S. White, *Citadel* (New York: Harper, 1956), p. 194.

[42] Cf. Fenno, *op. cit.*, pp. 314-315.

committees, the JCAE does not wait for crisis issues to take it by surprise; instead, its members study constantly and exercise oversight continuously.

Shared labor pulls members together, but not all equally. Some devote more time and energy to their duties than others. Holifield is perhaps the prime example of a legislator who has devoted most of his time to the Joint Committee. In order to study on weekends and until eleven or twelve most evenings, he has forsaken Washington's social life and has given up golf, hunting, and fishing. "My wife and my doctor reproach me for it," he says, "but I have no time now." [43] Senator Russell, because of his commitments as chairman of Armed Services and his duties on Appropriations, is quite another case. He seldom attends JCAE meetings or hearings. Although he tries to keep up with the written record of the Committee's activities and consults his colleagues from time to time, he cannot be considered one of the more active members of the Committee.[44]

Despite their assignments on other committees, most members are in particularly favorable positions to devote considerable time to atomic-energy affairs. In Congress, where politicking for votes back home is a constant preoccupation of members, those who come from relatively safe states or districts have more time to devote to legislative business. Relatively few members of the Joint Committee have had to worry seriously about re-election, since most come from districts or states which have become fairly safe for their candidacies. This has permitted House members, especially, who otherwise would have had to spend about one and a half of their two-year terms campaigning for votes, to devote considerable time to Committee work.

A glance at the "safety" of the seats of the thirty-eight men who have been on the Committee since, and including, 1946 is instructive. Only four were defeated in general elections, and these defeats were unexpected. Otherwise, members have had little to fear about returning to Washington after the next election. Russell since 1946 has had no opposition in general elections and only token opposition in primaries. Holifield has never received less than 70 per cent of the two-party vote and three times was nominated by both the Democratic and Republican parties of his Los Angeles district. During his Committee tenure, Sterling Cole generally garnered about 70 per cent of the vote in his upper New York State constituency. In six elections, Representative Price's plurality has ranged from a low of 65 per cent to a high of 76 per cent, and Representative Durham in seven elections has received between 63 and 100 per cent of

---

[43] *N.Y. Times,* Aug. 24, 1959.

[44] According to a member of Russell's staff, the Georgian only goes to the organization meetings of the Committee at the beginning of each Congress. This is an exaggeration, but it comes closer to the truth than not.

the vote. In only one of seven campaigns did Van Zandt's margin fall as low as 56 per cent; otherwise, it hovered around 63 per cent. Henry Jackson won six elections for his House seat and two for the Senate without ever losing or coming close to defeat. In primaries as well as general elections, the large majority of JCAE members have had little serious opposition.

On some Congressional committees, authoritarian rule by the chairman militates against cohesion. A chairman's authority is, of course, likely to be resented by minority party members if they see their proposals arbitrarily buried while proposals favored by the chairman are given expeditious attention. But, whatever the policy disagreements or partisan splits, the chairman who proceeds "democratically" is more apt to keep his membership united than the one who tries to maintain authoritarian control. The standing committees of the two houses vary enormously in their recognition of democratic procedures. On some, there is fair treatment of all matters that come before the committee, whereas on others procedures seem to be purely according to the whim of the chairman. Although Section 133 of the Legislative Reorganization Act provides certain ground rules for committees, in practice wide discretion is vested in the individual committees. If the rules of a particular committee are such that the chairman's authority is unlimited or nearly so, members are likely to rebel eventually.[45]

There has been little doubt as to who exercised paramount authority on the Joint Committee. But the several chairmen—Senators Hickenlooper, McMahon, and Anderson, and Congressmen Cole, Durham, and Holifield—have ruled with self-restraint and consideration of the views of other members. Whether aggressive like Clinton Anderson, adamant like Sterling Cole, or mild and soft-spoken like Carl Durham, the chairman has always been the key Committee personage. Within broad limits, his attitudes, preferences, and style have set the course for the Committee's activities. Yet, the chairman has been able to move the Committee only in directions underwritten by a majority. If too many members balk, the chairman must slow down or reverse his field.[46]

Preferences of other members, Republicans and Democrats, have usually been weighed before decisions have been made by JCAE chairmen.

---

[45] House Education and Labor until 1957 was an example of an "unreformed committee." Its rules were brief and vested complete power in the chairman. Finally, a bipartisan group of members pushed through rules similar to those followed by the "democratic" Interior Committee. See Stewart Udall, "In Defense of the Seniority System," *N.Y. Times Magazine,* Jan. 13, 1957.

[46] This is generally true of other Congressional committees, as well. The powers of Senators James Eastland and Harry Byrd, chairmen of the Judiciary and Finance committees, respectively, depend less on their personal leadership than on the acquiescence of conservative majorities in both groups.

Prior to announcing a Committee policy, scheduling controversial hearings, or making major demands of the executive branch, chairmen have consulted with other members of the Joint Committee. Most important have been the prior consultations between chairmen and ranking members of the opposite party. If an immediate decision is required and it is impractical to call the full Committee together, the chairman will contact ranking members by telephone or in person.[47] They, in turn, will be expected to communicate relevant information to other members, to discuss pros and cons, and finally to inform the chairman of their opinions on the matter. When a majority of Committee members desires, meetings are called or hearings scheduled. It is almost impossible for the chairman to unilaterally sweep aside issues which a number of members wish to discuss or to pigeonhole bills supported by a majority. The fair play of JCAE chairmen, from the time when McMahon permitted Hickenlooper's one-man investigation of the AEC in 1949 to the present, has enabled an unusually high degree of cooperation to prevail on the Committee.

The organization of the JCAE after its early years into permanent subcommittees has strengthened internal democracy. At first glance, it might appear that subcommittees with any degree of independence would tend to diminish Committee unity. The contrary has been the case. By providing members, and especially majority members, with clear fields of jurisdiction and expertise, subcommittees have given all active members channels for their energies. JCAE chairmen have respected the opinions of subcommittees, which has encouraged the latter to work energetically in their assigned areas. Chairmen of the full Committee have seen that all majority members have had the opportunity to chair a subcommittee, and, when necessary, new or special subgroups have been established partially to find chairmanships for those who did not yet have them. Members have been allowed to choose subcommittee assignments on the basis of their own interests, and seldom has the Committee chairman had to decide a dispute over placement.[48] The effect of subcommittees has been threefold: first, some of the wide powers of the JCAE chairman have been transferred to subcommittee chairmen; second, subcommittees have been permitted to initiate policies in the name of the full Committee, and their recommendations have usually been accepted by the Committee; and, third,

---

[47] For example, if a sensitive matter arose, one interviewee recalled, Chairman Anderson would call Sterling Cole and say: "Look, Stub, we know each other's views on this matter. It seems appropriate . . . , or do you have other feelings?"

[48] In the Second Session of the Eighty-sixth Congress, the JCAE was organized into the following subcommittees: Agreements for Cooperation, Communities, Legislation, Military Applications, Raw Materials, Research and Development, Security, and the Special Subcommittee on Radiation. Of the ten Democratic members, all but the chairman, the vice-chairman, and Senator Russell (who had insufficient time) were subcommittee chairmen. Holifield headed two.

the fact that small groups of members have worked closely together in specific areas and have been responsible for Congressional leadership in these areas has helped develop similar views and almost identical stakes in atomic-energy programs. Just as Congress is prone to follow the lead of the Joint Committee, so members of the full Committee are prone to follow the lead of expert subgroups.[49] Members therefore rely on one another for specialized leadership. This mutual reliance has been especially evident between Holifield, who for many years chaired the Subcommittee on Legislation, and Price, who headed the Subcommittee on Research and Development.

A few examples of the authority of JCAE subcommittees may prove useful. In 1951, the Reactor Development group under Durham gave an ultimatum to civilian and military authorities that, unless a decision on a reactor project were made within a specific time, executive officials would be requested to testify as to the reason for deferring judgment.[50] The subcommittee arrived at and announced its demand independently of any controls from the Committee chairman or the full Committee. When Carl Hinshaw was chairman of the same subcommittee in 1953, he announced publicly that he hoped to convince the full Committee of the need for hearings on private enterprise and atomic energy. In any case, he said, he was determined to hold hearings whatever the response of the full Committee, and he did.[51] Perhaps the most influential subcommittee since 1955 has been that on legislation, formerly chaired by Chet Holifield. This group has conducted hearings on the Commission's annual authorization requests, rewritten authorization bills, and brought its recommendations to the full Committee for only cursory consideration. It is no exaggeration to state that this subcommittee, usually in conjunction with the JCAE chairman, has made the basic Committee decisions shaping the AEC's new-construction program. The unifying force of a subcommittee is well illustrated by the case of that on Research and Development, headed by Melvin Price. Consensus on that body, whether with respect to the Aircraft Nuclear Propulsion program or increased basic research, has made itself felt on the full Committee as well. Thus, if it is possible to achieve cohesion within a subcommittee, and the very smallness of the

---

[49] In the two houses, relationships between subcommittees and committees vary considerably. At one end of the spectrum are committees such as House Appropriations or Labor and Senate Labor and Public Welfare, whose subcommittees are quite independent of the full committee. At the other end are the subcommittees of the two foreign relations committees, House Banking and Currency and Senate Finance. The JCAE is probably nearer in this respect to those committees which have fairly autonomous subcommittees.

[50] The required decision was made on the next-to-last day. See S. Rep. No. 1041, 82d Cong., 1st Sess. (1951), p. 4.

[51] *N.Y. Times,* March 25, 1953.

group makes this likely, chances of cohesion in the larger group are excellent.

If prior consultation by chairmen with the rank and file, nonauthoritarian leadership, and articulation by subcommittees have played a unifying role, another factor has also been significant. Whatever the rules and structure of the Committee, the chairmen might have been tempted to override the wishes of minority members had not the banner of "nonpartisanship" always been held high by Democrats and Republicans alike. The Joint Committee, probably more than any other Congressional group, has carefully cultivated a tradition of nonpartisanship, based on the unusually harmonious working relationships of members and also on the historical fact that, during the first years, few issues likely to provoke partisan sensibilities arose. Along with the foreign affairs committees of both houses, the Joint Committee has prided itself on the fact that it "has conscientiously sought to meet its responsibilities and to approach the nonpartisan problems of atomic energy in a nonpartisan spirit." [52] Over the years, members have claimed to be above party so frequently that the claim itself has become something of a shibboleth and has exerted independent influence. Undoubtedly, the Committee has been more cohesive purely as a result of this continuing tradition than might otherwise have been the case.

In a legislature where the most salient difference among members is determined by the side of the aisle on which one sits, a committee that boasts a firm tradition which precludes partisan considerations is something of an oddity. It is one to which JCAE members make glowing reference, even under the most inappropriate circumstances. In 1954, for example, in introducing a bill which had caused deep dissension on the Committee, Vice-Chairman Hickenlooper admitted "areas of disagreement," but quickly disclaimed partisan influences. He stated:

> . . . This committee has been free from partisan political motivation in the discharge of its responsibilities. . . . I can envision no situation where unpartisanship and nonpartisanship have been more in evidence than in the 8 years' history of the joint committee's operations.[53]

Repeated claims that the Committee operates in the "broad public inter-

---

[52] S. Rep. No. 1041, 82d Cong., 1st Sess. (1951), p. 2. An example of the nonpartisan solidarity of the Committee occurred in early 1953, when former President Truman was quoted as stating: "I am not convinced Russia has the [atomic] bomb." Democratic and Republican members of the JCAE, alarmed that Truman's statement might result in a reduction of support for the atomic-energy program, issued a bipartisan statement: ". . . the ex-President's statement is highly unfortunate in that it contradicts indisputable evidence. . . ." Recounted in Strauss, *op. cit.*, p. 331.

[53] *Leg. Hist. 1954 Act*, v. 3, p. 3045.

est" without concern for party position seem to have taken hold. Therefore, a popular conception is that the Committee, instead of being divided into Republican and Democratic factions, is monolithic. No longer, it is said, are the chief antagonists the two political parties, but rather the Committee, representing the legislative, and the AEC, representing the executive branch of government.[54]

Whether or not the claims of nonpartisanship have accorded with the facts, the claims themselves have given Committee members a sense of solidarity above and beyond party. As we shall see, nonpartisanship, though generally true of the pre-1954 Joint Committee, has since that time been a will-o'-the-wisp as far as certain crucial issues have been concerned. Yet it continues to be paid homage, whether in the breach or in the observance.

- Divisive Influences

The centripetal forces just discussed are certainly not without qualification. In contrast to most Congressional committees, it is true, the Joint Committee on Atomic Energy has been subject to a great number of unifying influences. Yet, nearly every pull toward unity has at one time worked in the opposite direction as well. Rule by Committee and subcommittee chairmen, for example, has tended to be loose and relaxed, but from time to time chairmen have been forceful enough to provoke opposition and destroy consensus. The nature of the Committee's subject matter at first set JCAE members apart from their colleagues, whose chores were more mundane. But, in time, even atomic energy came to be a less fashionable subject, and, as it lost its glamor, there was a corresponding decrease in the Committee's feelings of uniqueness. More important, and certainly more identifiable, have been the following divisive influences: first, rivalry between House and Senate members, which partially reduces the effectiveness of a unicameral committee; second, personality and general ideological differences among Committee members, which are by no means unique to the Joint Committee; and, finally, differences which can be traced to partisanship and traditional public-policy conflicts between Democrats and Republicans.

Important to how members work together but having little impact on policy cohesion is the rivalry between Senate and House members on the Joint Committee. For some time, the House has been resentful of the superior public prestige and status automatically accorded members of "the other body." From time to time, the lower house has felt obliged to reiterate its coequality. Members have developed a collective inferiority

[54] Jackson, *op. cit.*, p. 77, and Dorothy Fosdick, "Legislative Watchdog of the Atom," *N.Y. Times Magazine*, June 26, 1955.

complex, sensitive to the merest slight by the Senate. This feeling largely explains why congressmen have been less inclined than their Senate brethren to establish more joint committees, which loom as potential threats to their separate-but-equal identities.

The first years of the JCAE provide a good illustration of the reasons for the lack of enthusiasm among House members for the joint-committee mechanism. Creators of the Atomic Energy Act, led by the Senate Special Committee, under McMahon, made only one provision for House equality on the new committee. The House would be represented by the same number of members as the Senate. But, on the crucial question of who should chair the new committee, there were no instructions in the act other than that "the joint committee shall select a chairman and a vice chairman from among its members." This might have led to domination by the House, or even equality, but in practice it meant Senate rule. Because other joint committees were chaired by Senate members, congressmen on the JCAE were slow to react to their underprivileged status. During the first seven years, although rotation of the chairmanship was occasionally discussed, the Senate dominated. McMahon, then Hickenlooper, and again McMahon held the key positions, while Congressmen Thomason, Cole, and Durham served as vice-chairmen. Nor did the fact that Senate members made graceful gestures, inviting House members to attend and even ask questions at confirmation hearings held before the Senate section, preclude discontent. Only a rotating chairmanship could assuage the hurt feelings of the congressmen.

With the death of McMahon in July, 1952, Congressman Durham became acting chairman. After the Republican Congressional victory in November and the reorganization of the Eighty-third Congress the following January, JCAE House members came to the Committee's first organization meeting resolved to elect one of their own as chairman. But Senate members refused to yield precedence over the lower chamber, and from January through April, 1953, the Joint Committee was ensnarled in a deadlock. Eight congressmen backed Cole, and eight senators backed Hickenlooper. At meeting after meeting, House members refused to concede, insisting they deserved a turn at the chairmanship. "We took the position on the House side," said Holifield a year later, "that the dignity of the House was just as great as the dignity of the Senate, and we were just as much entitled to have the chairmanship of the committee for two years as the Senate was." [55] But the senators felt differently. A senator should be chairman, they argued, because of the Senate section's responsibility for confirmations and treaties. The House, after all, had no parallel duties. This was met with the counterargument that the lower body initiated

---

[55] *Leg. Hist. 1954 Act,* v. 3, p. 3964.

appropriations measures, and so it went. The deadlock was finally broken when Hickenlooper stepped aside, and a congressman, Cole, assumed the chairmanship for the first time.

In Chapter 17 of the Cole-Hickenlooper revision of the McMahon Act, the Committee wrote into law what it had already decided by informal agreement. Section 203 provided that "the chairmanship shall alternate" and that the chairman would be selected only by members from that house entitled to the position. The vice-chairman, on the other hand, would be chosen from the house other than that of the chairman and by members of that chamber only. Thus, members of the House of Representatives finally achieved equal dignity for their parent body. After 1954, the chairmanship rotated every two years, and there were no further arguments over the matter. The 1953 squabble disabled the Committee for three important months, since it proved impossible for a Republican majority to proceed under a Democratic acting chairman. Moreover, it left lasting scars. Even after the issue was effectively settled, mutual jealousies between House and Senate members continued, although in muted tones. Congressmen were much more disturbed than senators, who considered themselves above rivalry with members of the lower chamber. Representative Holifield doubtless spoke for the other seven Committee congressmen when he claimed that "75 per cent of the work of this joint committee has been done by members of the House." The Californian kindly pointed out that he did not intend criticism of senators, who had many more committees on which to serve, but, he stated confidently, congressmen "have established a far superior record of attendance and hours put in and hard work done to that of the Members from the other body." [56]

Privately, House members still complain that they carry the burden while their Senate friends share only the credit. Though this division has endured as an undercurrent—one that is probably inevitable when senators and congressmen must work together—it has not dominated the relationships of Committee members. Of considerably more divisive effect has been the contrast in personalities, approaches, and general ideologies of both House and Senate members of the JCAE.

"Political personality" is a term not easily defined. Approximate synonyms might be "style," "manner," or "approach." In any case, these characteristics and their influence on the interrelationships of members have affected JCAE cohesion. Plainly, the wider the difference in style and approach, the more difficult the task of maintaining unity. Given any issue, no matter how controversial or potentially divisive, a committee that can work harmoniously will have a better chance of reaching a satisfactory compromise than one on which members are personally as well as politically

---

[56] *Loc. cit.*

at odds. Consensus, according to this reasoning, results not only from the similarity of preferences and interpretations of fact, but also from the abilities of members to sit down together to try to resolve disagreements.

The JCAE was probably most adept at maintaining solidarity during the early years, chiefly because of the nonpartisan character of most of the issues it faced, but also because of the personal skills of a few key members. Brien McMahon, the driving force behind the JCAE in those years, was highly respected by Committee members. Even though his skillful handling of the Committee could not forestall occasional disagreements, by presiding over contentious matters wisely and with restraint he did much to preserve the essential unity of the Committee. To bridge likely partisan divisions, McMahon, and Hickenlooper before him, relied heavily on those men who acted as "mediators" and proved helpful in reconciling differences of outlook. The critical mediator was Vandenberg, the renowned architect of bipartisan foreign policy. He worked to unite Republicans and Democrats, Commission critics and defenders, and other conflicting groups on the Committee.[57] Vandenberg's abilities were particularly valuable in the fight between proponents of military control and those of civilian control during the fashioning of the 1946 Atomic Energy Act.

Undoubtedly, the principal mediator in recent years has been Carl Durham, who, however heated the intracommittee squabbles, always stood somewhat apart and "smoked his pipe in peace." [58] An excellent illustration of the North Carolina congressman's desire to avoid conflict is provided by the "principal-officer" controversy of 1954. Although other Democrats on the JCAE sharply challenged the scope of Lewis Strauss' authority as AEC chairman, Durham sincerely wished that the issue had never arisen and believed that it could be settled without public airing. He addressed his colleagues as much as Chairman Strauss when he remarked at a hearing:

> I do not like to get into personal difficulties. I just do not like cat fights. . . . We cannot settle these little things by coming here before this committee, and in my opinion it is something that could have been settled without ever getting to this stage of the game.[59]

Representatives Carl Hinshaw and Melvin Price also helped, by dint of

---

[57] Significantly, the Michigan senator associated himself with neither the majority nor minority report on the 1949 Hickenlooper investigation into the AEC, whereas other JCAE members aligned themselves in partisan camps.

[58] The characterization is by JCAE member Jack Westland, made on the occasion of Durham's retirement from the Committee and Congress. *Cong. Rec.,* 106 (Aug. 31, 1960), 18913.

[59] *Leg. Hist. 1954 Act,* v. 2, p. 2454.

their political personalities, to bring opponents on the Joint Committee closer together.

Some other members have been less inclined to brush over differences. For example, once "Stub" Cole—as he was nicknamed by his colleagues—formulated his views, he was not easily budged. He was not one to compromise on what he considered to be basic principles and would persist even if he were a minority of one. His *laissez-faire* outlook on problems involving government-industry relationships more than once threatened to prevent intracommittee agreement. In 1954, for instance, almost singlehandedly he pushed his patent provision through the House and into conference, even after it had been soundly beaten in the Joint Committee. Cole was absolutely wedded to the idea of free patents and held steadfast in the conference committee for some time before finally giving in to the majority. Even then, he promised that he would continue fighting for his patent amendment, and this he did.[60]

Like his Republican colleague, Democrat Chet Holifield has not been given to easy compromise. However salutary the effects of muted compromise on Committee consensus may be, Holifield has been little disposed to play down differences. During his years on the JCAE, he has firmly held to his belief that, no matter what the consequences within the Committee, "clean controversy and clean statements of position are demanded of all of us in our different responsibilities in a democratic society. . . ." Holifield's actions have reflected his hope that "no feeling of timidity will cause any of us to stand back from stating our position on a thing." [61] This attitude occasionally led to divisions that might not otherwise have occurred or been brought to public attention. In 1959, for

---

[60] On another feature of the 1954 act, Cole again bypassed his Committee colleagues in attempts to have his proposals adopted on the floor. After having suggested in executive session that a majority of the full Committee should select the chairman instead of having a biennial rotational system with the chairmanship changing from one house to the other, Cole brought the amendment up on the floor. The discussion which ensued is revealing:

> *Mr. Holifield:* This is not an amendment that was agreed to in the Committee?
>
> *Mr. Cole:* No, I did not offer it as such. . . .
>
> *Mr. Durham:* This is the amendment we discussed in the Committee and turned down, is it not?
>
> *Mr. Cole:* That is true.
>
> *Mr. Durham:* As I recall, it was turned down by a pretty substantial vote.
>
> *Mr. Cole:* I am not certain of that because, as the gentleman will recall, I was not in the room at the time. I fear that it might be considered that I have a personal interest in the matter, and of course I do not.

Leg. Hist. 1954 Act, v.3, p. 2958.

[61] *FY 1960 Authorization Hearings* (1959), pp. 82-85.

example, AEC Chairman John McCone made his first public appearance before the JCAE in hearings on the development, growth, and state of the atomic-energy industry. Holifield, without waiting for McCone to complete his testimony, issued a press release expressing disappointment and concern over the "pitifully small program" proposed by the AEC. Handed a copy of the release, McCone was visibly shocked and exclaimed:

> I just don't know why I am here. . . . I have spent 2 days now trying to give you the background, the reasoning why we are doing these things, which we arrived at after months of work. I find that Mr. Holifield makes a press release criticizing everything. He had it all printed and written up before he even heard what I had to say. . . . If you want me to come up and testify, listen to me and then make up your mind what you think about what I say.

Although Holifield reminded the chairman that there was nothing personal or intentionally offensive in what he did, he made his position as to the rules of the game perfectly clear: "All I have to say is this: It is an old, old axiom, 'If you can't stand the heat, don't go into the kitchen.' " At that point, Republican James Van Zandt sprang to the defense of the AEC chairman, simultaneously attacking Holifield for improper behavior. The Pennsylvania congressman said he disagreed with distribution of news releases before witnesses had completed their statements and added that this was not the first time such a breach had occurred.[62]

Another influential member, Clinton Anderson, has taken a similar approach to his role on the Joint Committee. What the New Mexico senator set out to do, he always did with single-minded determination. Whether his self-chosen task was assuring that the JCAE be kept "fully and currently informed," loosening AEC classification restrictions, or blocking the confirmation of Lewis Strauss as secretary of commerce, Anderson played a bruising political game. Much of the Joint Committee's history between 1954 and June, 1958, was colored by the personal enmity between Anderson and Strauss. Conflict between the two men resulted not only from the clash of irreconcilable ideas, but also from noncomplementary chemistries of personality.[63] Most important, Anderson felt that Strauss failed to regard Congress as a responsible partner in the business of making public policy—a tragic disregard for any executive official. To make matters worse, Strauss was extremely rough in battle, but not always wise in the selection of his foes or field of contest. Few, if any, executive officials would have dared attack the chairman of the committee having jurisdiction over their agency's affairs in his home state or district. In 1956, Strauss

[62] *"Sec. 202" Hearings* (1959), pp. 100-105.
[63] *Time,* June 15, 1959, p. 21.

did just this,[64] and from then on personal rapprochement between the AEC Chairman and Anderson was virtually impossible. Even apart from his feud with Strauss, the New Mexico senator was not the type to retreat from combat or hastily declare a truce. He was seldom reluctant to state just where he stood and just what he intended to do to bring others into line with him.[65]

Inescapable as a force which divides the Committee is the variance, not only in political styles, but also in political preferences of Committee members.[66] Each member naturally prides himself on his "independence" —his ability to follow personally formulated principles rather than dictates of party, interest groups, constituents, or even the majority of his JCAE colleagues. Nevertheless, on most issues, such as atomic development for defense purposes, the international sharing of information and weapons, nuclear testing, and Congressional and Committee controls over executive policy-making and policy execution, consensus has been considerable. On these matters, disagreements have never been sufficiently intense to divide Committee members into sharply defined and opposed camps. Only one force—party loyalty—has succeeded in seriously breaching Committee consensus, and then only on certain issues. This does not mean that the Congressional party or the party in control of the administration has dictated to members of the Committee. Only occasionally has that been necessary. It does mean, however, that, in certain areas of public policy, Republicans and Democrats have significantly different policy preferences. Party allegiance does not determine these preferences exclusively, for in large part a man chooses a party label because he shares certain beliefs dominant in that party but not the other. The party, therefore, not only shapes political attitudes, but also reinforces them. Traditionally, the two parties and the large majorities of their members have differed substantially on the extent and nature of governmental intervention in domestic economic affairs.

This traditional polarization of the parties has had a noticeable influence on JCAE affairs. Questions relating to federal leadership in the

---

[64] At Anderson's request, Strauss spoke before a gathering of New Mexico newspaper executives in Albuquerque. In the course of his address, he remarked that there had been complaints about the AEC's release of information, but that these could not be taken seriously, since the complainers had only "a limited understanding" of what was involved. A persistent critic of AEC secrecy, Anderson properly took this as a personal slap. See *Washington Post and Times Herald,* Jan. 22, 1956.

[65] During hearings on AEC proposals to amend the Atomic Energy Act in 1958, for example, Anderson made it plain that, if the administration refused to abandon one of its proposals, it would jeopardize passage of the entire bill. At one point, he warned: "I can't imagine anything that I would enjoy more than trying to organize another period of protracted debate as I did on tidelands and Dixon-Yates. These are good things. You can have a lot of fun with it." *Military Exchange Hearings* (1958), p. 113.

[66] Cf. Dahl, *Congress and Foreign Policy, op. cit.,* Chap. 1.

development of the domestic reactor program and exploitation by private- and public-power groups since 1954 have persistently divided the Committee along partisan lines. That this is to be expected—no matter how cohesive the Committee is on defense, international, and Congressional-authority issues—can be demonstrated by a brief examination of members' preferences on issues involving questions of public versus private power. Roll call analysis reveals that Democrats on the JCAE have been remarkably friendly to public power, whereas Republicans have been just as noticeably hostile.[67] Only 24 per cent of 384 votes have seen Republican members in favor of bills supported by public-power groups. In sharp contrast, Democratic Committee members have supported public-power legislation on 198, or 81 per cent, of 243 roll calls. (See Table II-3.) In the estimate of public-power groups, such legislators as Jackson, Price, Aspinall, Holifield, and Anderson have perfect or near-perfect records on power and resources issues. In the other camp are men like Bricker, Millikin, Bennett, and Cole. If JCAE members have been at odds on questions of conventional power, chances were that Democrats and Republicans on the Committee would also disagree on questions relating to electric power from atomic energy. A subsequent chapter will show that, since 1954, this has been the case.

Even before the atom became embroiled in the conflict between public and private power, there was evidence of partisanship among JCAE members. Most participants and observers agree that these were rather isolated instances in an era of Committee nonpartisanship. The JCAE was definitely unhampered by the types of partisan controversies that occurred constantly in committees like Senate Labor and Public Welfare, House Education and Labor, and many others. But the Lilienthal confirmation hearings, the Pike confirmation proceedings, and the Hickenlooper investigation revealed divergences between Committee Democrats and Republicans.

Probably the plainest case of partisanship prior to 1954 occurred during consideration of bills to extend the terms of AEC commissioners in 1948, aptly characterized by a *New York Times* editorial as purely "a

---

[67] Of necessity, pro–public-power votes are rather arbitrarily defined as those in accord with the views of one leading public-power group, the National Rural Electric Cooperative Association (NRECA). Our tabulation is based on that organization's publication, *Voting Records on Rural Electrification and Related Federal Wholesale Power and Rural Telephone Issues* (Washington, D.C.: NRECA, August 1956, April 1958). Taking the thirteen Senate and fifteen House members of the Joint Committee during the period 1954-1960, our task was to determine who voted in accord with NRECA's policy preferences—the pro–public-power position—on thirty-four power issues (exclusive of atomic energy) arising between 1943 and 1958. Only "yea" and "nay" votes were counted. Since not all members served equal lengths of time and not all voted on every roll call, total votes for each man differ.

Table II-3

JCAE MEMBERS VOTING ON POWER ISSUES

DEMOCRATS

JCAE member	*Total yea and nay votes*	*Number of pro–public-power votes*	*Percentage of pro–public-power votes*
Congressmen:			
Price	32	32	100
Aspinall	20	20	100
Holifield	24	23	96
Dempsey	14	11	79
Kilday	31	22	71
Durham	25	12	48
House totals	146	120	82
Senators:			
Jackson	14	14	100
Anderson	22	20	91
Gore	13	11	85
Russell	29	20	69
Pastore	19	13	68
Senate totals	97	78	80
Total Democrats	243	198	81

REPUBLICANS

JCAE member	*Total yea and nay votes*	*Number of pro–public-power votes*	*Percentage of pro–public-power votes*
Congressmen:			
Cole	15	1	7
Van Zandt	31	5	16
Bates	18	3	16
Jenkins	33	6	18
Patterson	31	6	19
Hinshaw	21	4	19
Hosmer	11	3	27
Westland	14	8	57
House totals	174	36	21
Senators:			
Bricker	28	2	7
Millikin	30	3	10
Bennett	18	2	11
Dworshak	26	3	12
Hickenlooper	25	4	16
Knowland	29	10	34
Cordon	22	8	36
Aiken	32	23	72
Senate totals	210	55	26
Total Republicans	384	91	24

Republican desire to determine the Commission's membership," which smacked of patronage.[68] The terms of the five original commissioners were to expire on August 1, 1948, and a New York newspaper story on April 19 announced that renominations were about to be made by President Truman. Later that day, the Senate Republican Policy Committee met, and Chairman Taft stated afterward that the GOP had decided "to go slow on all confirmations and appointments made by the President." The next day, Truman renominated the five commissioners for new terms commencing August 1, giving Lilienthal a five-year appointment, the longest permitted under the staggered-system requirements of the Atomic Energy Act. It became evident that the Republicans would not go along when, on April 23, Senator Taft repeated the Republicans' "go-slow policy" on television and added that "it included Lilienthal."

A fight over renominations loomed, and scientist groups advised JCAE senators that, if the nominations—especially Lilienthal's—went before the Senate for confirmation, there would be "a dirty political fight." Such a quarrel, they advised, would gravely impair the work of the AEC. To avoid a floor battle, Republican members of the JCAE's Senate section suggested that the terms of the commissioners be extended for a year. McMahon objected, but the Republicans insisted on their "compromise solution," and the party leadership stood behind a bill introduced by Hickenlooper on behalf of himself and Sen. Edwin C. Johnson (D., Colo.). This proposed extending the terms of the five commissioners automatically for two years from August 1, thereby precluding a confirmation battle but also giving a new president—and there was little doubt at the time that he would be a Republican—power to appoint an entirely new Commission during his term.[69]

Despite Vandenberg's plea that controversy be avoided, Democratic members of the JCAE contested the Republican proposal. The Committee on May 17 divided, with the exception of cosponsor Johnson, along party lines in reporting out the bill—ten Republicans and one Democrat in favor and five Democrats opposed—and both majority and minority reports were issued. When the legislation came to the floor of House and Senate, there were charges by Democrats of "partisan politics" and weak denials by the Republicans, but the measure passed quickly by voice vote. The President signed the bill, but accompanied it with a statement of strong disapproval. Said Truman: "I consider that this bill is not in the best public interest, since it invests the atomic-energy program with an aura of uncertainty and of partisan politics. . . . Politics and atomic energy

---

[68] July 4, 1948.

[69] *Cong. Rec.*, 94 (June 18, 1948), 8953-8954; (June 19, 1948), 9060-9073.

do not mix." Not until the Dixon-Yates outburst were politics and atomic energy again to be tied up with one another to this extent. There has not been a complete disentanglement since that time.

The bitter conflict over the Republican administration's attempt to block the expansion of TVA by encouraging private-power development in the Memphis area proved to be a milestone in the histories of both the AEC and the Joint Committee. The former became embroiled in bruising political controversy for the first time, while the latter became a battleground whenever policies appeared to affect public- or private-power interests. On Dixon-Yates, the Committee publicly split right down the middle—ten Republicans in favor of the contract and eight Democrats opposed. But, even before the Joint Committee made its decision, partisanship was in evidence. Democratic members pressed for hearings on Dixon-Yates at the end of the Eighty-third Congress. Fearing the Democrats would have a profitable election issue if the contract were aired before November, 1954, the Republican majority succeeded in postponing the hearings until after the election. Two days after Election Day, the hearings commenced.[70] Once the affair had been settled, JCAE members tried to keep discussion and recriminations out of their public deliberations.[71] But the resulting rancor persisted for several years. In 1958, Anderson pointedly noted:

> We never had any real trouble in the Joint Committee until we got into the Dixon-Yates controversy, and we hope we never get into another one . . . this was the most unified committee I have ever seen. . . . We got into a hassle that left a lot of scars.[72]

It seems, however, that, even without that hangover, the Joint Committee in the years following passage of the 1954 act would have been extremely hard-pressed to remain united on issues concerning domestic power development. The two parties were too far apart on questions of public and private power and the role of governmental intervention in domestic economic affairs. And, even when JCAE Republicans privately sympathized with programs aggressively espoused by their Democratic

---

[70] Aaron Wildavsky, *Dixon-Yates: A Study in Power Politics* (New Haven: Yale University Press, 1962), pp. 127-128.

[71] In the 1955 "Sec. 202" hearings, after lengthy discussion of the contract, Cole introduced a motion to halt further discussion. The motion carried by unanimous consent. *"Sec. 202" Hearings* (1955), pp. 383-386. In opening the following year's hearings, Anderson announced: "This year we hope to have no collateral issues which will take our time, and one particular issue which has been barred by unanimous consent." *"Sec. 202" Hearings* (1956), p. 1. When Strauss's confirmation as secretary of commerce came before the Commerce Committee and the Senate in 1959, Dixon-Yates was resurrected by the admiral's opponents.

[72] *Military Exchange Hearings* (1958), p. 113.

friends, as on the Gore-Holifield bill to accelerate civilian reactor development, pressure from their party leadership within the administration and Congress was sufficient to convert their support to opposition.

Although partisan controversies over domestic atomic power have probably been less significant than the consensus achieved in so many other areas, they cannot be overlooked. Their recurrence certainly weakens the JCAE claims of nonpartisanship. By 1956, there could be little doubt that the Committee was no longer harmonious on all issues. On the floor of the House, Sterling Cole made explicit reference to the new relationship of atomic energy and partisan politics. Although he gracefully omitted accusing his Democratic Committee colleagues, centering his attack on Chairman Clarence Cannon of the Appropriations Committee and the Democratic Congressional leadership, by implication they, too, shared blame.

> Regretfully [he said] I have observed a growing tendency by some in the present majority party in the Congress to attempt to use atomic energy for political advantage. . . . Pique over failure of the Gore bill to pass was apparently the basis for the refusal of the Democratic leadership of the House and Senate to consider and pass the measure, which the atomic industry has been awaiting and without which real progress will be seriously hindered.[73]

However, since 1958 there has been a notable diminution of partisanship on the Committee, owing largely to the replacement of Strauss as AEC chairman and to a general reassessment of the possibilities for rapid development of reactor technology.

■ THE COMMITTEE'S RIGHT ARM

Senators and congressmen on the JCAE share with members of other Congressional committees the feeling that the executive branch has entirely too many advantages over Congress. One of the most important of these is a fund of information made available by an army of bureaucratic experts. Special knowledge, inside information, and seemingly unlimited manpower, congressmen suspect, have been used by the Executive not only to formulate policies, but also to confound Congress and keep it dependent on the Executive. One good remedy, according to many legislators, is the employment of staff personnel who help to redress the balance of expertise and information and restore independence to its committees. Few other legislative committees have made as great use of staff assistance in both technical and policy areas as has the Joint Committee on Atomic Energy. The JCAE has permitted, even encouraged, an unusual degree of creative

[73] *Cong. Rec.*, 102 (July 27, 1956), 15716-15717.

initiative on the part of its staff. The staff has played such a crucial role, in fact, that one might properly inquire, not whether the Committee has maintained its expertness independently of information volunteered by the Executive, but rather whether it has not surrendered a portion of its prized independence to its own staff.

Besides the impressive abilities of staff professionals (which are indeed difficult to weigh against those of the staffs of other committees), there are four persuasive reasons for the effectiveness of the JCAE staff. First, the Committee's business has always covered a much narrower range than that of other committees; atomic energy has been a manageable field of endeavor for members and staff alike. Second, the relatively light legislative load, especially in the early years, and the fewer time-consuming, routine chores have allowed the JCAE professionals more time for studies in depth and self-education. Although by no means unharried, staff members have had comparatively ample opportunity to investigate, analyze, and think through policy alternatives. Third, there has been considerable continuity of personnel on the JCAE staff. Continued service has increased the staff's collective familiarity with the atomic-energy program and its influence on Committee members and executive officials. Finally, JCAE members have regarded the staff as unique [74] and have taken unusual interest in its selection and activities. Unlike most committee staffs, there is no separate majority and minority staff. A single group of professionals services members of both parties and all of the subcommittees.[75] Staff members are chosen by an informal subcommittee composed of the two ranking Democratic and the two ranking Republican members of the JCAE. This helps to ensure bipartisan support of the staff's operations.

Although the duties of JCAE staff professionals have covered a wide range—from preparing speeches for members to setting up hearings, arranging for witnesses, and preparing Committee documents for publication—undoubtedly the main job has been continuing liaison with, and scrutiny of, the AEC. The first report of the Committee to Congress emphasized the oversight function:

> Close liaison with key personnel of the Commission also has been maintained through continuous contact by the committee staff members with the Commission headquarters in Washington. Numerous conferences have been held with the chiefs of the statutory divisions, other division heads, and with personnel at varying levels within the organization both in Washington and in the field.[76]

---

[74] Remarks of Senator Hickenlooper, *Cong. Rec.*, 100 (June 28, 1954), 9061.
[75] *Utility Proposal for Hanford Powerplant Hearings* (1962), pp. 16-17.
[76] Reprinted in *Cong. Rec.*, 94 (Jan. 30, 1948), 752.

This close association has endured. In 1961, a Committee document explaining the functions of the JCAE stated that "close daily liaison is maintained between the staffs of the Commission and the Joint Committee." [77]

McMahon probably established the precedent of close and constant scrutiny by the staff. According to one former staff man, the Connecticut senator wanted the JCAE professionals to "know more about what was going on in the Commission than the commissioners did." The staff men have accomplished this objective by going directly to the sources of information, the Commission's operating personnel. This direct contact has been maintained not only with personnel in AEC's Washington headquarters, but with field personnel as well. A former JCAE professional noted the results of staff field trips: "We got to the point where we knew better than Mr. *X* did about individual installations; because he had his full-day problems here in Washington, he couldn't begin to get to the field offices the way we did." [78]

Seldom has the AEC attempted to escape the watchful eye of Committee staff members, who have generally been welcomed on their visits to AEC headquarters and field offices.[79] That staff liaison has been so successful is due partly to the obligations imposed on the AEC by the statutory "fully-and-currently-informed" provision, partly to the cordial personal relationships between Committee and Commission staffs, and partly to the fact that the JCAE offers a promising avenue of appeal to bureaucrats and scientists who have had their proposals turned down by the Commission.[80]

---

[77] Joint Committee on Atomic Energy, "Membership, Publications, and Other Pertinent Information through the 86th Congress, 2d Session, of the Joint Committee on Atomic Energy," 87th Cong., 1st Sess. (1961), p. 15.

[78] During the early years, staff members annually spent a total of about 100 days on the road, visiting field offices, installations, and laboratories. Although they have done less traveling in recent years, they still maintain astonishingly direct contact with all levels and phases of the Commission's far-flung operations.

[79] Several other departments and agencies, however, have taken a rather different view of oversight by the staffs of their jurisdictional committees. For example, a Defense Department official stated: "The chairmen of committees are the point of contact for us in Congress. We rarely deal with the staff members. . . ." Quoted in Marver H. Bernstein, *The Job of the Federal Executive* (Washington, D.C.: The Brookings Institution, 1958), p. 109. Departmental officials often work directly with committee members in order to bypass an aggressive staff. One official commented: "Our experience has been that we have had to develop a direct relationship with committee members as an offset to some of the pet objectives of the professional staff." *Loc. cit.*

[80] On only a few occasions have JCAE professionals encountered difficulty in their quest for information. During the Dixon-Yates controversy, for example, the flow of information from executive agencies to the JCAE staff was almost completely cut off. But JCAE professionals were not to be denied. Their quest for a particular piece in a larger puzzle is worth recounting, since it indicates their resourcefulness.

Two members of the staff believed that a key adviser to the AEC and the Bureau of the

A major purpose of continuing surveillance by the staff has been to assure JCAE members that they would either be kept informed or would be able to obtain reliable information on a moment's notice. It has been the staff's responsibility to keep members apprised of significant happenings in the atomic-energy field. "Periodic reports . . . are made to the committee," stated one JCAE document, "which keep the constantly developing picture available to its members." [81] Staff members or the executive director have taken every opportunity to talk with Committee members to "try to soak them full of details" about the conduct of the atomic program. Even more information has been filed away for ready reference. Finally, staff members have rendered valuable on-the-spot services to the JCAE in evaluating testimony and reports of the commissioners and expert witnesses and in either posing questions themselves or suggesting questions to Committee members. Although the staff professionals may not have known the answers, their close and continuous contact with the atomic-energy program has suggested the questions that needed to be asked.

In addition to the collection and processing of useful information, the staff has also played a more creative role. It has suggested problems for exploration, launching the Committee on investigations that otherwise might not have taken place. In 1958 and 1959, for example, members of the JCAE and the Committee staff became concerned about the safety and custody of nuclear weapons, particularly those assigned to NATO. In the summer of 1960, the staff embarked on a classified study, and in the winter staff members accompanied a special subcommittee on an inspection trip of nuclear-weapons installations in Europe. The outcome of JCAE

Budget was at the same time an executive of the First Boston Corporation, a Wall Street investment house which had a financial stake in seeing that the Dixon-Yates contract went through. They thought that a vice-president of the First Boston Corporation, Adolphe H. Wenzell, had attended meetings at the AEC and that this could be shown, since AEC rules required that everyone entering the building fill out a security pass with his name, organization, address, clearance, and name of the person who had escorted him. As related by one JCAE staff member:

> One of the JCAE employees jumped into a cab, went to the security officer at the AEC, and asked to be shown copies of every security pass that had been issued to Wenzell. Meeting with considerable hesitation and hedging, the Joint Committee employee decided to try a ploy. He said that Senator [Lister] Hill [a leading opponent of Dixon-Yates] knew that Wenzell had been to the AEC. If there was no record of Wenzell's visits, the AEC officer would be accused of serious violations of security procedures designed to protect the nation's defense secrets. The AEC security officer retorted that nobody was going to get him on that kind of charge, and, inside of two hours, the JCAE official had photostatic copies of Wenzell's security passes.

Wildavsky, *op. cit.*, p. 231.

[81] Reprinted in *Cong. Rec.*, 94 (Jan. 30, 1948), 752.

investigation was a classified report to the president recommending electronic devices on nuclear weapons. "The idea of utilizing various electromechanical devices to improve U.S. custody and control of nuclear weapons," said Senator Anderson, "originated with the staff of the Joint Committee and, more specifically, our staff director." [82]

Generally, staff members have worked up preliminary plans for hearings and then have discussed their ideas with the JCAE chairman. Their arguments have usually been so persuasive that hearings have been scheduled.[83] The staff then determined the agenda of hearings, screened the information upon which members relied, participated in executive sessions, drafted Committee reports and recommendations, and assisted on the floor of the two chambers. By the subtle processes of inclusion and exclusion, it has been able at every stage of the decision-making process to structure alternatives and thereby influence the outcome.[84]

Sometimes the Committee staff has felt it unnecessary to burden busy members with decisions that could be made at lower echelons. By working closely with AEC professionals, JCAE staff men have exerted influence even before problems have reached the attention of either commissioners or Committee members. Staff professionals have made special investigations of the AEC, during which they have been able to informally inject their views. Their influence thus extends well beyond the limits that their nominal positions would imply. They have conferred with AEC officials on policy questions in the effort to work out compromises and solutions on an informal basis.[85] Thus, JCAE professionals have had the opportunity of participating in preliminary negotiations and have consequently influenced the nature of subsequent decisions.

Despite the powers delegated it, the JCAE staff has been limited in the arrangements it could negotiate independently of its patrons' desires or without their knowledge. Staff professionals have realized that the

---

[82] *Cong. Rec.* (daily ed., July 10, 1962), 12163.

[83] Before the creation of permanent subcommittees, this was more difficult to accomplish, since members would sit only on the most important problems. The JCAE staff was a prime mover in the establishment of subcommittees, since its ideas would have greater chance of acceptance and development in small, specialized groups.

[84] A dramatic example of staff influence precipitated the Oppenheimer investigation. William L. Borden, who had resigned as director of the JCAE staff several months earlier, in a November, 1953, letter to J. Edgar Hoover initiated charges against the scientist. A month later, AEC Commissioner Smyth sent a memorandum to Chairman Strauss in which he noted: "Borden's letter of accusation is important not because it brings forward new evidence of any consequence but because of the position he has held as head of the staff of the Joint Congressional Committee on Atomic Energy." Strauss, *op. cit.,* p. 275.

[85] Professional staffs of many legislative committees operate in similar fashion. For example, the staff of the House Armed Services Committee frequently holds meetings with departmental representatives in order to iron out problems before actual submission of a legislative proposal.

Committee, or at least the chairman and majority, must be sympathetic to the course they were taking. However aggressive and free-wheeling the JCAE staff in its dealings with the executive branch, it undoubtedly reflected the natural tendency of the Joint Committee itself. As long as the staff has worked in a direction approved by the chairman and Committee majority, it has been permitted wide scope for its energies. As one former staff man explained:

> The staff member up there is extremely powerful and the chairman has to trust him. . . . I had a period with Senator Anderson when frequently he'd sign letters without even reading them, letters to Charlie Wilson, Secretary of Defense, on critical matters of the missile program. He wasn't negligent; he was one of the most diligent senators on Capitol Hill in this respect. But after a period of time he has to trust, he knows what you are trying to accomplish, what direction you are going.

The staff's influence on JCAE policies has depended largely on its ability to produce results which satisfied Committee members. This is a far cry from staff control of the Committee. On the contrary, the experience, personal competence, and political power of JCAE chairmen and ranking members have been sufficient to preclude dependence on hired professionals. The staff has served the Committee and has served it well.

III | Relations with The Executive

The JCAE cannot be considered only from the standpoint of its role in the conventional legislative processes. Although it performs functions common to all standing committees of Congress, it must also be considered from the standpoint of its special relationship with, and considerable impact on, the executive branch. The JCAE has progressively carved out a thoroughly distinctive role in the formulation of national policy relating to atomic energy and, in the course of so doing, has developed a unique position with respect to those functions of government which have generally been regarded as reserved to the executive branch.

A discussion of the relationship between the JCAE and the executive branch does not end with a restatement of the traditional separation-of-powers doctrine, but it may fairly begin there. Although the Constitution does not expressly state adherence to the doctrine, it is implicit in the three broad areas into which governmental powers are divided. Thus, Article I establishes the legislative branch, which makes the law; Article II, the executive branch, which implements and enforces the law; and Article III, the judiciary, which dispenses justice under the law. From this broad division, it has been inferred that the three functions of government are reciprocally limiting, that each department should be able to defend its characteristic functions from intrusion by either of the others, and that none of the departments may abdicate its powers to either of the others.[1] The Supreme Court has often restated its support of this doctrine as a viable principle of American constitutional law in such terms as these:

> It may be stated then, as a general rule inherent in the American constitutional system, that, unless otherwise expressly provided or incidental to the powers conferred, the legislature cannot exercise either executive or judicial power; the executive cannot exercise either legislative or judicial power; the judiciary cannot exercise either executive or legislative power.[2]

On the other hand, it has always been recognized that the three branches of government cannot exist as "watertight compartments" [3] in complete isolation from each other. Thus, separated powers have often come to mean in practice shared powers.

American political history since the adoption of the Constitution is in part a chronicle of struggle and accommodation among the three branches of government. Each has striven to enlarge the area in which it might exercise power, and each has had its period of ascendancy. At the same time, the three branches have by unwritten law developed the many methods of accommodation which have permitted the system to continue to operate effectively.

In the relationship between Congress and the Executive, an important issue has been the right of the former to demand information in the custody of the latter versus the right of the latter to withhold it. This controversy first arose in Washington's administration and has flared up constantly since. It is especially likely to arise where the president and the majority in Congress belong to opposing political parties.

Although the primary function of the legislature is to legislate, it is more than a mill inexorably grinding out legislation. At least equal in importance to the law-making function is that of "oversight of administration." The legislature also functions as both a reflection and molder of public opinion. To perform these roles, it requires information as the basis for intelligent action.

It is well recognized that Congress, acting as a whole through statute or resolution or through a duly constituted committee has the right to obtain information concerning executive policies and actions in order to adequately discharge its functions. The Executive has usually been

---

[1] Edward S. Corwin, *The President: Office and Powers* (4th ed.; New York: New York University Press, 1957), p. 9.

[2] *Springer* v. *Government of Philippine Islands,* 277 U.S. 189, 201 (1928); see also *Kilbourn* v. *Thompson,* 103 U.S. 168 (1881).

[3] Dissent of Justice Holmes in *Springer* v. *Government of Philippine Islands, op. cit.,* 211.

willing to provide such information to Congress, to its committees, and —although there may be some question of their right to demand such information—to individual members.

On the other hand, the Executive in innumerable instances has found it advisable to deny Congress access to requested information.[4] It should be recognized, of course, that the refusal of the Executive to make information available to Congress is largely a function of time and circumstance. Information of a kind held back from Congress on one occasion may be made available without protest on another. The fact remains, however, that in no instance has a Congressional committee prevailed in its efforts to obtain information or documents where the Executive has taken a firm position against disclosure.[5]

Issues relating to separation of powers have not been confined to controversies over access to information. The separation-of-powers question has arisen also in connection with the power of the president to hire and fire subordinate executive officers [6] and with respect to the president's obligation to comply with legislative enactments which he regards as violative of his prerogatives under the separation-of-powers doctrine. On a number of occasions in American history, various presidents have in one way or another resisted compliance with laws enacted by Congress. For example, President Fillmore took the position in 1851 that Congress lacked the power to restrain the president's use of troops to suppress insurrection

---

[4] Its reasons for refusal have included the following: (1) disclosure would be detrimental to the national security; (2) disclosure would prejudice the rights of wrongdoers entitled to a fair trial; (3) disclosure of information on wrongdoing within the executive branch would interfere with the Executive's own efforts to clean house; (4) disclosure of personnel files or applications for employment would interfere with the president's appointment authority; (5) disclosure would interfere with current negotiations; (6) disclosure is inconsistent with the right of the president in performing his constitutional role; (7) heads of executive departments "are subject to the Constitution, and to laws passed by the Congress in pursuance of the Constitution, and to the directions of the President, but to no other direction whatever"; (8) the information was requested by Congress for purposes other than legislation; (9) disclosure of the transcript of a presidential conference was not advisable and would restrain the president's discussion with the press; (10) disclosure would prejudice law enforcement; (11) disclosure would interfere with proper government functions; (12) the information was received by the Executive on a confidential basis; (13) agency heads should be able to receive confidential advice from their subordinates; (14) disclosure of advisory or preliminary opinions not representing final official actions would violate the separation-of-powers doctrine; and (15) disclosure would reveal investigative techniques and discourage flow of information from confidential informants. See Staff of Subcommittee on Constitutional Rights of the Senate Committee on the Judiciary, *The Power of the President to Withhold Information from the Congress—Memorandum of the Attorney General,* 85th Cong., 2d Sess. (Committee Print; Part I, 1958; Part II, 1959).

[5] The most recent instance of the use of executive privilege occurred in 1962, when President Kennedy refused to permit the secretary of defense to make certain information available to the Preparedness Subcommittee of Senate Armed Services.

[6] *Kilbourn* v. *Thompson, op. cit.,* and *Myers* v. *United States,* 272 U.S. 52 (1926).

except by decreasing the size of or abolishing the Army and Navy. In 1896, President Cleveland warned Congress that he could refuse to mobilize the Army if Congress declared war against Spain. Pres. Theodore Roosevelt asserted that, had he remained in office, he would have refused to comply with legislation enacted in 1909 which forbade appointment of presidential commissions without specific legislative authorization. In 1920, President Wilson refused to comply with a statute authorizing and directing him to give notice of termination of certain treaties not consistent with the statute. In 1942, Pres. Franklin Roosevelt told Congress in effect that, if it did not repeal a provision of the Emergency Price Control Act, as he requested, he would nevertheless treat it as repealed. Finally, in 1955, President Eisenhower indicated that he would ignore a provision of the Defense Appropriations Act requiring prior consent of the House and Senate Appropriations committees before the Department of Defense could transfer functions performed by it to private industry.[7]

In practice, the interplay of power between executive and legislative branches is based largely on practicalities of politics and not on legal principles.[8] Congress has a legitimate interest in overseeing the manner in which the president executes the laws of the land. It has the right, if it is displeased with executive action, to enact new laws to correct the situation. Such laws are, of course, subject to veto by the president, and the veto, in turn, may be overridden by a two-thirds majority of the House and Senate. Upon enactment of law pursuant to presidential approval or over the president's veto, the executive branch is obliged to comply with the will of Congress. In some cases, the president, believing that a law violates the inherent rights and powers of the Executive under the Constitution, has refused to comply or has exerted less than complete diligence in implementing the law. Such action squarely raises the conflict between executive and legislative power. In no such case has the conflict been resolved by the judiciary; rather, the issue has been resolved in a practical, political manner. Congress has immense pressure available through its ability to withhold appropriations, to enact legislation opposed by the Executive, and to defeat legislation desired by the Executive. Most important, perhaps, is Congressional power to harass executive officials through repeated criticisms of, and unfavorable publicity for, programs and policies

---

[7] President Eisenhower, on advice of the attorney general, told Congress that he would have vetoed the bill if the funds provided had not been urgently required by the Department of Defense, since the bill "seeks to encroach upon the proper authority of the Executive." Under the circumstances, he said, the executive branch would regard the provision as invalid "unless otherwise determined by a court of competent jurisdiction." H.R. Document No. 218, 84th Cong., 1st Sess. (1955); *Cong. Rec.,* 101 (July 13, 1955), 10459-10460.

[8] Questions of separation of powers as between Congress and the Executive can come before the courts only if there is a "justiciable controversy" involving private rights.

with which Congress disagrees. The president, on the other hand, has immense pressure available through his official prestige and his power to withhold patronage and other favors from Congressional foes. Furthermore, lines separating the president and Congress often are not sharply drawn, since in many cases the president can command the support of members of his own political party. Executive-legislative conflicts have therefore usually been resolved by some kind of compromise solution.

Short of open conflict between the president and Congress, there is constant interplay between various officials of the executive branch at all levels, on the one hand, and individual members of Congress, blocs of members, and Congressional committees on the other. These Congressional components inevitably seek to influence or shape presidential policies, often with the active or tacit endorsement of executive officials. By the same token, the president and his agents invariably seek to influence the course of legislative decisions. Thus, inherent in our structure of government is some degree of pressure exercised by each of these branches on the other.

Against this background, the relationship between the JCAE and the executive branch appears extraordinary. To a large extent, the peculiar link between the two is a direct consequence of the organic law which establishes the JCAE and defines its relationship to the executive branch. But the strength of the JCAE rests not only on this statutory basis. It has acquired considerable power vis-à-vis the Executive from a combination of factors which have been implicit in the political, social, and technical environment in which the atomic-energy program has been conducted.

■ INSTITUTIONAL BASES OF POWER

• Isolation of the AEC

When the AEC was established in 1946, it took over the very substantial program previously run by the Manhattan Engineer District. Since this program had been forged behind a curtain of security, few members of Congress knew or were able to learn very much about its details. Although all members were concerned in general terms with the atom after revelation of the atomic-bomb program, few had a special interest in it. After the 1946 act became law, this state of affairs continued. Unlike most other government agencies, the AEC had no significant constituency; there were no important segments of American society with a special interest in the atomic-energy program which might serve as sources of strength or influence. The program was obscured by secrecy and was at best difficult to understand. Furthermore, there was no particular reason why the average member of Congress should attempt to understand it. As a consequence, the AEC was almost completely isolated from the entire

Congress, with the exception of the JCAE and the Appropriations committees. Necessarily, the AEC was forced to look to the Joint Committee for sympathy and support, and this dependence in turn increased the JCAE's own importance and stature.

• The Anomalous Position of the President

The structure of the atomic-energy program has made it doubtful from the very beginning whether the AEC is primarily responsible to the executive or to the legislative branch of government.

From 1946 to 1954, the AEC was almost exclusively an operating agency carrying on research, development, and production activities, most of which were in direct furtherance of the national defense effort. It was not until 1954 that the Commission acquired a significant regulatory role, but acquisition of this role has not altered its primary nature as an operating agency.[9]

In the traditional scheme of American government, programmatic and operational functions have almost always been carried on by the cabinet departments, headed by a secretary, or by special agencies, headed by a single administrator. In either case, these functions have been carried on under the president's direction by executives subject to his control. The multiheaded form of administration reflected in a commission has traditionally been used for regulatory bodies performing quasilegislative (i.e., rule-making) and quasijudicial (i.e., adjudicating) functions. In such cases, the commission or board structure has been used to permit a more balanced judgment than would be possible with a single head and, also, by giving members fixed tenure and staggered terms, to permit greater insulation from presidential control and political pressures.

In terms of this scheme, it would appear that the atomic-energy program would have been more appropriately placed under a single administrator than under a five-man commission. Choice of the commission form seems to have been based on the feeling that the novelty and complexity of atomic energy required the mature consideration and judgment of a group of men with varied abilities and experience and that this was particularly important in view of the secrecy with which the program was to be conducted. Finally, it was felt that the commission form would add an element of continuity to the administration of the program.[10]

---

[9] As of 1960, members of the Commission were spending less than one-fourth of their time on regulatory matters. *Staff Report on AEC Regulatory Process* (1961).

[10] For a discussion of these considerations see William H. Berman and Lee M. Hydeman, *The Atomic Energy Commission and Regulating Nuclear Facilities* (Ann Arbor: University of Michigan Press, 1961), pp. 240-252.

Whatever the considerations may have been which underlay the choice of the commission form of organization, the result has been to place the AEC in a "no-man's land" between the president and Congress.[11] Members of Congress can claim, with considerable basis, that the AEC was established as a creature of Congress and not as a part of the executive branch, responsible to the president. Moreover, the 1946 and 1954 acts, in fixing the tenure of the commissioners and making them removable only for cause, clearly indicate a Congressional intent that AEC be largely independent of the president. As a practical matter, therefore, the president's role has been largely confined to the duties imposed on him by the act,[12] to exercising indirect control over the Commission through the budgetary process, and to directing policy through appointment of the commissioners and chairman.

This situation has tended to reduce the president's effective control over the atomic-energy program and probably his interest in it as well. For the most part, the president has played a positive policy role only on an intermittent basis by "rubber-stamping" noncontroversial recommendations or programs initiated by the AEC, by resolving conflicts between the AEC and other parts of the executive branch, or by defending the AEC budget. For example, President Truman made the decision to proceed with the H-bomb program only after differences of opinion arose among the AEC, the Department of Defense, and the Department of State. On the other hand, the major AEC expansion program for greatly increased production of U-235 appears to have been formulated in 1951 largely by the JCAE and AEC, without presidential direction.[13] Presidents Truman and Eisenhower both permitted vacillation in the aircraft nuclear propul-

[11] The AEC, under Chairman Seaborg and the Kennedy administration, seeking to readjust the balance of power between the AEC and the Joint Committee, in 1962 endorsed a proposal to substitute a single administrator for the five-man Commission. After discussing the idea with the President, JCAE Chairman Holifield announced that the Committee would hold hearings in 1963 on legislative proposals for reorganizing the AEC, including consideration of a single administrator. *N.Y. Times,* May 18, 1962.

[12] Under the act, the president is responsible for appointing the commissioners (42 U.S.C. §2032 (1958)) and designating the chairman of the AEC (§2031); appointing the chairman of the Military Liaison Committee (§2037) and the members of the General Advisory Committee (§2096); assenting to the designation of new source materials (§2091) and new special nuclear materials (§2071); determining annually the quantity of special nuclear material to be produced (§2061 (b)) and directing the number of nuclear weapons to be produced (§2121(a)(2)); directing delivery of weapons or special nuclear material to the Department of Defense and authorizing that department to produce weapons or reactors (§2121 (b)); exempting actions of the AEC from provisions of law relating to contracts (§2202); approving agreements for cooperation (§2153); and authorizing certain nuclear-weapons cooperation with other nations (§2164(c) and (d), §2121 (c)).

[13] See Chapter VII, *infra.*

sion program (ANP) at an expense of about $1,000,000,000, allowing it to be buffeted about by the AEC, the Department of Defense, and the JCAE for fifteen years without any evidence of firm direction and control. It should not be inferred that the president has never taken an active role;[14] Eisenhower, for example, fought both the Gore-Holifield bill and some JCAE additions to AEC authorization legislation. Neither Truman nor Eisenhower, however, had marked interest in the extent to which the JCAE nibbled away at the integrity of the Executive's position under the doctrine of separation of powers, although in areas other than atomic energy they took vigorous action to preserve the executive position. It would appear that the structure of the atomic-energy program has isolated the president from the AEC and that the absence of strong presidential interest, control, and leadership has created a power vacuum into which the JCAE could be expected to move.

• Atomic-Energy Subject Matter

The highly technical subject matter of atomic energy and the intense secrecy which surrounded almost the entire program before 1954 and much but not all of the program since then have also tended to enhance the JCAE's position of strength within Congress and therefore to increase the AEC's dependence on the Committee. Many members of Congress, including some of the ablest and most prominent ones, have publicly stated their inability to understand atomic-energy matters and therefore to legislate effectively.[15] Members of the Joint Committee have shown little reluctance to invoke their years of study of this highly technical area and their access to classified information (which they cannot reveal) to persuade Congress to follow their lead.[16]

---

[14] *Loc. cit.*

[15] In 1950, Sen. Owen Brewster (R., Me.) told the Senate that "it is very difficult for the Members of the Senate, outside of those on the committee, to pass upon a subject like the one being considered [Pike confirmation] because there is so much involved that is of a classified nature" *Cong. Rec.*, 96 (May 25, 1950), 9765. In 1951, Sen. J. William Fulbright (D., Ark.) acknowledged that senators must look to the chairman of the JCAE "to construe the approach . . . because there is really not much we can do about it." *Cong. Rec.*, 97 (Sept. 18, 1951), 11500. In debate on the Gore-Holifield bill in 1956, Rep. Howard W. Smith (D., Va.) said: "I have been unable to learn the merits of it, and I think you will be unable to learn the merits, because none of us are scientists." *Cong. Rec.*, 102 (July 24, 1956), 14246. Rep. Keith Thomson (R., Wyo.) went even further: "Congress has no business legislating in this field because it lacks the information necessary to direct the Executive Branch intelligently." *Ibid.*, 14252. In 1958, Rep. Ben F. Jensen (R., Iowa), a ranking Republican member of the Appropriations Committee, told the House that anyone who is not a nuclear scientist has to take the word of the AEC and its scientists on requests for money. *Cong. Rec.*, 104 (July 22, 1958), 14655.

[16] See Representative Holifield's recital of this litany, *Cong. Rec.*, 103 (Aug. 5, 1957), 13685.

• Continuity of Personnel

Another advantage of the JCAE lies in the strength and continuity of its personnel in comparison with the AEC personnel.[17] As the years pass, the senior members of the JCAE are building up a substantial advantage over Commission members in terms of the years they have been associated with the atomic-energy program. But, in addition to their advantage in tenure, these Committee members clearly have a broad comprehension of the atomic-energy subject matter, and time and time again have demonstrated an almost amazing knowledge, whereas AEC members have shown inadequate grasp of the same material. In part, this is due to exceptional staff work within the JCAE. During most of its existence, the JCAE has had a relatively stable and skilled staff. The ability and dedication of the staff, in conjunction with the continuity of membership on the JCAE, has been a tremendous source of strength to the Committee and has contributed to the position of inferiority and defense in which the Commission has almost constantly found itself in the last decade.

■ STATUTORY BASES OF POWER

Equally as significant as the institutional factors in the JCAE's unusual accretion of power has been the authority conferred by the organic statute. The atomic-energy law has given the Joint Committee sweeping jurisdiction and authorization powers, the authority to require cooperation from all executive agencies, and, most important, the power to demand full and current information from the AEC and the Defense Department on all matters within its jurisdiction.

• Jurisdiction

Section 202 of the Atomic Energy Act of 1954 explicitly gives the JCAE jurisdiction over "all bills, resolutions or other matters in the Senate or the House of Representatives relating primarily to the Commission or to the development, use, or control of atomic energy." This provision not only enhances the position of the JCAE as against other Congressional committees which might have a claim to jurisdiction over particular matters, but also effectively serves notice on the AEC and other executive agencies concerned with atomic-energy matters that they must deal with the Joint Committee. The AEC has been forced to look directly to the Joint Committee for support; it has not been able to develop sources of

---

[17] During the period 1946-1960, nineteen persons served on the Atomic Energy Commission for an average of about three and one-half years each. Only three of the nineteen served as long as five years, the equivalent of a full-term commissioner. Additional data appear in Chapter II, *supra.*

support in other committees. Indeed, the AEC's reliance on the JCAE has served to alienate other committees. In 1950, for example, members of the House Appropriations Committee complained that the AEC, seeking relief from an appropriations rider, wrote to JCAE members rather than to the Appropriations Committee. Members of the JCAE responded by vigorously defending the AEC and stressing that the AEC *must* notify the JCAE of matters of that kind. In 1951, the AEC requested the help of the Joint Committee in obtaining funds for construction of access roads to uranium facilities. When Senator Anderson, on behalf of the Committee, tacked a rider for this purpose on to an appropriation bill, Sen. Dennis Chavez (D., N. Mex.), chairman of the Senate Public Works Committee, rose indignantly to complain that the Joint Committee was attempting to do his committee's work. Although Senator Chavez' point of order was sustained, Senators Hickenlooper and Anderson argued vigorously that the JCAE and not the Public Works Committee had jurisdiction over the matter.[18]

• Authority to Use Executive Facilities

Section 205 of the 1954 act, carried over intact from the 1946 act, authorizes the JCAE "to utilize the services, information, facilities, and personnel of the departments and establishments of the Government." So far as the public record indicates, this authority has not been well defined in terms of actual exercise. To some extent, the Committee has used this authority in recent years to borrow technical personnel from the executive branch. The JCAE staff in 1962, for example, included an Army colonel and two Navy captains. For all practical purposes, these officers are integrated into the Committee staff, and the military services are reimbursed by the JCAE.

Basically, however, this provision seems to be regarded as a sort of reserve power to be used in buttressing the JCAE's authority to obtain information from the Executive. For example, when the patent commissioner was resisting Senator Anderson's interpretation that the responsibility of the Patent Office under Section 202 of the 1954 act superseded its general mandate under Title 35 not to disclose information concerning patent applications, the *coup de grâce* delivered by Anderson was reference to this Section 205 authority. The patent commissioner responded: "We are still not dead down here, I am happy to say, although that last shot was devastating." [19] The statutory language is intriguingly broad. It suggests that the JCAE might call on the FBI to perform security, espionage, or other investigations; on the CIA to develop or provide intelligence

[18] *Cong. Rec.*, 96 (May 5, 1950), 6511; 97 (July 26, 1951), 8937-8940.
[19] *Patent Hearings* (1959), pp. 42-52.

data;[20] on the Department of Defense to oversee on the Committee's behalf activities of the National Aeronautics and Space Administration (NASA) or AEC (or vice versa); or on the Department of Justice to represent the Committee in litigation.[21] Senator Hickenlooper characterized the scope of this provision in these terms:

> Under a strict interpretation of the law . . . , while I doubt if we would have occasion to go this far, yet if we should say to the Attorney General, "Detail X number of people on the staff of the FBI and have this matter investigated," I think, under the law, he would have to do it. If we determined, for instance, that the Department of Defense should perform certain acts in the interest of the furtherance of the atomic energy program, I think a strict interpretation of the law would require the Department of Defense to take our orders on that score, provided it went to the development of the atomic energy program.[22]

It is not difficult to stretch Senator Hickenlooper's statement to encompass a situation in which the Committee directs the AEC to have certain research performed or reports written on the basis of which the JCAE might sponsor legislation authorizing JCAE nuclear projects.[23]

The only instance in which the extent of this power was actually raised involved the Committee's authority to receive reports of FBI investigations. During consideration of the nominations of the original members of the Atomic Energy Commission in 1947, the Senate section of the JCAE requested the president to make available investigative reports of the FBI and the military intelligence agencies on the nominees. At that

---

[20] In 1954, the CIA reported that the JCAE is the only Congressional committee "which receives reports from CIA on a regular basis." *Cong. Rec.*, 100 (March 10, 1954), 2989.

[21] At one time, the JCAE considered formal intervention in an administrative proceeding before the AEC. *"Sec. 202" Hearings* (1957), p. 487. This proceeding, "In the Matter of Power Reactor Development Co.," arose as a result of intervention by some labor unions in opposition to a construction permit granted by the AEC for a power reactor to be constructed by PRDC. The JCAE, or at least certain Democratic members, regarded issuance of the construction permit as palpably improper and strongly endorsed the unions' intervention. The broad language of §205 raises the question whether the JCAE could have utilized the services of the Department of Justice in contesting this matter before the AEC.

[22] *Cong. Rec.*, 100 (July 16, 1954), 10696.

[23] This has in fact happened, although not on the basis of §205. For example, in the AEC Authorization Act for Fiscal Year 1958, 71 Stat. 402, there were requirements for the AEC to "proceed with sufficient design work, together with appropriate engineering and development work, necessary for the Commission to begin construction as soon as practicable after authorization by the Congress," of certain specified reactors which the AEC was strenuously opposed to constructing. The legislation further required the AEC to submit to the JCAE a report on its designs for these projects, including cost estimates and schedule of construction, by a specified date. The obvious purpose of these provisions was to give the JCAE an adequate basis for directing in subsequent authorization acts that these reactors be built despite the AEC's objections.

time, the JCAE contended that it had the right to such investigative reports and stated that it had in fact received and reviewed such investigative reports on a number of subordinate AEC personnel. Apparently, however, the Senate section of the JCAE, which considered the nominations, was regarded as a Senate committee not possessing the full authority of the Joint Committee itself. President Truman denied this request, basing his denial on,

> . . . the established policy that all such investigative reports are confidential documents of the executive department of the Government and that congressional or public access to them would not be in the public interest.[24]

As a result of this episode, Senator Knowland, a member of the JCAE, introduced a bill, S. 1004, requiring that an FBI report on any nominee to the Commission be submitted to the Senate members of the Committee at their request. The bill was passed by the Senate on April 12, 1948, and by the House on May 3, 1948. It was thereupon vetoed by the President, who stated in his veto message:

> S. 1004 is objectionable in that it would permit an unwarranted encroachment of the legislative upon the executive branch. Five Senators would be authorized to direct the Federal Bureau of Investigation, a bureau of the Department of Justice, to make investigations for them. The complete independence of the executive branch renders it imperative that the Executive have sole authority over the officers whom he appoints. . . . It would authorize the Senate members of the Joint Committee to utilize a bureau of an executive department and direct its head to perform functions for the legislative branch, at the same time that he was performing similar functions as part of the executive branch, with the possibility of confusion and misunderstanding as to which branch controlled.[25]

In debate on sustaining the veto, Hickenlooper, then JCAE chairman, pointed out that the President had signed the 1946 act without objecting to the provision authorizing the Committee to utilize the services, information facilities, and personnel of the executive branch and, indeed, had not objected to the Committee's "request and direction" to the FBI that it investigate all JCAE staff employees.[26] The veto was ultimately sustained by the Senate.

The language of the statute, in effect approved by President Tru-

---

[24] *Cong. Rec.*, 93 (March 28, 1947), 2804-2806.

[25] *Cong. Rec.*, 94 (May 17, 1948), 5895.

[26] *Ibid.* (May 21, 1948), 6247. As a matter of fact, the JCAE has called on the FBI to conduct full background investigations of its staff members and consultants, and the FBI has always complied with such requests.

man when he signed the 1946 bill and by President Eisenhower when he signed the 1954 bill, seems on its face to raise precisely the issue which caused President Truman to veto S. 1004 in 1948.[27] Although the full scope and effect of this provision is presently unclear, in view of the JCAE's evident self-restraint in exercising the authority to date, the provision appears to have potentially substantial implications for executive-legislative relationships.

• Power to Authorize Appropriations

The Atomic Energy Act of 1946 contained a blanket authorization for the appropriation to the AEC of such funds as might be necessary for carrying out the purposes of the act. Although such a blanket authorization was not unique (the most significant precedent was the authorization for the Tennessee Valley Authority), it was somewhat unusual, since, in the case of most government agencies with programmatic responsibilities, Congress has reserved the right to authorize activities by statute before funds could be appropriated for them.

Commencing with its 1949 investigation into charges of "incredible mismanagement" by the AEC, the Committee considered the desirability of amending the 1946 act to require authorization of AEC appropriations for acquisition or construction of real property and facilities. In this effort it was opposed by the AEC and the Bureau of the Budget, largely because introduction of a two-step process (authorization plus appropriations), the Executive contended, would delay AEC appropriations and thereby delay vital programs. It was not until 1954 that the JCAE finally obtained the authorizing power as a part of the over-all revision of the Atomic Energy Act of 1946. As originally enacted, Section 261 of the 1954 act required specific legislative authorization of all appropriations for "acquisition or condemnation of any real property or any facility or for plant or facility acquisition, construction, or expansion." Then, in 1957, when the AEC interpreted the term "facility" to exclude from the requirement for authorization certain experimental reactors, Section 261 was amended at the Committee's initiative to make it clear that authorization was required for any nonmilitary experimental reactor designed to produce more than 10,000 kilowatts of heat or to be used in the production of electric power. At the same time, Section 261 was also amended to require authorization for any AEC cooperative program involving the use of AEC funds directly or indirectly for development and construction of demonstration reactors

---

[27] It is somewhat surprising that President Truman, who was always exceptionally conscious of the prerogatives of the executive branch, apparently did not question, when considering the Atomic Energy Act of 1946, the exceptional powers vested in the Joint Committee.

or for commercial provision of materials or services for civilian use. Since the AEC's efforts to encourage private enterprise to invest in reactor projects and other phases of the atomic-energy industry were based largely on such cooperative programs, the 1957 amendment brought this entire program squarely within the JCAE's cognizance.

Although there is nothing per se unusual in the JCAE's authorization power, it has been imaginatively exercised to assume positive direction of the atomic-energy program. As the JCAE chairman pointed out in 1957, it is normal for Congress, in handling authorization legislation, "to take what the administration proposes and either reject it or revise details to suit the Congress," but the JCAE is not reluctant to make "significant revisions" in what the administration recommends or to "add its own projects or requirements when it sees fit." [28] In fact, it has become the systematic policy of the Joint Committee to review the AEC's budget *de novo* and to add projects which it considers desirable, although these projects may have been rejected or withdrawn by the AEC itself or by the Bureau of the Budget in the course of the budget-formulation process. For example, Representative Holifield, chairman of the JCAE during the Eighty-seventh Congress, in introducing the AEC's authorization bill for fiscal year 1962, told the House:

> As in the past, the Joint Committee—through its close review and continuous monitoring of AEC activities—reserves the right to recommend projects and levels of support which the Committee believes necessary or important to national interests. As the Chairman of the Joint Committee, I wish to assure my colleagues that I will encourage the Joint Committee to continue to exercise its expert judgment which in the past has proven on so many occasions to be correct.[29]

This policy was reflected in the JCAE's handling of the authorization legislation for fiscal year 1959. The president had directed that only the "most essential" projects be submitted by the various agencies to the Bureau of the Budget for inclusion in the 1959 budget. Acting on this basis, the AEC eliminated from its budget submission fourteen physical-research projects involving expenditures of about $30,000,000 and requested approval of a $462,779,000 budget. The Budget Bureau slashed this amount to $193,379,000, eliminating primarily a number of reactor projects. The Committee reported out the bill increasing the AEC authorization from the $193,379,000 recommended by the Bureau of the Budget to $386,-679,000 including six projects which had been eliminated by the bureau as well as the fourteen physical-research projects which had not been

---

[28] *Cong. Rec.* (daily ed., May 2, 1961), 6522.

[29] *FY 1962 Authorization Hearings* (1961), p. 444.

submitted to the bureau by the AEC because of the president's directive.[30] Congress enacted the authorization bill with all the items added by the JCAE.

Budget Bureau reductions have caused the JCAE to express serious concern over the "dominant role assumed by the Bureau of the Budget in the atomic energy construction program." [31] The bureau's activities have been viewed by the Committee as an attempt by an administrative body to justify economic decisions on scientific and technical grounds. Thus, during consideration of the fiscal year 1959 authorization legislation, the Committee assailed the bureau for withholding funds previously authorized and appropriated by Congress. The Bureau of the Budget had withheld these funds pursuant to the apportionment system required under the Anti-Deficiency Act, calling for "careful apportionment of all types of funds expended by Federal agencies." According to its deputy director, the apportionment process was utilized to review the AEC's 1958 construction program "in order to develop a coordinated program which would insure the most effective use of funds for both fiscal years 1958 and 1959," emphasizing the "most urgent requirements that could be accomplished within funds expected to be available" and placing the balance of the appropriation temporarily in reserve.[32]

Another illustration of the JCAE's handling of budgetary processes is to be found in the 1962 authorization bill. As reported out by the Joint Committee, this bill included three projects which had not been requested by the executive branch.

One of these projects, a physics building to be constructed at the University of Chicago at a cost of $800,000, was recommended to the Commission by the AEC's Division of Research, but was eliminated from the AEC's formal submission to the Bureau of the Budget for fiscal year 1962, since the Commission felt that "this item could be deferred for a year without unduly jeopardizing the program." [33] AEC officials gave no public indication that construction of this project was urgent, stating that the Commission was planning to build the facility in fiscal year 1963. Nevertheless, the Joint Committee included the project in the bill which it reported in June, 1961, maintaining that it had become "urgent" to construct the facility.[34] The second of these projects was a controlled-

---

[30] H.R. Rep. No. 2108, 85th Cong., 2d Sess. (1958), pp. 14, 26.

[31] *Ibid.*, p. 6.

[32] Testimony of Robert Merriam, *FY 1959 Authorization Hearings* (1958), pp. 61-62. He pointed out that part of the problem was that the Bureau of the Budget had to deal with a budget item added by the JCAE without prior detailed consideration with the bureau, so that additional information was needed before the bureau could have "a thorough understanding of how the money will be best used." *Ibid.*, p. 49.

[33] *FY 1962 Authorization Hearings* (1961), p. 444.

[34] S. Rep. No. 441, 87th Cong., 1st Sess. (1961), p. 14.

environment laboratory to be constructed at a cost of $1,000,000 at Brookhaven National Laboratory. This item was regarded by the AEC as "desirable" but was eliminated by the Bureau of the Budget "purely on the basis of its priority with respect to other projects." The third project was an animal bioradiological laboratory to be constructed at the University of California at a cost of $700,000. This project had not been formally submitted by the AEC to the Budget Bureau, since it was felt that the project could be deferred until fiscal year 1963. However, a subsequent decision on a date for dismantling a cyclotron apparently impelled earlier construction of this laboratory.[35]

What had actually happened was that, prior to the first "formal" submission by the AEC of its proposed budget to the Budget Bureau, it held informal meetings with the bureau. At these meetings, the bureau recommended the elimination of specific projects planned by the Commission. Commission officials met subsequently with the Joint Committee staff and brought to its attention projects in addition to those included in the administration bill which were considered "urgent" by the Commission. Five such items were listed in order of priority, and the Committee adopted three. According to a member of the JCAE staff:

> Whereas the AEC and its officials could not formally request these projects, without possible retribution by the Administration or the Bureau of the Budget, they could informally bring these to the attention of the Committee when questioned. This is indicative of the Joint Committee and its staff in that they are not content to take formal presentation on face value but investigate the actual facts and where appropriate take the initiative.

With the tacit support of the AEC, the Committee substituted its own judgment for that of the Budget Bureau.[36]

The Joint Committee handled the AEC's 1963 authorization request somewhat differently. The Commission transmitted its proposed authorization bill on January 19, 1962, and on March 13 submitted a revised draft. Neither of these draft bills was introduced, the JCAE having made it clear that no authorization bill would be considered unless it contained provisions for civilian reactor projects deemed adequate by the Committee. Finally, on May 14, a satisfactory draft bill, including authorization for civilian power projects, was submitted and was promptly introduced by the JCAE chairman and vice-chairman.[37]

---

[35] *FY 1962 Authorization Hearings* (1961), pp. 441, 444-445.

[36] The JCAE's report points out, however, that these projects, totaling $2,500,000, were offset by three other projects, totaling $3,640,000, which the Committee deleted. S. Rep. No. 441, 87th Cong., 1st Sess. (1961), p. 14.

[37] S. Rep. No. 1671, 87th Cong., 2d Sess. (1962), p. 3.

To aid it in evaluating authorization requests, the Committee systematically goes behind the executive budgetary processes by requiring the AEC to submit to the Committee an analysis of its requests to the Bureau of the Budget showing the bureau's action on each. It also requires an analysis of the budget requests submitted by AEC divisions to the Commission, showing the action of the Commission on each request. Then the Committee, in its hearings, probes the considerations underlying the deletion or reduction of any requests. The JCAE appears to be the only Congressional committee which systematically reviews the internal budget-making process of an executive agency and the Bureau of the Budget in this manner.

Another unusual aspect of the Committee's exercise of the authorization power is its use of the imperative in authorizing legislation. On several occasions, it has reported out bills which not only authorized appropriations but also stated that the AEC "shall" proceed with certain projects and "shall" conduct design and engineering studies on other projects, reports of which had to be submitted to the Committee by a specified date. For example, the Authorization Act of 1958 directed the AEC to proceed with design, engineering, and development work on two reactors and to submit a report, including cost estimates, to the JCAE by a certain date. It also directed the AEC to proceed with design, engineering, and construction of another type of reactor to be owned and operated by the government.[38] These projects had not been requested by the AEC; in fact, the AEC was strongly opposed to them.[39]

• The Legislative Veto [40]

In 1951, when the executive branch sought an amendment to the 1946 act permitting a limited exchange of restricted data with other nations, the JCAE initiated the use of another device for exercising power.

---

[38] §101 (b) (8), §101 (e) (14), §110 at 71 Stat. 404, 405, 408 (1957).

[39] Although authorization acts for other agencies frequently include some language of direction, authorization legislation is seldom used as a vehicle for attempting to compel the Executive to undertake unwanted large-scale projects. In 1962, however, in authorizing funds for the 1963 defense budget, Chairman Carl Vinson's House Armed Services Committee sought to direct increased spending on the Air Force RS-70 reconnaissance strike bomber. The committee's report to the House included mandatory language. But, after a compromise agreement was reached among Vinson, President Kennedy, and Defense Secretary Robert S. McNamara, the directive language was removed from the authorization bill, although funds allocated to the RS-70 were considerably greater than desired by the executive branch.

[40] Although the device discussed in this section is not precisely a "legislative veto," it falls within a broad category of devices which require executive acts to come before Congress or its committees before they become final, thereby giving Congress an opportunity to block them. Use of such devices is discussed in Robert W. Ginnane, "The Control of Federal Administration by Congressional Resolutions and Committees," *Harvard Law Review,* LXV (February 1953), 509, and Joseph and Ann Cooper, "The Legislative Veto and the Constitution," *The George Washington Law Review,* XXX (March 1962), 467-516.

It incorporated into this amendment a requirement that, before the AEC consummated any arrangement for exchange of restricted data, the Committee must have been "fully informed for a period of thirty days in which Congress was in session." [41]

This technique was carried over into the 1954 act, which requires that a number of actions lie before the Joint Committee for a specified period while Congress is in session before they become effective: (1) any determination by the AEC that a material is "special nuclear material," (2) any determination by the AEC that a material is "source material," (3) any agreement for cooperation, and (4) any long-term contracts for electric-utility service.[42] Subsequent amendments to the act extended a similar requirement that the AEC establish fair-price periods for special nuclear material produced by licensees and establish criteria for waiving use charges for special nuclear material.[43] In addition, authorization legislation since 1957 has extended a similar requirement to any cooperative arrangement whereby the AEC gives financial support to a licensed activity when the basis of the arrangement has not been included in the program-justification data submitted to the JCAE in support of authorization legislation.[44] All these provisions authorize the JCAE to waive by resolution the waiting period except in connection with agreements for cooperation contemplating the transfer of weapons items or certain weapons data. With the same exception, the contemplated action can be legally blocked by the Committee only if it obtains enactment of prohibiting legislation which would be subject to presidential veto. In the case of transfer of weapons items and data, however, a concurrent resolution, which does not require presidential approval, would legally bar the contemplated action.

The obvious purpose of these provisions is to give the Joint Committee an opportunity to block the contemplated executive action. It should be noted that the JCAE cannot legally do this itself, but requires the support of Congress as a whole. It has not been necessary, however, for the Committee to press its power, since, predictably, the AEC has been responsive to informal JCAE pressures and "moral suasion" in the few cases in which problems have arisen.[45] Indeed, in only one case have members of

---

[41] 65 Stat. 692 (1951), amending §10 of the 1946 act, 60 Stat. 766 (1946).

[42] §51, 68 Stat. 929 (1954); 42 U.S.C. §2071 (1958). §61, 68 Stat. 932 (1954); 42 U.S.C. §2091 (1958). §123 (c), 68 Stat. 940 (1954); 42 U.S.C. §2153 (c) (1958). §164, 68 Stat. 951 (1954); 42 U.S.C. §2204 (1958).

[43] §58, adding 71 Stat. 275 (1957); 42 U.S.C. §2078 (1958). §59, 71 Stat. 274 (1957); 42 U.S.C. §2017 (1958), amending 68 Stat. 960 (1954).

[44] This requirement is contained in Section 111 of the Authorization Act for Fiscal Year 1958, 71 Stat. 403. Authorization of cooperative programs for subsequent fiscal years has been made by amending Section 111.

[45] The JCAE's first exercise of this power after the 1954 act became law is a good example of this "moral suasion." Sen. John O. Pastore (D., R. I.), chairman of the JCAE

the Committee actually found it necessary to introduce disapproving legislation.[46]

The legislative veto power of the JCAE is not unique as a limitation on executive discretion. Other Congressional committees have the authority to require that the Executive "come into agreement" with the committee or obtain its approval before performing certain acts.[47] But the Joint Committee's legislative veto power stands alone in its breadth, encompassing several key areas in the administration of the atomic-energy program.

• Access to Information

In many respects, the most significant source of the JCAE's power lies in those two sentences of Section 202 which provide:

> The Commission shall keep the Joint Committee fully and currently informed with respect to all of the Commission's activities. The Department of Defense shall keep the Joint Committee fully and currently informed with respect to all matters within the Department of Defense relating to the development, utilization, or application of atomic energy.

The first of these sentences was carried over from the 1946 act, with the word "all" added in 1954 to emphasize the AEC's duty. The second sentence, imposing a similar duty on the Department of Defense, was also added by the 1954 act.

As contemplated in this provision, the Committee from the earliest days enjoyed access to vast amounts of information concerning the atomic-energy program. In its first annual report to Congress in 1948, reference was made to the "constant liaison and flow of information" from the AEC

Subcommittee on Agreements for Cooperation, wrote the Commission shortly after the bilateral agreement with Turkey had been submitted to the subcommittee stating that JCAE review of the agreement ". . . discloses a problem on which I believe the Commission should take immediate action." This problem involved the possibility that quantities of U-235 in excess of the amount specified could be transferred to Turkey under a particular clause, thereby turning the agreement into an "open-ended agreement." He requested that the AEC give the Joint Committee "firm assurances . . . as to the limits within which the Commission intends to exercise the authority retained by it. . . ." The Commission responded with such assurances, indicating that the language of future bilateral agreements would be changed to clarify the Commission's intent. *Cong. Rec.,* 101 (May 26, 1955), 7083.

[46] In this case, Senator Anderson and Representative Holifield introduced concurrent resolutions intended to block adoption of a proposed AEC power-demonstration-reactor-program contract with the Pennsylvania Power and Light Company and Westinghouse Electric Corporation. *Cong. Rec.,* 104 (April 1, 1958), 5878-5880. The AEC withdrew the proposed contract before action was taken on the resolutions by the JCAE.

[47] See, e.g., 57 Stat. 52 (1943); 58 Stat. 190 (1944); 65 Stat. 365 (1951); 66 Stat. 606 (1952). Also William E. Rhodes, *Committee Clearance of Administrative Decisions* (East Lansing, Mich.: Michigan State University, Bureau of Social and Political Research, 1959).

to the JCAE "designed to keep the Joint Committee fully and currently informed." [48] This information flowed not only from top headquarters officials, but also from staff personnel at the AEC's headquarters and field offices. By 1948, the precedent had already been set for JCAE review of FBI investigative files on personnel in the atomic-energy program, for JCAE access to intelligence sources and reports, and for constant liaison with respect to international atomic-energy developments.

The scope of the Committee's statutory right to be kept fully and currently informed is by no means clear and requires interpretation in practice. Certainly, its right to be informed on "all of the Commission's activities" is not to be interpreted as requiring the AEC to inform the Committee of a contract for procurement of pencils or desks or of its employment of a new messenger. Some rule of reason is necessary for determining what information should go to the Committee. Similarly, the precise meaning of "currently informed" is uncertain. Does it mean that the Committee is to be informed simultaneously with the occurrence of an event, before it occurs, an hour later, or a week afterward? Indeed, there may be some question as to when the reportable occurrence itself takes place. If the AEC decides to let a major production contract which should be reported to the JCAE, should the JCAE be informed when the decision is reached, when the contract is executed, or when an announcement is made to the public?

Despite these niceties of interpretation, it does not appear that there was any serious friction during the early years between the AEC and the JCAE concerning the implementation of this provision. Certainly there were no public complaints by the JCAE that it was not receiving the information it wanted as early as it wanted. The Committee seems to have assumed that the AEC would willingly and in good faith provide in good time all information of interest. The AEC seems to have assumed that the Committee would act with common sense and restraint in its requests for information.

Generally, information concerning the Commission's actions was sent after the actions took place and not while they were pending. The JCAE, as a rule, reviewed what had been done and was not in the position of reviewing what the Commission was about to do. There were, of course, exceptions: where the Commission was struggling with a major problem, and particularly where it felt its decision would require JCAE support, it did not hesitate to discuss the problem and its proposed course of action with the JCAE in advance of its decision. For example, the Commission

---

[48] S. Rep. No. 850, 80th Cong., 2d Sess. (1948). The JCAE did not fulfill its original intention of producing a regular annual report. Since 1948, its reports to Congress have been submitted on an irregular basis.

sought the advice and guidance of the Committee in formulating a policy for handling labor disputes at AEC installations.[49]

During the early years, the Commission seems to have held the line against making available to the JCAE information concerning internal AEC affairs, working papers, and AEC files.[50] This reluctance was usually respected by the JCAE. Even here, however, individual exceptions were sometimes made, especially by subordinate staff members in the AEC's field offices who were hesitant to oppose and eager to appease the Committee's investigators. These exceptions were not based on Commission policy and hence were not really precedent-setting.

The first public discussion of the scope of the "fully-and-currently-informed" requirement occurred during the hearings on the 1954 act. At that time, members of the JCAE made sweeping claims as to their authority to obtain information. Chairman Cole argued that the AEC had the responsibility to keep the Joint Committee informed of all its activities "with the possible exception of those areas where the Commission's activities may be related or connected in some way with national defense plans." Senator Hickenlooper refused to accept this limitation and stated that the AEC had the duty to give the JCAE "immediate and full access" even to information on war plans where the Commission had any activities in this area connected with its official duties. Chairman Cole hastily retreated and said he did not mean to admit that the Committee was excluded from this area, but only to suggest that this area might be "debatable." In a somewhat different vein, Hickenlooper contended not only that "every contract, every action of the Atomic Energy Commission, is subject to the scrutiny, examination and information of the Joint Committee on Atomic Energy," but also that "without exception all such matters [other than "routine day-by-day housekeeping operation"] are reported to the Joint Committee on Atomic Energy prior to final action." [51]

The broad dimension of the Commission's responsibility under the 1946 act was made even broader by the 1954 act. The law was changed to

---

[49] *Labor Policy Hearings* (1948); see also Morgan Thomas, *Atomic Energy and Congress* (Ann Arbor: University of Michigan Press, 1956), p. 32.

[50] Representative Jackson said in 1952: "Should we on the committee have access to the confidential FBI reports on atomic employees? We do in fact have such access—the only committee of Congress that does. Should our committee insist upon seeing the internal staff papers of the Commission and the minutes of Commission meetings? We have never insisted—because we respect the Commission's need for a certain privacy in its internal functioning. Should we be informed of Commission decisions before they are reached or only afterward? In fact we know about the big issues far in advance of any solution but on lesser matters we are sometimes advised after a decision is made." Address at the Atomic Energy Institute of the University of Michigan Law School, June 28, 1952; reprinted in *Cong. Rec.*, 98 (July 5, 1952), A4472. Members of the JCAE staff state that they often are shown staff papers and other internal AEC documents at AEC field offices.

[51] *Leg. Hist. 1954 Act*, v. 2, pp. 2310-2311; v. 3, pp. 3180-3186.

require the Commission to keep the JCAE "fully and currently informed with respect to *all* of the Commission's activities." Inclusion of the word "all" was intended to underscore the nature of the Commission's obligation and came about as a result of a difference of opinion during the hearings.

The Joint Committee wrote the Commission on May 20, 1954, while the hearings on the 1954 legislation were under way, requesting information concerning the date and hour of Commission meetings during the preceding ten-month period; a list of the commissioners present, absent, and absent for a portion of the meeting; and a list of the general subject matter of each meeting. This request raised considerable question within the Commission concerning the privacy of its own discussions and was regarded as an unprecedented intrusion by the JCAE into the internal affairs of the Commission. For this reason, the Commission referred the Committee request to the attorney general for his advice as to the propriety of furnishing the information. Before an opinion was rendered by the attorney general, the JCAE adopted and transmitted to the Commission a formal resolution demanding that the data in question be furnished. On May 28, 1954, six days after the original request from the JCAE was received, the Commission acceded and transmitted the information, stating:

> In the interest of cooperation with the Joint Committee, the Commission is furnishing the information requested although the Commission has been advised that perhaps it would have been proper to have declined to furnish some of the information on the basis of invasion of executive privacy. The Commission does not wish to raise the issue. Neither does the Commission wish to set a precedent by having furnished this information.[52]

On June 3, 1954, several days after the Commission's capitulation, Chairman Strauss again testified before the JCAE on the pending 1954 act, and the following colloquy took place with respect to Section 202:

> *Chairman Cole:* Mr. Strauss, I wanted to ask you with reference to a section of existing law. Section 15 of the present law, subparagraph B, says:
>
> "The Commission—"
>
> meaning the Atomic Energy Commission—
>
> "shall keep the joint committee fully and currently informed with respect to the Commission's activities."
>
> My interpretation of that sentence and that responsibility imposed on the Commission is all-inclusive with respect to the

[52] *Strauss Confirmation Hearings* (1959), p. 811. This was apparently the first and only occasion in the history of the AEC-JCAE relationship that such a resolution was adopted. *Loc. cit.* and *Leg. Hist. 1954 Act,* v. 2, p. 2311.

> Commission's activities, with the possible exception of those areas where the Commission's activities may be related or connected in some way with national defense war plans. In other lesser areas, it is my view that it is a statutory obligation of the Commission to keep this committee informed on all of its activities.
>
> *Mr. Strauss:* That is the view of the witness, and any respect in which I have failed to do that would be dereliction.
>
> *Chairman Cole:* You will agree there have been instances recently where that has not occurred?
>
> *Mr. Strauss:* If I am thinking of the same thing that the Chairman is, there have been instances recently in which the word "promptly" has certainly been violated.
>
> *Chairman Cole:* I will express it differently. You will agree there have been recent instances where that principle has been resisted, where the Commission has resisted informing the Committee on matters which the Committee requested of the Commission?
>
> Now my purpose in bringing that out is at this time to write into the bill language which may be even stronger than what is in there now, and I do not know what stronger language could be used than to say, it is the duty of the Commission to keep the Joint Committee fully and currently informed on all the Commission's activities.
>
> *Mr. Strauss:* Would you accept the change in wording, Mr. Chairman, that instead of resisting it has been delayed? I do not believe there is anything which the Joint Committee has requested that the Commission has failed to comply. Nor in respect to such information as crosses the desk of the Chairman has there been any delay in furnishing, as a matter of fact.
>
> *Chairman Cole:* It may not be in your memory, but it certainly is within mine, that for the first time within the history of this Committee it was necessary for the Committee to adopt a formal resolution to get information from the Commission.
>
> *Mr. Strauss:* I am aware of that.
>
> *Chairman Cole:* You may not call that resistance, but I do.
>
> *Mr. Strauss:* I should not absolve myself from that at the disadvantage of my colleagues.[53]

When the bill was subsequently reported, the word "all" was written in, and the JCAE report, discussing the "fully-and-currently-informed" provision, stated: "It is the intent of Congress that the Joint Committee be informed while matters are pending, rather than after action

[53] *Leg. Hist. 1954 Act,* v. 2, pp. 2310-2311. Cole, in a letter of June 15, 1954, to the *Richmond News Leader,* stated that his criticism was directed at the Commission as an agency and not at Strauss personally. He pointed out that the Commission vote was a split one, with Strauss in the minority favoring the release of information to the Committee. Strauss, *op. cit.,* p. 383.

has been taken." [54] Thus, the addition of the word "all" to Section 202 and the above language in the Committee report were direct consequences of the "resistance" of the Commission to making the information on its meetings available to the JCAE.

This discussion of the "fully-and-currently-informed" provision in 1954 was but a prelude to continuing controversy. In sharp contrast to the pre-1954-act period, the years since enactment of the new statute have been marked by considerable wrangling over the meaning and implementation of the clause. The JCAE has sharply increased its demands for information and has become highly critical of the AEC's failure to furnish information and to furnish it with sufficient promptness. It should be noted that this new attitude coincided with an evaporation of the previous spirit of joint venture and close collaboration which had prevailed between the JCAE and the AEC from 1947 to 1954. This spirit was replaced by controversy between a Democratic JCAE leadership dedicated to an aggressive, expansive atomic-energy policy, including a large-scale government investment in nuclear-power development, and a Republican administration which was extremely budget-conscious and desirous of minimizing government nuclear-power development. As Senator Pastore expressed it:

> . . . there has been a continuing struggle and disagreement among the members of the committee and the members of the Commission, not particularly the Chairman, as to whether or not matters that were to be brought to the attention of the Joint Committee were coming up rapidly enough.[55]

In 1958, Strauss retired as chairman of the Atomic Energy Commission and shortly thereafter was nominated by President Eisenhower as secretary of commerce. Hearings on confirmation were held in 1959 before the Senate Committee on Interstate and Foreign Commerce, and, after lengthy floor debate, the nomination was rejected by the Senate. Although the attack on Strauss had many facets, one of the principal charges against him, documented by specific cases, was his alleged failure to keep the Joint Committee "fully and currently informed," in accordance with his statutory duty. Review of these cases provides the best available picture of the significance of this JCAE power and the manner of its exercise.

1. *Records of Commission meetings.* The episode relating to hearings on the 1954 act, discussed above, was a prime example cited by the Strauss opposition in support of its contention that the Commission has

---

[54] S. Rep. No. 1699, 83rd Cong., 2d Sess. (1954). A report of a Congressional committee on pending legislation obviously can state only the intent of the committee and not that of Congress.

[55] *Strauss Confirmation Hearings* (1959), p. 690.

the statutory responsibility to provide the JCAE with information as to its meetings, at least on request.

2. *The "Nautilus" episode.* In 1955, the executive branch desired to amend the agreement for cooperation with the United Kingdom to provide the U.K. with restricted data concerning the nuclear submarine "Nautilus." For various reasons, there was considerable doubt and difference of opinion within the executive branch as to the legality of such action under the Atomic Energy Act of 1954. After the AEC's general counsel rendered an opinion that the action would not be legal, the Department of Defense referred the question to the attorney general, who ruled by letter of January 26, 1956, that Section 144 (a) of the act authorized the communication of these data pursuant to an agreement for cooperation, but cautioned:

> In view of the sensitive subject matter here involved, I believe that, in this instance, the matter should be discussed with the Joint Committee before the agreements are entered into. This, presumably, would be undertaken on an informal basis in the interest of ascertaining preliminarily the views of the Committee, and, at the same time, permitting the Committee to become aware of proposed developments in the field of international cooperation which might have significant effects upon the atomic energy program.[56]

This letter, which was addressed to the secretary of defense, with a copy to AEC Chairman Strauss, was not brought to the attention of the JCAE, nor was the Committee informed of the pending amendment to the agreement until June 8, 1956, when the amendment had already been submitted to the President for his approval. A copy of the attorney general's opinion was not sent the JCAE until June 29, 1956, twenty-one days after its existence was apparently inadvertently revealed to the Committee. Under Section 123 of the 1954 act, the amendment could not become effective until it had lain before the JCAE for thirty days. However, the JCAE let this period pass without public objection and permitted the amendment to become effective before voicing its objections for the record.[57] Thereafter, the JCAE unanimously agreed, on July 26, 1956, to request the President to suspend implementation of the exchange until the

---

[56] *Ibid.*, pp. 511-512.

[57] *Cong. Rec.*, 102 (July 17, 1956), 13066. During an executive session on June 9, Committee members of both parties objected to the agreement. The JCAE chairman, Senator Anderson, assailed the agreement, but pointed out that the Committee had deliberately maintained official silence during the thirty-day waiting period to avoid the impression that "we were trying to upset an agreement with the British." *Loc. cit.* Anderson felt that the Committee "was put in a position where we could not effectively protest." *Strauss Confirmation Hearings* (1959), p. 1027.

Committee and Congress had an opportunity to consider the matter further. The President acquiesced in this request and did not authorize the initiation of the exchanges until February, 1957.[58]

The Strauss critics castigated him, first, for not informing the JCAE immediately of the negotiations for the amendment of the agreement and, second, for his tardiness in giving the JCAE a copy of the attorney general's letter. The nub of the Joint Committee's position seems to have been that it is entitled to know about important negotiations such as these in sufficient time to participate in the policy decisions involved, over and above its statutory responsibility to review the final agreement for a period of thirty days before it becomes effective.[59]

3. *The "clean-bomb" press release.* In July, 1956, Strauss issued a press release referring to development in the then-current Pacific weapons tests of the so-called clean bomb. Neither the JCAE nor any of its members had advance notice of either the information or the release, and the release did not reach the Committee until eighteen hours after it was given to the press.[60]

4. *The PRDC case.* On June 28, 1956, the JCAE requested that AEC send it a copy of the report of the Advisory Committee on Reactor Safeguards (ACRS) concerning health and safety aspects of a contemplated power reactor for the construction of which Power Reactor Development Corporation (a group of companies headed by Detroit Edison Co.) had applied for an AEC license. The request was renewed on July 9. On July 13, the AEC wrote the Committee contending that the report had been prepared by an advisory group and was one element to be considered by the Commission in passing on the license application and that the Commission was acting in this case in a quasijudicial capacity. The AEC noted also that it would be ". . . inappropriate to disclose the contents of advice and recommendations which are currently under review" and that disclosure of the report would seriously impair the independence of the AEC staff and advisory committees. Finally, the AEC letter pointed out that the attorney general had previously advised the Securities and Exchange Commission that, "it would not be consistent with the orderly conduct of the

---

[58] *Ibid.*, p. 1018, and pp. 702-708 for a detailed chronology of this episode.

[59] It should be noted, also, that the JCAE believed the proposed agreement to be in violation of the 1954 act. Although the Committee appears to have been unanimous in the view that the new agreement with Britain was improper and unwise, there was apparently no general agreement among members, even the Democrats, that information had been improperly withheld from the Joint Committee by the AEC. Senator Pastore, chairman of the Subcommittee on Agreements for Cooperation, felt that it was "a gray area that could be debated one way or the other" as to whether "all of the negotiation detail should have been discussed with the Committee, detail by detail," particularly since the agreement had to come before the JCAE in any event before it could become effective. *Ibid.*, p. 602.

[60] *Cong. Rec.*, 102 (July 20, 1956), 13711-13712.

administrative process of your agency to subject to concurrent Congressional review the manner in which the Commission is discharging its quasi-judicial functions on any pending application." Nevertheless, the AEC sent a copy of the report to the JCAE "with the understanding that the Commission does not regard this as constituting a precedent" and with the "request that the letter be treated as administratively confidential by your committee." On the same date, the JCAE returned the ACRS report unread on the ground that the Committee could not receive the report under those conditions.[61]

A few days later, the Committee again wrote the Commission, renewing its request for the report and rejecting the AEC's contention that the report was privileged because the AEC had received it in a quasi-judicial capacity. The JCAE's position was based on its right to information, on its proper legislative purpose in making the request, and on the contention that the AEC had not previously treated the PRDC matter as a quasi-judicial proceeding. The AEC was reminded that it had not notified the Committee of any quasijudicial hearings, formal presentation of evidence, or rules for receipt of and handling of reports in quasijudicial proceedings. Three days later, the AEC capitulated and transmitted the document in question.[62]

5. *The uranium-policy speech.*[63] On Monday, October 28, 1957, Jesse Johnson, director of the AEC's Division of Raw Materials, delivered an address outlining a major AEC policy decision with respect to uranium procurement. A copy of this speech had been delivered to the JCAE office at 4:30 P.M. the preceding Friday, October 25. The Johnson speech had been approved by the Commission two days earlier, on October 23. During testimony before the Committee in January, 1958, Johnson indicated that the actual decision reflected in his speech had been made about two weeks before October 23. Strauss contended that Johnson was wrong in his statement, and an official AEC communication to Chairman Anderson in May, 1959, stated that Commission records reflect that the Commission on September 24, 1957, authorized "the development of an ore-procurement policy statement" for inclusion in Johnson's contemplated speech and that the "policy announcement made in the speech was cleared by the Commission" on October 23.

Senator Anderson's contention was that the AEC should have regarded this as a "pending matter of sufficient significance that the Joint

---

[61] *Staff Study of AEC Procedures and Organization in Licensing* (1957), pp. 117-119. JCAE staff members point out that the report had been made available by the Commission to the Power Reactor Development Corporation.

[62] *Ibid.*, pp. 110-121.

[63] A complete chronology of this episode is included in *Strauss Confirmation Hearings* (1959), pp. 1042-1052.

Committee should have been informed prior to the formal clearance of the speech on October 23, 1957," especially since the announcement "caused all kinds of trouble in the uranium industry." Considering Anderson's views in context, his main concern seems to have been that the Committee was not given the opportunity to influence the Commission's policy along lines more palatable to the Committee.[64] Subsequently, the JCAE extracted a commitment from the Commission not to take any final action on "stretch-out of certain domestic and Canadian uranium-procurement contracts" without prior discussion with the Committee.

6. *The Patent Office.* During the hearings before the JCAE on legislation in April, 1959, the question arose whether the Committee was entitled to have access to patent applications pending in the U.S. Patent Office. Under Section 151(d) of the 1954 act, the commissioner of patents is explicitly required to provide the AEC with access to all patent applications on inventions or discoveries useful in the atomic-energy field. This requirement apparently carves out a single exception to the general mandate of Section 122 of Title 35 of the United States Code that: "Applications for patents shall be kept in confidence by the Patent Office and no information concerning the same shall be given without authority of the applicant or owner." The Patent Office, a branch of the Department of Commerce, took the position, supported by Strauss, who was then acting secretary of commerce, that this general mandate barred it from giving the JCAE access to the patent applications, despite the provision of Section 202 requiring all government agencies to "furnish any information requested by the Joint Committee with respect to activities or responsibilities of that agency in the field of atomic energy." In taking this position, the Patent Office and the Acting Secretary of Commerce acknowledged that it was "incongruous to provide the Committee with the breadth of this information on atomic matters to which it is entitled by law and then deny direct access to patent information" and urged that Section 202 be amended to clearly authorize the patent commissioners to give the JCAE such access. The issue was largely an academic one, since the JCAE could easily obtain access to the same patent application through the AEC,[65] but the JCAE seemed

[64] According to Anderson, the JCAE "had to institute an investigation and bring out the fact and impel a modification" in the program which had been announced in Johnson's speech. *Ibid.*, pp. 1042, 1048. In his memoirs, Strauss comments that earlier notification "would have extended our responsibility to keeping the Joint Committee informed as to our thoughts as well as our actions." *Op. cit.*, p. 386.

[65] *Patent Hearings* (1959), pp. 42-52. AEC sources state that the JCAE had not requested access to patent applications prior to this occasion, but that, if it had, the AEC would have obtained the information from the Patent Office and made it available to the Committee. The commissioner of patents conceded that the JCAE had the right to "indirect access to pending applications for patents" through the AEC. *Ibid.*, p. 52. This question apparently arose in a hypothetical context, and not in connection with any Committee re-

determined to assert vigorously its claimed statutory authority to direct access and subjected the commissioner of patents to highly critical questioning.

These cases illustrate some of the controversies which have centered on the question of the JCAE's right of access to information and, more particularly, the AEC's responsibility to furnish information to the Committee. Numerous other examples may be found showing the extent to which the Commission has acquiesced in JCAE insistence for full and current information. These range from the AEC's simultaneous assertion and waiver of executive privilege with respect to furnishing opinions of its general counsel [66] to its furnishing the JCAE with advance copies of new AEC regulations before publication in *The Federal Register* [67] and to a "treaty" requiring twenty-four hours advance notice to the JCAE of AEC press releases.[68]

There is considerable reason to believe that the JCAE's running attack on Strauss for not keeping the Committee "fully and currently informed" was primarily a device for harassing the Commission and keeping it off balance. The Commission's position is well illustrated by an event of 1958. During JCAE hearings on the nuclear-power program, Strauss displayed a telegram he had just received from Pacific Gas and Electric Company indicating its desire to build a boiling-water reactor with private funds. Senator Anderson assailed Strauss' action as a device "to show that here stands private industry just itching to build these power plants" aimed at countering the efforts of JCAE Democrats to have the AEC build power reactors. Strauss replied:

> You will appreciate that the Commission is somewhat on the horns of a dilemma. I received this telegram this morning. . . . I thought I should present it. Had I not done so and this material been released to the press, as undoubtedly it will be later in the day in San Francisco, I am caught in the nutcracker of not keeping you fully and currently informed.[69]

It was to be expected that Strauss, under attack from the early months of his chairmanship for allegedly failing to keep the JCAE informed, would exert every effort to placate the Committee. In fact, communications from

---

quest for access to a particular patent application. The example indicates the vigilance of the JCAE in policing the breadth of its claimed right of access to information.

[66] *Strauss Confirmation Hearings* (1959), p. 704.

[67] *"Sec. 202" Hearings* (1955), p. 104.

[68] Statement by Representative Holifield, *Cong. Rec.*, 103 (May 28, 1957), 7923.

[69] *"Sec. 202" Hearings* (1958), pp. 6-8. Strauss' "dilemma" was probably complicated by the fact that there had been an agreement made before the opening of the hearings to postpone any discussion of the controversial power-demonstration-reactor program until after the hearings.

the AEC to the JCAE sharply increased in number during the Strauss era.[70] Strauss was nevertheless assailed by Anderson, who said his technique was "to deluge the Committee with considerable numbers of individual letters and reports" while on key questions holding out important information.[71] In the Committee members' view, therefore, a heavy burden rests on the AEC to keep the JCAE apprised of all matters which the AEC believes are or could become important. At the same time, it is expected to refrain from deluging the JCAE with trivia. From the AEC's standpoint, its position, when faced with a hostile JCAE or hostile JCAE members, is, "we're damned if we do and damned if we don't." [72]

The intimidating effect of the JCAE's exercise of its right to be informed, and particularly the fate of Strauss, has not been lost on recent commissioners. All indications are that Strauss' successor, John McCone, was exceedingly conscious of the practical necessity for giving the Committee what it wanted in the way of information. There is no indication in the public record that the JCAE found significant fault with McCone's performance in this respect.[73] In addition, the JCAE has adopted the practice of extracting a "commitment" from nominees to the Commission. In 1957, during confirmation hearings on the nomination of John S. Graham, the Committee elicited his commitment that he would inform the JCAE of his own votes as a commissioner and that he would personally bring to the attention of the Committee any matter on which he felt that the JCAE should be informed if it were not otherwise informed. The latter pledge was also made by Commissioner John F. Floberg.[74] Commissioner Robert E. Wilson was asked to, and did, subscribe to the "fully-and-currently-informed" requirement, although he pointed out that "currently" must be interpreted with reason.[75] Commissioner Loren K. Olson

---

[70] According to information furnished by the AEC, it transmitted 654 communications to the JCAE in 1954; 824 in 1955; 1,331 in 1957; 1,212 in 1958; and 1,375 in 1960.

[71] *Strauss Confirmation Hearings* (1959), p. 510.

[72] Obviously, the line between the significant and the trivial is difficult to draw and varies with time and circumstance. It is clear that the AEC frequently has a difficult decision as to whether and when information should be conveyed to the JCAE. For example, some Committee members complained in 1955 that Strauss had failed to live up to his obligations when he did not immediately report to the JCAE that the AEC's general manager had told him informally and in confidence of his intention to resign. *"Sec. 202" Hearings* (1955), pp. 38-41.

[73] McCone's relations with the JCAE were generally good. During his chairmanship, the AEC did not offer serious objection to Joint Committee direction of the civilian reactor program. Perhaps, had McCone found himself in opposition to the Committee on substantive issues, the JCAE would have found reasons for criticizing him on grounds of failing to keep it fully and currently informed.

[74] "Hearings Before the JCAE on the Nomination of John W. Graham and John F. Floberg to the Atomic Energy Commission, August 13, 1957," transcript, pp. 18, 28, 49-51.

[75] Senator Anderson replied: "If I did not think you were reasonable, I certainly would not favor your confirmation." "Hearings Before the JCAE on the Nomination of Robert E. Wilson to the Atomic Energy Commission, March 15, 1960," transcript, pp. 50-52.

was asked whether he had any reservations about the requirement and replied in the negative.[76] The present chairman, Dr. Glenn T. Seaborg, pledged that he would keep the JCAE informed on pending matters, rather than after action had taken place, and, specifically, that he had no reservations about making reports of the General Advisory Committee available to the JCAE.[77] Similar commitments were extracted from Commissioner Leland J. Haworth.[78]

It seems clear that the JCAE's right to information is substantially greater than that of any other committee. Relations between other Congressional committees and the executive branch are at arm's length in the sense that the other committees receive as a practical matter only that information which the Executive deems it necessary, desirable, or expedient to furnish. Where the Executive raises the question of privilege, other committees cannot obtain the information except through the exercise of normal political interplay. The JCAE, however, can also rely on the Commission's statutory duty to provide requested information. This circumstance, coupled with the unusual reliance placed by Congress on the JCAE and the Commission's dependence on the Committee for support, makes it extremely difficult for the AEC to assert any claim of privilege. This is evidenced by the scope of the Committee's access and, in particular, by those instances in which the AEC has in fact delivered information to the JCAE despite its belief that executive privilege applied.

It seems to be generally accepted by Congress that, whatever the legal position of Congress with respect to obtaining information from the Executive, the AEC and JCAE occupy a special position. Thus, during the 1955 hearings on the Dixon-Yates contract before a subcommittee of the Senate Judiciary Committee, Sen. Joseph C. O'Mahoney (D., Wyo.) rejected the contention that AEC Chairman Strauss could assert any privilege, arguing:

> . . . the Atomic Energy Act which established the Atomic Energy Commission was a delegation of congressional powers to the Commission. . . . It was not a conveyance to the President of any powers as in the case of the Department of Justice, or the Department of the Interior, or the Department of Agriculture. And Congress was so certain about this that it established the Joint Committee on Atomic Energy, and gave that Committee special power to keep in touch with your Commission. The purpose of the Atomic Energy Act, as I recall it,

[76] "Hearings Before the JCAE on the Nomination of Loren K. Olson to the Atomic Energy Commission, May 27, 1960," transcript, p. 14.

[77] "Hearings Before the JCAE on the Nomination of Dr. Glenn T. Seaborg as Chairman of the Atomic Energy Commission, Feb. 23, 1961," transcript, pp. 8-10.

[78] "Hearings Before the JCAE on the Nomination of Dr. Leland J. Haworth to the Atomic Energy Commission, March 29, 1961," transcript, pp. 8-10.

> . . . was to establish the closest liaison between the Congress and the Commission, so that nothing could be done without the knowledge of the people's representatives in Congress. . . .[79]

And Sen. Eugene McCarthy (D., Minn.) contended in 1959:

> The withholding of information from the Joint Committee on Atomic Energy is in a completely different category from the withholding of information from other committees of Congress. In the statute creating the AEC there is a specific provision in which Congress with the approval of the President, set forth that this particular problem was one which had such great economic, political and even moral significance that Congress was to be included in any basic decision regarding atomic energy.[80]

For its part, the JCAE has aggressively and vigorously policed the "fully-and-currently-informed" provision to ensure the broadest possible interpretation and to contest any tendency to narrow it. The Committee clearly believes that there is no information of any kind which the Commission has the right to withhold from it. In 1956, the JCAE chairman, responding to a Congressional inquiry as to the occasions on which an executive agency refused to provide the JCAE with information, stated that Section 202 of the Atomic Energy Act imposes an "absolute requirement" on the AEC to keep the Committee fully and currently informed and that,

> . . . the Joint Committee is of the opinion that it has the authority and power to obtain, on any given occasion, any information that it may desire from the Atomic Energy Commission. However, on particular occasions, the Joint Committee may, if it deems it advisable, elect not to exert its full statutory powers.

Then, citing two instances in which the AEC had declined to furnish information to the Committee on the basis of executive privilege, the JCAE chairman stated: ". . . the Joint Committee could have obtained the information sought, but elected to refrain from exercising its powers to the fullest extent permitted by the law." [81] It is clear, moreover, that the JCAE does not recognize the validity of any claim of executive privilege with respect to atomic-energy information possessed by the AEC and the

---

[79] "Hearings Before the Subcommittee on Antitrust and Monopoly of the Senate Committee on the Judiciary, Dixon-Yates Contract," 84th Cong., 1st Sess. (1955), pp. 1161-1164. Senator O'Mahoney's position, if tenable, would have cloaked Congress, including other committees, with the powers of the JCAE.

[80] *Cong. Rec.,* 105 (June 12, 1959), 10651.

[81] "Hearings Before the Subcommittee on Constitutional Rights of the Senate Committee on the Judiciary, Freedom of Information and Secrecy in Government," 85th Cong., 2d Sess. (1958), p. 356.

Department of Defense. Any executive privilege which may have existed was, the Committee contends, waived forever by the acquiescence of the President, the Secretary of Defense, and the AEC in the 1954 act which included the "fully-and-currently-informed" provision.

It is extremely difficult to compare the amount or kind of information flowing from the executive branch to the JCAE with the flow of information to other committees.[82] It appears, however, that the JCAE is an unusually well-informed committee and that it receives more information from the Executive than most other committees. It is also difficult to relate this JCAE access specifically to the "fully-and-currently-informed" provision. Although there is no doubt that this provision has enabled the Committee to obtain some information which would otherwise have been considered privileged and remained undisclosed, it is not clear that the JCAE would, all other factors being equal, obtain markedly less information in the absence of this provision. Former members of the JCAE staff have expressed the view that, during their tenure, this provision was not of great significance in obtaining information required by the Committee and attributed the quantity and depth of the information they obtained primarily to their personal contacts with a multitude of lower- and intermediate-echelon AEC employees, particularly at AEC field offices. Such AEC employees, it has been stated, would frequently make information and documents available, although Washington would probably regard the same information as privileged. Nevertheless, Section 202 of the act and its predecessor provision in the 1946 act undoubtedly tended to discourage resistance and objections to giving information to the Joint Committee.

■ IMPACT ON EXECUTIVE POLICY-MAKING

The JCAE's passion to be kept fully and currently informed is, of course, not based merely on a thirst for knowledge for the sake of knowledge. Rather, knowledge is desired to permit the Joint Committee to play what it regards as its proper role in the formation and implementation of the nation's atomic-energy policy. As early as 1952, Rep. Henry Jackson characterized the AEC-JCAE relationship as unique, pointing out that "present-day students of our Constitution seem almost unaware of its growth." He said:

> In considerable degree both Committee and Commission jointly run the atomic program. Basic Commission policy decisions tend to be made with the advice and consent of the congressional Committee. In the case of two vital policy matters . . .

[82] Knowledgeable observers have remarked that some other committees request and obtain more information, and that of a type which the JCAE would not think of requesting.

> the drive and the urging from the Committee played so powerful a role that in a very real sense it can be said that the Committee made the decision with the advice and consent of the Executive Branch.

The basic reason for this singular relationship, Jackson maintained, was the JCAE's right to be "fully and currently informed."

> At first glance this might seem a frail foundation for Committee authority—merely the right to know with no legal jurisdiction whatever to direct or to supervise. Yet, in this atomic energy business, this simple right to know the highly secret facts in and of itself confers immense powers of moral suasion. Here, in a most literal sense, knowledge is power.
>
> If powerful and unanimous protests were ever to issue from the Committee, I presume they would be heard in every corner of our land, for the Committee serves as the only substitute for public opinion, the sole conduit for transmitting what in a normal and nonsecret operation might be the popular will. The Commission has therefore come to consult more and more with my colleagues and myself on the Committee and to take our view into account.[83]

The general principles stated by Jackson have, in one form or another, been repeated in the years since 1952 by other members of the Joint Committee, as well as by members of Congress who are not JCAE members.

There is nothing particularly complex in the JCAE's conversion of information into policy action. Where information is received while matters are still pending, the Committee can take action to shape the final decision. Had the JCAE possessed advance information concerning the AEC's 1957 uranium decision, it could have attempted to change that decision, instead of bringing about its reversal months later. Had it been informed of the contemplated 1956 exchange of classified information with the British on nuclear-propelled submarines, it undoubtedly could have blocked consummation of the agreement for cooperation. Its advance knowledge of the H-bomb controversy in 1949 enabled it to play what it regards as a decisive role in bringing about the ultimate decision to proceed with the project.[84] Its advance knowledge of the AEC's internal policy discussions enables the Committee to play a role not only in making atomic-energy decisions, but in their implementation as well.[85]

---

[83] *Cong. Rec.*, 98 (July 5, 1952), A4472.

[84] "The original decision by President Truman to proceed with the vigorous development of the hydrogen bomb was influenced more by Sen. Brien McMahon, then chairman of the Joint Committee, and some of his associates, than by members of the Atomic Energy Commission." Anderson and Ramey, *op. cit.*, pp. 85, 88.

[85] Indeed, it has been well recognized that the right of Congress to be fully informed and to know all the facts leads directly to involvement in administration of the laws. This was pointed out with great clarity by Sen. Forrest C. Donnell (R., Mo.) at the time the Senate

The Joint Committee has over the years developed a distinctive approach. It favors a vigorous, imaginative, and aggressive atomic-energy program, demanding boldness and risk-taking rather than caution and economy.[86] Claiming that the Executive "was failing to initiate programs vital to the national welfare,"[87] the JCAE has consistently initiated, supported, and encouraged certain broad policies: the H-bomb program; expansion and diversification of nuclear weaponry; expanded production of fissionable material, especially plutonium; development of nuclear-propelled submarines and aircraft; and an accelerated program for developing nuclear power. The Committee has supported the AEC and the executive branch when they have taken the initiative, but it has usually prodded and pulled the Executive in its direction, believing that the Executive was lagging behind. Generally, the JCAE has desired more and bigger programs than the Executive deemed prudent or economical. It has lobbied actively for these programs within the executive branch, so that they have emerged from executive consideration bearing the JCAE imprint. Thus, the Committee achieves its program objectives by persuasion, negotiation, and pressure, not through legislation. In some cases, the efforts of the AEC and JCAE to work out a program involve, in effect, negotiations between two sovereign bodies.[88]

The Committee's approach was candidly discussed in 1960 by Sen-

---

was considering the Legislative Reorganization Act of 1946. Objecting to a provision in that legislation which called on each standing committee of the House and Senate to "exercise continuous surveillance" of each agency within its jurisdiction, he argued that it was inadvisable for Congress to take upon itself the "responsibility of seeing that there is a proper administration of the law which it has itself passed and the administration of which it has cast upon specific persons or agencies." *Cong. Rec.,* 92 (June 7, 1946), 6445. The Senate eliminated "surveillance" and inserted the word "watchfulness." 60 Stat. 832 (1946).

Similarly, in 1957, Senator Fulbright objected to an amendment to the Mutual Security Act which would have required the Executive to furnish Congress with any information requested by it concerning administration of that act. He argued that the effect of this amendment was to have Congress take over the function of administering the act by requiring full and current reports. He said: "If we are fully informed, then I suppose we should take the responsibility of administering the law day by day." *Cong. Rec.,* 103 (June 14, 1957), 9150.

[86] In concluding a 1951 report to Congress on the atomic-energy program, the JCAE said: ". . . if the Committee has a single general comment to offer, it is this: Greater boldness and more scientific and technical daring should be brought to bear upon the program." S. Rep. No. 1041, 82d Cong., 1st Sess. (1951), p. 7.

[87] Remarks of Representative Holifield, *Cong. Rec.,* 103 (Aug. 5, 1957), 13685.

[88] On November 27, 1957, the JCAE invited the AEC to cooperate in developing a realistic statement of nuclear-power objectives and an accelerated program to carry them out. The AEC accepted the invitation and, from December, 1957, to the end of June, 1958, there were four meetings between the commissioners and members of the JCAE and more than a dozen meetings between their respective staffs. H.R. Rep. No. 2108, 85th Cong., 2d Sess. (1958), p. 10. The effort was to achieve a "mutually acceptable compromise." Anderson and Ramey, *op. cit.,* p. 89.

ator Anderson, then chairman, and James T. Ramey, then executive director.[89] Pointing out that Section 202 of the 1954 act explicitly recognizes the JCAE's function of making policy recommendations to Congress, they commented that "it remained for the Joint Committee to apply this concept to the executive branch." This function of recommending policy, they said, had been carried on "informally" in the past, principally through "classified discussions and executive sessions with top AEC and military officials and the White House." More recently, they noted, "the efforts of the Joint Committee to initiate various policies and projects has [*sic*] not only involved informal methods, but has [*sic*] also taken on more of a public and formal character by means of public hearings and debate followed by legislative action in some cases."

The impact of the JCAE on the executive policy-making process has taken many forms. In addition to enthusiastically supporting pet projects, the Committee has attempted to play some role in the selection of key atomic-energy personnel. JCAE members were apparently instrumental in blocking the appointment of Richard Cook to be AEC general manager [90] and in protecting the position of Admiral Hyman G. Rickover. They strenuously attempted to influence the organization and staffing of the NASA-AEC effort with respect to nuclear space applications.[91] Similarly, the Committee has on at least one occasion attempted to direct AEC's choice of a particular contractor-operated AEC laboratory for conduct of a nuclear-power project.[92] In another case, the Committee asked the Commission

---

[89] *Ibid.*, pp. 87-88.

[90] *Cong. Rec.*, 101 (July 21, 1955), 11129. The objection to Cook was based on his role in the Dixon-Yates controversy.

[91] The JCAE threw its influence against Harold B. Finger of NASA and in favor of Col. Jack Armstrong of the AEC for appointment as director of the joint AEC-NASA nuclear rocket program. Four members of the Committee (Durham, Holifield, Price, and Van Zandt) wrote NASA urging that Armstrong be appointed and asked that, before any change in organization be effected, there be "an executive session of the Joint Committee to explore the desirability of the change and the qualifications of personnel recommended for the top positions." Notwithstanding JCAE pressure, Finger was appointed. *Nucleonics,* 18 (1960), 23-24.

[92] In reporting out the AEC Authorization Bill for fiscal year 1958, the JCAE recommended construction of a gas-cooled reactor and stated that "it would appear essential that this project be assigned to the Naval Reactor Branch under Admiral Rickover," which meant that Westinghouse Electric would obtain the contract. S. Rep. No. 791, 85th Cong., 1st Sess. (1957), p. 26. The AEC did not follow this advice. The Committee has on several occasions exerted pressure to prevent the Navy's retirement of Rickover. In 1961, Representative Van Zandt served notice on the Navy that, when Rickover comes up for retirement again in 1964, "we will be after them again," since the "AEC has programs that will need Admiral Rickover's advice and leadership beyond the year of 1964." *"Sec. 202" Hearings* (1961), p. 49.

"to change its interpretation" of one provision of the Atomic Energy Act of 1954, and the AEC acceded to the request.[93]

In 1962, the JCAE for the first time made a determined effort to dictate appointment of a particular person as a member of the Commission. It became known early in 1962 that, in addition to the vacancy to be created with the expiration of the term of Commissioner Loren Olson, another vacancy would occur with the resignation of Commissioner John S. Graham. The JCAE brought heavy pressure to bear on President Kennedy to nominate for one of these vacancies James T. Ramey, who had been executive director of the JCAE staff since 1955. Ramey had obvious qualifications for the post, but also had many foes within the executive branch. He had been the chief architect of the JCAE strategy which achieved dominance over the atomic-energy program during the Strauss and McCone eras and had antagonized several commissioners and numerous members of the AEC staff. At least one member of the Commission and several senior members of the staff were said to have served notice that they would resign if Ramey were appointed. In addition, the President and his advisers must have had considerable concern at the prospect of appointing to the Commission a man who had fought so vigorously and effectively to subordinate the executive position and to pierce the separation of powers. The President's reluctance to name Ramey was matched by the JCAE's insistence that it would block any other nominations to the Commission. The stand-off sorely taxed the AEC's operations, since, with only three commissioners on duty, it was frequently difficult to muster a quorum. Ultimately, if not inevitably, the President yielded, and Ramey was nominated and confirmed.

Aside from such influences on "housekeeping" phases of the AEC's operations, there has also been a profound JCAE influence on major policy decisions. It is worth noting that such influence had not been exercised at the outset. In 1948, David Lilienthal, characterizing the JCAE as an example of "political inventiveness," expressed the belief that,

> increasingly . . . the country will come to look to this committee as a principal means whereby the broad policy decisions that atomic energy will require may be studied, weighed, and

---

[93] *Forum Memo,* January 1956, p. 7. According to Senator Anderson, the 1954 act was satisfactory if the AEC would interpret and administer the law more liberally. *Loc. cit.* To some extent, the JCAE has regarded itself as a court of law to pass on and control AEC interpretations of the law. In 1956, the JCAE claimed that it "had to examine the operations of the Commission to see whether or not such operations came within the law since there is no way that the Commission's operations can be reviewed by a court." H.R. Rep. No. 1746, 84th Cong., 2d Sess. (1956).

> recommendations reported to the Congress as a whole and to the people. . . .[94]

The same year, the JCAE in its first report to Congress stated that

> the joint committee does not attempt to pass judgment on specialized scientific or technical procedures involved in the program and is not equipped to be an authority in highly specialized fields of research or technology. Moreover, the committee has not assumed the responsibilities for administrative policies that are clearly vested in the Atomic Energy Commission under the act, but is attempting to gain as much information and knowledge from an overall standpoint as will enable the committee to recommend . . . any legislation which may be desirable and to keep abreast of the potentially changing needs and requirements of a tremendous program. . . .[95]

It seems clear from these statements, as well as from the actual history of the early years of the Committee, that the JCAE's extraordinary powers were then recognized as being ancillary to substantially normal relationships between the executive branch and the Committee.

Within a short time, however, the Committee's role had undergone considerable change. By 1951, Senator McMahon was calling attention to the JCAE's role in policy formulation, describing the AEC-JCAE relationship as "peculiar" and characterizing the JCAE as, in a sense, "an operating committee." [96] From this interplay there has emerged an impression, skillfully nurtured by the JCAE, of Committee leadership in most of the principal accomplishments of the atomic-energy program during the first five years. Documenting its leadership role, the Committee in 1951 informed Congress that it had accomplished the following: [97]

> 1. encouraged the discovery and development of new uranium reserves in the North American continent and overseas;
>
> 2. played an "active role" in international arrangements that increased uranium deliveries from abroad;
>
> 3. called the AEC's attention to a significant domestic source of uranium that was not being adequately exploited;
>
> 4. "exerted continuous pressure" resulting in "seizure of opportunities" to step up plutonium production;

---

[94] Address before the annnal convention of the New York State Publishers Association in New York City, Jan. 19, 1948, reprinted in *Cong. Rec.*, 94 (Feb. 2, 1948), A708-A709.

[95] S. Rep. No. 850, 80th Cong., 2d Sess. (1948).

[96] *Cong. Rec.*, 97 (Oct. 8, 1951), 12753.

[97] S. Rep. No. 1041, 82d Cong., 1st Sess. (1951).

5. "vigorously sought to communicate its sense of urgency" to personnel in the AEC's reactor development program; and
6. contributed in large part to initiation of the AEC's Savannah River and Paducah facilities for production of fissionable material.

In addition, the Committee report noted that, when the JCAE subcommittee on reactor development concluded that a major policy decision on a vital reactor project had been too long delayed, it informed AEC and Defense authorities that, "unless the necessary decisions were reached within a specific time period, they would be requested to appear and explain the reasons for deferring judgment." (According to the Committee, "the decision was made on the next-to-last day of the stipulated time period" and was endorsed by the subcommittee.)

In all these instances, results were achieved by the Committee without the introduction or enactment of a single item of legislation. With the exception of its defense of AEC appropriations requests, the JCAE played a largely nonlegislative role, participating in policy formulation primarily through the informal exercise of political influence. In doing so, it encountered no opposition from the Truman administration, which, as a matter of political reality, recognized the basic power and usefulness of the Committee.

Through the years of the Eisenhower administration, the JCAE's "positive policy-recommending function" was recognized by Committee members as coordinate with its legislative, watchdog, and information functions.[98] But, because of policy conflict between the Democratic-controlled Committee and the Republican administration, informal and cooperative policy formulation between the AEC and JCAE was largely replaced by Committee pressure on a reluctant executive branch. During this period, the Executive often accepted the JCAE point of view simply in order to avoid open battle, which the Executive might lose or, if it won, win in a Pyrrhic sense only.

Thus, the Joint Committee has added a new and distinctive dimension to the concept of the Congressional committee, operating informally, in a manner not at all analogous to that of other committees, in the formulation of policy. Even when the JCAE, in order to accomplish its objectives, has taken more formal action by way of legislation, it has made a strenuous

---

[98] Address of Rep. Melvin Price before the Atomic Industrial Forum, Sept. 25, 1956. Price referred to the positive policy-recommending function as perhaps the most important JCAE role. He characterized the Committee as "a sort of over-all board of directors for the atomic-energy enterprise in coming up with recommendations and suggestions as to courses of action which may end as legislative proposals or *may be implemented by the Executive within existing statutory powers*." (Emphasis added.)

effort to persuade the Executive to reach an accommodation with it.[99] In recent years, the Committee has utilized authorizing legislation as a novel device to shape atomic-energy policy. The tactic of directly relating the JCAE's demands to AEC authorizations makes it more difficult for the Executive to resist and, especially, to veto the JCAE's legislative efforts.

In addition, legislating JCAE policy through the authorization process is significant from the standpoint of executive responsibility for orderly management of the federal budget. The Budget and Accounting Act of 1921, as amended, requires that the president each year submit his budget to Congress. The budget, theoretically at least, represents the president's views on the amount of money to be spent by the government and the manner in which the funds are to be allocated among executive agencies and departments and among the many proposed projects and activities. Congressional committees performing authorizing functions pass on the president's requests, approving them, rejecting them, or modifying them (usually by cutting the amount of funds to be authorized below the level requested). Further eliminations or reductions may be made by the Appropriations committees. Although it is not unheard of for legislative committees to report out bills authorizing expenditures for purposes not requested by the Executive, the tendency is to curtail executive programs rather than to expand them.

The Joint Committee, on the other hand, actively and systematically intervenes in the budgetary processes of the executive branch. In effect, the JCAE has become an important participant and pleader in the formulation of the atomic-energy budget, and what it wants and cannot obtain by negotiation it seeks to impose through authorization legislation.[100] In doing so, it finds allies within the executive branch,[101] thereby complicating the position of the president in his effort to take an over-all executive branch posture in budgetary matters. By thrusting funds for major projects on a reluctant Executive, the Committee is impinging on what the Executive conceives to be its proper role in budgetary and management processes. Although the dollar effect of the JCAE's additions may be relatively small,

---

[99] As Congressman Holifield put it: "It makes it easier, frankly, for us to pass it on the floor, rather than to again go through all the arguments about things which we may have mutually discarded or may have mutually agreed to add between ourselves on the committee, and the Commission and ourselves." *FY 1960 Authorization Hearings* (1959), p. 619.

[100] The Committee extracted a commitment from AEC Chairman Seaborg in 1961, before confirming his appointment, that he would faithfully carry out any projects authorized by Congress included in the bills signed by the president. "Hearings Before the JCAE on the Nomination of Dr. Glenn T. Seaborg as Chairman of the Atomic Energy Commission, Feb. 23, 1961," transcript, p. 33.

[101] In 1959, Admiral Rickover told the JCAE, in hearings aboard the N.S. "Skipjack," that the AEC had eliminated funds which he had requested for a natural circulation reactor, so that, "unless the Joint Committee acts, nothing will be done." *Review of Naval Reactor Program Hearings* (1959), p. 19.

this practice, if successfully followed by all committees, would strip the president of much of his present control over the budget and administration of the executive branch.

In an effort to ensure executive implementation of the Committee's reactor program, the JCAE has frequently employed imperative language in authorization legislation. It has done so in the face of widespread Congressional recognition that the legislature does not normally have the complete power of decision and that it "is not empowered to mandamus the executive branch to require use of the authorizations and appropriations granted." [102] Such use of the imperative raises a fundamental question as to the propriety of a Congressional requirement that a government agency, with broad responsibility and authority for implementing an over-all national program, undertake as a detail of that over-all program a major project with which it is not in sympathy.[103] This is not to say that Congress cannot validly and properly enact legislation requiring the AEC to undertake a national program for construction of government-owned reactors. The real question is whether, after a national policy is formulated through basic legislation, the specific steps in implementation of that policy should be left primarily to executive initiative.

■ THE JOINT COMMITTEE AND SEPARATION OF POWERS

The Joint Committee on Atomic Energy appears to be unique among Congressional committees in its relations with and influence on the executive branch. However, one can find precedent for almost all the instances of apparent JCAE encroachment on the doctrine and practice of separation of powers. Other committees have desired and attempted to

---

[102] Remarks of Senator Russell, *Cong. Rec.* (daily ed., May 15, 1961), 7938-7939. The inability of Congress to ensure that authorizations and appropriations are indeed expended was made dramatically clear during 1962. At that time, Representative Vinson, chairman of the House Armed Services Committee, retreated from the mandatory language of his committee's authorization report which directed the Air Force to spend formally unrequested budgetary funds for the RS-70.

[103] The Executive would be within its prerogatives in declining to undertake such projects despite the statutory mandate, but in the case of the atomic-energy program such defiance would be politically hazardous. Likewise, it is relatively difficult for the president to veto a money bill, particularly in the face of JCAE power and influence in Congress. A Legislative Reference Service report entitled "Some Illustrations of the Use of Executive Power in Relation to the Power of Congress," reprinted in *Cong. Rec.*, 102 (April 9, 1956), 5927-5929, discusses a number of instances of refusal by the president to expend funds for specific purposes designated by Congress in appropriation acts. See also the House Armed Services Committee report authorizing funds for aircraft, missiles, and naval vessels, H.R. Rep. No. 1406, 87th Cong., 2d Sess. (1962), pp. 5-6. In the case of unrequested funds appropriated by Congress in 1962 for the RS-70, it was expected that the Pentagon would spend no more than about 30 per cent.

achieve similar domination over the executive, and from time to time they have succeeded. But what makes the JCAE stand out is that its involvement in executive processes and its domination of certain areas of the atomic-energy program have become thoroughly institutionalized and accepted—the *modus operandi* and not merely an occasional occurrence.

Viewing the history of the Joint Committee, this outcome cannot be regarded as particularly surprising. Though the Committee's control over the atomic-energy program did not come about immediately, its eventual pre-eminence was implicit in the Atomic Energy Act of 1946, which created the JCAE and endowed it with unusual power. From 1946 to 1954, this power gradually expanded, reaching full maturity in the period between 1955 and 1960.

The Joint Committee's weighty contributions to the atomic-energy program during the Truman administration were made for the most part in a spirit of harmony and cooperation with the Executive and without any tangible indication that the line of separation between executive and legislative power had been traversed or even approached. So far as is known, the Executive during this period made only one major concession to the JCAE: it permitted the Committee to have access to FBI investigative material. This concession was made despite the President's vigorous, if not belligerent, refusal to extend a like privilege to other organs of Congress. There is little doubt that President Truman could have legally withstood JCAE demands for this information, on the ground that to interpret the statute so as to require the furnishing of such data would violate the inherent authority of the Executive under the Constitution. The political realities of atomic energy required, however, that there be the closest executive harmony with the JCAE, and the Executive accommodated itself to the Committee's demands, thereby establishing a precedent difficult to overcome in the years following.

Open conflict between the JCAE and the Executive did not arise until the Eisenhower administration. Time after time, the Committee demanded access to information of a kind not previously requested or given, and time after time the AEC acquiesced, although occasionally under protest and with the vain expression that such assent was not to be regarded as precedent. In each of these instances, the President could have stood his ground on the basis of constitutional separation of powers, but chose not to do so. Although he should have been aware of the implications of his action from the standpoint of the integrity of his constitutional position, he apparently felt that the JCAE's leverage over the AEC was too strong to contest as a matter of political reality.[104] While McCone was AEC

---

[104] The JCAE's attitude is that any document received by the AEC chairman in his capacity as such, including directives from the National Security Council, "ought to come

chairman, this acquiescence appeared to become completely institutionalized.

During the Eisenhower administration, the JCAE's policy-making role became established, and its influence vis-à-vis the Executive reached new heights through skillful use of the authorization process as an instrument for positive direction of the atomic-energy program. Although the Executive has from time to time fought the enactment of authorization legislation directing that projects opposed by the Executive be undertaken, its opposition has not rested on constitutional grounds. Moreover, impingement on executive prerogative has never been invoked as a reason for executive refusal to implement JCAE projects. Beyond this, the Executive has acquiesced in the AEC's breaking budgetary discipline by, in effect, cooperating with the JCAE in overriding actions taken by the Bureau of the Budget on behalf of the president.[105] At any one of a number of points, the Executive could have taken a stand against what it clearly recognized as JCAE encroachment. Instead, the Executive has chosen, in effect, to countenance and live with it. As a result, the predominant position of the Joint Committee has become an accepted fact.

It would be incorrect to characterize the Committee's history and record as one of aggrandizement or active assault on executive powers. It would be more correct to say that the JCAE, starting from a position of unique power and responsibility, has shown no reluctance to exercise this power to achieve goals which it strongly believes are essential in the national interest. If the power or privileges of the Executive have been sapped and if the JCAE has crossed the traditional line of separation, this is primarily attributable to executive abdication of its own responsibilities. In a sense, the expansion of JCAE power during the Eisenhower administration reflects the general expansion of Congressional power which can be expected in a period when one party controls Congress and the other party the administration, especially when the president has a passive

---

to this committee," and the AEC has apparently accepted this view. *FY 1956 Authorization Hearings* (1955), p. 92. An interviewee stated that, on at least one occasion, the AEC refused to accept a document in order to keep it away from the Joint Committee. It is noteworthy, however, that other executive agencies, particularly the Department of Defense, have stood their ground against JCAE demands for information. Although the "fully-and-currently-informed" requirement (as interpreted to include pending matters) applies equally to the Defense Department, that department reports to the JCAE only on "significant" matters and only after final action has been taken. Address by James T. Ramey, executive director of the JCAE, before the 1960 annual meeting of the American Political Science Association in New York City, Sept. 1, 1960.

[105] According to one observer, "the Eisenhower 'team concept,' under which virtually all executive decision-making was delegated to department and agency heads, invited congressional intervention as a broker of conflicting interests within the Executive Branch itself. Congress was quick to sense the absence of a hard center in the Administration. . . . It launched an ambitious campaign to make subordinate executive officials the vassals of the legislature." H. L. Nieburg, "The Eisenhower AEC and Congress," *Midwest Journal of Political Science,* VI (May 1962), 133.

view of his responsibilities. But the Joint Committee's power expansion has been much more dramatic and far-reaching than that of other committees or of Congress as a whole and has established precedents which may be hard for the Executive to live with in the future. Although general Congressional power may recede with a strong president whose political party controls Congress, it is somewhat difficult to visualize the recapturing by even a strong president of all the ground lost to the JCAE during the Eisenhower administration. Certainly, the first two years of the Kennedy administration have revealed no significant diminution of JCAE power.[106]

The problem of executive-legislative relationships in the context of the over-all structure and operation of American government in the twentieth century can by no means be frozen into a mold set by principles of constitutional law. The JCAE, as established by the Atomic Energy Act of 1946, and especially as its power and influence have grown since then, represents a new governmental technique. In the atomic-energy area at least, the existence of a Congressional body which participates decisively in a major governmental program has righted the balance of power which in this century has passed from Congress to the Executive. But the influence and techniques of the Joint Committee on Atomic Energy represent a considerable departure from traditional principles and raise substantial issues as to the manner in which government policies should be made and carried out. Granting that the role of Congress requires expansion and strengthening to counterbalance the enhanced position of the Executive, there remains the very important question whether the techniques exemplified by the JCAE represent an appropriate means for accomplishing this objective.

[106] It should be noted, however, that the Kennedy administration's plan to establish a single administrator in place of the five-man Commission represents a distinct threat to JCAE dominance. According to one Washington reporter, a major reason for the reorganization plan is the desire by executive branch officials to readjust the balance of power between the AEC and the JCAE. The lukewarm reaction of some Joint Committee Democrats to the proposal is reportedly due to fear of losing control over Commission appointments and also the possibility of a realignment of power. *N.Y. Times,* May 18, 1962.

IV | Legislative Techniques and Decision-Making

Today, as in the past, only a small part of the activities of the Joint Committee on Atomic Energy is directly concerned with legislation, and only part of the JCAE's influence derives from its legislative skills. With the significant exceptions of authorization and appropriation bills, policy-making in the atomic-energy field is usually accomplished without recourse to statutory enactment. As has been stressed, decisions are made, policies initiated or changed, and programs undertaken more often than not without deliberation by Congress as a whole.

There still remain persuasive reasons for examining the Committee's role in the processing and enactment of legislation. Despite ample scope for policy-making by other means, legislation is often a major instrument of policy determination. The desire for the prestige and authority conferred by statute, the utility of legislation as a dramatic announcer of policy initiation or change, and the requirements of existing statute all make some legislation in the area of atomic energy inescapable.

Furthermore, legislation affords the observer a more complete view of the Committee's activities on a particular issue. Unlike much of the JCAE's business, legislation must at some point be brought from behind the closed doors of the committee room for Congressional and public examination. A public record is made available—one that, although by no means complete, is voluminous compared to information in the public domain on many other issues. Hence, the legislative process can provide insight into the Committee's role in policy formulation and its influence on executive branch proposals.

Finally, any evaluation of the Joint Committee as an agency of representative government would be incomplete without consideration of its methods of handling legislation. Here we are concerned less with the product and whether that product reflects executive desires, Committee wishes, or public or private needs than with the way the product comes into being. The Committee's practice in processing, considering, and debating legislation is just as important today as in 1884, when Woodrow Wilson wrote that "that legislation which is not thoroughly discussed by the legislative body is practically done in a corner." Wilson's words are not very different from those of JCAE Chairman Chet Holifield, who in 1960 said on the floor of the House: "Unless we can bear the burden of new challenges, through the exercise of our historic democratic processes of discussion, debate, and publicly arrived at decisions, then our way of life is doomed." [1]

Ideally, a legislative proposal should be given full, critical, and open scrutiny. All contestants—those for and against a particular measure—should have approximately equal access to the legislative arena to make known their opinions. Even this does not ensure equal consideration of alternative positions, but at least those responsible for decisions have had the opportunity to hear conflicting arguments. Since Joint Committee members represent divergent points of view on many issues, two sides are usually presented throughout the debate. Dissimilar views by Committee members create controversy, at the same time ensuring closer examination. When the Committee is unanimous, however, full debate becomes even more appropriate; otherwise, the significance of the legislative proposal may not be brought to public light.

One side of the full-debate coin is the availability of relevant information. The other side is the careful processing and intelligent use of this information. Raw data are requisite, but not sufficient. Members of the JCAE should have sufficient time to consider and reconsider information before fashioning their legislative recommendations. Then other members of Congress—theoretically responsible for approving, disapproving, or amending—should have enough time to understand and reach a decision. The question—and, again, even a tentative answer depends on one's judgment—is whether legislation proceeds at a pace which permits full understanding.

---

[1] *Cong. Rec.*, 106 (Feb. 9, 1960), 2363.

Unless Committee members or other legislators have the ability to make sense of contradictory facts and opinions, time and availability of information are of little value. Much depends on the analytical and integrative powers of the individual legislator; much depends, also, on the clarity and focus of the over-all debate. Not every member of Congress will be competent to decide independently and wisely on complex issues; he will, or should, be able to turn to colleagues or experts for helpful advice. As long as there are those—normally Committee members—who are sufficiently familiar with atomic-energy issues and as long as they seek to clarify rather than to becloud, the lay legislator should be able to choose intelligently.

A caveat is in order. The Joint Committee's activities, methods, and influences are neither entirely unique nor wholly its own affair. Although we concentrate in this study on distinctions, this should not preclude an awareness that there are more similarities than differences between the JCAE and other committees. Moreover, although the Joint Committee may be largely responsible for its methods of formulating and steering through Congress legislative measures, the milieu in which it operates is not entirely of its own making. For example, the scheduling of legislation for floor debate often depends on factors beyond the Committee's control—the over-all initiative of the executive branch, the work of other committees, how crowded the House and Senate calendars are, and the wishes of the majority and minority leaderships in Congress. The course of debate, especially in the Senate, which operates under permissive rules, may be determined by non-Committee members. Particularly on controversial issues, the party leaderships of Congress influence the nature of discussion. Lyndon Johnson, for example, who was Democratic leader during the period dealt with in this chapter, never believed in lengthy and exhaustive floor debate. It was his view that good legislation was not the product of oratory, but of negotiation behind the scenes.[2]

■ EVOLUTION OF THE COMMITTEE'S LEGISLATIVE ROLE

Before 1953, the Joint Committee's legislative load was extremely light. In a report to Congress in late 1951, the Committee commented that, "among the unusual aspects of the Joint Committee and its work is the fact that, thus far, it has found only one major amendment to the original organic law to be necessary." That amendment, authorizing limited atomic-energy cooperation with other nations, was reported unanimously to Congress in 1951 and approved by the Senate and House without dissent and

---

[2] Ralph K. Huitt, "Democratic Party Leadership in the Senate," *American Political Science Review,* LV (June 1961), 340.

with little debate. Another Committee-sponsored bill, calling for JCAE access to FBI reports on nominees to the Commission, had been vetoed in 1948 by President Truman. In addition, several minor items of legislation had been recommended by the JCAE and enacted into law. By its own admission, however, the Committee's principal activities were those of oversight and "investigation, and 'a constant scrutiny of the unfolding atomic enterprise.' "[3]

Any explanation of the Joint Committee's delayed entrance on the legislative stage must be largely conjectural. The Committee did not, at a particular point, decide to accomplish its purposes without legislation. Rather, its early purposes suggested other approaches and other solutions; legislation was simply not necessary. During the first years, and especially under the chairmanship of Bourke Hickenlooper, attention was centered on problems of atomic-energy secrecy and security. Adequate security and secrecy did not require legislative amendment to the already-restrictive McMahon Act, but only careful selection of atomic-energy personnel and strict enforcement of existing requirements. Under the leadership of Brien McMahon, from 1949 until his death in 1952, the Committee was concerned with expansion of atomic-energy plant and weapons capacity, a program which could be carried out without specific legislation. The Commission already had adequate statutory authority for this program, and only ratification, through the appropriations process, was necessary.

The years 1953 and 1954 mark a watershed in the Joint Committee's legislative role. From that time on, the Committee's legislative powers became more than nominal; indeed, they proved a necessary and effective policy-shaping tool. The JCAE's new orientation was due to a number of factors. First, this nation's nuclear monopoly had ended, and foreign policy officials were beginning to realize that the United States would soon have to share its nuclear secrets with its allies. This would require new legislation. Second, with the Dean-McMahon weapons-expansion program well underway, Committee members felt an inclination to concentrate on peaceful applications of the atom; at the same time, there was pressure from private industry for a more active role in reactor development. Not only were the electric utilities anxious to foreclose the possibility of exclusive government development of the atom for peaceful purposes, but they were genuinely optimistic about the economic potential of converting atomic energy into electricity. If the field were to be opened to private enterprise, basic revision of the law would be needed.[4] Finally, atomic

---

[3] S. Rep. No. 1041, 82d Cong., 1st Sess. (1951), p. 2.

[4] Section 7 (b) of the 1946 act specified that, whenever atomic energy had been sufficiently developed to be of practical value, "the Commission shall prepare a report to the President stating all the facts with respect to such use, the Commission's estimate of the social, political, economic, and international effects of such use and the Commission's rec-

energy was no longer the novelty it had been in the years immediately after World War II. Members of the House Appropriations Subcommittee who examined the AEC budget were growing restive at the agency's independence of normal Congressional controls. Members of the JCAE shared this feeling and sought authorization powers for the Committee. When the JCAE received these powers, as it did under Section 261 of the 1954 act, its legislative activities naturally increased.

During the period preceding 1954, the JCAE had concentrated on its watchdog function; thereafter, circumstances required the Committee to devote greater attention to its legislative role. By examining the component phases of the legislative process, one can analyze the Joint Committee's behavior, methods, and influence and assess the legislative performance of an unusual Congressional institution.

■ LEGISLATIVE INITIATIVE

It is generally impossible to ascertain the parentage of a legislative proposal. Legislation is a complex production. The origin of a bill depends on many people, opinions, and influences, not at one point in time, but often over the course of years. A draft proposal may bear little resemblance to the bill which is finally passed by Congress and signed by the president. Nevertheless, considerable influence inheres in the power to initiate legislation. To initiate is to determine the problem which needs remedy and to control, at least at the outset, the scope and nature of Congressional consideration.

Although it is often difficult to discover the precise locus of initiative for atomic-energy legislation, it is clear that the area is indeed narrow. Usually, an atomic-energy bill receives its first impetus from either one, but normally a combination, of the following: the executive branch, the Joint Committee on Atomic Energy, or the interest groups directly concerned with atomic power. Few bills are sponsored and introduced by rank-and-file members of Congress. In fact, in comparison with bills on other subjects—housing, agriculture, health, labor, education, and even defense—bills dealing with atomic energy are seldom dropped into legislative hoppers. This is due in part to the average legislator's lack of familiarity with atomic-energy matters and in part to the fact that few constituents perceive themselves to be *directly* affected by atomic energy. Probably more important, those constituent groups that are affected address their appeals directly to either the Commission or the Joint Committee and

---

ommendations for necessary or desirable supplemental legislation." The president was then to transmit this report to the Congress together with his recommendations. Although the Commission never did prepare the 7 (b) report, it sent recommendations for legislation to the Joint Committee.

call on their particular representatives for support, rather than for initiative.[5]

Sometimes the source of the thrust behind a particular bill is easily located. Like other Congressional committees, especially in times of divided government, the Joint Committee has proposed legislation which has been clearly opposed by the executive branch. The Gore-Holifield bill of 1956 is an example. Senator Gore felt, as did other Democratic Committee members, that legislation was necessary if the United States was to economically produce electricity from atomic power before the Soviet Union. By the middle of 1955, he and other Democrats were convinced that the government should embark on a program of government nuclear-power development, as opposed to the administration's policy of relying primarily on private development. Naturally, the Commission had little to do with the initiation of this legislation.

When a bill is not formulated within the Joint Committee, it is probably the product of a department or agency within the executive branch. Not only in atomic energy, but in all areas, there has been an increasing tendency on the part of Congress and its committees to expect the various departments to prepare legislation affecting their interests. Although most legislators accept their limitations as initiators of legislative proposals, they will not rubber-stamp a measure recommended by the executive branch, but insist on being given an opportunity to modify it. In this respect, the JCAE is much like other Congressional committees.

There is a difference, however. Because of the "fully-and-currently-informed" provision and the close informal contacts between the Committee and the Commission, the JCAE generally becomes involved in legislation at a very early stage. Consultations between the Commission and the Committee begin long before the actual introduction of a bill. For example, the AEC forwarded to the JCAE on January 27, 1958, several amendments to the 1954 act to permit greater exchange of military information and materials with this nation's allies, and within a few days the bills were introduced, by request, in the Senate and House.[6] But almost

[5] If a member of Congress wants a proposal considered, he is likely to attempt to interest one of the ranking members of the JCAE in his idea. For example, when Rep. John F. Baldwin was asked by a city in his district to help clarify a section of the 1954 act, he spoke to his California colleague, Chet Holifield. At Baldwin's request, Holifield introduced a remedial bill in the House, and Clinton Anderson sponsored an identical bill in the Senate. Within three weeks, the AEC indicated its approval. After Baldwin testified at JCAE hearings, Holifield assured him that the proposal had the support of the AEC, the Bureau of the Budget, and the Committee and added: "The committee, I am sure, will act favorably on it, and probably pass it onto the floor within the very near future." *AEC Omnibus Bill Hearings* (1958), pp. 1-8.

[6] Introduction "by request" does not commit members to sponsorship or advocacy of a particular bill. It merely opens the way for hearings, discussion, and modification by a Congressional committee.

two months earlier, even before legislation was drafted, the Commission had laid its plan before the Committee. According to Chairman Strauss: "I got hold of Mr. Durham and asked him if he would not get whoever he could corral of the Joint Committee together so I might tell him what was being talked about." [7]

The JCAE's early role in framing legislation is of crucial importance, since it permits the Committee to develop its own information, discuss alternatives, and make known its ideas to representatives of the executive branch. For example, the Federal-State Cooperation bill was introduced, by request, by Senator Anderson and Representative Durham in mid-May 1959. But, prior to introduction, the Committee had the opportunity to make a complete examination of the problem of federal-state relationships in the atomic-energy field. In 1956 and 1957, Anderson and Durham had introduced bills so that state authorities might have a chance to study the problem before hearings were held. Meanwhile, the JCAE and AEC continued their study of the problem. In January, February, and March of 1958, two JCAE subcommittees held hearings on industrial radioactive waste disposal and employee radiation hazards and workmen's compensation, problems relevant to the issue of federal-state cooperation. At the conclusion of the Eighty-fifth Congress, the chairman and the vice-chairman of the JCAE instructed the Committee staff to make a study of existing laws and regulations in the atomic-energy field at federal, state, and local levels, in preparation for hearings scheduled for the spring of 1959. The Commission, in response to a JCAE request, prepared a bill and forwarded a draft to the Committee on March 5.[8] By the time hearings began, the ground had been well prepared.

The initiation of the legislation which eventually became the Atomic Energy Act of 1954 illustrates the interrelationships, overlappings, and blurred lines of responsibility and accountability connected with the germination of a legislative idea. Moreover, it shows that the Joint Committee has not been content to wait for the executive branch to submit legislation according to its own schedule; when the JCAE has decided that a problem needs remedy, it has relentlessly prodded the Executive for action. In this case, it was successful in quickening the pace of AEC deliberations, as the following exchange between the chairman of the Atomic Energy Commission and the chairman of the Joint Committee indicates:

> *Chairman Cole:* . . . the policy of the Commission was not something which was conceived and generated entirely

[7] Since Congress was not then in session, the job of rounding up members was not at all easy. Strauss, at one point, testified that he informed Durham "a month before anybody put pen to paper even to try to draft an amendment." *Military Exchange Hearings* (1958), p. 66.

[8] See S. Rep. No. 870, 86th Cong., 1st Sess. (1959).

> and exclusively within the Commission offices; but on the other hand . . . it was something which was shared to some extent at least, by an initial inquiry, an impetus, a suggestion, and a request, from the joint committee.
>
> *Mr. Dean:* Oh, that is quite true, Mr. Chairman, quite true.
>
> *Chairman Cole:* So, your policy statement is pretty much the response to a request from the joint committee.
>
> *Mr. Dean:* This is very true.[9]

Even after the AEC proposed draft legislation, the Committee felt no obligation to hold hearings on it. The proposals were merely the starting point; even before introduction, the JCAE had completely rewritten and expanded the AEC draft bills and had drastically altered many of their principal elements. Thus, the Committee's shaping of the legislation long antedated formal introduction and open consideration.

Despite the Commission's belief that the government monopoly was undesirable for the long term and that eventually the atomic-energy industry would be opened up to private enterprise, the AEC did not commence serious consideration of a broad revision of the 1946 act until 1951. The predominant feeling was that it was better not to "fiddle with the act," or, as the problem was frequently posed, "Are we ready to open that can of worms?" [10] Even in mid-1952, with the Commission staff working intensively on draft legislation permitting private participation, Chairman Dean stated that the time had not yet arrived for opening atomic development to industry. He believed that the need for restraints on private enterprise in the atomic program was "greater than the need for doing away with them." [11]

But members of the Joint Committee were becoming interested in the prospects for industrial participation. Carl Durham probably expressed the majority sentiment:

> No one wants this completely socialized industry to continue forever. . . . It has been in the minds of the members of the original committee ever since the beginning . . . that when we met the military problem, it was our duty . . . to get this interest started into the private enterprise system. . . .[12]

By the summer of 1952, Durham, then acting chairman of the JCAE following McMahon's death, informed the AEC that he would propose a series of meetings on industrial participation during the next session of Congress. He requested the Commission to submit a written statement of

---

[9] *Atomic Power Development Hearings* (1953), p. 60.

[10] Arnold Kramish and Eugene Zuckert, *Atomic Energy for Your Business* (New York: David McKay, 1956), p. 128.

[11] *Congressional Quarterly Almanac,* X (Washington, D.C.: Congressional Quarterly, 1954), p. 535.

[12] *Leg. Hist. 1954 Act,* v. 2, pp. 2134-2135.

its policy views on the subject in advance of these meetings. Two weeks later, Dean informed the Committee that policy discussions were proceeding within the Commission and that he hoped they might be crystallized for presentation to the JCAE at the beginning of 1953.[13]

The new year came, and the AEC had not yet responded to the Committee's request for a policy statement. Finally, on March 24, at the urging of Representative Hinshaw, chairman of the Reactor Development Subcommittee, Dean promised a Commission power-policy statement within two or three weeks. Still no statement came. The new JCAE chairman, Republican Sterling Cole, continued to prod the Commission for its policy views, asking that Dean make them clear at an executive session on May 26. Cole also specified that, in accordance with Dean's commitment to the Reactor Subcommittee, his statement be coordinated within the executive branch prior to presentation. Finally, he asked the AEC to recommend legislation necessary to permit private industrial participation in the field of atomic-power development.[14]

At the May meeting, the Commission finally submitted both a policy statement and a legislative draft to the JCAE. The draft, however, had not been cleared by the Budget Bureau and was therefore considered informally by the Committee and not made public. But Chairman Cole and Vice-Chairman Hickenlooper felt that they could proceed expeditiously, whatever the delay in the executive branch. In June, they issued a joint statement announcing public hearings and indicated that "the Joint Committee feels that it is necessary to develop a public understanding of the subject before determining whether a legislative expression of national policy should be made." It is extremely doubtful, however, that any determination was thought necessary, for one sentence later the statement continued, "In the next session of Congress we will be able to direct our attention to the question of the desirable legislative language." [15]

The aim of the June and July hearings was not to discuss specific legislation, but rather to examine the broad field of problems and come to some sort of agreement. The Committee fully accomplished its purpose. Four of the five industrial groups which had been conducting studies in cooperation with the AEC to determine the practicability of private atomic-power development sent representatives who testified in favor of private participation. AEC prime contractors, equipment manufacturers, and other

---

[13] *Atomic Power Development Hearings* (1953), p. 62.

[14] *Ibid.*, pp. 2, 63. One of the reasons for the AEC's hesitation is clear. In November, 1952, after twenty years of Democratic control of the administration, a Republican had been elected president. Eisenhower naturally needed time to consider his administration's atomic-energy policies. Furthermore, it was apparent by early 1953 that Dean would be replaced as chairman of the Commission.

[15] *Ibid.*, pp. 1-2.

industrial representatives urged changes in the atomic-energy law.[16] The executive branch, represented by officials of the AEC; the General Advisory Committee of AEC; the Federal Power Commission; and the departments of State, Defense, Interior, and Commerce also favored private participation. Most important, Lewis L. Strauss, who took over the chairmanship from Dean on July 1 and who spoke with the full confidence of President Eisenhower, testified that he had earnestly hoped, as early as 1947, that in his lifetime "conditions will improve to the point where atomic energy can be freed of government monopoly and placed in the framework of [*sic*] American system of free, competitive enterprise." [17] In concluding the hearings, Chairman Cole announced that legislation to revise the 1946 act would be considered at the next session of Congress.[18]

But, before the second session of the Eighty-third Congress convened, a new development had intruded. On December 8, 1953, President Eisenhower delivered his Atoms for Peace speech before the General Assembly of the United Nations, calling for the establishment of an international agency to further peaceful atomic development. A month later, in his "state of the union" address, the President proposed that the U.S. share information on the tactical uses of nuclear weapons. In his budget message on January 29, 1954, he called for amendments to the Atomic Energy Act which would achieve three goals: first, allow the exchange of more classified atomic information with this country's allies; second, permit the transfer of fissionable materials to friendly nations for "peacetime atomic-power development"; and, third, encourage wider participation in atomic-power development by private industry in the United States. Eisenhower's ideas were further spelled out in a special atomic-energy message sent to Congress on February 17 which recommended fifteen changes in the McMahon Act.[19]

Simultaneously, the AEC forwarded two draft bills to the Joint Committee, one dealing with international and security aspects and the other with private participation. The administration urged that the former be enacted without delay; with the latter there was less urgency. Neither

---

[16] Only witnesses from rural electric cooperatives, the National Rural Electric Cooperative Association, the Cooperative League of the U.S.A., and labor organizations expressed fear of revision and hoped that the act would remain unaltered.

[17] *Ibid.*, p. 565. Strauss later recalled his 1947 attitude toward the McMahon Act: "I disagreed with the whole atmosphere of it because it was out of step, out of spirit, with the free-competitive-enterprise system in which I had been brought up, but I believed, I was confident, that at some time in the future atomic energy could be turned to the free-competitive-enterprise system, and that in that belief I was prepared to serve." *Leg. Hist. 1954 Act,* v. 2, p. 2299. See also his memoirs, *op. cit.*, pp. 318-319.

[18] *Atomic Power Development Hearings* (1953), p. 570.

[19] See H.R. Doc. No. 328, "Message from the President of the United States Transmitting Recommendations Relative to the Atomic Energy Act of 1946," 83d Cong., 2d Sess. (1954).

of the bills was introduced by the Committee chairman or any other member, nor were the texts of the draft bills made public until July 17, at the height of Congressional debate on the legislation, when Vice-Chairman Hickenlooper, under criticism on the floor of the Senate, inserted them into the *Congressional Record*.[20] The AEC drafts were found objectionable by the Committee chairman, who stated that they gave the president such complete and unrestricted authority, both in the domestic and international fields, that he would not even introduce them. Cole maintained that the JCAE and Congress would not accept such wide latitude of executive authority.

But neither the full Committee nor Congress was given an opportunity to decide. Without any public consideration of the administration proposals, Cole, Hickenlooper, and members of the JCAE staff drafted a new bill. They took both executive drafts (which involved the minimum amendment of the 1946 act necessary to accomplish the desired purposes) and merged them into a single bill which completely revised the 1946 act. Cole explained:

> It had been my personal purpose and thought to treat these 3 phases of the amendments to the Atomic Energy Act of 1946 in 3 separate bills. However, as we got into this subject, we discovered that the three problems were very interlocked and interwoven. We realized also that the act itself was in dire need of being overhauled and modernized and brought up-to-date. We therefore concluded that all 3 of our objectives, along with the overall revision, would be treated as 1 bill. So the bill was drafted by the chairman and vice chairman.[21]

Another factor, not mentioned by Cole, was that of political strategy. The JCAE staff director pointed out, and Cole and Hickenlooper readily agreed, that either proposal by itself would be difficult to push through Congress. The domestic measures might be opposed by Democrats as a government "giveaway" to private industry, whereas the international and security proposals might be opposed by a coalition of isolationists and secrecy-conscious Republicans and Democrats. If the two features were joined, however, the opposition would be hard pressed to decide whether the advantages of one outweighed the disadvantages of the other.[22]

After Cole and Hickenlooper revised the executive drafts, they submitted their own draft to the full Committee, which then spent about five

[20] Two weeks after that, in debate on the House floor, Chairman Cole still referred to the AEC draft legislation as "a bill" sent to the Committee by the Commission. *Leg. Hist. 1954 Act,* v. 3, pp. 2873, 3241-3245.

[21] *Ibid.,* p. 2873.

[22] "Credit is due the staff of the Joint Committee for the political sagacity of seeing that, separated the two parts would have a hard time passing either House of Congress; together, they couldn't miss." Kramish and Zuckert, *op. cit.,* p. 129.

weeks examining it paragraph by paragraph, line by line, and item by item. During this period, the Commission and officials of the executive departments testified in executive session on the draft bill, and there was extensive and intensive discussion between the JCAE and executive staffs. The result, after a series of draft bills printed as "confidential committee prints," was a bill reasonably, but not completely, acceptable to most members of the Committee. On April 15, Cole introduced H.R. 8862 in the House, where it was immediately referred to the JCAE. In introducing the bill, the chairman announced that it would be subject to revision by the Joint Committee during and after public and executive hearings. Four days later, Hickenlooper introduced the companion bill, S. 3323, in the Senate and made a similar announcement.[23]

The AEC commissioners were generally in favor of the Cole-Hickenlooper bill, but were opposed to some of its provisions. Furthermore, they clearly recognized that the Committee bill was not their own. "The record should show some place," Strauss stated, "that . . . we are talking about a piece of legislation, defending a piece of proposed legislation, as to which we are, shall I say, the beneficiaries, but not the authors." Cole agreed, but phrased it differently: "You are the foster parents. You may not be the natural parents." [24]

■ COMMITTEE CONSIDERATION AND DECISION

During debate on the Cole-Hickenlooper bill, the Joint Committee chairman told his colleagues in the House, "if ever there was a bill that was figuratively hammered out on the anvil of the legislative process, this bill represents such a piece of proposed legislation." [25] The "legislative process" Cole referred to was the Committee's deliberation over the particular provisions of the measure. In bare skeleton, JCAE deliberation appears to be similar to that of any other committee. After a bill is introduced and referred to the JCAE, it is placed on the calendar, and hearings are scheduled. The staff lines up a panel of witnesses, both experts and others who may wish to be heard. Before public hearings, the JCAE usually holds executive sessions to consider the pending legislation. When public hearings commence, witnesses, many of whom have previously testified in executive session, give their testimony publicly. Following the hearings, the Committee staff drafts a report summarizing the information obtained and setting forth the Committee's proposed conclusions and legislative recom-

---

[23] *Leg. Hist. 1954 Act,* v. 3, pp. 2797, 3009-3010.
[24] *Ibid.*, p. 2549.
[25] *Ibid.*, p. 2873.

mendations. Committee members may then spend many hours in executive session refining the staff document.[26]

There is obvious and significant difference, however, between the consideration given atomic-energy legislation and that given other types of bills. With respect to the latter, proposals are almost always heard and discussed by parallel committees of the House and Senate. A foreign aid bill, for example, receives attention from both the Senate Committee on Foreign Relations and the House Committee on Foreign Affairs; an education bill must undergo the scrutiny of the Committee on Labor and Public Welfare in the Senate and the Committee on Education and Labor in the House. But legislative proposals in the atomic-energy field are referred to and considered by only one committee. There are both advantages and disadvantages to this procedure. On the one hand, it is efficient in conserving the time and energies of busy officials of the executive branch, who theoretically spend only half as much time on Capitol Hill explaining and defending administration bills. Similarly, it reduces the burden on agents of private interest groups testifying on particular legislation.

Deliberation by one committee alone, however, reduces the avenue of appeal for participants in the legislative struggle. In the usual situation, a decision by a House or Senate committee can be appealed to and modified by the cognizant committee in the other body. On atomic-energy legislation, however, the JCAE is the court of first and, probably, last resort. If the Joint Committee opposes an executive proposal, there is no chance that it will ever see the light of legislative day. Neither house of Congress will consider it. If legislation the Executive does not like is reported out by the JCAE, there is no other committee to reconsider, and the only courts of appeal are the Senate and House floors. Thus, unique pressure falls on the executive branch to come to terms with the JCAE if it hopes to have atomic-energy legislation enacted.

In terms of debate, examination by one committee is by no means the same as consideration by two committees. The orientation of committees varies; some will probe thoroughly in certain areas, others will touch on entirely dissimilar aspects. Seldom, if ever, do corresponding committees of the Senate and House ask the same questions of witnesses or report out major legislation in identical form. In the case of the JCAE, no matter how thoroughly a legislative measure is discussed, the area of debate is definitely restricted.

With this framework established, other distinctive characteristics of the Joint Committee as legislator bear examination. The first concerns

---

[26] Description by Congressman Hosmer, *Cong. Rec.*, 106 (Jan. 13, 1960), 473.

the staging of Committee hearings on legislative proposals, the second the purposes of hearings and Committee deliberation, and the third JCAE's great striving for consensus.

• Staging of Legislative Hearings

Once a bill is introduced and referred to the Joint Committee, the first question that arises is whether and when a hearing should be held. The decision to hold hearings is not a difficult one for the Committee, since few legislative proposals, whether initiated within Congress or by the executive branch, come as a surprise to JCAE members. Largely because of the Committee's aggressive and studious approach to legislation, sufficient groundwork is laid before a specific decision on a bill's hearing is necessary.

Major bills have generally been given prompt hearings. Especially since 1954, the Committee has usually responded quickly to legislation recommended by the executive branch. Whatever the Committee's objections to administration proposals and whatever modifications it may have made during subsequent deliberation, executive bills usually have received prompt consideration. An excellent example is the Committee's quick response in the case of the 1958 military-exchange legislation. On Monday, January 27, 1958, Chairman Strauss forwarded proposed amendments to the 1954 act providing for broader exchange of weapons information and material with U.S. allies. The next day, Durham and Pastore introduced the bill by request. The following afternoon, the Subcommittee on Agreements for Cooperation opened hearings. Strauss, in his opening testimony, complimented the JCAE on its prompt handling of the matter.[27]

A second question which arises before hearings actually begin pertains to witnesses who will be permitted to testify in behalf of or against a particular measure. Since 1945, when Representative May's Military Affairs Committee held "quickie" hearings on the May-Johnson bill, all those wishing to testify on atomic-energy legislation have been given the opportunity. Wherever possible, the Joint Committee, in anticipation of the introduction of a major bill, has compiled and distributed prints with valuable information on the problem in advance of public hearings. It is fair to say that the JCAE has made an effort to inform potential witnesses from outside government as thoroughly and as far in advance as time and staff facilities permit. The Committee's press releases, which are

[27] He stated: "When one considers that you only received this on the afternoon of Monday, and that this is Wednesday and you are having a hearing, it is extremely gratifying to us." *Military Exchange Hearings* (1958), p. 12. It should be noted that the Committee was prepared for the administration's request. Strauss had informed Durham almost two months before and had also spoken about the objectives of the legislation with Congressional leaders when they met with the President early in December of 1957.

mailed to a long list of interested groups and individuals, have been aimed at affording witnesses sufficient time to consider the subject and prepare testimony.

On legislation which has been the subject of considerable study prior to introduction, the Committee has been able to notify the public well in advance of scheduled hearings. With plans for the federal-state hearings well underway, a letter was sent, about three months before hearings were to begin, to each state governor, informing him of the schedule and inviting him to attend or send a representative.[28] However, when legislation is urgently requested by the executive branch, the Committee has usually chosen to satisfy the administration's urgings for speed rather than give the public sufficient opportunity to prepare testimony. Even then, as in the case of the military-exchange hearings, the Committee has provided some advance notice to public witnesses.

The Joint Committee goes to great lengths to inform the public of legislative hearings and to invite testimony from public groups. In JCAE hearings on legislation (as distinguished from the statutory "202" hearings held annually and for a different purpose), however, nongovernmental witnesses usually play a small role. Representatives of private and public utilities, reactor manufacturers, cooperative associations, labor organizations, and other public groups are able to testify at length, but their testimony is seldom the focal point. Public witnesses simply provide a backdrop for the performance of the more important actors—executive officials and Committee members. Furthermore, although public witnesses may have been fully briefed about the general problems and aspects of the proposals being considered, on some occasions they have not been apprised of the specific proposals being discussed.

After hearings have begun, Committee members and staff (often jointly with executive officials) necessarily continue to refine legislative language and compromise differences, changing provisions substantially or dropping them entirely. Sometimes, by the time a new draft bill has been prepared, public witnesses have already testified on provisions which are no longer under active consideration. On federal-state legislation, for example, a JCAE print was held up so that the AEC's proposed bill of March, 1959, could be included in distribution to the public. But the AEC draft had been forwarded by the Commission before study had been completed and before the views of other executive agencies could be coordinated. Before hearings began, therefore, the AEC drafted another bill, which it sent to the Committee on May 13. This revision, containing an important provision which had not been included in the earlier draft, was introduced in Congress on May 18 and May 19, the day the hearings

---

[28] *Federal-State Hearings* (1959), pp. 1-2.

started. Obviously, public witnesses had no time to consider it. After the May hearings were adjourned, the Committee and the Commission continued redrafting. As a result, two new bills were introduced which were similar, but not identical, to the AEC's May proposals. On August 26, hearings were reopened, but with testimony only from AEC witnesses. Although the U.S. Chamber of Commerce protested to Chairman Anderson that the Committee was about to report a bill without benefit of public hearings, Anderson insisted that modifications in the legislation followed advice given by public witnesses in the May hearings. The Chamber thereupon withdrew its objection in order to permit the JCAE "to go ahead and get something done. . . ." [29]

The practice of holding hearings and then reporting out revised, or "clean," bills is common to all committees. There have been objections to this procedure as followed by the JCAE, but these objections seem to have been caused less by the Committee's methods than by the substance of the legislation under consideration. On the relatively noncontroversial Euratom proposals, for instance, the facts that the JCAE introduced clean bills after hearings had closed, then discussed the new drafts with the AEC in executive session, and finally filed a clean bill stirred no public criticism. The controversial Cole-Hickenlooper bill, however, produced an entirely different response. At the outset, the JCAE chairman made the ground rules for the hearings clear to all concerned. After the Committee had received testimony from all those who wished to appear, a revised bill would be prepared and made available to the executive departments and agencies. Their representatives would then be asked to testify in open session on the first revision of the bills. On the conclusion of comments, including those from private individuals and groups who wanted to submit written statements on the revised proposal, the Committee would undertake a final revision. Representative Holifield, who opposed the domestic provisions of the Cole-Hickenlooper bill, objected to this procedure, claiming that the revised bill might require public hearings. But Senator Hickenlooper pointed out that the Committee had inherent power to determine at the end of the hearings whether additional public testimony was necessary.[30]

Holifield was hardly satisfied, and the fact that the bill was in constant revision as the hearings progressed irritated him further. Members of the Committee, as well as public witnesses, often had no idea precisely

---

[29] *Ibid.*, pp. 293-300, 485-486.

[30] *Leg. Hist. 1954 Act*, v. 2, p. 1637. Holifield made his recommendation as a matter of record, and Cole held firm in stating: "The course of action will be determined by the full committee . . . just as it has in the past." *Ibid.*, p. 1658.

which draft bill they were discussing. An April print of the bill served as a starting point, but that draft supplied almost as much confusion as guidance. During the public hearings, it was revised and re-revised, so that witnesses, Committee members, and even author Cole were never quite sure which draft was current.[31] Even after a clean bill was printed on May 21, changes continued, and confusion ensued.[32] Thus, after public and governmental witnesses had been heard—on one or another draft—and the Committee had gone behind closed doors, the bill had already been significantly transformed.

After the May hearings, the original bill was revised and a draft dated May 26 was transmitted to the AEC for comment. In June, hearings on the revised bill were held with only government witnesses present. While proponents remained silent, opponents were visibly dissatisfied. Representing the National Rural Electric Cooperative Association (NRECA), Clyde Ellis, who had requested at the May hearings that he be allowed to comment again on any clean bill, wrote to Cole on May 28 asking for an opportunity to testify on the revised draft. Cole replied that, since it was necessary to have the legislation considered in that session of Congress, Ellis should send his views in writing instead of appearing again in open hearings. On June 9, Ellis again wrote Cole to say that he would rather appear in person. There is no record that Cole answered the letter.

Meanwhile a staff member of the NRECA telephoned Walter Hamilton, a member of the JCAE staff, who allegedly advised him against submitting even a written statement on the second bill, because a print of still another bill would be available in a few days for public examination. Hamilton indicated that, before the Committee acted, the public would have one week to submit written views on the third bill, but within a few days legislation was reported out of committee. Alex Radin of the American Public Power Association and Benjamin C. Sigal of the CIO also complained about the manner in which Cole had conducted the hearings.[33]

Toward the close of the hearings, the Committee met to discuss whether to hold hearings on the revised bill. Cole and Hickenlooper were adamantly opposed, since time was running out, and they were determined that the bill be passed before adjournment. They had no reason to fear discussion of the new bill, for by that time it was evident who were the

---

[31] At one point, a sorely confused Holifield addressed the chairman: "We are at a little bit of a disadvantage because we do not have a clean bill before us and we are not aware of the language changes that have been made by the staff." *Ibid.*, p. 1957.

[32] Holifield and Cole disputed the number of changes that had been made, the latter insisting that only one important revision had been made and the former complaining: "I think I have several galley copies and I believe all of them are different." *Ibid.*, p. 2405.

[33] *Ibid.*, v. 3, pp. 3860-3861.

supporters and who the opponents of the substantive revisions that had been proposed.[34] Each Committee revision could have been subjected to additional public discussion and criticism, but it is unlikely that additional consideration would have changed anything, especially since the major issues had already been raised and opinions had become set. In any case, JCAE members were acting less as judges than as adversaries, each of whom had entered the hearings with attitudes crystallized by ideology and experience.

• Objectives of Deliberation

Hearings on proposed legislation are not held to enable the public to draft legislation or change the basic views of legislators. Instead, much like other Congressional committees, the JCAE holds hearings (1) to make a public record available to Congress; (2) to clarify as many issues as possible; (3) to provide by means of bargaining and accommodation a basis for agreement within the Committee and especially between the Committee and the executive branch; and (4) to protect, and sometimes enhance, the powers of Congress, and of the JCAE in particular.

1. *Making a public record.* The Joint Committee has often gone out of its way to make public a record of its deliberations. Security considerations necessitate hearings behind closed doors, but even then the JCAE sometimes releases a transcript of the proceedings with classified discussions deleted.[35] Occasionally, the Committee has also published extremely revealing records of sessions held *in camera* with executive officials for purposes of "marking up a bill"—resolving disagreements and drafting appropriate legislative language. On the other hand, the JCAE has had numerous executive-session hearings on legislation which have not been released, even though there were few, if any, problems of security classification involved. For example, there are voluminous executive-session transcripts of hearings on the 1954 Cole-Hickenlooper act which have not been published or otherwise released for inspection.[36]

---

[34] *Ibid.*, v. 2, p. 1940. Pastore, for example, asked Ellis if he felt that the bill should not pass in *any* form. Ellis replied that it should not pass in any form which "we can conceive of . . . at the moment." *Loc. cit.*

[35] The military-exchange hearings in 1958, for instance, were held primarily in executive session—a total of ten days of closed-door hearings and only four days of public hearings. But all testimony taken in executive session was submitted to the departments and agencies concerned, with a Committee request that the testimony be reviewed for accuracy and for identification of classified information. After classified discussion was deleted, a 527-page record was published.

[36] This is unfortunate, since most of the basic aspects of the 1954 act were considered and resolved in these executive sessions and are not reflected in the published hearings. From time to time, portions of this unpublished legislative history have been tantalizingly but inconclusively revealed. For example, when a controversy developed over the "no-

2. *Clarifying issues.* During hearings, Committee members try to clarify chiefly for themselves—but also for other members of Congress and the public—the factual situation, the legislative provisions, and the policy implications associated with a particular bill. The individual members, whatever their motives, usually succeed in casting light on issues which are extremely complex and easily confused. Sometimes, on the other hand, analysis is buried in polemic, repetition, and irrelevance.

The military-exchange hearings of 1958 illustrate how clarification can be achieved by pointed questioning of witnesses. Both Senator Pastore, who chaired the subcommittee holding the hearings, and Representative Holifield, who attended, helped bring out facts and policy implications which might otherwise never have been volunteered by representatives of the executive branch testifying in behalf of the proposed bill. Pastore's admonition to AEC Deputy General Manager R.W. Cook set the tone: "You have got to answer these questions. . . . I am not going to allow you people to straddle. . . . I want positive categorical answers . . . and if my questions are not categorical enough I want you to ask me to rephrase them. . . ."[37]

There was a difference of opinion about whether the Executive's legislative proposal would allow the U.S. to provide nuclear weapons to allies. Administration witnesses denied that such was either the intention or even a remote possibility. Holifield felt differently, bringing to light the basic issue in this exchange with Chairman Strauss:

> *Mr. Strauss:* We have not recommended in this legislation that we provide any weapons.
> *Representative Holifield:* Mr. Chairman, on that point, may I respectfully contest that with you?
> *Mr. Strauss:* If I am wrong, I would like to have it brought out. . . .
> *Representative Holifield:* Does not this language of this bill provide for you to furnish all of the nonnuclear components of a weapon?
> *Mr. Strauss:* Of certain weapons; yes.
> *Representative Holifield:* All right. Does it not also allow you to furnish the material for the cores of weapons?
> *Mr. Strauss:* No. It allows us to furnish material out of which to fabricate a core. We do not provide the core.
> *Representative Holifield:* . . . Does not the language also permit you to furnish the design of the core of the weapons?
> *Mr. Strauss:* Not necessarily of that weapon; no sir.
> *Representative Holifield:* I am not going to differentiate be-

---

subsidy" provision of §169 of the Atomic Energy Act, the unpublished legislative history was brought to light in order to ascertain the intent of the JCAE in drafting that provision. *"Sec. 202" Hearings* (1955), pp. 159-160.

[37] *Military Exchange Hearings* (1958), pp. 211-212.

> tween weapons, because you may have 3 weapons in mind and I may have 8 weapons in mind. But let's just keep it to weapons. Does it not permit the furnishing of designs for any weapon? I will put the word "any" in quotes. . . .
>
> *Mr. Strauss:* Yes, sir.
>
> *Representative Holifield:* So when you say we are not furnishing weapons you are technically correct, of course. But the effect of the whole bill is to furnish the materials, the design, and the information with which to construct the weapon. So the end result is a weapon.
>
> If you want to hide behind the technicalities or evade the impact of the whole language by saying we technically do not furnish a completed weapon, why that is a position you will have to take on your own responsibility. As far as I can read it we are furnishing weapons.[38]

Holifield pursued this line of inquiry with other administration witnesses. He elicited a concession from Donald A. Quarles, deputy secretary of defense, that it would be possible to transfer nuclear material, design information, and components, thereby giving the recipients the wherewithal for assembling nuclear weapons.[39] Holifield went on to suggest possible implications in a broader context of foreign policy. To him, the basic issues which the JCAE had to face in deciding on the administration bill were whether its implementation would increase the likelihood of nuclear war and whether its implementation would enhance the international prestige of the U.S.[40]

3. *Bargaining for consensus.* The Joint Committee's use of legislative hearings for bargaining with the executive branch is particularly noteworthy. Such use of hearings is by no means unique, but it represents an unusually strenuous effort on the part of the Joint Committee to reach some kind of agreement with the executive branch. The achievement of Executive-Committee consensus assures the JCAE that its legislative recommendations will be accepted with little or no debate by Congress and protects the Committee against the dissipation of control over the atomic-energy program which would result from long and controversial floor discussion.

The process of compromise to reach consensus works both ways. When the JCAE wants legislation enacted, it must be prepared to compro-

---

[38] *Ibid.*, pp. 61-62.

[39] *Ibid.*, pp. 102-103.

[40] *Ibid.*, p. 369. AEC Commissioner Vance answered Holifield by saying that he did not believe that Soviet propaganda, which had charged the U.S. with distributing hydrogen-weapons information and component parts, would place this country at a disadvantage in the opinion of the uncommitted nations. The congressman remarked pointedly: "You believe that the uncommitted nations will understand this is all in good fun." Sarcasm is an interrogating tool Mr. Holifield employs often and effectively.

mise with the administration on its original request. A case in point is the Gore-Holifield bill, by means of which the Democratic majority tried to push through a policy proposal in the face of firm executive opposition. During Committee deliberation, conscientious efforts were made by both Democratic and Republican members to achieve a workable compromise so that the Committee could go to Congress with legislation backed by the Executive and the JCAE. Even before hearings opened, the AEC and the administration had expressed hostility to the proposal. But Committee members, hoping to effect a compromise, altered the bill substantially in an effort to win the administration's support or, at least, its neutrality. Consequently, when the bill was finally reported out by the JCAE, it bore little resemblance to the bill Senator Gore had originally introduced.[41] The Committee recognized that if any part of the Gore-Holifield program were to be enacted, it had to eliminate many of the features of the original Gore bill which were regarded as pro-public power. According to Senator Anderson, the JCAE strategy was dictated by the following consideration:

> I think we could have reported a straight out-and-out public power bill if those concerned had been disposed to do so. We did not do so; we took a very substantially compromised route, in the hope that a political controversy or a fight between public and private power would not develop.[42]

But on another divisive aspect of the bill, there was no compromise possible. Language stating that the AEC was "authorized and directed" to proceed with the new program was objected to by the Commission, which recommended that the legislation be permissive, not mandatory. But, in view of the AEC's unyielding insistence that its existing reactor development program was adequate and that no governmental acceleration or expansion was necessary, JCAE Democrats decided to retain the key word "directed" in the bill as finally reported. The Committee's position is illustrated by the following exchange between the AEC chairman and Democratic members:

---

[41] Compare S. 2725, reprinted on p. 1 of the first part of the hearings, to the June draft, printed on pp. 1-2 of the second part. *"Gore-Holifield" Civilian Power Hearings* (1956), pts. 1 and 2. The following modifications were made in the course of Committee deliberation: (1) Reactors were to be located only at AEC sites, rather than in six regional areas, and the power produced was to be used only in AEC operations at these sites. (2) The AEC was given discretion as to the number of reactors to be built rather than required to build six reactors as specified in the original bill. (3) Although policy guidance as to criteria for the selection of reactors was contained in the bill and spelled out in the Committee report, the AEC was not restricted to those criteria. (4) Foreign atomic-power assistance was changed to indirect support instead of direct construction of reactors. (5) It was specified that the new provisions would be supplementary and would in no way restrict the current AEC power-demonstration-reactor program.

[42] *Cong. Rec.,* 102 (July 26, 1956), 14724. Republican Committee members agreed with Anderson's statement. *Ibid.* (July 12, 1956), 12461.

> *Mr. Strauss:* Senator Pastore, do you feel that you cannot rely upon the Commission's good faith to carry out this policy . . . but that we have to be directed to do it?
>
> *Senator Pastore:* I will tell you very frankly, I would leave the word "directed" out, if you gentlemen would say that you believe this ought to be done, but you keep saying that we are doing enough, and we don't think that we ought to do any more.
>
> That is what frightens me.
>
> *Mr. Strauss:* Do you think for a moment if you passed this bill, and the Congress passed the bill, that we would go at it half heartedly?
>
> *Chairman Anderson:* You have testified that you don't think anything needs to be done.
>
> *Senator Pastore:* I don't think that you would build the reactors.[43]

Committee and Commission agreement on inclusion or exclusion of this key word depended on whether they considered an accelerated government reactor program necessary. Without such agreement, solid support for Gore-Holifield seemed unlikely.

Loyalty of the Committee Republicans was divided between the JCAE and the Eisenhower administration. Carl Hinshaw was furthest from the party fold, but even he demurred at the Committee's directive to the Commission.[44] Other Committee Republicans were notably unenthusiastic about the acceleration program. Although Hickenlooper was instrumental in suggesting and pushing through several compromises during Committee discussion, he feared passage of the bill would slow down private reactor development. He saw no necessity for mandatory legislation, but nevertheless said, "If it was necessary to have a bill, I hoped it would come as near to being a good bill, and not a bad bill, as possible, but I did not know whether I would support it." [45]

The Republican JCAE members were on the spot. They found it difficult to oppose the intent of the legislation, to ignore the advice of Dr. W.H. Zinn, the Committee's renowned reactor consultant, and to split the Committee. On the other hand, they disapproved of the slap at the Commission's program and the implied criticism of the Eisenhower administration and the domestic provisions of the 1954 act. Cole and Hickenlooper could hardly be expected to admit that the policies underlying

---

[43] *"Gore-Holifield" Civilian Power Hearings* (1956), pt. 2, p. 9.

[44] "Some people," he stated, "were a little more enthusiastic about telling somebody to do something than some of us on the committee were; we would rather authorize them to do it than direct them to do it." *Cong. Rec.,* 102 (July 24, 1956), 14256.

[45] *Ibid.* (July 12, 1956), 12458. Anderson noted that Hickenlooper contributed much to alterations which were aimed at making the bill, so far as possible, acceptable to all concerned. *Ibid.* (July 2, 1956), 11576.

the bill they had authored and steered through Congress were in need of radical revision within two years.[46] Because of these fundamental disagreements, no real compromise could be reached between Committee Democrats and Republicans or between the Committee majority and the Commission. Gore-Holifield faced a stormy battle on the floor of Congress.

Ordinarily, however, it is not the JCAE which must make concessions. When the executive branch wishes to have legislation enacted, it must be prepared to accept somewhat less than it originally requests in order to obtain JCAE support. When the Committee is united on a point, the Executive, unless it prefers no legislation at all, has little choice but to accede to JCAE views. Executive officials will sometimes make known their opposition to JCAE suggestions, but this is frequently only token criticism.

The indemnity legislation of 1956 and 1957 provides a graphic example of the concessions the Executive makes to obtain JCAE support. After considering two indemnity bills, one prepared by the JCAE staff and introduced by Senator Anderson, the other an administration bill prepared by the AEC and introduced by Representative Cole, the Committee agreed to report a slightly revised version of the Anderson bill. During hearings, Commissioner Vance stated that the AEC would be willing to support the Committee proposal on the assumption that it would "have a better chance for passage at this session." He believed that the immediate passage of some bill was more desirable than the AEC's insistence on its own bill. Despite the Commission's capitulation, indemnity regulation died on the House calendar in 1956. It came up again the next year, but by this time Anderson had revised it by adding amendments relating to the AEC's handling of reactor licensing cases. Although the executive branch was extremely unhappy about the new statutory role given the Advisory Committee on Reactor Safeguards by Anderson's amendments, it gratefully

---

[46] Cole's dilemma, which reflected that of other JCAE Republicans, is illustrated by the following colloquy on the House floor:

> *Representative Dies:* If the Commission is ready and willing to embark upon this new field, what is the necessity for this legislation?
>
> *Representative Cole:* . . . I feel this legislation is not necessary; that the Commission now has the authority to do everything that this bill intends to cover.
>
> *Representative Dies:* I understood the gentleman was one who helped to prepare the bill and that he was in favor of it.
>
> *Representative Cole:* I did help to prepare the bill because I am in favor of accelerating and stepping up the program if there is any area in which greater progress is needed. I am not going to allow myself to be in a position of resisting legislation which has as its purpose the acceleration and stepping up of the program and not give heed to the advice of such an outstanding expert as Dr. Zinn.

Ibid. (July 24, 1956), 14248.

accepted the Committee bill in the belief that further delay on governmental indemnification would halt the entire civilian reactor program.[47]

Occasionally, the Executive must pay an even higher price for legislation it sponsors. In order to ensure passage of certain parts of its proposal, it must abandon others. When it referred to the Committee its proposed amendments to make possible the exchange of military information and materials with U.S. allies, the suggested bill included an amendment to Section 55 of the Atomic Energy Act. This amendment would have authorized the Commission to enter into fifteen-year contracts to buy plutonium produced in atomic-power plants abroad and to make these purchase contracts in excess of available appropriations by using a revolving fund of $200,000,000. Committee Democrats, not without some sympathy from their Republican colleagues, immediately objected to the proposal as a subsidy to American exporters of reactors, which was extraneous to the basic purpose of the bill.[48] During hearings, the JCAE used reasoned argument, sympathetic advice, and veiled and not-so-veiled threats to convince administration witnesses that this amendment should be withdrawn.

When the Commission attempted to justify the "buy-back" amendment on the basis of military need for additional plutonium for defense purposes, JCAE members questioned the development of a sudden need for foreign plutonium when the AEC and Department of Defense had for years rejected the Committee's request that plutonium production facilities be increased. Strauss explained that the AEC's proposal would not necessitate spending one or two billion dollars on domestic plant expansion, but Pastore could not understand how a different method of financing plutonium purchases could justify a suddenly increased need.[49] In any event, Committee members were wary of the paradoxical position in which the U.S. would find itself if the buy-back subsidy provision were enacted, for the U.S. would be fostering the development of reactors for peaceful purposes, they argued, by buying plutonium, useful only for military purposes, at a subsidized price. The U.S. would not receive any buy-back plutonium until after 1963, the military would not project its

---

[47] *Indemnity Hearings* (1956), pp. 318-319; *Cong. Rec.*, 103 (Aug. 16, 1957), 15057-15059.

[48] On this issue, the JCAE was bolstered by the support of senators and congressmen from the uranium-producing states in the Rocky Mountain region.

[49] Pastore commented: "The committee has been talking month after month about increasing the supply of plutonium and there has been a consistent, consistent, consistent resistance on the part of the military and the Commission that we do this." *Military Exchange Hearings* (1958), pp. 74-75. Commissioner Vance explained that the military would not recommend the expenditure of several billion dollars for additional plutonium capability except on the basis of a definite military requirement, and such a requirement was a short-range one. *Ibid.*, p. 233.

plutonium needs much beyond that date,[50] and the State Department opposed the provision; why, Senator Pastore wondered, was the Commission insisting that Section 55 be amended "when the rebound could be cataclysmic, propagandawise"? [51]

Holifield objected along slightly different lines. He pointed out that the proposal reversed a well-established AEC policy of paying only fuel value for special nuclear material produced in civilian reactors in order to encourage construction of reactors directed toward the production of electric power rather than plutonium. The effect of the proposed $30 buy-back price would be to encourage construction of reactors producing plutonium rather than power. This change of policy, moreover, would discourage, particularly in foreign countries, development of the use of plutonium as fuel. Durham was concerned with a possible importation of $200,000,000 worth of plutonium by the AEC, fearing that uranium plants at home might have to shut down and thus harm the national defense.[52]

It was unlikely that argument alone would persuade the AEC to withdraw its proposed amendment. Although the JCAE could easily report the legislation without the controversial amendment to Section 55, it wanted firm guarantees that there would be no administration-inspired floor fight to restore the provision. The AEC had to be persuaded to abandon its request. The tactic adopted was to make it clear that insistence on the amendment would endanger the more vital items in the bill. Anderson made no bones about his position; he was opposed to the $30 buy-back provision. It would have to go, he threatened, or the fight on the floor of the Senate might last just as long as the fight over Dixon-Yates. Anderson told the AEC chairman that, if the Commission insisted on the provision, the chairman could "confidently count on one very difficult fight on the floor of the Senate. . . ." [53] What this might mean, he stated later, is that,

> If there is extended debate in both House and Senate, that debate will be reported in the press all over the earth, and a lot of things will be said that may not be complimentary to the British or the French. . . . I think you ought to weigh those

---

[50] The date itself was deleted from the published record; in context, however, it seems to be either before 1963 or certainly not much after that date.

[51] *Ibid.*, pp. 217, 221.

[52] *Ibid.*, pp. 202-204.

[53] *Ibid.*, pp. 42-43, 76. Anderson evidently presumed that, even if the JCAE Democratic majority reported out a bill without the buy-back provision, the administration, unless it acquiesced beforehand, would have a minority member introduce the provision as an amendment from the floor.

> along with the narrow advantages that seem to come from trading.[54]

Anderson, however, was not opposed to trading. To make his bargaining terms clear, the Senator noted that although he was wholeheartedly in favor of liberalizing the information-exchange provisions of the bill, he had reservations on the material-exchange sections and was strongly opposed to the buy-back amendment.[55] From this it appears that Anderson was suggesting that he might abandon or modify his reservations on the exchange of material if the AEC withdrew its amendment to Section 55.

Subcommittee Chairman Pastore was more diplomatic than his colleague, but the implication of his remarks was plain. He suggested that the Commission introduce its amendment to Section 55 separately at a later date, since he would not want "to see anything destroy the other program we have been talking about which is so important to world peace and the common defense." Strauss, impressed less with the Committee's logic than its power, agreed that, if the buy-back amendment resulted in delay of favorable action on other provisions, it could be considered a separate measure. But Strauss first suggested, as an alternative to deferring consideration of the Section 55 amendment, that the contract period be cut from fifteen to seven years. For the next month, the Commission retained this compromise offer. The Committee similarly continued to explain to administration witnesses the dangers if the provision were not withdrawn. Republican member Van Zandt even told one witness that, as long as the bill contained an amendment to Section 55, it would not even get out of committee. He frankly advised, ". . . we had better face up to [it] and then let's get the bill on its way without the Section 55 amendment." To clinch his case, Van Zandt hinted that Senator Gore's Subcommittee on Raw Materials might hold special hearings to take testimony from domestic uranium miners and then a real furor would develop.[56]

Although the Commission had been cajoled and threatened, it tenaciously clung to hopes of salvaging its amendment, even in a diluted form. In addition to limiting the terms of contracts to seven years, the AEC went a step further by suggesting that the total amount of contractual authority be reduced from the original $200,000,000 request to only $50,000,000.[57] Senator Pastore, however, did not have compromise in mind.

---

[54] *Ibid.*, pp. 114-115. This threat was followed by an off-the-record discussion which, unfortunately, does not appear in the published hearings.

[55] *Ibid.*, p. 87.

[56] *Ibid.*, pp. 43, 54, 202-203.

[57] The effect would have been to authorize contracts for purchase of plutonium abroad for a term equal to the seven-year period for which the AEC was then authorized to guarantee prices domestically. Without the revolving-fund provision, purchase arrangements would have had to be made on an annual basis, subject to the availability of appropriations. *Ibid.*, p. 207.

In response to the new AEC proposal, he read a letter from the comptroller general replying to the senator's inquiry of February 19. The General Accounting Office did not recommend favorable consideration of the AEC amendment because it would remove the long-term plutonium-purchase contracts from Congressional review and control. In view of the GAO criticism, the Commission that afternoon offered to concede that the purchase contracts be treated as agreements for cooperation and lie before the Joint Committee for thirty days before going into effect. But the Committee held firm against inclusion of any buy-back provision, and, two days later, the Commission capitulated. In a letter to the JCAE, Commissioner Vance wrote that the AEC still favored the amendment, but, since its retention might delay favorable action on other sections of the bill, a change in Section 55 could be deferred without harmful military effect.[58]

Executive surrender was not absolutely necessary. Had the JCAE reported out the bill without this amendment, the administration could have carried the fight to salvage its plutonium policy to the floor of Congress. But neither the Executive nor the Committee wanted the arena of debate enlarged. If floor debate were acrimonious, the executive branch risked losing the basic provisions of the bill, which it regarded vital to national security. The Joint Committee, on the other hand, risked losing prestige and its unquestioned leadership of Congress on atomic-energy affairs if its recommendations were overridden, or even challenged, by Congress.

On issues involving new or altered atomic-energy policies, the Executive and the JCAE have persuasive reasons for reaching agreement before a bill is reported to Congress. Otherwise, the results are unpredictable enough to upset those who have been delegated primary responsibility for atomic-energy decisions. On issues of legislative and executive prerogatives which do not directly involve policy, pressures on the Executive to agree with the Joint Committee are increased, for Congress considers every request from the executive branch for vague and broad authority another challenge to its dwindling power.

4. *Preserving legislative authority.* Congress has seldom been adventurous. For this reason, and also because of its concern about its own power, Congress has often applied checks to daring programs offered by executive departments. The JCAE has probably been more adventurous than most Congressional committees, but it has insisted that atomic ventures be either of its own choosing or subject to its persuasive influence.

When the Executive, for example, proposed to enter a full-scale Euratom program, the Joint Committee not only made substantive revisions, but also included certain safeguards to preserve continued Congres-

---

[58] *Ibid.*, pp. 208-210, 265, 277.

sional control of the program. Its approach was to extend only as much approval as was considered absolutely necessary for the program to be launched. The JCAE resolved to keep the administration on a short rein as the Committee report noted:

> The Joint Committee, with the concurrence of the Atomic Energy Commission and the Department of State, recommends that the Congress authorize United States participation in Euratom arrangements *in such a manner that the Congress during the next and succeeding sessions can review and authorize* the proposed arrangements as to specific projects after the terms and conditions have been worked out more fully.[59]

Acting Secretary of State Christian Herter was not happy with the JCAE Euratom bill, but, after talking it over with advisers, he told the Committee that he thought the bill was "all right" and would not be difficult to administer. To make certain of executive acquiescence, Van Zandt asked Herter whether "all segments of Government, as far as the administration is concerned, are in accordance with the position you do take here today." Herter replied that they were.[60]

The Committee's concern for legislative authority was nowhere more clearly evidenced than in consideration of the executive proposal that agreements for the exchange of military information and materials be handled in the same way as nonmilitary agreements for cooperation.[61] Although there was general Committee acceptance of the need for closer scientific and military cooperation among Western allies, members were concerned about the broad delegation of power requested by the Executive.[62] Holifield pointed out that the provision for keeping a bilateral agreement before the Committee for thirty days conferred little or no review authority on the JCAE. If the Executive made tentative agreements, engaged in negotiations, or entered into international commitments, the Joint Committee would have to deny the agreement by reporting a regular bill to both houses of Congress. Such action would create two problems, Holifield maintained. First, it would be a public, and perhaps embarrassing, display of opposition to diplomatic arrangements. Second, both houses of Congress would have to pass a special bill of disapproval. A subsequent presidential veto would require a two-thirds vote to override.[63]

---

[59] S. Rep. No. 2370, 85th Cong., 2d Sess. (1958). Emphasis added.

[60] *Proposed Euratom Agreements Hearings* (1958), pp. 486-494.

[61] These agreements, according to §123 of the 1954 act, would lie before the Joint Committee for thirty days before becoming effective, with no explicit Congressional veto provided.

[62] It was not only the delegation that troubled the Committee, but also the fact that the administration proposal might accelerate the atomic arms race by spreading weapons among more nations.

[63] *Military Exchange Hearings* (1958), p. 63.

The purpose of the amendments, JCAE members thought, could be achieved either by treaty or international arrangement; the former would have to be approved by a two-thirds vote of the Senate and the latter by a majority vote of both houses. The Committee's concern was clearly shown by the following exchange between Pastore and the AEC's counsel:

> *Senator Pastore:* If you come in under section 121, it will mean that the Congress of the United States by concurrent resolution will have to pass on every item in the proposed agreement which does not become an agreement until the Congress acts affirmatively.
>
> . . . If it comes in by way of treaty, the Congress of the United States through the Senate will have to pass on item by item of that agreement before it even becomes an agreement and be ratified by two-thirds of the Senate. That is not the case under the proposed recommendation. . . .
>
> Under the prepared recommendations you are bringing in this under section 123, which means that you have the power to consummate the agreement, which becomes an effective agreement after it rests here for 30 days.
>
> The only way that you can repudiate that is by affirmative action by both branches of the Congress signed by the President of the United States.
>
> Otherwise you have to override him by a two-thirds majority, am I right or wrong?
>
> *Mr. Diamond:* That is technically correct.
>
> . . . .
>
> *Senator Pastore:* . . . In order for the Congress to repudiate that agreement you have to pass a law repudiating that agreement and that repudiation has to be signed by the man who sent it up here in the first place.
>
> In all probability he will veto it. Therefore, you have to override his veto. I think that ought to be clear in the record. . . .
>
> *Mr. Diamond:* I think your analysis is correct, Mr. Chairman.[64]

But the executive branch was determined to gain administrative flexibility in the distribution of weapons, parts, or information to a particular ally or allies. Certain general assurances could be given the Committee, however, without any radical modification of the executive request. First, the JCAE was assured that, if military agreements were carried out under Section 123, the Committee would, of course, be kept informed. Commissioners Strauss and Vance promised that the Commission would discuss with the Committee any bilateral agreement, even before it was

[64] *Ibid.*, p. 302.

signed. Informal prior consultation would prevent disputes when the agreement was finally referred to the Joint Committee. Gen. Herbert B. Loper, assistant to the secretary of defense (atomic-energy matters), indicated that problems could be resolved in the formative stages "before we proceeded with the actual formation of an agreement for consideration by the President." If accord could not be reached, Loper added, the views that would finally prevail would depend on the administration's estimate of the importance of the disputed provisions.[65]

Second, Strauss also assured the legislators that, if they objected to any agreement referred to the Committee, he "would find it extremely doubtful to think that any Commission would bullheadedly go ahead and force you to take the kind of legislative action to which you have referred." Commissioner Vance said that, if a question were raised by the Joint Committee, he personally would reconsider his earlier recommendation to the President regarding any agreement for cooperation. Deputy Secretary Donald A. Quarles told the JCAE that the Defense Department "would not proceed against the objections of the committee." [66]

Third, Strauss casually pointed out that the Joint Committee had its own stake in the matter. He implied that the proposed arrangement would protect the Committee's jurisdiction in atomic-energy affairs, whereas under the treaty process the JCAE would forfeit its control to the Senate Foreign Relations Committee. It was imperative, Strauss argued, that the Joint Committee maintain its key position, since classified matter in military-exchange agreements could not be debated on the floor, but could be disclosed only to the JCAE. "This is the very purpose for which the Joint Committee was created," concluded the AEC chairman, "namely, 18 men specially trusted by the two bodies with all information." Pastore and others were impressed, but hardly diverted, by that line of reasoning.[67]

Holifield sympathized with the administration's plight, since it was simpler and quicker for the Executive to act than for Congress to deliberate. But he noted repeatedly that, in view of the revolutionary weapons involved (". . . and we have lived with them now in this committee to the point where I sometimes think familiarity breeds contempt . . ."), exchanges were so important that each one should be considered individually. Otherwise, Congress would not be discharging its responsibility "on the most important subject that it can possibly act upon, which is the spreading of nuclear weapons throughout the world." Instead, it would

[65] *Ibid.*, pp. 66, 320.
[66] *Ibid.*, pp. 63, 292, 320.
[67] *Ibid.*, pp. 68, 187.

be abdicating legislative jurisdiction by placing entire power within the hands of one man, the president.[68]

Largely because of Holifield's efforts, a compromise was arranged which permitted administrative flexibility but did not make Congressional disapproval of agreements difficult enough to be practically impossible. Under a new subsection of Section 123, military-exchange agreements would have to lie before the Joint Committee for a period of sixty days, and such agreements would not become effective if both houses of Congress disapproved by concurrent resolution.[69]

Committee solidarity preserved for both Congress and the JCAE significant control of military and diplomatic policy relating to atomic weapons. Van Zandt stated to his House colleagues, "The bill does not go as far as originally requested by the executive branch. Certain authority requested has been eliminated, and in other sections, additional standards and safeguards have been written into the bill." [70] What was not expressed, however, was that the Committee retained for itself the crucial role of review. Any concurrent resolution to disapprove an agreement would naturally be referred to the JCAE for action. It could, therefore, block objections raised by non-Committee members simply by not reporting the referred resolution or by reporting it adversely.[71] At the same time, the

[68] *Ibid.*, pp. 303, 248-250, 364. Anderson noted that the Finance Committee, on which he sat, debated reciprocal-trade problems dealing with trivialities, and then the Senate had to ratify a trade treaty by a two-thirds vote. "If Congress," the senator asked one executive witness, "can be trusted to do the right thing by bicycles and mushrooms, can't it be trusted to do it in hydrogen weapons?" *Ibid.*, p. 333.

[69] Unlike a regular bill expressing Congressional disapproval, a concurrent resolution does not require the president's signature in order to become effective. Thus, Congress, by majority vote, rather than by two-thirds vote overriding a likely veto, could reject a proposed agreement for the exchange of military information or materials. The concurrent resolution procedure was patterned after §6 of the Reorganization Act of 1949; 63 Stat. 205 (1949); 5 U.S.C. §1332-1334 (1958). That act provided that a reorganization plan submitted by the president to Congress would not take effect if, within a sixty-day period, *either* house passed a disapproving resolution. Members of the JCAE concluded, however, that proposed international agreements for military cooperation would not be disapproved unless *both* houses joined in the *concurrent* resolution. S. Rep. No. 1654, 85th Cong., 2d Sess. (1958), pp. 16-17.

[70] *Cong. Rec.*, 104 (June 19, 1958), 11780-11781. For some members of the JCAE, even the safeguards incorporated by the Committee appeared inadequate. Senator Anderson offered an amendment both in executive session and later on the floor which would have limited the transfer of restricted data and special nuclear materials to nations that had made "substantial progress" in the development of atomic weapons. His amendment was rejected in committee. *Ibid.* (June 23, 1958), 11934.

[71] In 1959, seven agreements for cooperation with NATO allies were submitted to the JCAE. The Committee, after a unanimous report from its Subcommittee on Agreements for Cooperation, reported favorably on the agreements to the Senate and House. Seven concurrent resolutions introduced in the House in opposition were adversely reported by the JCAE and were not adopted by Congress. See JCAE press release, July 13, 1959.

JCAE, if it disapproved of an agreement, could report a resolution recommending its rejection. Congress would, of course, give any such recommendation by the Joint Committee sympathetic consideration.

• Limits of Agreement

Considering the numerous possibilities for disagreement within the Executive, within the Committee, and between the Executive and the Committee, it is astonishing that JCAE actions are unanimous so much of the time. No JCAE member nor executive official finds all provisions of every bill to his liking; forces for agreement, nevertheless, are stronger than those for dispute. The pressures to preserve solidarity and enact something outweigh individual, departmental, or partisan wishes for the whole loaf. This explains the JCAE's success in voting out a bill unanimously; writing a report with no dissenting, separate, or minority views; and going to the floor united.[72] Technical amendments to the 1954 act, community facilities legislation, governmental indemnity, military-exchange amendments, and federal-state cooperation legislation are examples of bills which have been taken to Congress by a "unanimous" Committee backed by the executive branch.[73]

On those bills, however, where splits are irreconcilable, the struggle continues beyond the stage of Committee deliberation. Sometimes the conflict is over a provision on which there has been a close vote in Committee; at other times, it is over an issue which only one member opposes. In either case, the minority has the option of continuing battle. To do so means to break down the solidarity of the Joint Committee, and this is

[72] Every bill is linked politically with other legislation. Where the Committee majority and the executive branch are in fundamental agreement, questions of political strategy are less likely to come to the fore, but, when there is a serious split, either between the Committee and Commission or within the Committee, each contestant will take advantage of the larger legislative situation. For example, the Gore-Holifield bill, sponsored by Committee Democrats, and the governmental indemnification bill and the proposed amendment to the Public Utility Holding Company Act, sponsored by the Republican administration, were considered a package by JCAE Democrats. Rejection of the first would, and did, affect enactment of the latter two. Strategy was also a factor when Euratom legislation was discussed. Whatever the intrinsic merits of the administration proposal, there were other factors to be considered. Whereas Committee members felt a responsibility to go far enough ahead with Euratom to preserve the enthusiasm that had been built up in the U.S. and abroad, the Democratic majority wanted to hold back the Euratom bill until an acceptable appropriation bill cleared Congress.

[73] "Unanimity" in this sense does not mean that every member of the Committee wholeheartedly favors the legislation or even goes along with the majority. It means that opposition is slight and mainly for the record. Holifield, for example, dissented and abstained on the governmental indemnification bills of 1956 and 1957, but he offered only token opposition. Anderson introduced amendments to the military-exchange bill on the floor of the Senate, which did not qualify his support for the basic purpose of the bill. Senator Russell voted against the military-exchange bill after making a brief statement in opposition.

done only with considerable reluctance. But there have been occasions, notably the disputes over the Cole-Hickenlooper and Gore-Holifield legislation, when a minority has carried the fight to the floor of Congress.

During consideration of the Cole-Hickenlooper bill, Committee members raised several points of serious contention, which were settled temporarily by votes.[74] No item was more controversial than the proposed Dixon-Yates contract. Both Democrats and Republicans on the JCAE opposed embroiling the Commission in this political battle, but the Republicans followed the President's wishes and voted down Democratic attempts to include a provision prohibiting negotiation of the contract. The vote settled nothing, however, for it was clear that the Democrats would renew their efforts on the floor. When a majority report on the bill was filed, Representatives Holifield and Price filed minority views rejecting Dixon-Yates.

Dissenters can take further action even though the Committee has tentatively agreed on a compromise so that a bill may be reported. Long discussion of the "principal-officer" clause, written into the bill by Cole and Hickenlooper, led to the substitute "official spokesman." Although the Committee had agreed unanimously to the substitution, the dissenting report of Holifield and Price called for deletion of the language.[75] Another outstanding issue settled by Committee vote without being permanently settled at all was the Bricker amendment. In executive session, it carried with only Pastore opposed,[76] but Pastore, with Holifield and Price subscribing, filed separate views and notified his colleagues that he would offer an appropriate amendment on the floor of the Senate. Similarly, no final resolution was achieved on the patent provisions. As originally written by Cole and Hickenlooper, the bill provided for normal patent rights, but, after considerable Committee debate, the overwhelming majority of members decided that a compulsory licensing provision was necessary to prevent a few manufacturers from achieving complete dominance. Cole would not accept the Committee decision, and his separate views on patents, subscribed to by Van Zandt, labeled the provisions adopted by the Committee unconstitutional, unnecessary, and hostile to the American system of private enterprise.[77] There could be no doubt that Cole, too, would offer an amendment when the bill reached the floor of the House. Finally, at least

---

[74] On less controversial items, it is seldom necessary for the Committee to vote formally. Decisions are made on the basis of nods, assents, and mutual understandings.

[75] *Leg. Hist. 1954 Act,* v. 2, pp. 2466, 2472; see also *N.Y. Times,* June 11, 1954.

[76] Several members were absent at the time of voting, but even those, there is reason to believe, shared Bricker's desire to enlarge the Congressional role in international agreements. *Leg. Hist. 1954 Act,* v. 3, pp. 3538, 3663.

[77] *Ibid.,* p. 3107; see also *N.Y. Times,* June 29, 1954, and H.R. Rep. No. 2181, 83d Cong., 2d Sess. (1954), pp. 96-99. According to Cole, "Compulsory licensing is not creeping socialism; it is socialism run rampant."

Holifield and Price were dissatisfied with the entire domestic program set forth in the bill. The Committee, they charged, had not undertaken a systematic review of all phases of the AEC's organization and management, despite the majority's claim that the bill represented a complete overhaul of the McMahon Act. Even more important, the entire private-participation program was premature. The President, they continued, sent to Congress a "two-package" proposal consisting of separate international and domestic bills. Yet Congress, in the closing days of the session, was faced with a "single package," an "all-or-none" proposition.[78] It was evident that neither Holifield nor Price would accept the legislation in the form reported to Congress.

Despite deep rifts over the Cole-Hickenlooper bill, obeisance was made to unanimity. The Committee report maintained that all differences concerning specific provisions of the legislation were resolved and consideration ended in "essential" unanimity of Committee members.[79] Similarly, in discussing his bill in the Senate, coauthor Hickenlooper claimed:

> . . . every member of the joint committee at one time yielded on some specific point or another. Yet none of us has compromised on fundamentals, and I think the fact that the committee has come into substantial accord on the essentials of the proposed legislation speaks well for it.[80]

Subsequent events demonstrated what was already evident from the dissents of Holifield, Price, Pastore, Cole, and Van Zandt; Hickenlooper was mistaken about the degree of Committee consensus. By that time, however, the decision was largely out of the hands of the Joint Committee. Congress would have to decide.

■ CONGRESS DECIDES

Once the Joint Committee on Atomic Energy files and reports a bill, both houses of Congress have an opportunity to accept, modify, or reject it. Theoretically, only the whole Congress has the power to enact atomic-energy legislation; in reality, however, the large majority of Committee decisions are passed on with only the most cursory consideration by each house. Generally, when the executive branch and Committee are in basic agreement, floor debate is perfunctory and ratification *pro forma.* If a debate does take place, it is usually irrelevant to Congressional decision, for the basic decision has already been made.

---

[78] *Ibid.,* pp. 106-107, 109, 120-124, 181.

[79] *Ibid.,* pp. 5-6. The word "essential" really meant that, since the JCAE could not reach agreement, it was necessary for members to agree at least to report out some bill and continue the fight on the floor.

[80] *Leg. Hist. 1954 Act,* v. 3, p. 3046.

JCAE bills fall generally into two categories, the noncontroversial and the controversial. On the former—the bills which are backed by the JCAE and executive branch—Congress often acts merely as a rubber stamp, taking little time to listen to explanation of proposals to which its delegates have already agreed. Sometimes there is brief debate, but never a close vote; in fact, there is never a record vote. On the latter—bills reported either by a divided Committee or with the Executive in opposition—debate is intense and involves not only JCAE members but other legislators as well. Amendments to controversial bills may be offered by JCAE members as well as by others. Both voice and record votes are taken, and, until votes are tallied, the result remains in doubt. The fight can go either way, since Committee, party, and regional loyalty affords no clear indication of how individuals will vote. The JCAE endeavors to retain control of the situation, but, rent internally, it offers only fragmented leadership. On these issues, control is exercised primarily by others.

• Effective Unanimity

Most of the Committee's bills are considered routine and are brought up for consideration by agreement between majority and minority leaders in the two houses. Minor proposals are usually passed with no debate at all, often with only a few legislators in attendance. AEC "omnibus" bills, consisting of technical amendments to the atomic-energy law, were enacted in 1953, 1956, and 1959 with little or no debate in either the Senate or the House.[81] Occasionally, on technical amendments, the JCAE members in charge of steering a bill on the floor—usually the chairman and vice-chairman—will explain the legislation and submit to questions. Members will normally then emphasize that the bill has been unanimously reported and is strongly endorsed by the AEC.[82]

Even on a measure which could provoke controversial discussion, objection on the floor is unlikely if the Committee works out a solution satisfactory to all members. Seeds of controversy were surely present when Senator Anderson used an AEC proposal concerning interim pay for commissioners to attach a rider bolstering the position of one commissioner in particular, but, since Committee Republicans and Democrats had come into agreement, the bill sailed through Congress. It passed in the House on the consent calendar and in the Senate with only a brief statement by Minority Leader William F. Knowland (R., Calif.), who pointed out that, although he supported the bill, the provision relating to full informa-

---

[81] S. 2399 and H.R. 6305 in 1953; S. 4203 and H.R. 12215 in 1956; and S. 2569 and H.R. 8754 in 1959.

[82] See, e.g., debate on S. 2399 in 1953, *Cong. Rec.*, 99 (July 20, 1953), 9225-9229; (July 21, 1953), 9438-9439.

tion for all commissioners was already in the law and, therefore, unnecessary.[83]

There are times when Committee members must answer certain questions so that other legislators may be sure their own interests will not be prejudiced. On the federal-state bill, for instance, Senator Humphrey made a legislative history to the effect that a provision for a Federal Radiation Council in no way prejudiced another bill, which would have given the Public Health Service primary responsibility for regulating radiation sources. Anderson answered Humphrey's questions, which had been presented to him beforehand, and the bill passed both chambers the same day.[84] Legislation granting the AEC the right to enter into long-term utility contracts was subject to slight delay in 1953, when Sen. Wayne Morse (Ind., Ore.) and Senator Gore objected to its immediate consideration. Morse wanted a legislative history and, therefore, submitted questions to Hickenlooper, who, two days later, inserted the answers into the *Record*. The next day, the bill was again called from the calendar. Hickenlooper stressed that there were no objections to the legislation by any member of the Committee. Anderson supported his colleague, Morse and Gore expressed satisfaction, and the bill passed by voice vote.[85]

As long as the Committee and the Executive are in accord, even important legislation can be enacted with only passing attention by the whole Congress. In 1951, the JCAE reported a bill providing for the limited exchange of certain classified information with friendly nations. During consideration in the Senate, Chairman McMahon stressed two factors: first, the many hours spent by the Committee working over the proposal to make certain that adequate safeguards were included and that national security would not be adversely affected as a result of information exchanges; second, the unanimity of the Committee and executive branch. The ranking Republican senator supported the chairman, again emphasizing

---

[83] During the first session of the Eighty-fourth Congress, the AEC requested an amendment which would permit commissioners whose appointments had not yet been confirmed by the Senate, because of either delay or recess, to receive salaries for the time they spent on the job before official confirmation. Anderson saw an opportunity to right what he thought was a wrong: the alleged failure of Chairman Strauss to keep other commissioners, principally Thomas Murray, adequately informed of AEC business. Therefore, Anderson tagged on to the AEC amendment a provision unrelated to salaries which affirmed that each commissioner should have "equal responsibility and authority in all decisions and actions of the Commission, . . . full access to all information . . . , and . . . one vote." *Ibid.*, 101 (July 29, 1955), 12147; (July 30, 1955), 12253. Despite the salary provision, which was the main reason for the bill's initiation, the measure has become known as "the Murray bill."

[84] Humphrey asked the JCAE chairman, "Does the bill in any way lessen the need for legislation along the lines stated in the bill [S. 1228] introduced by Senator Hill?" Anderson replied that Hill's bill was a corollary measure, which would also "more clearly define where authority is. . . ." *Ibid.*, 105 (Sept. 11, 1959), 19044-19046, 19169.

[85] *Ibid.*, 99 (July 6, 1953), 8002; (July 9, 1953), 8339.

JCAE and administration unanimity "from topside to bottomside." With less than a dozen senators on the floor, the bill passed by voice vote. Debate in the House echoed that in the Senate. The bill was passed after Durham assured the chamber that the Committee had "exhaustively explored and weighed the issues," had "conscientiously evaluated all factors and had rendered its thoroughly considered judgment." [86]

The Euratom debate in Congress provides another interesting example of perfunctory handling of an important issue. There was little doubt that the Committee had significantly modified the administration's proposal, but, when Sen. Jacob K. Javits (R., N.Y.) inquired whether the JCAE-reported Euratom cooperation bill went far enough, floor manager Pastore replied, as if according to script:

> This was a very complex and complicated arrangement. It came to us toward the close of this session. We worked upon it very scrupulously, carefully, ardently, fervently, and enthusiastically. I consider this a fine project, and it has the concurrence of the Atomic Energy Commission and the concurrence of the State Department. Both of them are satisfied with it; and we are more than satisfied with it.[87]

Sen. Frank A. Barrett (R., Wyo.) was the only other non-JCAE member who had anything to say about the Euratom proposal. Only one JCAE member, Sen. Henry C. Dworshak (R., Idaho), opposed Euratom, and he made a long, uninterrupted speech detailing his reasons. But, significantly, Dworshak prefaced his statement with the comment: "I am a realist so I do not intend to make an extended effort to oppose the taking of favorable action on the bill as reported by the committee." Both the Euratom bill and the resolution passed the Senate by voice vote. When the bill was taken up in the House, no JCAE member disapproved, and there was no debate. Durham explained the measure briefly. Then Van Zandt and Hosmer, after announcing support, asked unanimous consent to have their written speeches on Euratom included in the *Record* as an extension of remarks; there was little need to take up the valuable time of the House when the conclusion was foregone. The bill was passed by voice vote.[88]

If a Committee member is resolute in opposition to a JCAE-endorsed bill, he can, if he desires, take issue on the floor. In 1956, Holifield was the only JCAE member voting against the governmental-indemnification bill during Committee deliberation. That year, because of the defeat of the Gore-Holifield bill, indemnification never reached the

---

[86] *Ibid.*, 97 (Oct. 11, 1951), 12940; (Oct. 16, 1951), 13311.
[87] *Ibid.*, 104 (Aug. 18, 1958), 18100.
[88] *Ibid.*, 18102; (Aug. 20, 1958), 18788.

floor.[89] In 1957, the Committee again considered the measure, made several changes, and reported a bill. This time, Holifield abstained from voting in committee, but his opposition had in no way diminished. When the bill came before the House, floor manager Price stressed the effective unanimity of the Committee and noted that the AEC and the President urged passage. After several minor amendments offered by the Committee were agreed on, Holifield offered an amendment which would have limited the government's insurance liability. Cole rose in opposition, pointing out that the Californian's proposal had already been rejected by the JCAE. Durham also spoke in opposition, and Holifield's amendment was rejected by a voice vote. After rejecting two more Holifield amendments, the House passed the bill by voice vote. The Senate followed suit shortly.[90]

• Disagreement and Controversy

If the power of the Committee over the fate of noncontroversial legislation is almost unlimited, its power on controversial legislation is drastically curtailed. When the Committee is divided against itself, Congress cannot turn to it for definitive advice. When the administration opposes a measure brought out by a JCAE majority, Congress faces an additional dilemma—whether to follow the lead of the executive branch or of the Committee majority. At this point, partisan and regional considerations may be injected. No longer does the Joint Committee make

---

[89] After the Gore-Holifield bill was killed, Democrats decided that it would not die alone. On July 25, 1956, when Republican Whip Charles A. Halleck of Indiana asked the Democratic House leader when the governmental indemnification bill would be called from the House calendar, Rep. John W. McCormack (D., Mass.) was vague. The next day, after Holifield and Price objected to consideration of the amendment to the Public Utility Holding Company Act, both Cole and Van Zandt noted that the Democrats were purposely pigeonholing two important measures. Two days later, Cole charged, "Pique over failure of the Gore bill to pass was apparently the basis for the refusal of the Democratic leadership of the House and Senate to consider and pass the measure which the atomic energy industry has been awaiting and without which real progress will be seriously hindered." *Ibid.*, 102 (July 27, 1956), 15717. Even a letter from the President calling the attention of the Senate and House to the indemnification bill had no effect on the Democratic leadership. *Ibid.*, 15126-15127. Pique, however, was not the main reason the Democrats blocked the indemnification bill. Primarily, Democratic Committee members hoped to use the bill as a bargaining point in their future efforts to enact Gore-Holifield in one or another form.

[90] *Ibid.*, 103 (July 1, 1957), 10710-10724; (Aug. 16, 1957), 15057-15059. That the Senate passed the bill quickly is not surprising. The proposal for a statutory Reactor Safeguards Committee contained in the bill had already been made satisfactory to the administration by a Committee-sponsored House amendment making the RSC "advisory." Furthermore, no Senate JCAE members opposed the bill. Most important, the indemnification legislation, having already passed the House, was purposely called up for consideration just after the Committee's controversial authorization bill had been passed by the Senate. No longer was the threat of bottling up indemnification legislation a necessary instrument for Democrats anxious to accelerate the civilian reactor program.

the crucial decisions. Rather, its members operate among a greater number of key participants as individuals in diminished, but still important, roles.

The Gore-Holifield bill divided the Committee and pitted the Democratic majority against a determined administration. At issue was the role of the federal government in the development of electric power facilities, a question that had long divided the two political parties. Here, partisan and constituency influences predominated, despite the expertise of JCAE members and their efforts to produce a compromise bill. Although the Gore-Holifield bill was unanimously reported by a fourteen-to-nothing vote, with Senate Republican members abstaining, it promised to provoke controversy on the floor of Congress. On the last day of JCAE hearings on the measure, Chairman Strauss had made the final and conclusive statement: "I hope, in view of the fact that we have been here and testified, that this bill will not be taken to mean that the Commission has indicated approval. . . ." [91]

With Democrats hopeful that they had the votes to pass Gore-Holifield and the administration and JCAE Republicans confident that they could amend or defeat the bill in the House, the civilian reactor legislation was put in the lap of Congress. It was called up in the Senate first, presumably because the Democratic leadership felt that it stood a better chance of passage in the upper chamber. Debate was brief, for both sides expected the crucial test to come in the House. There was no attempt by either side to delay a vote, and on a roll call the Senate passed the JCAE bill by forty-nine to forty.[92] For the third time—the other instances are the Dixon-Yates fight of 1954 and the Lilienthal confirmation—both Committee and Senate were split along strictly partisan lines. Of the forty-nine affirmative votes, only three were cast by Republicans; of the forty negative votes, not one was cast by a Democrat. The voting pattern among JCAE members was the same, with Anderson, Russell, Pastore, Gore, and Jackson voting "aye" and Hickenlooper, Millikin, Knowland, and Bricker voting "nay."

On the House side, the bill was brought to the floor with Durham's

---

[91] *"Gore-Holifield" Civilian Power Hearings* (1956), pt. 2, p. 45. Earlier in the hearings, Strauss had made plain his opposition to legislation which *directed* the Commission to perform in the manner specified. He said, "We are anxious to go forward, but we hate to be flogged as tardy schoolboys. . . ." *Ibid.*, p. 10.

[92] *Cong. Rec.*, 102 (July 12, 1956), 12452-12469. Three years later, Senator Anderson recalled that, when the bill was reported, he was under the impression that there would be little trouble. Then he noted rumblings in the Senate, and "the next thing I knew somebody told me that a couple of Senators had been pledged to vote against it. We immediately began to canvass the cloakroom and found there was a vigorous drive going on to kill the bill." The fight, Anderson reflected, was because of "a change in attitude which came directly from the Atomic Energy Commission." Evidently, Anderson believed that the administration would neither support nor oppose the Gore-Holifield bill. *Strauss Confirmation Hearings* (1959), p. 516.

statement that "it is one of the few bills which has been brought out of this committee without full and complete agreement between the committee members, the Atomic Energy Commission, and the Administration. . . ." Durham stressed the unique competence of the Joint Committee, but admitted that the issue before the House was extremely complex, involving scientific information difficult for laymen to evaluate. Along similar lines, Rep. Howard Smith, chairman of the House Committee on Rules, in reporting a rule on the bill,[93] noted "violent disagreement" between the Commission and the Joint Committee and questioned how Congress could decide when scientists and statesmen disagreed.

Whenever the AEC and the Committee are in conflict, the JCAE can be relied on for a reminder of the Committee's past omniscience. Thus, Durham and Price pointed out that the Joint Committee had proved right in overruling the Commission on the hydrogen-bomb crash program. This bill, they maintained, provided an analogous situation.[94] But unlike in the hydrogen-bomb controversy, which saw the JCAE united (with the exception of Cole), the Committee in this instance was split into majority and minority factions. Sterling Cole, acting on behalf of the administration, announced that, although he supported the general principle of the legislation, he would offer several amendments. He also introduced into the *Congressional Record* a letter from Strauss announcing the formation of a group of reactor specialists to examine the entire reactor program. Administration strategy was by then clear: in return for delay, it proposed further study of the problem.

More important than Cole's activities were the "position statements" made by party leaders of the House. At the very beginning of debate, Rep. Charles A. Halleck (R., Ind.), the Republican whip, stated that he was dissatisfied with the bill and suggested that it be amended. Toward the end of debate, even after Cole's amendments had reduced Gore-Holifield to the most innocuous proportions, Halleck insisted that the bill was still unacceptable to the administration. Democratic leader

---

[93] *Cong. Rec.*, 102 (July 24, 1956), 14249-14250. The bill was held up briefly by the Rules Committee. On July 17, after brief consideration, the committee failed to give the Senate-passed bill a rule. Chairman Howard Smith told Senator Gore that his committee "may or may not" clear the Senate bill for House action before adjournment. *N.Y. Times*, July 18, 1956. By the next day, however, the situation was reversed. The Democratic Congressional leadership was determined that the bill come to a vote, so that responsibility for lack of progress in achieving economic nuclear power could be fastened to the Republicans. If the bill passed the House, President Eisenhower might veto it. If the bill were rejected, Republican votes would be the cause of its defeat. In either case, Democrats imagined they might have an issue that would net votes in the approaching election. Smith was, therefore, prevailed upon to permit the bill to come to the floor, and, on July 18, the Rules Committee, by a five-to-four vote along party lines, reported a rule for Gore-Holifield. Smith and one other Democrat abstained.

[94] *Cong. Rec.*, 102 (July 24, 1956), 14266.

John W. McCormack (D., Mass.) accepted Halleck's challenge, stressing two points: first, if the bill failed to pass, there might be some delay on two other atomic-energy bills—governmental indemnification and amendment of the Public Utility Holding Company act; and, second, if the bill were rejected, responsibility would be placed on the Republican Party and particularly on Charles Halleck.[95]

Not only were party lines hardening, but another factor soon became important. Congressmen from coal districts had their own objections to the bill. The United Mine Workers had been active in persuading them that atomic power loomed as a threat to the coal industry.[96] Thus, congressmen from Pennsylvania and West Virginia, Democrats and Republicans alike, took the floor to oppose enactment of Gore-Holifield.

Within the framework set by partisan lines and regional interests, JCAE members were faced with important tasks on the floor. Cole had the job of rendering the bill ineffectual by a series of amendments. The first deleted the directive language from the legislation; the second provided that private industry be given a six-month first option to build each new reactor proposed for construction. With the acceptance of these amendments on teller votes, the bill's survival, rather than its palatability, became the sole issue. Halleck announced that the administration would not accept even the watered-down Gore-Holifield bill, for fear that in conference the Senate bill would prevail, much to the displeasure of the Republican Party. The main business now was the vote on Van Zandt's motion to recommit, offered on behalf of the Republican leadership. The motion passed by a 203-191 roll-call vote, and the civilian reactor acceleration bill was dead. For an inconsequential moment, the Joint Committee was almost united. Only Van Zandt and Patterson voted for the motion to recommit; Hinshaw, Cole, and Democratic members voted against it. Once the bill had been rendered relatively harmless to the administration's position, JCAE Republicans were free to vote according to their own conscience. Except for the defection of a few Republicans and a number of coal-district Democrats, the vote was strictly along party lines. Of the 191 votes for Gore-Holifield, 174 were cast by Democrats and only seventeen by Republicans. Of the 203 opposed, 176 were Republicans, and twenty-seven were Democrats.[97]

In the tumult created by the private–versus–public-power battle,

---

[95] *Ibid.,* 14248, 14281, 14287.

[96] *N.Y. Times,* July 30, 1956.

[97] Of the Democrats who voted, or were paired, against the bill, seven were from Virginia, five from Pennsylvania, and four from West Virginia. A switch of seven Democratic representatives from coal regions would have saved at least what was left of the original Gore-Holifield bill and permitted a House-Senate conference to restore other provisions included in the Senate bill. Of interest is the fact that, of the thirty-eight members not voting, twenty-nine were Democrats.

the alleged effects of atomic power on the coal industry, the heightened sense of partisanship, and the efforts to fix party responsibility to gain electoral advantage, the role of the Joint Committee on Atomic Energy was significantly reduced. In the House, where the crucial battle took place, Committee members defended or attacked the legislation and proposed or opposed weakening amendments, but the most influential decisions were made by others. The floor of the House was not the setting most favorable to effective Committee leadership on an issue as divisive as Gore-Holifield, nor were the cloakrooms or individual congressmen's offices. It was up to party leaders in the House, representatives of the executive branch, and lobbyists to collar votes. The Joint Committee's failure to come to the floor united behind its legislative proposal was, in a sense, an abdication, however involuntary, of its powers to lead. These powers depend on cohesion, which could not always be maintained.

• Partisanship versus Committee Leadership

On another occasion, the Joint Committee lost control of a bill it reported to the Senate and House. That the final version of the Atomic Energy Act of 1954 bore a marked resemblance to the original Cole-Hickenlooper bill was less because of the ability of the Committee than because of the skills and resources of other participants in the legislative process. Several factors had immediately precluded *pro forma* ratification of the bill by Congress; for, although the legislation had been reported unanimously, few JCAE members were entirely satisfied with the compromises that had been worked out in committee. Nevertheless, the JCAE might still have retained control had it not been for another factor: the injection of the Dixon-Yates controversy into consideration of the atomic-energy legislation.[98]

The role of the Joint Committee as legislative leader was shaped by an issue over which it had little control. Members functioned as individuals for or against particular sections of the legislation and joined the various blocs that coalesced during the public–versus–private-power battle. In the House, Holifield was a key strategist for the opposition and Cole a key defender of his own legislation. In the Senate, Hickenlooper pushed for expeditious action, assuring his colleagues that the provisions had already been fully debated as a result of eight years of "intensive and continu-

---

[98] Another result of Dixon-Yates, as Kramish and Zuckert note, was that the AEC was politically "deflowered," and its "above-politics" stature was replaced by a deep distrust of almost all actions of the Commission, particularly by the Democratic members of Congress who opposed the Dixon-Yates arrangement. *Op. cit.,* p. 130.

ous study" by the JCAE.[99] Anderson, on the other hand, did his utmost to delay passage of the reported bill until public-power senators had the chance to make significant modifications.[100] To illustrate the ineffectiveness of the Committee during this period, two slights to ranking members may be cited. Chairman Cole and Vice-Chairman Hickenlooper, seeking to shield their bill from controversy, appealed unsuccessfully to high administration officials that Dixon-Yates be dropped.[101] On another occasion, the ranking Democratic senator on the JCAE, Clinton Anderson, was ignored by his minority leader. After floor discussion had gone on for more than ten days, Lyndon Johnson introduced a unanimous-consent request to limit debate without showing the proposal to Anderson before its introduction. Moreover, Johnson took directly on himself the task of controlling time for the Democrats, a function which would normally have been performed by the ranking Democratic member of the Committee.

The Joint Committee's failure to achieve agreement, as well as the injection of an issue which aroused traditional ideological attitudes and constituency interests, resulted in a leadership vacuum which was naturally filled by other legislators. Among the first to take an active role were the public-power lobbies and their advocates in the Senate, who saw in the Cole-Hickenlooper bill an ideal opportunity to rally forces against not only Dixon-Yates, but also against the entire power program of the Eisenhower administration. By July 15, two days after Cole-Hickenlooper had been called up from the Senate calendar, lines had been firmly drawn against the legislation.[102]

---

[99] "I am not in any way saying," the Iowan maintained, "that the Senate should not debate the bill fully and understandingly, but I wish to give assurance that the legislation now proposed is not the result of any hasty or precipitate action on the part of the Joint Committee on Atomic Energy." *Leg. Hist. 1954 Act,* v. 3, p. 3216.

[100] On July 16, Senator Anderson gave a luncheon for other Democrats to review strategy and gain time in the fight. *N.Y. Times,* July 17, 1954. Anderson objected to hasty consideration of Cole-Hickenlooper primarily to allow opponents time to marshal their forces for key amendments. Meeting again on July 18 and July 20, Democrats made plans to amend the bill, and an amendment committee was appointed. If the liberals did not succeed with amendments, a second line of strategy was to split the bill into international and domestic sections so that the former would be enacted and the latter blocked. *Leg. Hist. 1954 Act,* v. 3, p. 3773.

[101] This information is based on interviews. See also Wildavsky, *op. cit.,* p. 118, and Strauss, *op. cit.,* pp. 304-305. Cole and Hickenlooper were not the only Republicans to take their case to the White House. Sen. John Sherman Cooper of Kentucky, a friend of TVA, tried on several occasions to persuade the President and White House advisers to withdraw the contract. Wildavsky, *op. cit.,* pp. 108-109.

[102] One participant has described events which preceded the atomic-energy debate as follows:

> Toward the end of 1953 a group of some dozen liberal Senators were giving serious consideration to "staging" an extended debate on public power. They felt that the cooperation between administration forces

While the "public-power liberals" argued vehemently against Dixon-Yates and the Cole-Hickenlooper giveaway to private industry, the Democratic leadership remained aloof.[103] Until about July 24, a self-appointed group of public-power advocates, led by Albert Gore of Tennessee, Lister Hill of Alabama, and Clinton Anderson of New Mexico, spoke on behalf of Senate Democrats. Then Johnson took over, having lost patience with the liberal tactics designed to delay votes on amendments. Disposition of the atomic-energy bill was necessary, Johnson believed, in order to permit action on several other important pieces of legislation which had to be considered during the brief time remaining to the Eighty-third Congress. Furthermore, the minority leader felt that continuation of the filibuster would be detrimental to the Democratic Party, and, accordingly, he decided to work out a compromise to expedite consideration of the atomic-energy bill.

On the Republican side as well, Committee members, including Cole and Hickenlooper, played only a secondary role. The administration had made plain its support for both the Dixon-Yates contract and the atomic-energy legislation.[104] White House officials were in constant communication, by phone and in person, with Republican Congressional leaders and other key GOP members of the Senate and House; the White

---

> and the private utilities should be brought forcefully to public attention. At that time a large number of high-tension speeches were prepared. They were to be "sprung" as a surprise to the conservative elements, and would occupy the time of the Senate for several days, if the liberals could get, and hold, the floor. But the right occasion never presented itself.
>
> In the spring of 1954 the idea was revived by a group of seventeen Senators. . . . But again, the opportune issue and moment for uncorking this effort to bring the situation forcefully to public attention did not arrive.

Barrow Lyons, *Tomorrow's Birthright* (New York: Funk & Wagnalls, 1955), pp. 327-330.

[103] Lyndon Johnson originally tried to hold the Democrats together by keeping one foot in each camp, voting with public-power advocates but taking no advanced position otherwise. The Senate Democratic Policy Committee, which almost always reflected the views of Johnson, met on July 14 and decided unanimously not to take a party position in the fight. *N.Y. Times,* July 15, 1954.

[104] Backing the Republican administration were the groups supporting private power. In early 1953, more than seventy-five electric-utility companies anticipated the coming struggle by launching a public-information program designed to "tell the story of investor-owned electric companies in simple terms so the people can decide the issues in the fight against socialization." In February of that year, an atomic-power committee was created by the Edison Electric Institute. It was headed by Edgar H. Dixon, president of Middle South Utilities, one of the firms which submitted the Dixon-Yates proposal. Allied with private utilities was the National Association of Manufacturers. By June and July 1954, private-power lobbyists were swarming through the corridors of the House and Senate office buildings.

House press secretary issued several public statements calling for rapid consideration of the bill.[105] During the night of July 23, as debate in the House was drawing to a close, Vice-President Nixon visited House Republican leaders to lend them support and encouragement. Perhaps the key Republican strategist was William Knowland, a member of the JCAE, who performed primarily as administration agent and Republican Party leader in heading the parliamentary fight against the liberals.

In neither chamber was the Joint Committee able to give much direction to the course of debate on its bill. In the House, although Cole and Holifield spoke at length and persuasively, floor debate was generally superficial. Under the five-minute rule, there was little discussion of amendments, and it is quite likely that many members were hardly aware of the issues on which they were voting.[106] In the Senate, too, debate on particular provisions was overshadowed by polemic and partisan maneuvering. Republicans were anxious to pass the bill with minimum discussion and then adjourn. Democratic liberals were chiefly interested in hammering home their themes that the Republican administration favored the rich, that the President was concerned only with the problems of large corporate interests, and that the Cole-Hickenlooper bill was a giveaway. For the liberals, extensive debate was necessary to win as many concessions for public power as possible, to educate the American people in anticipation of the approaching election, and to have as many roll-call votes as possible so that local public-power groups might hold their senators accountable.[107]

Thus, Congressional debate, especially in the Senate, was more a study in political strategy and parliamentary tactics than a close scrutiny of atomic-energy legislation. Debate was a one-sided affair. Issues were seldom joined, especially since Republicans hardly bothered to answer the charges of Democrats, but contented themselves with attacking Democratic obstruction. Although the Dixon-Yates contract was, no doubt, important, discussion of it largely obscured from both public and Congressional view some of the other extremely important provisions of the Cole-Hickenlooper bill. As for discussion of these provisions, Senator Hickenlooper characterized it most accurately: "I have heard some of the longest, most repetitious

---

[105] On July 23, for example, Press Secretary James Hagerty reflected the President's views when he commented on delay by the Democrats: "Everyone here in the White House is concerned that such action is jeopardizing enactment of key items in the legislative program. . . ." *N.Y. Times,* July 24, 1954.

[106] Majority leader Halleck argued that extensive debate was unnecessary, since members had talked about the provisions of the bill for three or four weeks preceding its consideration and had read newspaper reports of the Senate debate. *Leg. Hist. 1954 Act,* v. 3, p. 2926.

[107] The last point, based on interview information, is reported by Wildavsky, *op. cit.,* p. 102.

speeches I have ever heard, regarding the same grist hour after hour, speaker after speaker. . . ." [108]

The partisanship which characterized floor debate was even more clearly evidenced in key roll-call votes. On every important Senate vote but the one on passage, each party followed its leadership.[109] In the House, JCAE decisions, as the vote on Cole's patent amendment illustrates, were handily overturned. (See Table IV-1, Vote 1.) The roll-call vote on the amendment saw only thirteen Democrats and six Republicans cross the aisle to vote with the opposing party. JCAE members also followed their

TABLE IV-1

HOUSE ROLL-CALL VOTES ON H.R. 9757

House voting	Vote 1		Vote 2		Vote 3	
	Yea	Nay	Yea	Nay	Yea	Nay
JCAE members:						
Democrats	0	4	2	2	2	2
Republicans	5	0	0	5	5	0
Entire House:						
Total votes	203	161	165	222	231	154
Democrats	13	154**	157	26	36	146
Republicans	190	6	7	196	195	7
Party cohesion: *						
Democrats	—	.84	.72	—	—	.60
Republicans	.94	—	—	.93	.93	—

* Party cohesion is based on Stuart Rice's "index of cohesion"; see note 109.
** Rep. Frazier Reams of Ohio, an independent, is not included in the party totals.

Vote 1: Cole amendment to grant normal patent rights for nonmilitary developments not invented under government auspices. Accepted (July 24, 1954).
Vote 2: Holifield motion to recommit bill to the JCAE. Rejected (July 26, 1954).
Vote 3: Passage of Bill (H.R. 9757) (July 26, 1954).

---

[108] *Leg. Hist. 1954 Act,* v. 3, p. 3566.

[109] The following voting tabulations are based on *Congressional Quarterly Almanac, op. cit.,* X, 563-565, 574. This determination of party cohesion is based on the "index of cohesion" given by Stuart A. Rice, *Quantitative Methods in Politics* (New York: Knopf, 1928), pp. 207-227. The basic formula for determining cohesion on a single-vote decision of the members of Party X is:

$$2\,\frac{(\text{Majority } X\ \ )}{(\text{All } X \text{ Voting})} - 1$$

Taking the Democratic vote on the Cole patent amendment (Table IV-1, Vote 1), for example: 167 Democrats voted, thirteen for and 154 against the amendment. The index of cohesion of the Democrats on this roll call is $2\,\frac{(154)}{(167)} - 1$, or .84, indicating a high degree of cohesion on a scale which ranges from zero to unity.

Congressional party leaderships, with the five Republicans voting for the amendment and the four Democrats voting against it. Under Majority Leader Halleck's prodding, several Republican Committee members changed their votes on the patent provision. On Holifield's motion to recommit the bill, the Republicans again held firm, whereas twenty-six Democrats, including Durham and Price, decided that some bill was better than no bill at all. (See Table IV-1, Vote 2.) After the Democratic recommittal motion failed, ten more Democrats deserted the leadership to vote for passage, but still the overwhelming majority of Democrats voted against H.R. 9757, whereas 195 out of 202 Republicans voted in favor. (See Table IV-1, Vote 3.) Holifield's motion to recommit, the critical vote, found Democrats from all areas except the South firmly behind leaders Rayburn and McCormack. The Republicans were even more cohesive, but to assume that they were following the lead of JCAE members would be to imagine that the tail wagged the dog.

In the Senate, under Knowland's leadership, Republicans were remarkably united, and a few Democratic defections—mainly Southerners—provided comfortable margins to defeat nearly all the amendments offered by the liberal Democrats. On the first important vote, the Anderson amendment, which would have voided the Dixon-Yates contract proposal, both the JCAE and the Senate as a whole split along party lines, except for several pro–Dixon-Yates Southern Democrats who voted with the Republicans.[110] (See Table IV-2, Vote 1.) With the exception of Pastore, the same lines formed on Knowland's motion to table reconsideration of the amendment offered by Sen. Homer Ferguson (R., Mich.) and, thereby, officially authorize Dixon-Yates. The vote on Sen. Edwin Johnson's public-power-preference amendment revealed a similar partisan split, but this time the public-power amendment carried because four pro–Dixon-Yates Republicans and six pro–Dixon-Yates Democrats voted for the Johnson amendment. (See Table IV-2, Vote 2.) Thus, although party lines were moderately firm, Republican cohesion was lower here than on any other of the key Senate votes. When Republican unity faltered and Democratic unity picked up, the JCAE's rejection of the Johnson amendment in Committee deliberation was overruled.[111]

Two other amendments, aimed at making important revisions in

---

[110] Generally, the Democratic South was split on Dixon-Yates, with senators and congressmen whose states were in the heart of the Tennessee Valley opposed to, and those outside the valley in favor of, the contract.

[111] According to Kramish and Zuckert: "In a strange sort of irony, the debate caused by the Dixon-Yates contract brought about the inclusion in the basic atomic energy law of several features (the preference clause being the most prominent) favoring public power agencies; a victory that the public power advocates would not have tasted except for the rallying point offered by the Dixon-Yates controversy." *Op. cit.*, p. 137.

TABLE IV-2

KEY SENATE ROLL-CALL VOTES ON S. 3690

Senate voting	Vote 1		Vote 2		Vote 3		Vote 4		Vote 5		Vote 6	
	Yea	Nay	Yea	Nay	Yea	Nay	Yea	Nay	Yea	Nay	Yea	Nay
JCAE members:												
Democrats	4	0	4	0	1	3	0	3***	1	3	3	1
Republicans	0	5	0	5	5	0	5	0	0	4***	4***	0
Entire Senate:												
Total votes	36	55	45	41	46	41	41	37	31	51	57	28
Democrats	33**	11	38	6	2	40	1	36	29	11	13	25
Republicans	2	44	6	35	44	1	40	0	1	40	44	2
Party cohesion: *												
Democrats	.50	—	.73	—	—	.90	—	.95	.45	—	—	.32
Republicans	—	.91	—	.71	.96	—	1.00	—	—	.95	.91	—

* Party cohesion is based on Stuart Rice's "index of cohesion"; see note 109.
** Senator Morse of Oregon, an independent in 1954, is not included in the party totals.
*** Russell not voting on Vote 4; Bricker not voting on Vote 5; Bricker "announced" or "paired for" on Vote 6.

Vote 1: Anderson amendment (in the nature of a substitute for Ferguson amendment) to limit AEC authority to contract for electric-utility services to persons supplying power directly to the AEC and require a review of such contracts by the JCAE. Rejected (July 21, 1954).

Vote 2: Edwin Johnson amendment to authorize the AEC to produce electric power and other forms of energy from nuclear fission and require that preference be given to public bodies and cooperatives in disposing of excess power from AEC plants. Accepted (July 22, 1954).

Vote 3: Knowland motion to table Pastore amendment (which would have permitted the president without making a treaty to deal with more than one nation in setting up an exchange of atomic information in an atomic pool). Tabling motion agreed to (July 23, 1954).

Vote 4: Knowland motion to table Kerr amendment (which would have maintained the existing law regarding compulsory licensing of patents obtained in the atomic-energy field by deleting language in the bill which required that such licenses be of primary importance in the production or use of atomic energy and to the purposes of the act). Tabling motion agreed to (July 23, 1954).

Vote 5: Stennis amendment in the nature of a substitute to strike from the bill all provisions except those pertaining to the international pooling of atomic information. Rejected (July 26, 1954).

Vote 6: Passage of House-passed bill as amended, substituting text of S. 3690 for the House language. Passed (July 27, 1954).

the Cole-Hickenlooper bill, were defeated on straight party-line votes. With the exception of Senator Johnson of Colorado, whose views on international affairs closely paralleled those of Bricker and Millikin, JCAE Democrats voted for Pastore's proposal to permit agreements with international organizations. Only one other Democrat crossed the aisle on this vote. (See Table IV-2, Vote 3.) Similarly, all but one Democratic senator voted for the amendment offered by Sen. Robert S. Kerr (D., Okla.) to retain the patent provisions of the 1946 act, whereas every Senate Republican voted against the amendment. Again, party lines held firm, firmer, in fact, than on the public-power amendments to the bill. (See Table IV-2, Vote 4.)

When the question, however, was not one of specific revision, but rather of wholesale change, as in the amendment proposed by Sen. John Stennis (D., Miss.) to delete all but the international provisions from the legislation, JCAE Democrats supported the bill the Committee had brought forth. Except for Anderson, who had aligned himself closely with the liberals, members closed ranks to prevent their legislation from being dissected. Although Minority Leader Johnson, primarily to keep peace with the liberals, voted for the Stennis amendment, it was easily defeated. (See Table IV-2, Vote 5.) Similarly, on the final roll call, JCAE Democrats joined their Republican colleagues to support Cole-Hickenlooper.[112] Even Anderson, who until that time had voted consistently with the liberals, cast his ballot with the rest of the Joint Committee. Lyndon Johnson also went along with the JCAE bill as amended; but twenty-eight senators, including Republicans William Langer of North Dakota and John Sherman Cooper of Kentucky, Democrat Richard Russell of Georgia, independent Wayne Morse, and Northern and Western Democratic liberals were left in opposition to S. 3690. (See Table IV-2, Vote 6.)

The Joint Committee on Atomic Energy, less as a result of its own efforts than those of the Republican Party leadership, had steered its bill through the two chambers of Congress. The next step would be to resolve several differences between the bill passed by the Senate and that passed by the House. This would be the job of a conference committee composed of members of the Joint Committee. The JCAE would have another opportunity to retire behind closed doors and deliberate on the Cole-Hickenlooper bill.

• The JCAE in Conference

Not all JCAE bills find their way to conference, but certainly the most controversial ones do. Even though the Joint Committee differs from

---

[112] Again, there was one exception. Senator Russell, who feared national security might be threatened if there were a relaxation of information controls, voted against passage and against the second conference report.

the other standing committees of Congress in that it reports identical bills to the two chambers, important atomic-energy legislation frequently emerges from the House and Senate in somewhat different forms. On minor matters, one chamber may accede to the other's bill without insisting on a conference; on major issues, however, the house where a bill originates will usually refuse to accept the other's amendments, thereby necessitating a conference. Members of Congress often consciously postpone serious conflict on the floor in order to let the conferrees hammer out compromises. Sometimes, committee members responsible for steering a bill on the floor will agree to an amendment that they oppose in the belief that it will be killed in the conference committee.[113] In the case of atomic-energy legislation, the most important provisions have generally been sharply debated on the floor of each house before discussion in conference.

The conference committee has considerable discretion in reconciling differences in, and recommending compromises for, a bill. Since its reports cannot be amended, but must be accepted *in toto* or recommitted, the conference committee exercises substantial powers. However Congress may decide an issue, the conference committee has an opportunity to modify that decision. Since conferrees are chosen from among the members of the committees which reported the bill, those who had an early voice in shaping controversial legislation also have a voice in its disposition. Theoretically, conferrees or managers serve on behalf of the chamber which appointed them. It is expected, therefore, that they will support the bill passed by their own house. Sometimes, and particularly with legislation on which the two parties are divided, this is not the case, and conferrees act primarily as Democrats or Republicans. Even then, loyalties to one house or the other affect the behavior of conferrees. When the JCAE acts as a conference committee, ties to the respective chambers are minimal, since the JCAE is practically a conference committee from the beginning of its deliberations.[114]

---

[113] During Senate debate on the McMahon Act, for example, Senator O'Mahoney of Wyoming offered a floor amendment which was opposed by JCAE member Millikin. Instead of objecting at that point, Millikin explained, "So, merely to get it out of the way, and although I am in complete disagreement with the theory of the Senator from Wyoming . . . I am willing to accept the proviso in the hope that the conference will eliminate the amendment." Quoted in Bertram M. Gross, *The Legislative Struggle* (New York: McGraw-Hill, 1953), p. 318.

[114] After the House had knocked a provision for the conversion of the Hanford reactor out of the AEC authorization bill of fiscal year 1962, the Republican leadership introduced an unusual resolution instructing House conferrees to uphold the action. Republicans feared that the Democratic-controlled conference would support the Senate bill, which restored the Hanford project. There was good reason for such fears; Representative Holifield himself admitted that his loyalty on this issue was not to the House. He said that, as chairman of the JCAE, he owed a responsibility to his committee, which, by a large majority, had reported favorably on the Hanford project. *Cong. Rec.* (daily ed., Aug.

In view of the fact that conference committees represent committee power in its most concentrated form, it might seem that JCAE members have, after all, the last word on the legislation to be enacted by Congress. In several instances, however, the behavior of JCAE conferees has been strongly determined by the positions of the Congressional parties, and the division of the Committee and Congress along party lines has barred the JCAE as a conference committee from effective exercise of control. Instead, individual conferees have performed as party representatives in accord with positions that had already been taken by their parties during Senate and House debate.

An illustration of the circumscribed role of JCAE members in conference is that on the Cole-Hickenlooper bill. The chief sources of controversy were the patent provisions and the public-power-preference clause. The Senate bill would have given the AEC authority for compulsory licensing of important atomic-energy patents for a ten-year period, whereas the House bill included the Cole amendment providing for normal patent rights. The second major difference between the two bills was that the Senate version contained the Johnson clause providing that publicly owned bodies and utilities in higher-cost areas be given preference in buying electricity from experimental plants.

The conferees met on August 4, but could not reach agreement on the patent sections, which were considered by Democrats to be the heart of the bill. Several compromises were suggested but failed to win approval. One was even presented to the liberal senators who had led the fight against the bill to see whether it was agreeable to them. Clearly, the conferees hoped to avoid the possibility of resuming the liberal "talk-athon." [115] But the author of the patent amendment, Sterling Cole, insisted that his amendment stand. He was supported by other JCAE Republicans, although Hickenlooper, who had experienced the arduous fight in the Senate, was less than enthusiastic. "I can't take this back to the Senate floor," the Iowan remonstrated with his fellow Republicans. "It will touch off another fireworks. We've got to compromise." [116]

Two days later, the JCAE conferees finally hammered out a report on the atomic-energy bill. The Republican majority in the conference committee succeeded in retaining the Cole patent provision and in watering

---

8, 1961), 13897. In 1962, the Hanford project was reconsidered by the JCAE in conference after the House had voted to delete the Hanford proposal from the AEC fiscal year 1963 authorization legislation. In this instance, with the proposal altered from its earlier form, only one of the JCAE conferees, Republican Representative Van Zandt, dissented. The other conferees agreed to a compromise permitting the use of the steam by-product from the new Hanford production reactor. *Ibid.* (daily ed., Sept. 14, 1962), 18373-18381; (daily ed., Sept. 18, 1962), 18656-18657.

[115] *Washington Post and Times Herald,* Aug. 5, 1954.

[116] Drew Pearson, *ibid.,* Aug. 10, 1954.

down the public-preference clause by adding the phrase "insofar as practicable." [117] Conferrees Holifield, Johnson, and Anderson refused to sign the report; the latter two urged that the Senate send the measure back to conference to avoid further debate.[118]

On August 9, the House adopted the conference report by a voice vote. In the Senate, however, Democrats were prepared to fight for its recommittal. Democratic liberals were assured by the minority leader that the party would hold firm. Through the buttonholing skills of Johnson, promises were obtained from almost all Senate Democrats to support a recommittal motion. On August 11, Johnson and Majority Leader Knowland joined in sponsoring a unanimous-consent agreement limiting debate on the conference report to three hours. The fact that this was done with the reported approval of the public-power Democrats, who had threatened another extended debate, was an indication of their confidence in the outcome.[119] When the conference report came before the Senate the following day, Lyndon Johnson took personal command of the drive to defeat it. Although floor manager Hickenlooper argued that, if the report was voted down, it would mean the death of the bill, both Johnson and Anderson insisted on a second conference and assured their colleagues that the conferrees could complete their work in a few days.

The Republicans used several devices in an attempt to salvage the conference report. Just before the vote, Hickenlooper introduced into the *Record* a letter from President Eisenhower urging that the report be accepted by the Senate.[120] Majority Leader Knowland, fearing that several Midwest Republicans would defect because of their objections to the phrase, "insofar as practicable," proposed that the conference report be accepted and that Congress then pass a concurrent resolution deleting the

---

[117] Thus, §44, on the sale by the AEC of excess energy, read: "In contracting for the disposal of such energy, the Commission shall *insofar as practicable* [emphasis added] give preference and priority to privately owned utilities providing electric utility services to high cost areas not being served by public bodies or cooperatives." H.R. Rep. No. 2639, Conference Report, 83d Cong., 2d Sess. (1954), p. 12.

[118] Anderson was most critical of the patent provision, which, he said "takes out all compulsory licensing and . . . makes it a bad bill." Edwin Johnson commented on the "insofar as practicable" phrase: "It sounds like innocent language, but it makes the whole preference clause meaningless." *Washington Post and Times Herald,* Aug. 8, 1954.

[119] *Ibid.,* Aug. 13, 1954.

[120] In his letter of August 12, the President assured Hickenlooper that the bill as it had emerged from conference would not be harmful in any way to the Rural Electrification Administration. He added that the bill's provisions regarding patents "adequately meet my recommendations on this subject and will prevent use of patents for monopolistic purposes." *Leg. Hist. 1954 Act,* v. 3, p. 3916. It should be pointed out, however, that President Eisenhower had initially urged a five-year compulsory-licensing period to safeguard against monopoly, as had the AEC and the JCAE. The Senate had extended the licensing period to ten years, and Cole's House amendment had deleted compulsory licensing completely.

phrase. The effect would be to compromise by retaining the Cole patent provision in exchange for removing the limitation on the preference clause. But Democrats refused to accept the Knowland proposal. Sen. Walter F. George (D., Ga.) condemned it as an attempt at "doctoring" the conference report, warned that it would be subject to a point of order in both houses, and said he would oppose it. Lyndon Johnson said that Knowland's proposal was "one of the most shocking announcements I have ever heard made in the Senate" and would, if accepted, "make a laughing stock out of the United States Senate." More important, Johnson noted that the majority leader's proposal ignored the other important issue at stake—the patent provision.[121]

On a roll-call vote of forty-one to forty-eight, the Senate rejected the conference report. As on the previous ballots, the voting on this bill was largely along party lines. Arrayed against the report were forty-two Democrats, five Republicans, and Independent Wayne Morse; supporting it were thirty-nine Republicans and two Democrats. Lyndon Johnson had rounded up every Democratic vote except those of Harry F. Byrd of Virginia and J. William Fulbright of Arkansas. What made the difference, however, was that the Democrats won the votes of Republicans Cooper, Dworshak, Langer, George W. Malone of Nevada, and Milton R. Young of North Dakota, the latter four being under great pressure from rural electric cooperatives in their states to safeguard the public-preference clause.[122] Thus, the JCAE conference majority had been overridden by the Democratic Party in the Senate.

A second conference committee of JCAE members was appointed, and, within an hour, conferrees unanimously agreed on two major changes in the earlier report: a five-year compulsory-patent provision was adopted, and the phrase, "insofar as practicable," was eliminated from the preference clause. JCAE Republicans, especially Cole, were dissatisfied, but, if an atomic-energy bill were to be enacted, the concessions were necessary, as the showdown vote in the Senate had proved. On August 16, the Senate adopted the second conference report by a fifty-nine–to–seventeen roll-call vote, and the next morning the House agreed to the report by a voice vote. Two weeks later, President Eisenhower signed H.R. 9757, and the Atomic Energy Act of 1954 became law.

---

[121] *Loc. cit.*

[122] On this vote, the index of Democratic party cohesion was .91; the Republican cohesion index was .77. Only seven senators did not vote; three Republicans were paired for, and three Democrats were paired against, the conference report. Sen. James H. Duff (R., Pa.) was the only member who did not vote or pair, but he was announced in favor of the report. For Senate debate, see *ibid.,* pp. 3892-3918, and *Washington Post and Times Herald,* Aug. 17, 1954.

V | Authorizing Techniques and Decision-Making

"The greatest power we have is the power of the purse." [1] This remark by a former chairman of the Joint Committee on Atomic Energy illustrates a predominant attitude in Congress today. Despite its diminished power in the area of policy formulation, or perhaps because of it, Congress is extremely reluctant to relax its control over the national purse. Control over funds, theoretically residing in the whole Congress, has come to rest primarily in the House Committee on Appropriations and secondarily in the Senate Committee on Appropriations. There is no doubt that the appropriations committees and their subcommittees are the most influential legislative agencies on review of the Executive's budget. Often overlooked, however, are the financial powers of other Congressional committees. As a rule, before funds can be appropriated for new government facilities and sometimes programs as well, they must be first specifically authorized by statute. Thus, legislative committees, by virtue of their role in the enactment of authorization legislation, have a significant voice in executive expenditures and programs.[2]

---

[1] Remarks of Senator Anderson, *Cong. Rec.*, 103 (Aug. 16, 1957), 15014.

[2] Recently, it seems, legislative committees have expanded their authorization powers. For example, §412 of the Military Construction Act of 1959, 73 Stat. 322, provides that,

Authorization power is a formidable instrument of control. For all practical purposes, use of this tool has been delegated to the standing committees, which review departmental and agency requests and make recommendations to Congress as to dollar expenditures and particular programs. In the case of the JCAE, the power to recommend authorizations for the Atomic Energy Commission has in the last six years been an effective device in shaping the nation's atomic program.

▪ THE QUEST FOR AUTHORIZATION POWER

Ironically, the 1946 Atomic Energy Act, which provided for a unique and potentially powerful joint legislative committee, failed to provide Congress and the JCAE with the power to authorize appropriations. Instead, the act authorized all "such sums as may be necessary and appropriate to carry out the provisions and purposes of this act." Under this "blanket" authority, the AEC was able to turn directly to the Appropriations committees to get funds for operations, equipment, plants, facilities, and real estate.

Within a few years, JCAE members decided that the Committee should have authorization authority, and, on July 7, 1949, Senator McMahon and Representative Durham introduced bills to require statutory authorization for (1) programs set forth in the annual AEC budget and (2) the total amount of money and contract authorization annually requested by the Commission. But these two bills were never acted on by the Committee, primarily because the AEC convinced McMahon that authorization legislation would cause delay in the atomic-energy program.[3] Two years later, the proposal for authorization was renewed because of controversy between the JCAE and the House Appropriations Committee. With its ever-increasing knowledge about and experience with the atomic program, the Joint Committee was becoming increasingly incensed with the way in which the House Appropriations Committee disregarded its advice. Moreover, the Appropriations Committee was encroaching upon the legislative area which the JCAE considered its exclusive domain. In 1950, for example, the House Appropriations Committee attached a rider to an AEC appropriations bill to restrict payments to private community management contractors. This particularly aroused Congressman Durham,

---

after December 31, 1960, no funds may be appropriated for the procurement of aircraft, missiles, or naval vessels ("military hardware") unless the appropriation of such funds has been specifically authorized by legislation. Before the enactment of this requirement, appropriations for aircraft and missile procurement on the basis of authorizations were exceedingly broad and general in language. See S. Rep. No. 253, 87th Cong., 1st Sess. (1961), p. 2.

[3] Thomas, *op. cit.,* p. 80.

who felt it was time that the Joint Committee obtain authorizing powers, if only to prevent other committees from legislating in the atomic-energy field. But the Commission and the Democratic administration continued to oppose any proposals for authorizations.[4]

Administration views notwithstanding, in June, 1951, Democrats McMahon and Durham introduced two new bills conveying authorization power to the Joint Committee,[5] but the Committee did not hold hearings until 1952, when a number of alternative proposals were considered. At this time, JCAE members argued that the Committee was unnecessarily deprived of an essential power. First, they said, the JCAE could not effectively review the Commission's budget. Previous efforts at review by a subcommittee had proved unsuccessful, since JCAE members, with no direct responsibility for acting on the budget, had become bored and paid little attention to the presentation. The dominant attitude, according to AEC Chairman Dean, had been: "Why are we listening to all of this . . . and what do we do about it as a subcommittee, because we are not authorizing?" [6]

Second, JCAE members contended that, without an opportunity for a thorough review of the AEC budget, they were hard pressed to defend the Commission's program from attack by the House Appropriations Committee. "When the Appropriations Committee brings the matter to the floor," stated Representative Holifield, "then the rank and file of the Atomic Energy Committee itself is not acquainted with the individual items in the budget because we have not scrutinized it that closely. . . ." The Californian maintained that the authorizing power was necessary to strengthen the Joint Committee in supporting the AEC program. Without authorization power, Holifield maintained, the House Appropriations Committee was free to chop AEC appropriations requests at will. But, if program and expenditures were authorized by the Joint Committee, the AEC would be bolstered by "the intent of Congress" as expressed in authorization legislation. Expressing agreement with his Democratic colleague, ranking Republican Senator Bourke Hickenlooper argued that the JCAE should

---

[4] *Community Policy Hearings* (1950), p. 40.

[5] H.R. 4330, introduced by Durham, and S. 1602, introduced by McMahon, would have required specific authorization for construction projects involving $500,000 or more. These bills further provided that, if either House failed to vote on an authorizing bill within twenty days, the president might nevertheless authorize the Commission to proceed. In commenting on the legislation, Commissioner Sumner Pike, in a letter dated August 15, 1951, cited many problems that might result. Budget Bureau Director Frederick Lawton was even more critical: ". . . it may be productive of potential conflict between the Congress and the executive branch. We should not attempt a hybrid process. The authority and responsibility embodied in the bill should rest in the Congress or the executive branch and not halfway between the two." *Amending the Atomic Energy Act Hearings* (1952), p. 101.

[6] *Ibid.*, pp. 60, 108.

receive authorization power and that the AEC should provide every assistance. Suggesting that the AEC adopt the major premise that the JCAE would receive authorizing power, he asked for the Commission's advice on the "best and most workable" provision.[7]

The JCAE offered the executive branch four alternative authorization proposals that had been formulated by the Committee staff. The first provided that there be annual legislation to fix the amounts to be appropriated for both operations and construction. The next three were limited to authorization of construction projects estimated to cost in excess of $500,000, with procedures varying according to the specific proposal. One provided for the AEC's "coming into agreement" with the JCAE. Another required an authorizing act, but would have permitted the AEC and the Budget Bureau to make exceptions in certain cases. The last also required authorizing legislation, but would have permitted the president to make exceptions in particular instances.

Budget Director Frederick J. Lawton was cool to all the proposals, which he believed would not only complicate the AEC budget and the over-all budget of the federal government, but would also cause delays in the atomic-energy program. He objected most vociferously to the alternative which would have the Commission come into agreement with the Committee. "We do not favor this approach," he stated, "because it represents an intermingling of congressional and executive responsibilities, contrary to the constitutional principle of the separation of powers, and creates difficulties for both branches. Under this device responsibility for program control would never really be fixed." Despite resistance, however, the Committee made some headway. AEC Chairman Dean said that, if authorization were to come, he would prefer it for the entire budget, rather than for individual construction items. The value of "a careful look," he believed, would be that the JCAE would be thoroughly informed, "so that the rest of the Congress then could look to the joint committee" and "get behind us when the appropriation time came." Even Lawton made a concession, indicating that he would not be "too adverse to," but "would welcome," some authorization on long-term construction if it were not an annual procedure.[8]

---

[7] *Ibid.*, pp. 106-109. "From these hearings," writes Morgan Thomas, "it appears that the Joint Committee desire for authorization power in the Dean period was a product of its desire to protect the AEC from the growing interference of the Appropriations committees, and not a result of its fear of being unable to control the AEC." *Op. cit.*, p. 134. This is certainly true, but more important was the Committee's desire to increase its own authority, not for any immediate purpose but as a goal in itself.

[8] *Amending the Atomic Energy Act Hearings* (1952), pp. 57, 99, 108. The budget director certainly was not without sympathy for the precarious position of the Joint Committee in defending the Commission's budget. He suggested to the Committee: ". . . if there is some basis on which you can make your judgment felt prior to the action of the Appro-

With the GOP in control of both the administration and Congress as a result of the November, 1952, election, the JCAE, now under Republican leadership, continued its efforts to obtain authorizing power. A provision was finally included in the 1954 act which required authorization for funds "necessary for acquisition or condemnation of any real property or any facility or for plant or facility acquisition, construction or expansion." In commenting on the bill, the AEC continued to oppose the requirement on the grounds that it would delay completion of programs vital to national security.[9] All the Commission offered the Joint Committee was continuing opportunity to review the AEC budget informally.

Notwithstanding the AEC attitude, Committee members, drawing on their experience with both atomic energy and military programs, concluded that the discipline of authorizing legislation was desirable for the Commission and that the increased powers that went with such authority were necessary for the Committee. It is interesting to note that, despite the administration's opposition to inclusion of Section 261, there was little public discussion of the matter. In lengthy debate on the 1954 act, the legislators raised no objection to the authorizing provision. They were apparently satisfied with Senator Hickenlooper's explanation that the section was merely "an attempt to follow the general purposes expressed repeatedly by Congress so far as the agencies of the Government are concerned."[10]

■ USE OF LIMITED POWERS

With its newly acquired powers, the Joint Committee during the next two years came to grips with two problems: management of the AEC

---

priations Committee by something less than complete Congressional action in the form of a joint resolution or bill, it might meet your problem, something that would be highly persuasive to the membership of the House and to the Appropriations Committee." But the JCAE had tried persuasion with little success. A JCAE annual report on the budget was suggested in committee, but members felt it would never be read. Formal JCAE recommendations on the budget, communicated privately to the Appropriations Committee, were proposed, but members considered it unlikely that their advice would be heeded. *Ibid.*, pp. 110-111.

[9] Unless the authorizations for construction projects were very general in nature, the memorandum held, the AEC would be tied to specific projects. If technical changes or military requirements dictated revisions, there would be harmful delays if specific authorization were necessary. The memorandum further pointed out that, although Congress enacted specific legislation authorizing certain construction projects of the Department of Defense, such legislation was not required for industrial-type facilities needed for production purposes. Not only was the bulk of AEC construction of this type, but it was precisely in this area that the Commission sought the greatest flexibility in making changes in the type and scope of individual projects without delay. *Leg. Hist. 1954 Act,* v. 2, pp. 2244-2246.

[10] *Ibid.*, v. 3, p. 3255. According to Morgan Thomas, the appropriations committees did not oppose the provision and did not feel that their own power was threatened. Thomas assumes that the close relationship between Rep. John Phillips (R., Calif.), chairman of the House Appropriations Independent Offices Subcommittee, and Sterling Cole forestalled any conflict. *Op. cit.*, p. 156.

budget and direction of the AEC programs. With respect to management, the Committee and Congress were united in laying down specific guidelines on just how funds could be spent, and the Commission's opposition to these restrictions was unsuccessful. With respect to direction, the Committee encountered substantial difficulty even in its limited effort to shape the atomic-energy program.

The chairman of the new Subcommittee on Authorizing Legislation, Representative Holifield, voiced the opinion of the entire Committee when, during the first hearings on authorizing legislation, he told AEC officials that the Commission would have to conform more closely to "regular procedures" than it had in the past.[11] Since the Committee believed that the agency's program had matured to the point where costs could be estimated, it restricted flexibility in Commission budgeting. Under the Independent Offices Appropriations Act for 1955, which was enacted before the JCAE acquired the authorization power, the AEC was permitted to embark on any project as long as it did not exceed the estimated cost as set forth in the budget by more than 35 per cent. Thus, if the Commission estimated in its budget that a certain plant would cost $1,000,000, it could still start the project even though a revised estimate brought the plant cost as high as $1,350,000. The JCAE now revised this "overrun" formula so that in projects where costs were difficult to calculate the overrun category was 25 per cent; where cost estimates were more easily calculated, the overrun was 10 per cent; and in those cases where costs could certainly be predetermined, no overrun was permitted.[12]

The Commission acquiesced in these restrictions and assured the Committee that the atomic-energy program could proceed despite the limitations. But another restriction appeared more serious. The 1955 Appropriations Act also permitted the Commission to begin any new project for which an estimate was not included in the budget if the new project was "a substitute therefor within the limits of cost included in the budget." The first draft of the JCAE authorizing bill eliminated the substitution provision entirely, but, after an appeal by AEC Chairman Strauss, Holifield agreed to have the AEC and JCAE staffs work out together precise language for a substitution provision. The JCAE was finally persuaded by the Commission to permit flexibility, but limited it to projects in weapons production, weapons logistic operations, and related special-nuclear-materials-production areas, that is, projects "essential to the common defense and security." Both the Commission and Committee seemed satisfied with the compromise.[13]

---

[11] *FY 1956 Authorization Hearings* (1955), p. 151.

[12] *Ibid.,* p. 150. In doing this, the Committee was following a pattern set by the armed services committees in restricting Defense Department expenditures. *Ibid.,* p. 147.

[13] S. Rep. No. 538, 84th Cong., 1st Sess. (1955), p. 4.

Whereas the Committee clearly established a measure of control over AEC procedures for the expenditure of funds, in considering specific elements of the atomic-energy program it merely reviewed items which had been requested by the AEC and approved by the Budget Bureau. In one case, however, the Committee added an item of $5,000,000 which had not been approved by the AEC or cleared by the bureau, and the Executive willingly went along.[14] More important, however, were the items struck from the administration request. By a narrow margin, the Committee voted to eliminate $21,000,000 for construction of a reactor for a nuclear-propelled cargo ship. The cargo ship had its genesis in a proposal by President Eisenhower in April, 1955, for construction of an atomic-powered merchant ship to demonstrate his Atoms for Peace program to the world. A request for $21,000,000 to pay for the power plant was then included in the AEC budget, and $12,000,000 for design and construction of the hull was included in the Commerce Department budget. Members of the Joint Committee, in special hearings before the Reactor Subcommittee as well as in the authorization hearings, were lukewarm toward the President's proposal on the grounds that another "Nautilus"-type reactor would add little to the art of reactor design.[15] In executive session on June 13, the Committee voted nine to seven to eliminate the President's project from the authorizing bill. The administration immediately declared its intention of fighting the cut on the floor of Congress, and Republican Congressional leaders announced plans to introduce amendments restoring the slashed funds.

When the AEC authorization bill came up in the House on June 27, there was little debate. There was some discussion about the merchant ship, but no attempt to amend the JCAE bill. The administration had tried without success to win over Representative Cole, but Cole had other ideas about a nuclear-powered ship. On the House floor, he was instrumental in silencing Republican objections, stating that the Committee did not oppose the President's purpose, "rather, a majority of the members . . . felt that the suggested means of carrying out the President's basic idea was not as practical as the amount of money involved should require." The authorization bill, as reported by the Committee, passed by a voice vote. In the Senate, Knowland and Hickenlooper led the attempt to amend the JCAE bill. There was little debate on Hickenlooper's amendment to restore

---

[14] This item was hastily included in the authorization bill after President Eisenhower suggested the project in a speech on June 11, 1955, only three days before the JCAE filed its report.

[15] Anderson called it a "museum ship," and Holifield referred to it as a "showboat." *N.Y. Times,* June 14, 1955. Of great influence on Committee members was Admiral Rickover's assertion that work on a merchant-ship reactor would retard the submarine-reactor program. *FY 1956 Authorization Hearings* (1955), p. 86.

the merchant-ship reactor. On a roll call, the amendment was rejected by a straight party vote of forty-one to forty-two. Every Republican voted affirmatively, and every Democrat, with the single exception of Strom Thurmond of South Carolina, voted negatively. Once the amendment was rejected, the authorization bill passed by a voice vote.[16]

By an extremely narrow margin, the Joint Committee had defeated a partisan attack on its one controversial alteration in the AEC authorization for fiscal year 1956. But, with almost no dissent, it had successfully placed limitations on the Commission's expenditure of appropriated funds. When the AEC came before the Committee with its 1957 request, these limitations were considered firmly established and not subject to major revision.[17] The Joint Committee made no important additions or deletions in the AEC request, and there was consequently no disagreement between the two bodies. If the AEC civilian reactor program was not up to the expectation of Democratic JCAE members, authorizing legislation was not yet seen to be the best means of shaping the program. Instead, attention was being focused on the Gore-Holifield acceleration bill, and hearings were scheduled to begin in May. Any battles to be fought would be over Gore-Holifield, not over authorizing legislation. Since the Committee reported the 1957 authorization bill unanimously and the administration was content with the legislation, there was no problem on the floor of Congress. The bill passed by voice votes,[18] with ratification a *pro forma* matter.

■ THE EXPANSION OF AUTHORIZATION POWER

Civilian power reactors, an important aspect of the AEC program, were beyond the scope of the JCAE's authorization power. The AEC had taken the position, supported by the comptroller general, that reactor experiments and certain civilian reactor projects with only temporary value were not "facilities" within the meaning of Section 261 and, therefore, did not require authorization. Furthermore, the AEC was placing primary reliance for power-reactor development on its Power Demonstration Reactor Program (PDRP), under which AEC funds would be used to support research and development on projects undertaken by private industry.

---

[16] *Ibid.*, pp. 165-167, and *Cong. Rec.*, 101 (June 27, 1955), 9284; (June 28, 1955), 9354.

[17] In the 1956 hearings, Holifield indicated satisfaction with the language in the previous year's bill. "To the best of my knowledge," he stated, "the Commission has not indicated that it has been handicapped in any substantial way . . . as a result of the passage of Public Law 141 last year." The AEC's draft authorization bill for fiscal year 1957 was almost identical in form and language to the one drafted by the Committee the year before. *FY 1957 Authorization Hearings* (1956), p. 2.

[18] *Cong. Rec.*, 102 (April 18, 1956), 6542-6545; (April 19, 1956), 6618.

Since the program explicitly precluded use of AEC funds in construction of the reactors, it was beyond the scope of the authorization requirement. When the Gore-Holifield bill was defeated, the JCAE recognized the infeasibility of legislating what it considered an adequate power-reactor program by usual means. Committee Democrats then sought to subject the entire PDRP to the authorization requirement. By putting itself in a position to control funds for the Commission's own reactor program, the Committee could more effectively compel the Commission to bargain on the JCAE's program. It is interesting to note that Republicans, who were not oblivious to the tactical motives of their Democratic colleagues, were happy to support the drive to expand the Committee's power. Since this approach would require amendment of Section 261 of the 1954 act, the real tactical problem was to avoid executive opposition.

JCAE members of both parties agreed that cooperative arrangements under the PDRP should be scrutinized by the Committee. They also agreed that all government-financed experimental reactors, except very small ones, should be authorized prior to appropriation of funds for construction.[19] Even before hearings on fiscal 1958 authorization legislation began on April 10, 1957, Democratic members were discussing among themselves the tactics for accomplishing these ends. Then, an extremely fortuitous or cleverly planned event occurred. Clarence Cannon, chairman of the House Committee on Appropriations, who, since Dixon-Yates, had been extremely critical of atomic-energy authorization procedures and distrustful of the AEC, launched a massive attack against the AEC.[20] He charged that in 1956 and 1957 the AEC had obtained 80 per cent of its funds as "operating expenses" without proper legislative authorization. Not only plants and facilities, but also research and development funds should be authorized, Cannon maintained. Implied in Cannon's broadside was the threat that his committee would block the appropriation of funds unless the Commission's reactor program were specifically authorized by Congress.[21]

The JCAE's response to Cannon was immediate and obliging. Holifield, chairman of the Subcommittee on Legislation, announced that, in view of Cannon's remarks, discussion of the reactor program items would be deferred until after the Easter recess of Congress.[22] In a speech delivered in California on May 22, Chairman Durham provided a popular rationale for what was about to happen. "There is a great deal of feeling in Congress

---

[19] H.R. Rep. No. 571, 85th Cong., 1st Sess. (1957), p. 2.

[20] Several interviewees suggested that Cannon and JCAE Democrats had discussed strategy before he launched his attack. This, however, has not been corroborated. For Cannon's attitude toward the Commission during Strauss's tenure, see Chap. VI, below.

[21] *Cong. Rec.*, 103 (April 16, 1957), 5790-5801.

[22] *FY 1958 Authorization Hearings* (1957), p. 73.

that greater review of the atomic power budget by Congress is necessary," he said. "As you may have heard, 'economy' is the watchword right now." [23] In the meantime, a series of informal meetings was being held between members of the JCAE, the Commission, and their staffs to consider various methods of increasing the scope of JCAE review of the Commission's reactor programs.[24]

On May 23, AEC witnesses, including Commissioner Libby and General Manager K.E. Fields, testified in executive session of the Subcommittee on Legislation on the substance of drafts that had been prepared. During this hearing JCAE members made it perfectly clear that the Commission's only choice was among the several proposed alternatives. Holifield's early statement set the tone:

> Some time ago your Commission was warned that the Atomic Energy Commission had lost its high estate in the minds of the Congress; that it had gotten itself embroiled in political areas and had made political decisions. . . . You are face to face with the grim fact of just exactly how you are going to be treated. You are going to be treated like the Agriculture Department and like the rest of the agencies from here on out, in my opinion, by the Congress. So you have to either make up your mind to work under that condition or not to work under it.[25]

The villain was clearly the Appropriations Committee, not the JCAE. Durham assured the AEC that the Joint Committee was only "trying to be helpful," but, "if you want to fight it out with the chairman of the Appropriations Committee, of course you can." Senator Gore added that Congressman Cannon was not the only obstacle AEC faced. Any one of the 435 members of the House, the Tennessean pointed out, could raise a point of order about the legality of appropriations. Republican Cole thought that the parliamentarian would be justified in not sustaining a point of order, but the issue was in doubt. "So to resolve any question or dispute," Cole advised, the Commission should comment on the JCAE proposals "and get down to something concrete here."

Commissioner Libby assured the subcommittee that the AEC would not be uncooperative, but his statement on behalf of the Commision was ambiguous. After much prodding, Libby finally admitted, "we do not want a change in the act." But he quickly qualified his statement by asking that, if the Committee thought such legislation necessary, "it be aimed as nearly as possible at specific phases of the program which are of concern to the Congress." Senator Anderson was hardly appeased:

---

[23] Remarks at General Electric Vallecitos Atomic Laboratory, JCAE press release, May 22, 1957.

[24] H.R. Rep. No. 571, 85th Cong., 1st Sess. (1957), p. 2.

[25] *Congressional Review Hearings* (1957), pp. 11-13.

> We have explained it over and over again. It isn't this committee which has raised the point of order. Now you tell this committee that you don't want authorizing legislation and then say "We hope you will use your judgment." We have no judgment to use. If the Commission feels it can get along without money for a power reactor development program and you have reached that decision, there is nothing we can do about it.[26]

Almost three weeks later, on June 10, the Committee met to put the finishing touches on a proposed bill which had been worked on by the JCAE and AEC staffs.[27] The effect of the bill was to increase markedly the powers of the JCAE over the civilian reactor program. It revised Section 261 to require the AEC to obtain authorization for funds before it could build any nonmilitary experimental reactor designed either to produce more than 10,000 thermal kilowatts of heat or to be used in the production of electric power and to require the AEC to obtain authorization for funds for cooperative programs (PDRP) with industry. In addition, it added a new Section 58 to require the AEC to submit to the Committee forty-five days in advance any plans to establish or revise any "fair price or guaranteed fair price period" for buy-back materials or "any criteria for the waiver of any charge for the use of a special nuclear material." [28] Not part of the JCAE bill but drawn up concurrently was a Committee proposal to include in authorization legislation a requirement that each AEC arrangement with private industry for reactor development be submitted to the JCAE for forty-five–day review.[29]

The "Durham bill," ostensibly framed to meet Cannon's objections, was informally cleared with the chairman of the Appropriations Committee of the House.[30] The Commission, said Strauss, was prepared to "live with" the revisions, but was by no means overjoyed. The AEC chairman added candidly: "If there is any implication or any feeling in your mind that we are going to take any steps to oppose this, let me disabuse you of that at once. But it would have been unfair and improper for me to have come in to give you the impression that we are happy about this."

---

[26] *Ibid.*, p. 12.

[27] On June 6, the Commission staff had indicated preliminary but reluctant agreement to the proposed bills to amend §261 and to add a new §111 to the annual authorizing legislation. The next day, Durham introduced the bill, H.R. 7992, in the House, and it was referred to the JCAE. Anderson introduced an identical bill, S. 2243, in the Senate on June 10.

[28] Thus the Joint Committee would be able in the authorizing process to review all price schedules to be paid for the production of plutonium under §56 or the waiver of use charges under §53 of the basic Atomic Energy Act. The forty-five–day prior notification could be waived by the JCAE.

[29] *Congressional Review Hearings* (1957), pp. 35-36.

[30] *Ibid.*, p. 73.

At this point, in order to impress JCAE views on Strauss, a Republican and three Democrats engaged in what appeared to be a less than spontaneous exchange:

> *Chairman Durham:* The only thing that I can see, and I feel that we are doing, is to try to act as an intermediary between the Commission and the Appropriations Committee. . . .
>
> *Representative Van Zandt:* While I am not a member of the Legislation Subcommittee, it appears that the wishes of one Member of Congress have forced this committee into our present position. I would like to know why, as a committee of Congress, we have to respond to the wishes of one Member of Congress.
>
> *Chairman Durham:* If you have a better solution, I would like to have it.
>
> *Representative Price:* We do not have to, but then, the only other recourse is to face points of order on the appropriations of the Commission. We do not have to do a thing.
>
> *Senator Anderson:* If we do not have to, why do we spend our time on it?
>
> *Representative Van Zandt:* Then it is not the whims and wishes of one individual.
>
> *Senator Anderson:* If the point of order is good, I do not think that is a whim. A point of order, I am pretty sure, is going to be good in the Senate, and they are pretty sure to be made in both places.
>
> *Representative Van Zandt:* If this Member's point of order is sustained, then the AEC receives no appropriations.[31]

Given a choice between two evils, the more extensive authorization requirement or a possible point of order and reprisal by Chairman Cannon, Strauss selected the former. The JCAE report indicated that the Commission agreed not to oppose the legislation and to cooperate in the future with the type of Congressional review and authorization proposed.

On June 10, immediately following executive hearings, the JCAE voted unanimously to report the Durham bill. Four days later, a report was filed. On June 19, after JCAE members explained that the bill satisfied the need for more extensive Congressional review of the atomic-energy budget and that the Committee was unanimous in its recommendation, the Senate passed S. 2243 by voice vote without debate. Five days later, the House passed the bill under suspension of the rules.[32] Thus the Senate

---

[31] *Ibid.*, pp. 42-43. It is interesting to note that, though the problem revolved around whether a point of order would be sustained, according to Durham no one on the Committee consulted with either the Senate or House parliamentarian on the question. *Ibid.*, p. 43. It seems, therefore, that JCAE members were less concerned with the merits of Cannon's charges than with the opportunity his attack afforded them for increasing their own authority.

[32] *Cong. Rec.*, 103 (June 19, 1957), 9635; (June 24, 1957), 10151-10156.

and House leaderships, in conjunction with a unanimous Joint Committee, provided another demonstration of the speed and ease with which a piece of important legislation could be sent through Congress when controversies were ironed out in advance.

■ USE OF EXPANDED POWERS

With the Durham bill enacted, the Committee then resumed its consideration of the authorization legislation for 1958 and proceeded to use its newly won prerogatives in shaping the substance of the civilian power program. That the Committee, or rather its Democratic majority, had less than complete success in this effort attests to the disparity between procedural powers per se and the successful utilization of those powers in a politically charged arena.

In the course of detailed scrutiny of each reactor project proposed by the Commission, the JCAE subcommittee sharply criticized the lack of progress in the reactor development program. On the conclusion of the public hearings, Holifield and members of the staff drafted a bill, and on July 9 Commissioners Strauss and Vance were given a chance to testify on the draft in executive session. Although the AEC had only one evening to study the proposal before being called on for comment, there was sufficient time for Strauss to become dissatisfied with several features of the JCAE draft. Strauss objected, first, to the fact that the Committee had added four reactor projects which had not been requested by the AEC or approved by the Bureau of the Budget.[33] He also objected to altering the basis of proposed cooperative arrangements under the second round of the power-demonstration-reactor program.[34] At the end of the hearing, Strauss

---

[33] In December, 1956, the Commission, yielding to JCAE pressure, requested from the Bureau of the Budget $150,000,000 for government construction of two large demonstration reactors and several small reactors. The request was reduced to $20,000,000 by the bureau, which felt that continuing reliance should be placed on private investment. At the same time, the AEC reached an understanding with the bureau that, if the Commission did not succeed in getting private industry to build two proposed reactors—a natural-uranium, heavy-water reactor and an aqueous, homogeneous reactor—the administration would support the AEC in a future request to Congress for funds for construction of these reactors by the government. The AEC thereupon solicited proposals for construction under the power-demonstration-reactor program, and two private groups responded. *FY 1959 Authorization Hearings* (1958), p. 663.

[34] The AEC had for many months been negotiating with five such organizations, but no contracts had as yet been concluded. Under the second round, the AEC contemplated that these consumer-owned utilities would provide land and conventional turbogenerating equipment at their own cost and would contract with a reactor manufacturer for construction of a power reactor for their systems. The AEC would then enter into a contract with the utility for financing the construction of the reactor on a fixed-price basis, with the utility assuming the risk of cost overruns. The AEC would own the reactor part of the power plant and would contract for the utility to operate the reactor for the AEC and to buy from the AEC the steam produced by it. The JCAE majority felt that this program was un-

stated that he had certain deep-seated convictions on the matters discussed, that he would give the JCAE proposal further consideration, and that he would then announce the Commission's views in a letter to the Committee.[35]

Not only was the AEC opposed, but the Committee itself was split on the contemplated revisions of the authorization request, with the Democrats in favor and Republicans in opposition. Holifield argued that, "sometimes we feel that maybe the Congress should set some of the policy in this Nation, and the administrative agencies should help to carry it out." Committee Republicans were not in disagreement on who should make policy, but only on what policies should be made. Nevertheless, in the few weeks following this session members of the subcommittee and the full Committee tried to work out compromises which would assure united support for the authorization bill. In addition, Durham, Holifield, and Strauss tried to reach agreement on the various provisions in dispute.[36]

Some progress was made as Democrats reduced their demands. Holifield's original bill called for construction by the AEC of four reactors (costing a total of $165,000,000) for which the AEC had not sought funds. After bargaining, the Committee's additions were considerably curtailed. One project, a heavy-water reactor, was dropped. A gas-cooled reactor and a plutonium recycle reactor were retained, and a dual-purpose reactor was changed from a $95,000,000 proposal for construction to a $3,000,000 proposal only for development-design and engineering. The total cost of Committee additions was therefore reduced by some $58,000,000. On another contentious issue, the status of the second-round cooperative and municipal projects, little headway was made. Democrats stood fast, and the bill retained the provision that the AEC contract directly with manufacturers for the entire second round. During Committee deliberations, Republicans made three unsuccessful attempts to amend this provision so that the Commission would have discretion in dealing directly with manufacturers or suppliers of equipment.[37] On July 23, the Subcommittee on Legislation voted four to three along party lines in favor of the authorization bill. Two days later the Committee voted eleven to seven, with Senator Dworshak joining the Democrats, in favor of H.R. 8996.

If the majority-sponsored bill was controversial, the majority report was even more so. It specified various technical features of the AEC reactor

---

realistic and economically unsound from the standpoint of the utilities and proposed that the AEC contract directly with the reactor manufacturers, thereby relieving the utilities of this burden. The AEC assailed the JCAE's action as unwarranted interference with its discretion in contracting and as upsetting all past negotiations, which in one or two of the five cases had reached the point at which execution of the contracts was imminent.

[35] *Ibid.*, p. 702.

[36] *Ibid.*, pp. 655, 686.

[37] *Cong. Rec.*, 103 (Aug. 16, 1957), 15012.

projects and went so far as to designate the location, contractor, and branch chief within the AEC who should be responsible. The report also prescribed in considerable detail the nature of the contractual arrangements to be made by the Commission with publicly owned and cooperative organizations and set forth general principles for altering contractual requirements with the qualification that they would need "adaptation to the circumstances of each contractual situation." [38]

The frustration of JCAE Democrats with the reactor program delays explains in part the tone and content of the report. All possible pressure, they believed, had to be exerted on executive officials who had demonstrated hostility toward governmental leadership in the reactor-acceleration field. But JCAE Republicans in a separate report vigorously disputed the majority document. Nor did the Executive show any signs of being cowed into submission as a result of Democratic criticism and detailed directives. In a letter to Rep. James Patterson, a Republican member of the JCAE, Chairman Strauss stated that, no matter how Congress might act on the authorization legislation, the Commission would not be bound by the Committee report.[39]

Four days after the Democratic report was filed, Republicans announced their strategy in the coming floor battle. At a meeting of Republican legislative leaders with President Eisenhower on August 6, the decision was made to fight the authorization bill on the basis of "public power favoritism." At this meeting, Strauss stated his objections to the Committee's detailed direction as to the types of reactors, locations, and contractors, considering such particulars to be a transgression on the powers of the executive branch. His main point, however, was that the provisions inserted by the Democratic majority "would constitute a substantial start toward a program for government-owned atomic-power facilities." The

---

[38] The report stated that it "would appear essential" that the natural-uranium gas-cooled reactor have higher-temperature fuel elements, that it be under the direction of Admiral Rickover, and that it be carried on by the Westinghouse Bettis organization. Quoting the testimony of W. E. Johnson, general manager of the Hanford Atomic Products operation of General Electric, the report concluded that, since plutonium-recycle work had been carried out at Hanford, "it would appear appropriate" that the experimental recycle reactor be constructed there. H.R. Rep. No. 978, 85th Cong., 1st Sess. (1957), pp. 26-27, 17-19. It is a common practice of the JCAE to write its legislation in rather general terms and to attempt to direct the AEC's interpretation and implementation of the statute through statements of intention and expectation. For example, in reporting out a bill in 1962, the Committee included at least fifteen references to its "hope," "expectation," and "intention." H.R. Rep. No. 1966, 87th Cong., 2nd Sess. (1962).

[39] Strauss wrote on August 8, ". . . if the bill is enacted in its present form, the Commission will have to determine in each case whether in its judgment the Nation's best interests will be served by following the majority report's approach in matters not mandatory under the authorization bill itself, reasonably construed, and take the course that the Commission's own discretion dictates." Reprinted in *Cong. Rec.,* 103 (Aug. 8, 1957), 14121-14122.

same day, the House Republican Policy Committee met, and Minority Leader Martin announced that almost all the members agreed to support the administration's effort to defeat the Democratic program.[40]

Democrats in the meantime were attempting to round up the votes necessary to put through their measure. Holifield took the floor of the House on August 5 to explain the authorization bill. He stressed the fact that the Joint Committee had usually been proved right in its recommendations to the Commission and Congress.[41] The next day, Anderson described the bill in the Senate, emphasizing that other atomic-energy legislation (a salary increase for AEC executives, the International Atomic Energy Agency (IAEA) participation bill, and governmental indemnification) was waiting on passage of the authorizing bill. The JCAE vice-chairman threatened that, if the Republicans succeeded in killing the Democratic program, "Congress should be consistent and consider saving the $500,000,000 or more in obligations in the indemnity bill and avoid any charge of favoritism to the private power companies." He went on to decry the raising of the public–versus–private-power controversy by the administration and Congressional Republicans and accusations of socialism hurled by House JCAE Republicans in their separate report.[42]

When the bill was brought up in the House on August 9, debate was lengthy and heated. It is doubtful that any attitudes were changed as a result of Republican charges of socialism, favoritism, public-power advocacy run rampant, and atomic-power federalism, or Democratic countercharges that the reactor program was at a complete standstill. Anyone familiar with the Gore-Holifield struggle in the House the year before could have ventured a good guess as to the outcome of this battle. Of course, in this case there was no possibility of recommitting the bill to the Joint Committee without threatening the entire AEC program. Republican stategy was therefore to strike out, by the amending process, sections of the authorization bill which did not satisfy the administration.

Led by JCAE Republicans, the committee of the whole passed three amendments striking out controversial sections of the Committee bill. First, Patterson's amendment to strike the $3,000,000 reactor design study was accepted. Then, Van Zandt's amendment to strike the two reactor

---

[40] *N.Y. Times,* Aug. 7, 1957.

[41] To demonstrate the Committee's superior judgment, the much-used illustrations of the hydrogen bomb, the "Nautilus," the weapons-expansion program, the Shippingport reactor, and the first five-year reactor program were cited. *Cong. Rec.,* 103 (Aug. 5, 1957), 13685.

[42] Anderson made a particular point of the fact that Republican Senator Dworshak voted for the bill in committee and mentioned: "I have heard the Senator from Idaho associated with many things, but nobody, in his wildest stretches of imagination, ever accused him of advocating socialism." In answering criticisms that the Democrats were trying to help certain private firms, Anderson jibed: "I do not know how we could favor great companies like that and still be socialistic. . . ." *Ibid.* (Aug. 6, 1957), 13740-13746.

construction projects was agreed to. Finally, the House passed Cole's amendment to strike the provisions concerning the second round, retaining only the authorization sum of $132,621,000. When the committee of the whole reported the bill, as amended, back to the House, Durham requested roll calls on the three amendments. (See Table V-1.) Voting paralleled

TABLE V-1

HOUSE ROLL-CALL VOTES ON H.R. 8996

House voting	Vote 1		Vote 2		Vote 3	
	Yea	Nay	Yea	Nay	Yea	Nay
JCAE members:						
Democrats	0	5	0	5	0	5
Republicans	4	0	4	0	4	0
Entire House:						
Total votes	197	201	211	188	213	185
Democrats	20	195	35	182	50	166
Republicans	177	6	176	6	163	19
Party cohesion: *						
Democrats	—	.81	—	.68	—	.54
Republicans	.93	—	.93	—	.79	—

* Party cohesion is based on Stuart Rice's "index of cohesion"; see note 109, Chap. IV.

Vote 1: Patterson amendment to eliminate $3,000,000 authorization for a plutonium reactor study. Rejected (August 9, 1957).
Vote 2: Van Zandt amendment to eliminate $40,000,000 authorization for construction of a natural uranium reactor and $15,000,000 authorization for plutonium recycle plant. Accepted (August 9, 1957).
Vote 3: Cole amendment to authorize $132,621,000 for the cooperative power-reactor-demonstration program and delete provision requiring the AEC to construct and operate the plants. Accepted (August 9, 1957).

closely that of the year before, when Gore-Holifield was defeated.[43] On each vote, Republican and Democratic House leaders, JCAE members, and Congressional rank-and-file stood united in opposing partisan camps. Only the Committee's plutonium reactor study was salvaged.[44]

Senate voting was another matter entirely. As in the House, Senate

[43] Tabulations are based on *Congressional Quarterly Almanac,* XIII, *op. cit.,* 312, 366. Besides Republicans, mainly conservative Southern Democrats and Democrats from coal-producing areas voted against the gas-cooled reactor and plutonium recycle reactor. Three were from Kentucky, four from Pennsylvania, five from Texas, eight from Virginia, and four from West Virginia. See *Forum Memo,* September 1957, p. 11.

[44] After roll calls on the amendments, H.R. 8996 was passed by a 383-14 vote, with all members of the Committee as well as Republican and Democratic leaders supporting the bill.

debate was extended and spirited, with all issues adequately discussed. First, Dworshak proposed that the $40,000,000 for the gas-cooled reactor be limited to $500,000 only for a development-design and engineering study. On a party vote, the Republicans were barely defeated. (See Table V-2, Vote 1.) Thereupon, Hickenlooper introduced an amendment similar to the one offered by Van Zandt in the House, but this was defeated by a wider margin, with Dworshak voting with Democratic members of the JCAE. (See Table V-2, Vote 2.) By this time, it was apparent that the Joint Committee would emerge unscathed. Thus, in introducing his final amendment—to eliminate the new second-round contract provision—Hickenlooper prefaced his remarks with the comment: "I think I am aware of the mood of the Senate in this matter. Action on the last amendment was certainly indicative." [45] When a vote was taken, Hickenlooper's amendment was easily defeated. (See Table V-2, Vote 3.) The entire bill, in the form reported by the JCAE, then passed by a voice vote. This time, the administration suffered the major setback. Differences between the House and Senate bills would have to be resolved by a conference committee.

The authorization bill which finally emerged from conference reduced the Democratic reactor program to very modest proportions. The $3,000,000 for the plutonium reactor study, which had gone through both houses intact (chiefly because of its implications for national defense), was included in the conference recommendation. Also retained was the $15,-000,000 for the plutonium recycle reactor, which had been struck from the House bill but included in the Senate version. But the natural-uranium gas-cooled reactor—originally proposed for construction at a cost of $40,-000,000—was limited to a design and engineering study costing $3,000,-000.[46] Although the compromises included at least a start on all the Democrats' approved additions to the reactor program, the outcome of the design and engineering studies was left in doubt. On the gas-cooled reactor, for example, even if the Commission reported that the project were feasible, funds would still have to be authorized for construction. Then Congress would be able to decide whether the government or private enterprise was to build the reactor. The administration showed no hesitancy on this score. In signing the authorization bill the day after the conference report was accepted by Congress, President Eisenhower repeated his opposition "to the expenditure of public money for the construction and operation by the Government of any large-scale power reactor, or any prototype thereof,

---

[45] *Cong. Rec.*, 103 (Aug. 16, 1957), 15038.

[46] The Commission was directed to submit to the JCAE not later than April 1, 1958, a report on its design for the gas-cooled reactor, including cost estimates and a schedule of construction. See H.R. Rep. No. 1204, 85th Cong., 1st Sess. (1957).

TABLE V-2

SENATE ROLL-CALL VOTES ON S. 2674

Senate voting	Vote 1 Yea	Vote 1 Nay	Vote 2 Yea	Vote 2 Nay	Vote 3 Yea	Vote 3 Nay
JCAE members:						
Democrats	0	5	0	5	0	5
Republicans	4	0	3	1	4	0
Entire Senate:						
Total votes	37	40	34	42	34	42
Democrats	4	37	2	38	2	37
Republicans	33	3	32	4	32	5
Party cohesion: *						
Democrats	—	.80	—	.90	—	.90
Republicans	.83	—	.78	—	.73	—

* Party cohesion is based on Stuart Rice's "index of cohesion"; see note 109, Chap. IV.

Vote 1: Dworshak amendment to authorize $500,000 for design and engineering work on a gas-cooled natural-uranium reactor, instead of $40,000,000 for construction of the reactor. Rejected (August 16, 1957).

Vote 2: Hickenlooper amendment to eliminate authorization of $40,000,000 for gas-cooled natural-uranium reactor and $15,000,000 for plutonium recycle plant. Rejected (August 16, 1957).

Vote 3: Hickenlooper amendment to authorize $132,621,000 for the cooperative power-reactor-demonstration program and delete provision requiring the AEC to contract directly with manufacturers and engineers for construction and with cooperatives for operation of the plants. Rejected (August 16, 1957).

unless private enterprise has first received reasonable opportunity to bear and share the cost." [47]

The Democrats won their most substantial victory on the question of contractual arrangements with cooperatives and publicly owned agencies. The conference report retained, but modified, the Senate language calling for the AEC to contract directly for construction of four power reactors under the second round of the PDRP. However, it permitted the AEC to continue with one project, the Consumers Public Power District of Nebraska reactor, under the original concept. The conference committee also added provisions for the AEC to dismantle the second-round reactors or sell them

[47] *N.Y. Times,* Aug. 22, 1957. During Senate consideration of the conference report, Senator Javits mentioned the inability of Congress to direct the executive branch to spend funds on projects it had opposed. "It is always difficult," said Javits, "to force money on a commission or governmental agency when it does not want the money. When we try to force it to take the money, we are likely to get the result that we saw when Congress tried to force President Truman to accept $8,000,000 for the Air Force. He would not be forced to take it." *Cong. Rec.,* 103 (Aug. 20, 1957), 15315.

to the utilities if it decided that their usefulness in research had ended, but in any case not later than ten years after construction. In no event would the government remain in the business of producing electric power.

Thus was resolved, temporarily at least, the question of public versus private power and the extent of the AEC reactor development program. Unresolved was an issue implicit in the authorization controversy —how far the Committee could go in determining the atomic-energy program. In the past, the JCAE had certainly "moved the Commission's program along." But there had been no conflict, because the JCAE and the Executive regarded themselves as joint venturers. Accordingly, implementation was left to administrative officials. Now the Committee majority and the Executive were at odds. As a result, Republicans charged that the Committee was specifying the implementation of certain policy decisions and involving itself in administrative details. "What is being attempted here," Hickenlooper maintained, "is to dictate to the Commission what it shall do . . . in a matter which should be within the administrative province of the Commission." Congress, in short, should remain concerned with broad policy only and ought not to usurp executive prerogative and responsibility.[48]

There is obviously no sharp demarcation between policy and administration. In the 1958 authorization legislation, the broad policy advocated by the Democratic majority was federal leadership in the civilian reactor program. This policy was clearly contrary to the wishes of the administration and the majority of AEC commissioners. Therefore, JCAE Democrats had good reason to doubt that executive officials would carry out the desires of Congress if they were phrased as nothing more than a general directive or formula. After years of frustration, climaxed by the defeat of the Gore-Holifield bill at the hands of the administration, JCAE Democrats naturally felt that, in order to ensure any action at all, they would have to spell out a program as fully as possible. They felt that they had authority to do this. Only a few months before the authorization battle, Congress had assumed significantly broader authority for the civilian reactor program. Republicans and Democrats on the Committee were united in seeking this authority, the only difference being that the latter had immediate plans for putting it to use.

Assuming that the Committee has, on behalf of Congress, a policymaking function,[49] the question remains whether authorization legislation is the best vehicle for substantive policy decisions. House Republican mem-

---

[48] H.R. Rep. No. 978, 85th Cong., 1st Sess. (1957), p. 54, and *Cong. Rec.*, 103 (Aug. 16, 1957), 15037.

[49] During debate in the House, Durham posed the problem as follows: ". . . who is setting the policy, and program, the Congress or the AEC? I believe it should be the Congress and that is what we are trying to do in a small way." *Ibid.* (Aug. 8, 1957), 14116.

bers of the JCAE declared that it was not, arguing that the place to resolve differences of political opinion was "not in connection with the legislation respecting the funding of the Commission's operations, but in connection with substantive legislation." [50] But, since the Democrats had failed in 1956 when they resorted to substantive legislation, they turned to authorizing legislation, which offered two distinct advantages. First, it was unlikely that an authorization bill would be defeated in Congress. It might be amended by the more conservative House, but it would probably be passed intact by the more liberal Senate, laying the basis for negotiation of a compromise in conference committee. In the case of substantive legislation, on the other hand, the House alone might kill the bill, and no conference could take place. Second, whereas the president might well veto substantive legislation with which he disagreed, it was unlikely that he would veto an authorization bill because of his objections to a few provisions.

For strategic reasons, JCAE Democrats in 1957 chose to effect their civilian reactor policy through authorization legislation. They made it clear that such issues would henceforth be resolved in authorization bills, rather than by substantive legislation. Congress has therefore never enacted a basic national policy with regard to the civilian reactor program; rather, it has legislated on a project-by-project basis from year to year.

Because of changed conditions in 1958, policy-making through authorization legislation aroused less controversy than it had the year before. Before the fiscal 1959 bill was reported by the Committee, Lewis Strauss was replaced as AEC chairman by John A. McCone. On July 2, McCone was approved by a friendly Senate section of the JCAE "without dissent," and a week later he was confirmed by the Senate. Both McCone and the JCAE Democrats were prepared to attempt to establish a new era of harmony and cooperation. As Chairman Durham stated in reporting the bill to the House, "In a sense, our consideration of the AEC authorization bill will be the first test of what could be a new era of relationship between the Congress, including the Joint Committee, and the executive branch, particularly the AEC with its new Chairman." Ranking Republican Van Zandt agreed, citing the authorization bill as "an effort by members of the Joint Committee to bury past differences of personality and policy to reach agreement." [51]

The new spirit of "sweet reasonableness" which resulted from the

---

[50] H.R. Rep. No. 978, 85th Cong., 1st Sess. (1957), p. 52. When the Gore-Holifield bill was debated on the floor the preceding year, Republicans had quite a different argument. At that time, they maintained that there was no need for the reactor-acceleration authorization, since the AEC already had the authority to embark on the program included in the legislation. All it had to do was request authorization from Congress.

[51] *Cong. Rec.*, 104 (July 14, 1958), 13696, 13698.

departure of Strauss and the Commission's new outline of a broad program of reactor prototypes and full-scale reactors for development and construction in the period 1959-1963 stilled the private–versus–public-power controversy in 1958.[52] Avoidance of this divisive issue enabled members of the Joint Committee to reconcile less important differences and agree on an atomic-power program more extensive than that desired by the Eisenhower administration. With the Committee united against a budget-minded Executive, the AEC, under its new chairman, remained benevolently neutral. The Bureau of the Budget, as presidential economy spokesman, replaced the AEC as the Committee's antagonist.

After hearings on the Commission's authorization bill, the JCAE decided to (1) include all the projects requested by the AEC and approved by the Bureau of the Budget; (2) restore some projects requested by the AEC and disapproved by the bureau; and (3) add some projects, which, though generally favored by the AEC because of budgetary ceilings imposed by the administration, were never formally submitted to the Bureau of the Budget. (See Table V-3.) The JCAE excoriated the bureau in its report on the authorization bill:

> The Joint Committee is seriously concerned over the dominant role assumed by the Bureau of the Budget in the atomic energy construction program. Again and again, the committee was advised that the Bureau had disapproved a project, or had withheld funds on a project recommended by the Commission and approved by the Congress. This the committee does not approve.[53]

The largest project added by the Joint Committee was a plutonium production reactor to be located at Hanford, which had been proposed by the AEC but eliminated by the Budget Bureau.[54] Although the AEC had originally requested $120,000,000 for the plutonium reactor, the Committee added another $25,000,000 to ensure that the reactor could later be converted to produce electric power as well as plutonium. In addition

---

[52] The AEC long-term program statement, according to Senator Anderson, represented a genuine step forward and an effort to be responsive to JCAE suggestions. Although the Committee found that the announced program had limitations, Anderson stated: "I am willing to let the dead past bury its dead, and go on to happier days. There is certainly a need for a new era in atomic power development." Address at fourth annual meeting, Nuclear Energy Writers Association, New York City, June 18, 1958; JCAE press release, June 19, 1958. See also *Forum Memo,* July 1958, pp. 3-9.

[53] S. Rep. No. 1793, 85th Cong., 2d Sess. (1958), p. 6.

[54] In the fiscal year 1958 authorization bill, it should be recalled, Congress authorized the Commission to make a development-design and engineering study on a plutonium production reactor. On April 1, 1958, the Commission submitted to the JCAE a report on the design of the reactor. The Committee studied the report and held hearings. The Subcommittee on Military Applications then appointed an advisory panel to look into the need for additional plutonium production facilities.

to the $145,000,000 for the Hanford reactor, the JCAE increased the scope of the Commission's physical-research program. Of a total of eighteen projects requested by the AEC Research Division for its 1959 budget, only five were included by the Commission in its submission to the Budget Bureau, and only three of these were approved by the bureau.[55] Since the Committee felt that the need for new research facilities was urgent, it requested and received from the AEC a list of high-priority physical-research construction items and simply added them to the authorization bill. Over the objections of the Bureau of the Budget, the Committee inserted under the category of "physical research" fourteen projects costing $39,000,000 in addition to the three items included in the original budget request. There was not a dissenting voice raised on the Committee on any one of these projects.[56] Finally, the Committee included in the bill several additional design and engineering studies of promising new reactor types. The Joint Committee increased the Bureau allowance from $193,379,000 to $386,679,000, nearly doubling the authorization request submitted by the executive branch. (See Table V-3.)

Despite the major Committee revisions and the opposition of the Bureau of the Budget, H.R. 13121, the fiscal 1959 authorization bill, had little difficulty clearing the House. Durham sounded the keynote, stressing the unanimity of the Joint Committee. To ensure that the controversy over public versus private power would not recur, he noted that many of the projects added by the JCAE related to national defense and basic research. Three other projects included by the Committee, the chairman pointed out, were restricted as follows: (1) they were limited to design and engineering studies; (2) they could be constructed either by private industry or the AEC; (3) none carried a commitment for later government construction; and (4) in any case, government construction would require specific Congressional authorization and appropriation. What was crucial, however, was that JCAE Republicans took the floor in favor of this bill. Patterson endorsed the Committee bill, though he noted that the Commission and White House were opposed to certain portions of it. The key address was undoubtedly made by the ranking Republican House member of the Joint Committee, James Van Zandt, who described the bill as a well-balanced program deserving of bipartisan support. "Therefore," he stated, "it was my hope and desire to avoid disagreement and a fight on the floor of the House today, and to be able to agree to a program which the new chairman of the Atomic Energy Commission can carry out in a spirit of cooperation and friendship. . . ."[57]

---

[55] S. Rep. No. 1793, 85th Cong., 2d Sess. (1958), pp. 14-17.
[56] *Cong. Rec.,* 104 (July 14, 1958), 13697, 13710-13711.
[57] *Ibid.,* 13696, 13698, 13707-13709, 13712.

TABLE V-3

FISCAL YEAR 1959 AUTHORIZATION LEGISLATION

Projects requested by the AEC, allowed by the Bureau of the Budget, and action taken by the JCAE

	AEC request to Budget Bureau	Budget Bureau allowance	JCAE action
Report submitted to Congress (S. 3788 and H.R. 12459)	$193,379,000	$193,379,000	$193,379,000
Department of Defense small plant reactors	30,000,000	0	0
Tanker propulsion plant	7,000,000	0	0
Heavy-water power reactor	65,000,000	0	0
Materials and engineering test reactors	35,000,000	0	0
Production reactor, Hanford	120,000,000	0	145,000,000
Design study, natural-uranium heavy-water reactor	*	0	2,500,000
Design studies on three reactors	4,000,000	0	6,000,000
Design study, advanced reactor	0	0	750,000
Metals and ceramics building, Oak Ridge	6,500,000	0	6,500,000
Metals development building, Ames, Iowa	1,900,000	0	1,900,000
Accelerator improvements, University of California Radiation Laboratory (UCRL), increase by Joint Committee			800,000
Two accelerator improvements, Pennsylvania State University	0	0	950,000
Cyclotron, UCRL	0	0	5,000,000
Central Research Laboratory addition, Oak Ridge	0	0	3,500,000
Chemistry building addition, UCRL	0	0	2,000,000
Chemistry hot laboratory, Argonne	0	0	4,400,000
Expansion of stable-isotope production capacity, Oak Ridge	0	0	900,000
High-energy physics building, Columbia University	0	0	500,000
Particle-accelerator program addition, Harvard-MIT	0	0	1,300,000
High-flux research reactor, Brookhaven	0	0	1,000,000
Research and engineering reactor, Argonne	0	0	1,000,000
Van de Graaff accelerator, Argonne	0	0	2,500,000
Cyclotron, Oak Ridge	0	0	3,000,000
Research reactor, Ames Laboratory	0	0	3,800,000
Total	$462,779,000	$193,379,000	$386,679,000

* Included in operations budget

Source: S. Rep. No. 1793, 85th Cong., 2d Sess. (1958), p. 26.

The only House opposition to the bill came from Rep. Cleveland M. Bailey (D., W. Va.), who argued that its passage would damage the nation's coal industry. Since the administration could round up few congressmen willing to make the fight against the JCAE bill, it was up to Democrat Bailey to introduce a letter from Eisenhower, which stated the President's objections to the convertible plutonium reactor, the added research facilities, and the reactor design projects with mandatory reporting requirements. The letter plainly had little effect on the outcome, for the bill passed a few minutes later by a voice vote.[58]

The story was almost the same when the bill came before the Senate a day later. Vice-Chairman Anderson, opening debate, noted that House passage without amendment was a tribute to the "harmonious consideration of the bill in the Joint Committee and the fact that the bill was reported without a dissenting vote." Although the President opposed nearly every project added by the Joint Committee, no Republican JCAE member was willing to take the administration's side on the floor of the Senate. It was left to Sen. Leverett Saltonstall (R., Mass.) to act on behalf of the administration. He introduced an amendment to reduce the authorization for the plutonium production reactor from $145,000,000 to $120,000,000 by striking its convertibility feature. Hickenlooper supported the Saltonstall proposal, describing the dual-purpose feature, no matter "how it is dressed up or how it is painted," as favoring public power; but, significantly, he did not oppose any of the other changes made by the JCAE. Although the Department of Defense had not laid down a requirement for more plutonium, and despite the fact that the President and the Bureau of the Budget opposed the plutonium reactor, Hickenlooper felt justified in supporting the item because the AEC had requested it from the Budget Bureau.[59] After perfunctory debate, the amendment was rejected by a voice vote and the AEC authorization bill then passed.

Because several amendments offered by Saltonstall were accepted by Anderson and agreed to by the Senate, a conference between the House and Senate was necessary. An amendment to have the Department of Defense certify jointly with the AEC the substitution of new military projects in the Commission's budget was abandoned by the conferrees because of strong objections by the AEC. The other Saltonstall amendment provided that the AEC should not be obligated to proceed with the gas-cooled reactor project, either as a government-financed project or as a cooperative arrangement with industry, if industry "is prepared and proposes to design, construct, and operate" such a reactor at its own expense. This amendment was changed significantly in conference. The conference report was sup-

[58] *Ibid.*, 13712, 13715.

[59] *Ibid.* (July 15, 1958), 13802-13803, 13810.

ported unanimously by JCAE managers (except for Senator Bricker, who was absent) and agreed to by the House and Senate. In concluding discussion of the fiscal 1959 bill, the Senate Democratic majority leader lauded Clinton Anderson for rapid action on the authorization measure in committee, on the floor, and in conference.[60]

President Eisenhower signed the bill into law, but at the same time issued a strongly worded statement opposing the JCAE additions. He said that he considered it unsound to proceed with the plutonium production reactor and its convertibility features. He advised Congress to withhold appropriations for the authorized gas-cooled power reactor and questioned the urgency of design studies for four more reactors and the construction of additional research facilities. In conclusion, the President said: "I feel obliged to urge the Congress to guard more vigilantly against the ever present tendency to burden the government with programs . . . the relative urgency and essentiality of which have not been solidly determined."[61] Despite Eisenhower's plea, Congress on August 20 passed an appropriations bill nearer to the wishes of the JCAE than to those of the Executive.

In 1958, there was little doubt that the Joint Committee had won its authorization battle with the President and the Bureau of the Budget.[62] Thus, when partisan considerations were not at stake and when ideological questions relating to public versus private power or the role of the federal government in economic affairs did not divide the Committee, it was assured of strong Congressional support, no matter what the attitude of the executive branch.[63]

---

[60] *Ibid.*, 13803, 13819; (July 22, 1958), 14641-14643, 14589.

[61] Quoted in *Forum Memo,* August 1958, p. 7.

[62] However, victory in the legislative arena was not necessarily final. Although the President might not veto either an authorization or appropriation bill, he did have the option of spending or not spending the funds appropriated for the projects he opposed. In fact, work on several of the physical-research construction projects authorized by the JCAE was not begun in 1959. *FY 1960 Authorization Hearings* (1959), p. 18.

[63] The reverse, however, is not true. In 1961 and 1962, the JCAE, supported by the AEC and the Kennedy administration, attempted to enact legislation to permit waste steam from the Hanford reactor to be converted into electricity. The Committee-sponsored bills—a 1961 authorization provision and a 1962 amendment to the authorization bill—were defeated in the House by a coalition of Republicans, Southern Democrats, and Democrats from coal-producing regions. In 1962, although the administration and all JCAE House members except Van Zandt supported a measure to permit the AEC to contract with a group of public utilities, it was overwhelmingly defeated. The Senate, however, agreed to the Hanford project, necessitating a conference. As in 1961, Van Zandt offered a motion to instruct the House conferrees not to agree to the Senate's action on the Hanford proposal. This time, however, the motion was defeated by the House, and the JCAE conference committee reported a bill authorizing the AEC to sell the steam produced by the Hanford reactor. In September, 1962, the House reversed its previous position by defeating Van Zandt's recommittal motion and approving the conference report. The Senate perfunctorily agreed to the conference report. See *Cong. Rec.* (daily ed., Aug. 29, 1962), 16952-16959; (daily ed., Sept. 14, 1962), 18373-18380; (daily ed., Sept. 18, 1962), 18656-

■ ISSUES, INFLUENCE, AND DEBATE

Certain additional conclusions emerge when the role of the Joint Committee on Atomic Energy in regular legislation (the subject of Chapter IV) is considered together with its role in authorizing legislation. Throughout its career as legislator, the ability of the JCAE to influence policy decisions has depended primarily on the nature of the issue at hand. Similarly, the role of Congressional debate has been closely tied to the nature of the legislative proposal before Congress. As a rule, there has been a remarkably close relationship among issues, Committee influence, and Congressional debate. The more controversial the issue, the less cohesive the Committee and the less decisive its recommendations to Congress are. The cohesion of the Committee and the decisiveness of its recommendations on the floor are naturally greater on a noncontroversial issue, and thus there is little floor debate on issues the Committee endorses unanimously and considerable debate on issues a JCAE minority—especially a partisan minority—opposes.

Since 1954, especially, three major types of problems have come before the JCAE for consideration, decision, and recommendation. The first has involved national security and foreign affairs. Those issues which have been encompassed in legislation—the Euratom bill, the IAEA proposal, information exchanges, and many items of authorization bills—have been handled by a cohesive and bipartisan JCAE. Differences either within the Committee or between the Committee and the executive branch on national-security proposals have been minor and easily reconciled.

A second type of problem has involved the respective powers of the legislative and executive branches. Although the JCAE has concerned itself with the protection and expansion of its own prerogatives, it has generally argued that the primary issue has been the necessity for Congressional safeguards in the face of an increasingly powerful Executive. Questions of safeguards arose during Committee consideration of several proposals: the 1954 act, Euratom, and the military-exchange legislation. The JCAE's drive to obtain and then expand its authorizing authority clearly illustrates the Committee's desire to achieve greater and more effective control of the atomic-energy program. On any question of Committee authority, JCAE members have united against an Executive reluctant to allow its flexibility to be curtailed by any further increase in Congressional power.

The most controversial legislation, however, has involved the ci-

18657. Also, *N.Y. Times,* Sept. 15, 1962. The controversy that began in 1959 was apparently ended. The Democratic majority had tailored its original demands to win the support of the Republican JCAE members (with the exception of Van Zandt) and with administration support had finally won the Hanford battle.

vilian reactor acceleration program, the thorny issue of public versus private power, and the role of government in nuclear power development. Here, the otherwise-cohesive Joint Committee has generally divided along partisan lines, with Democrats supporting an expanded program under government leadership and Republicans defending the privately led program under an economy-minded administration.

On the first two types of problems, the JCAE has been amazingly cohesive and therefore very influential. Its recommendations, or compromises not too wide of the mark, have generally been accepted by the Executive and later ratified by Congress. On the third problem, however, the usually monolithic committee has fragmented into two opposing wings. As a result, JCAE influence on domestic power issues has been significantly reduced.

Nevertheless, whatever the type of legislative issue, the JCAE has been an unusually influential Congressional committee. It has not only considered bills submitted by the AEC, for example, but has been instrumental in fashioning the bills prior to actual introduction and formal referral to the Committee for action. During the several stages of JCAE consideration of a bill, the overriding goal of both the Committee and the AEC has been consensus. If the proposal were initiated within the executive branch, JCAE modifications have had to be accepted lest no bill at all be reported to Congress. If, however, the proposal were initiated by the Committee or, as has most often been the case, by the Democratic majority, the JCAE has had to meet executive objections in order to preclude serious opposition when the bill was reported. Thus, consensus has served the interests of both the Committee and the Executive, and each has consequently modified its demands from time to time. On issues involving national security or foreign arrangements, the Joint Committee has been eminently able to tailor executive requests to its own wishes. On issues relating to legislative or Committee powers, the JCAE has also been successful in writing restrictions into executive proposals. On both types of issues, the executive branch has been more disposed to satisfy the Committee than to risk JCAE opposition and thereby jeopardize its legislation altogether.

Even on the civilian power issue, there have been meaningful attempts to reach agreement. In an effort to win at least neutrality from the Republican administration, the JCAE Democratic majority repeatedly scaled down its original reactor acceleration demands in order to bridge the wide gap between the two political parties. But whenever the administration took a strong stand against a JCAE bill, as on Gore-Holifield, or against Committee additions to an AEC bill, as on the fiscal 1958 authorization, final decision was taken from the Committee and placed with Congress. And even when the Committee majority and the administration were in agreement, as on the Cole-Hickenlooper bill, if issues were politically charged, decisions were made by Congress, not by the Committee. The Committee sometimes has had a last chance to reshape the legislation in conference, but here, too, significant restraints have been imposed on its discretionary powers.

When the Committee and Executive are at odds and JCAE members follow their party leaderships, debate is usually extensive and probing. Both sides have ample opportunity to argue their position. But when the Committee and the Executive have ironed out disagreements in advance and have come before the Congress united behind a legislative proposal, there is little or no debate at all. JCAE members pride themselves on their unanimity and the endorsement of the executive branch. In 1959, for example, when the Committee reported an AEC authorization bill, JCAE unanimity was illustrated by glowing comments from members about the new era of Committee-Commission cooperation. But the authorization legislation was hardly discussed. This brought forth an interesting response by Rep. Thomas B. Curtis (R., Mo.), who said:

> Unanimity sometimes results from an overzealous desire on the part of the committee to control the decisions. Frequently the most helpful manner in which a committee can explain a matter to the House is through pointing up the differences of opinion that occurred within the committee during the hearings and in executive session. Certainly unanimity should never be used as an excuse, as it has been here, to avoid discussion and explanation to the House membership.[64]

Representative Curtis did not single out the JCAE for criticism, but noted that its behavior was a manifestation of the growing tendency of committees to decide for the House issues that came before them.

Although committees are theoretically creatures of their respective houses, delegated the duties of studying matters within their jurisdictions and then reporting their findings and recommendations, they have in fact exercised decisive leadership on legislative matters. For example, the House Committee on Ways and Means exercises overwhelming influence on revenue measures. These usually come before the House with "closed" rules, under which debate is limited and amendments—except those sponsored by members of the committee itself—forbidden. Similarly, there is little Congressional debate on military appropriations after members of the military appropriations subcommittee assure their colleagues that they have not been approving "blank checks" but have been supporting programs based on voluminous justifications, plans, and statistics.

It is not unusual in the legislative process for deliberation and

---

[64] *Cong. Rec.*, 105 (June 15, 1959), 10829.

crucial decisions to take place outside the legislative chamber. There is certainly discussion of proposals, but emphasis is on discussion in committee.[65] If the committee, after examination, reaches agreement on a bill, the function of the legislature may be reduced to merely authenticating the agreement. Therefore, the nature of committee discussion is of paramount importance. The Joint Committee on Atomic Energy, as we have seen, takes its role as discussant quite seriously. There is little danger that problems will not be thoroughly explored.

Also of importance is the Joint Committee's responsibility to Congress as a whole, since it decides so many issues for Congress. In a sense, the members are more or less representative in their own political preferences, but, more important, they represent the views of the political parties to which they belong. If the parties agree on issues, it is not surprising that JCAE members also agree. Agreement apparently benefits all those concerned with atomic-energy policies. The executive branch runs fewer risks if its proposals have the solid support of the Joint Committee. The JCAE preserves its leadership of Congress if it can unanimously report legislation which has the Executive's approval. Finally, when there is Executive-Committee accord, Congress conserves time and energies that might be devoted to other problems. The system obviously makes for an efficient legislative process; matters are handled expeditiously. But it should be recognized that decisions reached in a narrow arena where most pressures support consensus are neither exclusively Congressional nor executive decisions. They are made by the Atomic Energy Commission and the Joint Committee on Atomic Energy, neither of which functions in a purely executive or purely legislative capacity.

---

[65] Cf. Fenno, *op. cit.,* pp. 316-317. The chairman of one subcommittee of House Appropriations remarked: "I tell them [the full Committee] we should have a united front. If there are any objections or changes, we ought to hear it now, and not wash our dirty linen out on the floor. If we don't have a bill that we can all agree on and support, we ought not to report it out. To do that is like throwing a piece of meat to a bunch of hungry animals." *Ibid.,* p. 317.

VI | Congressional Surrogate

The Joint Committee's activities in Congress are by no means limited to matters of substantive and authorizing legislation. Its Congressional activities are continuous, and its prestige within the national legislature depends on this continuing performance, not only on occasional flurries of legislative activity.

One of the Committee's most important nonlegislative activities is its role in keeping Congress and the public informed about atomic energy. This role is one to which members in recent years have paid increasing attention. In an address of 1956, for example, Rep. Melvin Price, having discussed the JCAE's watchdog, legislative, and policy-making functions, went on to describe a fourth function of the Committee, that of informing the Congress and the public of developments in the atomic-energy field.[1] In this capacity, the Joint Committee not only has added a wealth of valuable information to the public domain, but also has fashioned a tool designed to influence executive policy and Congressional response.

---

[1] Address before a meeting sponsored jointly by the Chicago Bar Association, Northwestern University Law School, University of Chicago Law School, and the Atomic Industrial Forum, at Chicago, September 25, 1956. JCAE press release, Sept. 25, 1956.

A second JCAE activity, one closely related to other Committee functions, is that of defending, perpetuating, and expanding its own jurisdictional authority and influence. The most direct tests of JCAE influence within Congress occur when its legislative recommendations are put to a vote. But the Committee's influence is at stake at other times as well, especially when the JCAE is challenged by other Congressional committees which seek to limit its sphere of control.

Finally, a significant Congressional activity of the Joint Committee is that of protecting the AEC and its program from criticism and attack. By maintaining relatively clear jurisdiction, it has isolated the Commission from either attack or defense by most other committees. Only the House Committee on Appropriations, especially its Subcommittee on Independent Offices, has persistently challenged the JCAE in its efforts to exercise sole Congressional leadership in the field of atomic energy.

■ SECRECY VERSUS PUBLIC INFORMATION

• Security through Secrecy

The early years of the nation's atomic-energy program, as we have seen, were marked by an intense concern to achieve national security through stringent secrecy. At that time, the JCAE did not conceive its mission to be one of informing Congress or stimulating Congressional and public discussion of atomic energy. On the contrary, the Committee's attitude seemed to be that the atomic-energy program could be debated in Congress only by those with immediate responsibility who were already privy to atomic secrets—in effect, only by members of the JCAE. "Because of secrecy necessary to preserve knowledge essential to the production of atomic weapons," the Committee stated in 1948, "the operation of this vast set-up is clothed with restrictions and mandates for security." This meant that "opportunity for public examination and evaluation of its progress and of the impact of its activities upon our normal peacetime or even potential wartime economy are non-existent." In such an unusual administrative situation, "solemn responsibility" was placed with the Joint Committee.[2]

The Committee took its commitment to preserve security so seriously that almost no information of substance was communicated to the rest of Congress. Although the JCAE and its subcommittees held hundreds of meetings during the years from 1947 through 1951, about three-quarters of them took place in executive session, because of secrecy requirements.[3] Through 1953, only a few Committee reports were submitted to the House and Senate. Paradoxically, the public hearings which shed most light on

---

[2] S. Rep. No. 1342, 80th Cong., 2d Sess. (1948).

[3] S. Rep. No. 1041, 82d Cong., 1st Sess. (1951). See also Jackson, *op. cit.*, p. 179.

the atomic-energy program—the 1949 Hickenlooper investigation into the AEC—were aimed at tightening both management and security procedures within the Commission.[4] The Hickenlooper investigation made everyone even more secrecy-conscious than before.

There were a few dissents by key people who wanted to increase access to information. Senator McMahon was by no means categorical in insisting on absolute silence.[5] Although he was uncertain as to how much, and what kind of, information could be made public, he believed that most matters were unnecessarily wrapped in secrecy. The main impetus for greater divulgence of information came from the Commission itself, especially from Chairman David Lilienthal. In a speech of 1948, for example, he stressed the overriding importance of public knowledge and the need to carry out AEC actions and programs "within the framework of rigorous public accountability and public criticism." [6]

Some JCAE members felt that Lilienthal was inclined to take too many risks with sensitive information. In January, 1949, when the Commission issued its fifth semiannual report, it was hailed by Lilienthal as a prime example of the AEC's attempt to fulfill its informational obligations. At a press conference, he described the report as "a turning point in the Commission's activities in balancing the interests of security through concealment and the interests of promoting security through progress and through public information." [7] Reaction from the Joint Committee was immediate, and a hearing on the report was held in early February. With the exception of Holifield, who maintained that the sensational headlines

---

[4] According to one observer, although Hickenlooper's charges of "incredible mismanagement" within the AEC were in large part "picayune, confused, frivolous, and, in not a few instances, outright humbug," valuable information was brought to light during the hearings. James R. Newman, "The Atomic Energy Industry: An Experiment in Hybridization," *Yale Law Journal,* LX (December 1951), 1339.

[5] *Cong. Rec.,* 96 (Feb. 2, 1950), 1343. In an address before the Economic Club of Detroit on January 31, 1949, McMahon discussed the problem posed by secrecy:

> This problem, I believe, may well cause the Joint Congressional Committee on Atomic Energy more anxious concern than any other. I cannot suggest an answer to the problem, for I have not yet arrived at a conclusion myself. . . . But in the case of atomic energy, Congress has purchased a defense package sight unseen. Congress has only a most general idea of what the atomic package contains. . . . So far as atomic energy is concerned, Congress simply lacks sufficient knowledge upon which to discharge its own constitutional duties. . . . There is a natural inclination in all of us, in Congress as well as out, to shy away from the implications of this problem.

Reprinted in *Bulletin of the Atomic Scientists,* V (March 1949), 66-68.

[6] Address before the New England Council at Boston, November 19, 1948; reprinted in *ibid.* (January 1949), pp. 6-8.

[7] Anne Wilson Marks, "Washington Notes," *ibid.* (May 1949), p. 159. The report summarized the atomic-energy program in some detail and included photographs of AEC facilities.

the report stimulated were the responsibility of the press, not the Commission, JCAE members were extremely critical of the AEC's information policies. Senators Millard Tydings and Tom Connally, in particular, asked Lilienthal why it was advisable to reveal so much about the nation's weapons progress. When Lilienthal justified the report on the basis of the Commission's responsibility to account for the expenditure of public funds, the following exchange took place:

> *Senator Connally:* Congress appropriated the money. Why is it necessary, because you spend public money, to go out and blah blah all over the country about these bombs?
> *Mr. Lilienthal:* It is the general principle of public accountability of reporting within the limits of security.
> *Senator Connally:* Reporting to whom?
> *Mr. Lilienthal:* Reporting to the Congress and to the country.
> *Senator Connally:* That is one thing. Reporting to the country is one thing, but to be running in to the press is another thing. It seems to me that Congress or the Executive, one or the other, ought to have discretion as to what ought to be given out and what ought not to be given out. I do not think it is the business of the Commission to conduct its own decisions on those things.[8]

The effect of this criticism, combined with the subsequent Hickenlooper investigation, was soon demonstrated. The sixth semiannual report of the Commission, in comparison with its predecessor, was a banal document. It read, commented *Time,* like a Soviet report on the current five-year plan. "There is not a firm figure to inform, alarm, or comfort the nation's potential foes or friends."[9] For the next few years, the Joint Committee clamped the lid down tightly on information and effectively excluded Congress from even rudimentary knowledge of the nation's atomic-energy program.

• Dissemination of Information

Since 1954, the JCAE, in deeds as well as words, has made an almost complete about-face. As a result of the Soviet Union's breakthrough in nuclear-weapons technology, the entrance of private industrial participation in the atomic-energy program, and an increasing clamor from Congress for greater AEC accountability, the Committee's concept of its informational role has shifted noticeably. Security through concealment is no longer the overriding consideration. Today, the Committee conceives of its informational responsibilities as specific and continuing and as important as

---

[8] *Atomic Energy Report to Congress Hearings* (1949), p. 8.
[9] Quoted in Marks, *op. cit.* (August-September 1949), p. 220.

its other duties. Recently, Representative Holifield summed up what he believed to be the JCAE's approach, stating that the Committee was peculiarly fitted for unearthing facts and informing the Executive, Congress, and the public. Not only is information necessary for intelligent formulation of public policy, but, also, unless facts are widely disseminated, "the formulation of policy in the political and diplomatic fields may lack the basis for understanding or justification." [10]

Two quantitative measures demonstrate that, as circumstances have changed, the Committee has, indeed, reversed its policy on the dissemination of information. First, it has made available a greater number of hearings, reports, and Committee prints. During the first six years of its existence, the JCAE issued only forty-seven publications, twenty-nine of which were hearings. From 1954 through 1960, it issued 129 publications, eighty-one of which were hearings.[11] During the first session of the Eighty-sixth Congress, for example, 161 public and executive hearings were held, and twenty-five publications, totaling eleven thousand pages, were issued. There has been a comparable increase in the number of JCAE meetings and hearings which are open to the public. Originally, 75 per cent were *in camera;* recently, more than half have been in open session. In fact, the percentage of closed JCAE meetings in the past few years is lower than that of several other standing committees, some of which are not concerned with problems of security and classified information. (See tables VI-1 and VI-2.)

The Committee's activities in making information available cover a wide field. In addition to hearings and reports on legislation and annual hearings on the development, growth, and state of the atomic-energy industry, the JCAE has rendered other informational services to Congress, in some instances displaying keen sensitivity to Congressional concerns. For instance, the Committee invited members of Congress to attend atomic tests, and more than two hundred legislators witnessed shots at the Nevada test site in 1953 and 1954. Other activities have included publishing a weekly summary of the AEC program and providing films on President Eisenhower's Atoms for Peace proposal for showing in each member's home district or state.[12]

From time to time, the Committee is called on to provide specific information or to satisfy general inquiries. In 1954, for instance, Rep. Thomas M. Pelly (R., Wash.) charged that many classified documents

---

[10] *Cong. Rec.,* 106 (May 10, 1960), 9908. See also Clinton P. Anderson, "The Test Debate: 'We Need to Know More,'" *N.Y. Times Magazine,* Feb. 25, 1962.

[11] For a list of publications, see Staff of JCAE, "Membership, Publications, and Other Pertinent Information Through the 86th Congress, 2d Session, of the Joint Committee on Atomic Energy," 87th Cong., 1st Sess. (1961), pp. 23-31.

[12] *Cong. Rec.,* 101 (Jan. 24, 1955), 608; (June 21, 1955), 8794, 8886.

TABLE VI-1

OPEN AND CLOSED HOUSE COMMITTEE MEETINGS
1958, 1959, AND 1960

Committee	Open	Closed	Total	Percent closed
Appropriations *	—	—	—	100
Foreign Affairs	119	205	324	63
House Administration	28	39	67	58
Ways and Means	135	153	288	53
JCAE	130	112	242	46
Public Works	107	75	182	41
Judiciary	282	188	470	40
Armed Services	297	172	469	37
Banking and Currency	163	93	256	36
Un-American Activities **	15	8	23	35
Agriculture	285	136	421	32
Education and Labor	264	105	369	28
Post Office and Civil Service	187	69	256	27
Merchant Marine and Fisheries	192	69	261	26
Government Operations	216	71	287	25
District of Columbia	102	31	133	23
Veterans' Affairs	111	28	139	20
Science and Astronautics	169	41	210	20
Interstate and Foreign Commerce	346	81	427	19
Interior and Insular Affairs	352	76	428	18
Rules	43	3	46	7
Total (excluding the JCAE)	3413	1643	5056	32

* The Appropriations Committee holds all of its meetings behind closed doors, so there is no reliable information on how often the committee and its subcommittees meet.
** Incomplete data.

Source: *Congressional Quarterly Weekly Report,* XVIII (Dec. 16, 1960), No. 51, 1957-1958.

were missing from the AEC's Hanford installation. When the Commission failed to reply promptly to Pelly's request for an investigation, he called the matter to the attention of the JCAE chairman. Representative Cole turned the matter over to the Committee staff, and, within a few days, Hanford assured the JCAE that no vital atomic secrets were missing. The Committee, in turn, notified Pelly that the investigation revealed no security leaks.[13] Similarly, during the course of the Dixon-Yates controversy of 1955, JCAE Democrats were requested by their Congressional colleagues to obtain information on the suspected violation of the conflict-of-interest law. In February, Sen. Lister Hill (D., Ala.) asked the Committee to

[13] *N.Y. Times,* March 13, 14, and 17, 1954.

TABLE VI-2

OPEN AND CLOSED SENATE COMMITTEE MEETINGS 1958, 1959, AND 1960

Committee	Open	Closed	Total	Percent closed
Rules and Administration	22	43	65	66
Foreign Relations	121	175	296	59
Finance	75	90	165	55
Armed Services	118	118	236	50
JCAE	130	112	242	46
Aeronautics and Space Sciences	30	24	54	44
Public Works	68	42	110	38
Agriculture and Forestry	104	55	159	35
Post Office and Civil Service	59	29	88	33
Interior and Insular Affairs	145	68	213	32
Labor and Public Welfare	174	76	250	30
Government Operations	71	30	101	30
Appropriations	397	147	544	27
Banking and Currency	121	37	158	23
Judiciary	370	99	469	21
Interstate and Foreign Commerce	284	68	352	19
District of Columbia	97	22	119	18
Total (excluding the JCAE)	2256	1123	3379	33

Source: *Congressional Quarterly Weekly Report,* XVIII (Dec. 16, 1960), No. 51, 1957-1958.

"obtain access to all available records and data in order that the full story . . . may be thoroughly investigated." A few months later, when Sen. Estes Kefauver's (D., Tenn.) subcommittee of Senate Judiciary was conducting hearings on the Dixon-Yates affair, the JCAE chairman offered to obtain the Commission's minutes if the Tennessee senator could not get them himself.[14]

Secrecy requirements, however, still limit the amount of information that can be subjected to Congressional and public scrutiny. Senator Anderson has often expressed his regret that JCAE members cannot discuss secret matters with other congressmen and has endeavored to persuade the Commission to declassify as much matter as possible without endangering security. Anderson's efforts have, at times, sharply illustrated the secrecy dilemma—the problem of maintaining security while keeping Congress and the public informed of developments. In 1957, Sen. Alan Bible (D., Nev.) forwarded to the JCAE a letter from a constituent requesting information on the effects of testing on the people of Nevada. Anderson

[14] *Cong. Rec.,* 101 (Feb. 18, 1955), 1715-1716; (July 21, 1955), 11124-11127.

wrote the AEC asking that Bible be given this information. Although the Commission responded to his request, the answer bore a "secret" classification, so Anderson could not tell the senator from Nevada what was in it.[15]

Probably the most effective means of communication for the Committee is the public hearing. Hearings not only inform JCAE members, but also bring facts and opinions to the attention of Congress and the public. By advance notice through announcements on the floor and distribution of press releases, the Committee tries to arouse interest in the hearings it has scheduled. Journalists covering atomic-energy affairs report the proceedings to the public, and the Committee publishes records and frequent summary-analyses of the information disclosed.

One purpose of holding public hearings on matters other than legislation is to provide Congress and the public with data that the Committee believes the Executive is withholding without good cause. In recent years, the JCAE has conducted hearings on several important technical problems which had been kept from public view either because of legitimate secrecy requirements or because of lack of candor on the part of the executive branch. For instance, had the AEC kept the public informed of facts about dangers from radiation, the Committee might not have held public hearings on this problem. The JCAE, and Representative Holifield especially, felt, however, that the Commission was "grossly tardy and negligent" in educating Americans about the "harsh realities" of the effects of atomic blasts, and Holifield charged that the AEC intentionally and dishonestly played down the dangers from radiation. Hearings on the nature of radioactive fallout and its effects on man began in late May of 1957 and lasted eight days.[16]

In reporting the hearings to the House, Holifield emphasized that public investigation was the only way to uncover vital facts. To bring the AEC out into the open, he said, the Committee was literally forced to squeeze information out of the Commission. He elaborated on the theme of unnecessary secrecy:

---

[15] *Ibid.*, 103 (Aug. 6, 1957), 13742. Anderson has been an especially forceful advocate of declassification, so that American industry might take advantage of opportunities in the field of atomic energy. He has been particularly critical of the unnecessary restraints imposed by the AEC access-permit program and the Commission's evasiveness in giving businessmen information vital to their operations. In a speech before the Nuclear Science and Engineering Convention in 1955, Anderson assailed AEC secrecy, stating that "it is easier for a camel to pass through the eye of a needle than it is for a businessman to receive frank and complete and unfettered answers from the Atomic Energy Commission." *Washington Post and Times Herald,* Dec. 16, 1955.

[16] *N.Y. Times,* Feb. 28, 1957. Holifield, chairman of the Special Radiation Subcommittee, which heard a long line of expert witnesses, was conscious that he might be accused of rigging the hearings against the AEC. He was careful, therefore, to point out that six witnesses from the Commission and twenty-five employees of, or consultants to, the AEC accepted the opportunity to testify.

> Except for the Congressional hearing, the AEC would withhold some important information that the public should have. Then, too, when the Commission releases information on its own initiative, it comes in forbidding technical form or in driblets through speeches of Commission members or other high-ranking personnel. Even skillful newspaper reporters, not to mention layman [*sic*] on the outside have difficulty piecing together the information or understanding its significance.[17]

The Committee continued to insist that all unclassified data on fallout be made public.

A few years later the fallout issue again assumed dramatic proportions. In grudging deference to the Department of Defense, the JCAE had withheld from the public new information on fallout. But when the department leaked hitherto-classified data on the Argus shots (high-altitude tests in the South Atlantic in September of 1958), Chairman Anderson was furious. The news of the Argus shots, which had apparently been undetected by the Soviet Union or any other nations, supported the Defense Department position that nuclear testing could not be easily detected. Since the Committee had not yet accepted this view, Anderson commented how curious it was that "at the same time the Department of Defense was leaking this secret information, it was gagging the Joint Committee on an unclassified but most important bit of information on fallout." He therefore revealed to the press that the Department of Defense had indicated, in correspondence with the JCAE, that radioactivity in the stratosphere had a residence half-life of two years, instead of the seven which the AEC had previously assumed. "In layman's language," the senator concluded, "it looks like Strontium 90 isn't staying up in there as long as AEC told us it would, and the fallout is greatest on the United States." He promised that the Committee would look into the matter at hearings to be held a few months later.[18]

In May, 1959, Holifield's special subcommittee heard four days of testimony. The announced purpose was to bring the data of 1957 up to date and to assess new information on increased dangers from radioactivity, but the implied aim was to expose the problem to public view and ques-

---

[17] *Cong. Rec.*, 103 (June 28, 1957), 10572. An amusing incident illustrates Holifield's determination to make radiation facts known. During the noon recess at the May 29 hearing, a Senate policeman asked the subcommittee chairman whether he wanted the "secret papers" guarded while the members ate lunch. "Don't worry about that," Holifield replied. "This is one time when we are going to get all this fallout information out in the open." *Washington Post and Times Herald,* May 30, 1957.

[18] JCAE press releases, March 19 and March 22, 1959. Anderson addressed his colleagues in the Senate on the issue: "I know of no obligation on the part of the Joint Committee on Atomic Energy to withhold the truth about fallout from the people of the United States." *Cong. Rec.*, 105 (March 23, 1959), 4880.

tion the AEC-Defense Department assumption that there was little danger from nuclear testing. Although the hearings did not convert any of the participants, a wealth of technical information was publicized, and an excellent summary-analysis was prepared by the Committee staff.[19]

Another purpose of hearings is to influence executive action and policy.[20] When the Joint Committee is engaged in a dispute with executive departments or agencies, it tries to shift the balance to its own favor by enlarging the arena of debate. This seems to have been a major consideration in its hearings on the aircraft nuclear propulsion program (ANP) of 1959. For ten years, the JCAE, spearheaded by Representative Price, had unsuccessfully urged the AEC and Department of Defense to accelerate the development of a prototype nuclear-powered aircraft. Matters came to a head in February, 1959, when the Committee was informed by Deputy Secretary of Defense Donald A. Quarles that the administration was postponing a decision on early nuclear flight. Quarles went on to say that criticism by JCAE members of the ANP program was intemperate. Price immediately retaliated by scheduling public hearings, although until this time no public sessions on the program had ever been held. He justified his action by stating publicly:

> If we are going to be charged with "hitting below the belt" and misleading the public, I think it is high time the American public be given the opportunity to hear the true facts of the situation and make their own judgment as to who has been misleading whom for the past decade.[21]

Hearings were held, and a lengthy record was published.[22] The Committee did succeed in increasing the amount of information available on the ANP program, but it failed in its effort to force the Executive into reversing the decision on early flight.

• Technical Hearings

How the Joint Committee on Atomic Energy conducts hearings on a highly technical problem deserves close examination. Committee members often enter the hearing room with definite opinions on the subject under discussion and attempt to elicit primarily information which buttresses their own views. Frequently, their own beliefs determine the course

---

[19] Staff Director James Ramey noted that the radiation hearings and summary-analysis had become valuable reference works for scientists, engineers, and laymen.

[20] Cf. Ralph K. Huitt, "The Congressional Committee: A Case Study," *American Political Science Review,* XLVIII (June 1954), 340-365, and David B. Truman, *The Governmental Process* (New York: Knopf, 1951), pp. 372-377.

[21] JCAE press release, Feb. 6, 1959.

[22] *ANP Hearings* (1959). Also *Staff Report on ANP* (1959). For a study of the Committee's efforts on ANP, see Chapter VII.

of the hearing and the information that is brought to light, no matter how objective they may try to be in questioning witnesses. If members are agreed among themselves, it is likely that hearings will move from a preconceived idea to a predetermined conclusion.[23]

The hearings of April, 1960, on technical aspects of detection and inspection controls of a nuclear-weapons-test ban [24] illustrate the Committee's methods in exploring a problem on which members have similar views. Before these hearings, the Committee had held intensive executive sessions with experts in seismology and detection. On the basis of the information elicited, JCAE members were convinced that the available technical facts on detection techniques did not justify the Eisenhower administration's optimism regarding a test ban. Furthermore, they believed that the administration had made political decisions ostensibly on the basis of technical data, and they were eager to bring to Congressional and public attention considerations which they felt had not been taken into full account.

The test-ban hearings were held as United States negotiators at Geneva were trying to arrange a ban on nuclear-weapons tests. In September and October of 1958, a series of tests, the Hardtack shots, had been held, and the results showed that detection was more difficult than previously believed. By late January, 1959, three months after the Geneva conference had begun, the Hardtack data had been carefully evaluated, and the American stand on inspection controls was changed. Nevertheless, President Eisenhower and Prime Minister Harold MacMillan of Great Britain announced, after their Camp David meeting, that the Soviet test-ban proposal would be accepted. The JCAE then decided that the difficulties of detection and inspection should be made clear.[25] Some members, in fact, believed that, by dramatizing the problem with testimony from the administration's own scientific witnesses, they could prevent further concessions to the Soviet Union on the test-ban issue, which was on the agenda for the summit meeting of May, 1960.[26]

In light of information received in executive sessions, one of the

---

[23] Douglass Cater, *The Fourth Branch of Government* (Boston: Houghton Mifflin, 1959), pp. 56-65.

[24] *Test Ban Hearings* (1960).

[25] Arthur Krock, "Nuclear Loopholes," *N.Y. Times,* April 24, 1960. Referring to the hearings as "an act of statesmanship," Krock added, "Even professional politicians can see that sometimes statesmanship is the best politics." He pointed out that the Committee was under Democratic control and Democrats feared that, if Eisenhower concluded a permanent agreement on testing, the Republicans might have a peace issue in the approaching election. Krock's charge seems dubious, especially since JCAE Republicans differed little from their Democratic colleagues in the opinion that an adequate detection system had yet to be discovered.

[26] *Ibid.,* April 20, 1960.

JCAE's objectives was to convince Congress and the public that a reliable control system was difficult, if not impossible, to establish. By prearrangement, discussion was confined to the technical aspects of detection and controls. Several times during the course of the hearings, Representative Holifield, who presided, pointed out that, although policy issues deserved great attention, the Committee's only job was to explore technical problems. The Committee would lay the technical facts on the table and leave the job of drawing conclusions to each member, witness, and citizen. Thus the "emotional and philosophical" issues inherent in questions of radioactive fallout and disarmament would be avoided, and, if a treaty were proposed, Congress and the public would be informed of the scientific facts.[27]

Because of the narrow scope of the inquiry, many related questions of undeniable significance were excluded. Witnesses opposed to further testing were not entirely satisfied with the ground rules, which, they thought, determined the outcome from the start. Dr. Harold Urey, of the University of California, felt that, to be completely fair, the Committee should look into other questions. Such information, he added, might be more encouraging and "might just make it [test-ban controls] success instead of failure." At one point, Urey suggested that the JCAE go beyond seismological data and consider other methods of obtaining needed information. Holifield, however, cut the scientist short. He conceded that political judgment was necessary, but pointed out once more that the purpose of the Committee was not to pass on nontechnical questions. Throughout the four-day session, therefore, no consideration was given to such crucial matters as (1) the importance of continued weapons development, (2) the physical effort required to carry out a violation, (3) what this effort could do for the violator if expended on other military projects, and (4) how great a possibility of detection would be an adequate deterrent to a potential violator.[28]

Within the narrow area of the Committee's stated concern, there was conscious effort to be fair. In order to hear scientists for and against a resumption of testing, Holifield and the JCAE staff took extreme care in selecting witnesses. Edward Teller and Harold Brown were identified with the scientific community favoring resumption; Hans Bethe, Richard E. Roberts, Jay Orear, and Harold Urey were outspoken opponents of further testing. As it happened, however, the scientists who opposed the test ban were directly involved in work on the technical aspects of detection and controls. Those on the other side, although extremely able, were less experienced in the particular technical field under consideration by the Com-

---

[27] *Test Ban Hearings* (1960), pp. 2, 203, 76, 104.
[28] *Ibid.*, pp. 218, 215, 76.

mittee. Anxious to avoid charges of bias, the JCAE went as far as to put into the record the fact that witnesses were testifying as individuals, not as spokesmen for positions held by any government agency. For example, after Dr. Richard F. Taschek, of the Los Alamos laboratory, had testified on the time schedule for achieving nuclear-detonation detectability, Hosmer asked point-blank, "Did anybody tell you to put in a pitch on it one way or another?" Somewhat startled, Taschek replied that while preparing his statement he had talked to no one but his secretary. To make the point even clearer, the congressman asked the witness:

> It is your own idea? . . . Did anybody in Government or out ask you to make detection look to the committee more difficult than it actually is?
>
> *Dr. Taschek:* No, absolutely not.
>
> *Representative Hosmer:* This is your honest answer?
>
> *Dr. Taschek:* Yes.

Hosmer concluded that the scientist's statement reflected his professional opinion based only on the merits of the scientific case.[29]

After Harold Brown's opening testimony, which effectively questioned the idea that detection controls were entirely adequate, Senator Gore complimented the witness for confining his statement to scientific opinions and not attempting "to become a diplomat or a politician." Holifield agreed and said he hoped all witnesses would do the same. The scientists were permitted to comment on technical aspects, to challenge opposing testimony, and to submit additional technical papers. But the ground rules were not exactly the same for all. Whenever opponents of testing digressed from the clearly technical, they were cut short. Discussing tactical nuclear weapons, a subject not too far afield, Bethe stressed that such weapons would not give either side an advantage in the event of war. Hosmer immediately pointed out that the subject was beyond the Committee's field of inquiry and shifted the discussion. Later, when Bethe, in an exchange with Sen. Wallace F. Bennett (R., Utah), expressed the opinion that the United States already had a large enough stockpile of tactical weapons, Holifield intervened. Dr. Herbert Jehle, who had requested and been given permission to testify, suggested that countries like China and Egypt would denounce the United States if testing were resumed. He, too, was quickly cut short.[30]

The record of the hearings indicates that however well-intentioned JCAE members may have been in their attempt to give both sides equal consideration, they were more sympathetic to testimony presented by Teller and others who favored a resumption of testing. For example, only two

---

[29] *Ibid.*, pp. 361-362.

[30] *Ibid.*, pp. 29, 178, 210, 414.

Committee members interrogated Bethe during his prepared testimony;[31] seven had questions to ask Teller. The questions and Teller's replies both strayed, on occasion, from purely technical issues. When Representative Van Zandt asked whether the physicist thought that the United States had lost its nuclear advantage as a result of the cessation of testing, Teller replied that, if the Russians had tested clandestinely, we might have lost much, or even all, of our advantage. Although Holifield here interposed that the record showed no information that the Russians had tested during the two-year moratorium, Van Zandt pursued this line of questioning. A few minutes later, Hosmer requested Teller's opinion of information about testing which was obtained through government intelligence channels.[32] Toward the end of his testimony, Teller was permitted to summarize his position:

> . . . if we enter a treaty where the pretense is made that we can be checking, where the fact that there are really great loopholes and possibilities of evasion, where these facts are not put clearly before the American people, then I feel that I must raise my voice as a scientist in protest.
>
> . . . the only really fruitful way toward any disarmament is the way toward complete openness. Once we have accomplished that, then the way toward disarmament and toward peace lies open before us. Without it, however, we are just inventing one method after another how to fool ourselves.[33]

It was difficult, no doubt, to keep matters within the prescribed area. Holifield ignored his own guide-lines several times. He asked a witness whether the Russians were making vital concessions in the Geneva negotiations and repeated the question to another expert, withdrawing it when Senator Gore reminded him of the inquiry's limits. Gore, himself, however, did not hesitate to wander from the purely technical aspects. On the first day of the hearings, he suggested that Ambassador James A. Wadsworth, the U.S. envoy to the Geneva negotiations, be called on to testify, preferably in public session. The following afternoon, Wadsworth appeared before the JCAE, but in executive session, so that policy issues might not intrude. After the meeting, no one objected when Gore, at the session of April 20, made a lengthy statement which was highly critical of

---

[31] It should be noted that during Bethe's testimony House members were called away for a roll-call vote. *Ibid.,* p. 176. Cf. David R. Inglis, "The Congressional Hearings on Technical Aspects of Test Control," *Bulletin of the Atomic Scientists,* XVI (June 1960), 205-207.

[32] *Test Ban Hearings* (1960), pp. 162, 164. At one point, Teller was allowed to discourse on the need for clean and more flexible nuclear weapons. *Ibid.,* p. 168. Bethe had not been given the same leeway.

[33] *Ibid.,* pp. 165, 167-168.

the manner in which the negotiations had been conducted.[34] In the meantime, the State Department, under pressure from the Committee, made public the transcript of the secret Geneva talks underway since October, 1958. Thus, although political issues had been barred from the hearings, they certainly loomed large in the immediate background.

From the first day of the hearings, the position of most JCAE members was obvious. According to one reporter: "Despite the stated objective of a purely technical, nonpolitical review of the test ban issue, the committee's underlying skepticism about the desirability of a test ban was exhibited by both Republican and Democratic members in their questioning and statements." [35] Republican Hickenlooper, for example, posed a question which assumed that detection in the foreseeable future was almost impossible. Republican Aiken's question assumed that underground tests would be valuable and that such tests would eliminate problems of fallout. Democrat Durham indicated that he favored underground testing when he asked whether the country could feel safe on the basis of detection knowledge.[36]

The information which reached Congress and the public through press reports, published hearings, and the JCAE's summary-analysis [37] had been common knowledge among scientists and statesmen before the hearings began. Nearly everyone, including those opposed to a resumption of nuclear testing, agreed that new concealment techniques had created difficult problems. It was also agreed that there would always be some explosions which could not be detected. Privately, Committee members were hopeful that they had impressed both Congress and the administration with the dangers of any hasty treaty with the Soviet Union. With the summit meeting opening on May 16, however, JCAE members were afraid that the hearings had come too late to cause the administration to abandon a proposed agreement based on what the JCAE considered inadequate controls.[38] How the Eisenhower administration responded to the Committee's findings is not known, for the U-2 flight on May 1, 1960, led to the cancellation of the Paris summit meeting and made the fears of the Joint Committee on Atomic Energy academic.

As the test-ban hearings demonstrate, the JCAE is not completely impartial in educating Congress and the public when the Committee has already established its position before hearings. Simply by scheduling hear-

---

[34] *Ibid.*, pp. 70, 23, 74, 103-104, 169. According to one account, the JCAE's reaction to Wadsworth's testimony illustrated the lack of harmony between the administration and the Committee on the test-ban issue. *N.Y. Times*, April 21, 1960.

[35] *Ibid.*, April 20, 1960.

[36] *Test Ban Hearings* (1960), pp. 27-29, 120.

[37] *Staff Summary-Analysis of Test Ban Hearings* (1960).

[38] *N.Y. Times*, April 23, 1960.

ings on a particular subject, determining the scope, and questioning witnesses, the JCAE determines the type of information to be made available. The Joint Committee should not be criticized for acting in this fashion. It would, in fact, be difficult to imagine a Congressional committee acting in any other manner and naïve to assume that releasing information—through hearings, press releases, or statements—has no political purposes.

Apart from its policy aims, the JCAE has placed before Congress and the public a vast amount of information which would never have been revealed or even assembled without the Committee's impetus. One can readily agree with the JCAE member who stated that ". . . the Joint Committee would still perform an invaluable public service if it performed no further function than such dissemination of authoritative information to the American public. . . ." [39] Representative Holifield, chairman during the Eighty-seventh Congress, expressed the Committee's attitude toward the secrecy surrounding atomic energy when he stated that the atomic-energy program was reaching the point at which it should be treated like any other national program. "Secrecy and security and all those mysterious banners behind which men have hidden in the past," Holifield concluded, "could no longer be used to prevent congressional scrutiny." [40]

■ THE PROBLEM OF JURISDICTION

On atomic-energy matters, the Joint Committee is comparatively independent of the remainder of Congress. Only occasionally do other committees become actively involved in affairs the JCAE considers within its own purview. When they do, conflict, rather than cooperation, is the usual mode of interaction, with the clash primarily concerning the bounds of each committee's jurisdiction. Congressional history has been constantly enlivened by such rivalries, and during its fifteen-year life, the Joint Committee has engaged in its share. All in all, the Joint Committee has been less than successful in its relations with rival claimants within Congress. As the applications of atomic energy have widened, more committees have indicated interest, and the JCAE has been gradually compelled to cede portions of its private preserve while its own efforts to expand jurisdiction have failed.

---

[39] Remarks of Representative Hosmer, *Cong. Rec.,* 106 (Jan. 13, 1960), 472-475. Others have agreed. Sen. Edward J. Thye (R., Minn.), for example, in introducing a resolution to set up a Joint Committee on Science, noted that the JCAE has "effectively kept Congress informed of all matters pertaining to atomic energy. . . ." *Ibid.,* 104 (April 1, 1958), 5888. *The Nation,* a magazine which has at times disputed JCAE policies, lauded Senator Anderson, then chairman, "who takes seriously the rights of citizens of a democracy to be informed." April 4, 1959.

[40] *Cong. Rec.,* 103 (Aug. 12, 1957), 14425.

• Anomalies of Jurisdiction

From the beginning, the JCAE has been an anomaly in the committee system. One reason for its creation was that Congress was originally unable to agree on referring control of atomic energy to any existing committee. In the Senate, for example, President Truman's special message on atomic energy was referred to the Military Affairs Committee although the Foreign Relations Committee had already been given several proposals and had even recommended action on one of them. Other bills on atomic energy had been referred to the Interstate and Foreign Commerce Committee. In the House, responsibility for the large number of measures introduced was similarly fragmented.

In calling for joint and special committees to consider legislation, Senators Vandenberg and Warren G. Magnuson (D., Wash.) noted this confusion. Fearing a battle between several committees and "a rush to get somebody's pet bill reported," Vandenberg proposed the establishment of a special joint committee to which all bills on atomic energy would be referred.[41] Magnuson announced that, because several committees of the Senate were operating at cross-purposes, hearings would be held before a joint session of the Military Affairs and Commerce committees. Until a special group was formed and was delegated responsibility, it was conceivable that every committee in the Senate might claim jurisdiction, hold hearings, and report legislation. A solution was imperative. Introducing his resolution to set up a special committee, Brien McMahon noted that there were at least twelve standing committees of the Senate which could argue that various aspects of this new subject matter came within their scope. His recommendation that one group be given the task of formulating and reporting an atomic-energy bill was accepted by the Senate, but not before a few senators voiced concern. Alben Barkley stated: "Legislation concerning many important discoveries and inventions has been handled by standing committees. I think that almost any one of a half dozen or more standing committees of the Senate would have been just as able to deal with this subject as any special committee. . . ."[42]

The report of McMahon's special committee, which recommended the establishment of a new group to handle atomic-energy affairs, created another jurisdictional problem. The Legislative Reorganization Act, signed into law just after the basic atomic-energy statute had been passed, attempted to define the areas of committee responsibility so that overlapping and duplication would be eliminated. The statute therefore specified in detail the subject matter to be handled by each legislative committee: the armed

[41] Hewlett and Anderson, *op. cit.*, p. 424.
[42] *Cong. Rec.*, 91 (Oct. 3, 1945), 9323-9329; (Oct. 22, 1945), 9888, 9890.

services committees, for example, were to exercise responsibility over the common defense and necessary strategic and critical materials, and the committees on foreign relations and foreign affairs were given responsibility for foreign policy. Creation of the JCAE made the change of rules brought about by the Reorganization Act little more than an academic exercise as far as atomic energy was concerned. The military committees were nominally responsible for the common defense, but the weapon on which that defense relied and the materials vital for its production were largely beyond those committees' purview. In Congress, production of weapons and special nuclear materials was primarily the business of the JCAE. The military committees controlled the naval establishment, but, when it came to the most revolutionary naval development of midcentury, the nuclear-powered submarine, they had to share authority with the JCAE. Similarly, the foreign affairs committees, responsible for American foreign policy, were excluded from control of bilateral exchanges which involved atomic information and materials.

Overlapping committee memberships alleviated only part of this fragmented authority. Some members of the JCAE did serve on the military committees of both houses and thus were able to correlate their duties, but members of the military committees who were not also on the JCAE had to rely on the advice of their colleagues who did have access to atomic-energy secrets. Communication of essential information from one member to another was impeded by the security requirements of the Atomic Energy Act, and only members of the Joint Committee could readily obtain needed restricted data.

• Cooperation and Conflict

Although close relations among Congressional committees are rare, the JCAE has at times cooperated with other committees, generally on an *ad hoc* basis. Sometimes it has voluntarily deferred jurisdiction, either because the issue in question was clearly not its business or because it was of little interest to JCAE members. In 1956, when the chairman of Senate Judiciary asked that a bill amending the Atomic Energy Act be referred to his committee because of its constitutional implications, the chairman of the JCAE voiced no objections. At other times, committees have referred matters to the JCAE. Sen. Edward J. Thye (R., Minn.), chairman of the Small Business Committee, received several communications in 1954 from rural electric cooperatives complaining about provisions in the Cole-Hickenlooper bill. Thye asserted that these complaints should be handled by the JCAE.[43]

Occasionally, other committees seek the advice and assistance of the

---

[43] *Cong. Rec.,* 102 (Jan. 12, 1956), 391; 100 (July 15, 1954), 10604.

JCAE. The Senate Government Operations subcommittee, which conducted a study of international health, in 1960 commended the Joint Committee's activities in radiation research. Before issuing a report, the subcommittee chairman consulted with JCAE Chairman Anderson. The report itself contained glowing praise of the JCAE, stating, "it is universally recognized that no group within the legislative branch is better qualified to appraise the contents of this or any other technical reports [*sic*] in this field than is the Joint Committee."[44] The JCAE has sought help from other committees, with varying results. In 1956, at the request of Senators Anderson and Gore, Sen. Mike Mansfield (D., Mont.) introduced in the Foreign Relations Committee an amendment to the foreign aid bill which would have set aside a portion of authorized funds for the construction of power reactors overseas. The amendment was easily defeated in the committee.[45] The same year, the JCAE was more successful working with the Senate Interstate and Foreign Commerce Committee. A bill to exempt certain private atomic-power combines from the Public Utility Holding Company Act had been introduced in 1955 by Senators Pastore and Charles E. Potter (R., Mich.). It was referred to the Commerce Committee, where hearings were held by a subcommittee chaired by Pastore. At his request, the bill was later referred to the JCAE, on which he also served. The committees worked out legislation that was mutually satisfactory.[46]

Much more typical than cooperation are intercommittee inroads and assaults. Some have developed when the JCAE saw itself threatened by rivals, others when the JCAE tried to capture new, uncharted areas of jurisdiction. The first such controversy concerned control of civil defense. The dispute of 1950 with Senator Kefauver's Armed Services subcommittee demonstrated that JCAE claims could be successfully resisted by older committees.

In 1949, after the first Soviet atomic-bomb explosion, Senator McMahon announced that the JCAE would hold civil defense hearings. At that time, the administration was preparing civil defense legislation, but had hesitated to send it to Congress until it had been determined whether the JCAE or the armed services committees would handle the matter. The Joint Committee opened executive hearings in February, 1950. Although no bill had been introduced yet, the JCAE knew that jurisdiction could be determined not only by referral but also by the subject on which a committee decided to conduct a study or hold a hearing. The Senate Armed Services Committee was fully aware of this maneuver. In late March,

---

[44] Staff of the Senate Committee on Government Operations, "Radiation Research in the Life Sciences," 86th Cong., 2d Sess. (1960), p. 5.

[45] *Forum Memo,* July 1956, p. 39.

[46] *"Gore-Holifield" Civilian Power Hearings* (1956), pt. 1, p. 207.

Kefauver wrote to McMahon (Senators Russell and Harry P. Cain (R., Wash.) countersigned the letter) calling attention to the JCAE hearings which appeared to duplicate the work of his own committee. McMahon replied that responsibility for civil defense rested with the JCAE. Other members were dubious. Representative Hinshaw, for example, knowing that past legislation on defense had emanated from the armed services committees, wondered about the validity of the JCAE's claim. McMahon assured Hinshaw that the JCAE hearings were only educational, but he added that "this business of preparing for total defense against a total war . . . is in some part within the jurisdiction of every committee of the Congress." The Armed Services Committee, in his view, would have a part, but only a part, since "defense against atomic attack would be the responsibility of the Joint Committee alone." [47]

By the end of the year, civil defense legislation was ready for introduction, and administration officials were worried that they might have to testify before three committees instead of one or two. Durham, a member of the Armed Services Committee and the JCAE, introduced the administration bill in the House. It was quickly referred to Armed Services, and Chairman Vinson appointed a subcommittee of members who also served on the JCAE to hold immediate hearings. McMahon introduced the bill in the Senate, but referral was delayed while the JCAE and Armed Services Committee skirmished over jurisdiction. At a continuation of the JCAE's civil defense hearings on December 4, McMahon announced that he had had several conversations with Kefauver and Russell, trying to devise a way of combining operations. Although he disclaimed any wish to dispute which of the two committees should have control, he stated "that in view of the abdication by the Armed Forces of responsibility in this matter," a committee other than Armed Services should handle civil defense.[48]

The matter was settled the same afternoon, much to McMahon's displeasure. Vice-President Barkley, presiding over the Senate, ruled that civil defense legislation be referred to the Armed Services Committee. For the record, McMahon stated that he would work out an arrangement with Kefauver, but this proved hopeless. The only arrangement that could be concluded was an invitation to JCAE members to observe the hearings. Commenting a year later, McMahon admitted that "under the Reorganization Act, Armed Services had a much sounder claim to it [the civil defense bill] than our committee had, and we had to recognize this." [49] Not only

---

[47] *Cong. Rec.,* 96 (April 13, 1950), 5153-5156, and *Civil Defense Hearings* (1950), pp. 118-119.

[48] *Ibid.,* p. 183.

[49] *Cong. Rec.,* 96 (Dec. 4, 1950), 16043, and "An Interview with Senator McMahon," *Bulletin of the Atomic Scientists,* VIII (January 1952), 12.

was the military committee's claim more convincing, but its members were also more influential with the Senate leadership.

Another dispute occurred in 1958 when Congressional attention was focused on the development of administrative and legislative organization for outer space. Throughout 1956 and 1957, JCAE members had been pointing out their Committee's potential role in supporting the nation's missile program. By 1958, they were giving prominent mention to the role of the AEC and JCAE in accelerating Project Rover (development of a nuclear-propelled missile) and asserting that there was no need for any other agency to carry on the project.[50] Nevertheless, the Preparedness Investigating Subcommittee of Senate Armed Services held extensive hearings on the missile and satellite programs late in 1957 and early in 1958. The subcommittee was headed by Democratic Majority Leader Lyndon Johnson.

The prospect of another group's gaining control of outer space impelled the JCAE to action. At the end of January, 1958, Anderson led the Committee's brief, abortive drive to win jurisdiction of outer space, including the missile program. Anderson, Gore, Durham, and Holifield introduced bills amending the Atomic Energy Act to provide for outer-space development by the AEC. They maintained that the facilities already available to the AEC—the network of national laboratories staffed with excellent scientists—could not be duplicated easily and that there was no necessity to create an additional agency to undertake the task. Moreover, as Anderson told his Senate colleagues, "The Joint Committee on Atomic Energy would be the watchdog committee of the Congress over such an enterprise were it assigned to the AEC and here the experience of its committee members would be of great value." [51] On the same day, Chairman Durham appointed a special subcommittee on outer-space propulsion. The new subcommittee, headed by Anderson, immediately held hearings.

The JCAE was too late, and the opposition was much too formidable. Majority Leader Johnson, who had become interested in outer space a year before, introduced a resolution creating a Special Committee on Space and Astronautics to frame legislation for a national space program. The resolution passed without contest. A month later, the House followed suit, establishing a Select Committee on Astronautics and Space Exploration. Senator Johnson and House Majority Leader McCormack were appointed chairmen of the respective groups, and, although Anderson and Hickenlooper were named to the Senate committee, no JCAE member was appointed to the House committee.

---

[50] *Cong. Rec.*, 102 (Feb. 1, 1956), 1763-1769; 103 (May 27, 1957), 7677; 104 (Jan. 16, 1958), 583-588.

[51] *Ibid.*, 104 (Jan. 23, 1958), 887-889.

The outcome of this brief controversy was that separate standing committees on outer space were established by the House and Senate. Since passage of the National Aeronautics and Space Act of 1958, the JCAE and the space committees have been engaged in intermittent conflict over their respective roles.[52] The primary question of which committee would handle space activities, however, had been settled by a Congressional leadership which was little impressed by the JCAE's claims to expanded authority.

If the Joint Committee has failed in attempts to enlarge its area of authority, it has been somewhat more successful in resisting assaults on its prerogatives.[53] Nevertheless, as other committees have become interested in atomic-energy applications, there has been some diminution of its jurisdictional authority. A case in point is the fight for control of a nuclear-powered merchant ship in 1955 and 1956. Here committee control was not the only consideration, but it was an important, and even explosive, one.

In May of 1955, House Merchant Marine Committee Chairman Herbert C. Bonner (D., N.C.) introduced an administration bill providing for the design and construction of a nuclear-powered merchant ship. An identical bill was introduced in the Senate. In July, the Senate bill was reported from Interstate and Foreign Commerce and re-referred to the JCAE. As originally introduced and reported, the bill placed prime responsibility for developing the merchant ship in the Maritime Commission. The Joint Committee then rewrote the bill to give the AEC sole responsibility for a long-range program to develop an economically competitive merchant ship, with the Maritime Commission providing only assistance. Thus, the JCAE, rather than the Merchant Marine and Commerce committees, would play the key Congressional role. The chairman of House Merchant Marine was incensed and attacked the JCAE publicly as a closed corporation which required that "nobody else should even mention the utilization of atomic energy." In the rush for adjournment, however, Congress failed to act on the JCAE bill. The following year, the bill was again considered by the Senate Commerce Committee, and in June it was

---

[52] In 1958, for example, Congressman Van Zandt expressed concern that the space committees "appear to be invading the jurisdictional field of this committee as far as Rover and Pluto are concerned." *FY 1959 Authorization Hearings* (1958), pp. 279-280. Also *FY 1962 Authorization Hearings* (1961), pp. 493-511.

[53] As early as 1954, for example, Rep. Sidney R. Yates (D., Ill.) objected to the JCAE's broad jurisdiction. He asked Hinshaw, a member of both the JCAE and the House Commerce Committee, why the former should have oversight for licensing atomic-power companies. Yates suggested that such oversight was the duty of the Commerce Committee, which also had jurisdiction over the Federal Power Commission. Hinshaw's first loyalty was apparently to the JCAE, for he told Yates that it is composed of "some very able and long-time Members of the House of Representatives . . . [who] are able indeed to decide all questions relative to atomic energy because of their familiarity with the subject." *Leg. Hist. 1954 Act,* v. 3, p. 2885.

reported in its original form. The JCAE was unhappy at the obstinacy of the Maritime Commission, which evidently refused to give up administrative control of the program, and of the Commerce Committee, which tenaciously supported its executive-branch constituent. Senator Hickenlooper, in particular, regretted the tendency of every department of government to get into the atomic-energy field. Nevertheless, the bill passed Congress, and jurisdiction over the merchant ship was parcelled out to the AEC, the Maritime Commission, the JCAE, and the Senate Commerce and House Merchant Marine committees.[54]

At least one group has recently seemed to pose a special threat to JCAE control of the international aspects of atomic energy. The Disarmament Subcommittee of Senate Foreign Relations, originally established as a special committee composed of members of Senate Armed Services, Foreign Relations, and the JCAE, has challenged the Joint Committee on a number of occasions.[55] Senators Pastore and Bricker represented the JCAE; Hickenlooper [56] sat as representative of the Foreign Relations Committee. Between 1956 and 1958, Senator Humphrey, who headed the special committee, appeared to be making an effort to keep the JCAE informed of his group's activities, but Humphrey was often compelled to appeal directly to the AEC for the data he required. There was one attempt, initiated by the two committee staffs, to set up joint hearings, but members of the JCAE objected, and the plan was abandoned.

Ironically, the very existence of the Humphrey committee was one factor in launching the JCAE into certain areas of inquiry. By announcing that he intended to explore a particular subject, Humphrey aroused the Joint Committee to make an investigation along the same lines. When the Disarmament Committee held hearings on fallout, the JCAE embarked on comprehensive hearings of its own, in part to prevent pre-emption by the Humphrey group. In 1957, Humphrey wrote to Chairman Durham

---

[54] S. Rep. No. 1269, 84th Cong., 1st Sess. (1955); *Cong. Rec.*, 101 (July 18, 1955), 10814; 102 (June 20, 1956), 10650-10657.

[55] Senator Humphrey, chairman of the Disarmament Subcommittee, was often critical of JCAE control in areas that concerned foreign policy. In 1959, a large package of bilateral agreements was submitted by the executive branch to the Joint Committee. Humphrey pointed out that sixty days of JCAE consideration was insufficient when several separate agreements were submitted at the height of the session. In any case, he asked on the Senate floor whether the Foreign Relations Committee should have jurisdiction over such agreements. His colleague, Sen. Frank Church (D., Idaho), also questioned whether bilateral agreements were receiving sufficient attention by the Congress, noting that the JCAE report on them was issued only three days before they went into effect. *Ibid.*, 105 (July 17, 1959), 13679, 13684; (July 24, 1959), 14219.

[56] It is reported that, when the special committee became a subcommittee of Senate Foreign Relations in 1958, Senator Hickenlooper opposed its continued existence on the grounds that the JCAE was perfectly capable of performing its functions.

suggesting that the JCAE focus public attention on detection of nuclear tests. Durham's reply was terse; weapons detection, he said, would be discussed in executive sessions, and classified information could obviously not be made available to outsiders.[57] Partially because of Humphrey's prodding, the JCAE finally held public hearings on test detection in 1960.

Pressure on another front has also impelled the Joint Committee to action. In March, 1959, a twelve-man National Advisory Committee on Radiation submitted its report, "The Control of Radiation Hazards in the United States," to the surgeon general. A principal recommendation was that primary responsibility for protection from radiation hazards be taken from the AEC and vested in the Public Health Service of the Department of Health, Education, and Welfare. Later that month, Sen. Lister Hill, prodded by HEW, announced that he was in complete agreement with the Advisory Committee's findings. Concurrently, the White House announced that a study of federal organization of radiological health activities would be made under the direction of the Bureau of the Budget. From this study emerged a Federal Radiation Council established by executive order and chaired by the secretary of HEW, with other members being the secretaries of defense and commerce and the chairman of the AEC. Identical bills had been introduced in April by Senator Hill and Rep. Kenneth A. Roberts (D., Ala.), chairman of the Subcommittee on Health and Safety of the House Commerce Committee. This legislation also would have vested primary responsibility for research on radiation hazards in the Public Health Service, but, to disarm opposition by either the AEC or the JCAE, the legislation stated that there would be no transfer of current AEC authority to the Public Health Service.

JCAE members, however, were dissatisfied. Several publicly opposed the Hill bill, although they realized that, as atomic-energy applications broadened, the JCAE would inevitably lose exclusive jurisdiction. In early May, Holifield, appearing on television, made his attitude plain. He said that the JCAE was willing to permit the AEC to cede radiation authority to the Public Health Service if the latter could get an annual appropriation of $20,000,000. However, continued Holifield, "on Capitol Hill it's very easy to get money for the AEC, but it's very difficult to get money for the Public Health Service." [58] Shortly thereafter, the JCAE reported legislation which included a provision making the Federal Radiation Council a statutory body under the Atomic Energy Act. Although Anderson pointed out that his Committee's bill in no way affected the Hill bill, there was

---

[57] S. Rep. No. 2501, "Final Report of the Disarmament Subcommittee," 85th Cong., 2d Sess. (1958), pp. 23-26.

[58] "Face the Nation" transcript, May 3, 1959; reprinted in *Cong. Rec.*, 105 (May 4, 1959), 7392.

little doubt that the JCAE's rapid response had completely eclipsed the HEW measure and preserved the positions of the AEC and JCAE.

It should be noted that the Joint Committee's efforts to retain exclusive control in the field of atomic energy have been supported by the AEC. The Commission's loyalty has stemmed from two factors: first, it has not wished to serve more than one board of directors in Congress; second, it has recognized that any diminution of the JCAE's jurisdiction might mean a corresponding reduction in the AEC's own authority. It has preferred, therefore, to deal exclusively with the JCAE and has kept it fully informed of its contacts with other Congressional groups.[59]

When the Committee attempted to capture control of outer-space development, the Commission lent support. Whenever the AEC felt threatened by another government agency or Congressional committee, first appeal was to the JCAE. Even Chairman Strauss, who might have been expected to seek allies elsewhere, showed no desire to bypass the JCAE. At one point, he even told the JCAE chairman: "There are many occasions, on which I have expressed concern to you about the fact that other committees in the Congress have called upon us repeatedly for testimony on various parts of our program, that originally was concentrated here, but there is nothing that we can do about it." [60] For once, the Committee sympathized with Strauss, because it was as anxious as he to safeguard its traditional preserve.

In addition to the normal jurisdictional disputes in which the Joint Committee has become involved, one committee has caused it serious concern. Some of the JCAE's hardest Congressional battles during the first years of its existence were fought against the House Committee on Appropriations and its Subcommittee on Independent Offices.

■ THE PROBLEM OF APPROPRIATIONS

A student of Congress has described the normal relationship between the appropriations and legislative committees as one of lingering conflict.[61] Although the intensity of this conflict depends on many factors, the three most important are the amount of funds cut from agency budgets, the nature of the restrictions imposed on agency programs, and the legisla-

---

[59] If a commissioner or staff member was scheduled to testify at another committee's hearings, prior notification was given the JCAE. When the AEC corresponded with other committees, a staff member, if he thought the matter would be of interest to the Joint Committee, usually notified its executive director. The phrase, "of interest to the Joint Committee," was interpreted liberally.

[60] *"Gore-Holifield" Civilian Power Hearings* (1956), pt. 2, pp. 36-37.

[61] Roland Young, *The American Congress* (New York: Harper, 1958), p. 115.

tive committees' feelings about the effects of cuts and restrictions recommended by the appropriations committees.[62] Since the JCAE has always felt directly responsible for the nation's atomic-energy program, it is not surprising that it has resisted any other committee's direction, especially attempts to limit AEC operations.

From the outset, it was clear that there would be an unusual relationship between the JCAE and the appropriations committees. Under the 1946 act, the JCAE was given no formal role in the determination of atomic-energy appropriations, but it was expected to play an important informal role in assisting the appropriations committees.[63] The House Committee on Appropriations, however, viewed the prospect of JCAE advice with little enthusiasm. Members took the view that the Committee on Appropriations had special obligations and prerogatives and was the most important and responsible unit in the whole appropriations process.[64] As one member of the Independent Offices Subcommittee (which, until 1955, had responsibility for the AEC budget) said to a Commission witness: "When you are dealing with the committee [*sic*] you are dealing not with five members of the United States Congress, but are in effect dealing with the entire Congress." [65] Since this was also the attitude of the JCAE toward itself, there was the question of which committee actually represented Congressional views.

The House Appropriations Committee regarded the JCAE as an irresponsible newcomer. Its reaction to the creation of the Joint Committee was well summed up by Rep. Clarence Cannon, who, in 1947, described the JCAE as,

> . . . the Committee popularly known as the Watch Lilienthal Committee. . . . We got the idea from Soviet Russia. . . . If any untoward influences affect the administration of the AEC, it will probably be due to the meddling of the political commissars appointed to watch Lilienthal.
>
> We have innumerable commissions and agencies in the Government. But this is the first time a committee of Congress has been appointed and financed to watch one of them. In

---

[62] Although the rules of the House forbid legislation in appropriation bills, there has never been clarification of what these rules mean. Sometimes limitations of a legislative nature pass unchallenged or, if challenged, are given favorable rulings by the presiding officer of the House. Moreover, when the Appropriations Committee wants to legislate, it usually can obtain from the Rules Committee a special rule to bar points of order against its bill.

[63] S. Rep. No. 1211, 79th Cong., 2d Sess. (1946), p. 29.

[64] Fenno, *op. cit.*, p. 311.

[65] Remarks of Rep. Albert Gore (later a Senate member of the JCAE). "Hearings Before the Independent Offices Subcommittee of the House Appropriations Committee," *Second Supplemental Appropriation Bill for Fiscal Year 1951,* 81st Cong., 2d Sess. (1950), p. 193.

> order to carry out completely the program of our Russian prototype we should appoint still another committee . . . to watch the committee. . . . The system has endless possibilities.[66]

This was the beginning of the stormy relations between the JCAE and the House Appropriations Committee.

In the Senate, the Joint Committee was far more cordially received. The Senate Appropriations Committee cherished no strong tradition of independence, as did its House counterpart. In fact, the Senate and House appropriations committees were competitors, and in this respect the JCAE became a welcome ally of the former.[67] From the beginning, members of the JCAE participated in the deliberations of the Senate Independent Offices Subcommittee when AEC appropriations were being considered. A resolution introduced by Senator Bricker in 1951 made this arrangement formal by providing that three JCAE members sit ex officio on the subcommittee when the AEC budget came up.[68] As a result of this device, one JCAE congressman wrote, the regular members of the Appropriations Committee had come to heed the counsel of their ex officio colleagues, so that the Senate was exhibiting "great responsibility and rare discrimination in its handling of atomic energy appropriations." [69] Efforts to institute a similar arrangement in the House were of no avail. Although several requests were made to the House Appropriations Committee, its chairman refused

---

[66] Cannon's attack came during consideration of the JCAE's $150,000 appropriation request, part of the Legislative Appropriations Act for fiscal year 1948. *Cong. Rec.*, 93 (July 15, 1947), 8932.

[67] Historically, the Senate Appropriations Committee has sat primarily in appellate capacity to restore cuts inflicted by the far more economy-minded House group. See Arthur W. Macmahon, "Congressional Oversight of Administration," *Political Science Quarterly*, LVIII (June 1943), 161-190; (September 1943), 380-414. As a result of the Senate committee's relative leniency with agency budgets, House Appropriations members regarded the Senate group as irresponsible. They did not believe that Senate proceedings were either as lengthy or as intensive as those in the House. *Ibid.*, p. 176. See also Elias Huzar, *The Purse and the Sword* (Ithaca: Cornell University Press, 1950), p. 37. Perhaps the outstanding clash between the two appropriations committees occurred in 1962, when Chairman Cannon disputed the Senate committee's habit of chairing joint conferences and complained about Senate restorations of House cuts.

[68] When the Senate reorganized its Appropriations Committee in 1922, it allowed chairmen and ranking members of certain legislative committees to participate in subcommittee discussions when funds for agencies within their jurisdiction were being considered. Macmahon, *op. cit.*, p. 175. The JCAE arrangement was by no means unusual. In the area of defense, the Senate Armed Services Committee could designate three of its members to serve with the Appropriations Committee during discussion of the budget for the Defense Department; the Foreign Relations Committee had the same privilege when State Department appropriations were being considered, but—significantly—not on foreign aid funds. See H. Bradford Westerfield, *Foreign Policy and Party Politics* (New Haven: Yale University Press, 1955), p. 114.

[69] Jackson, *op. cit.*, p. 80.

to permit ex officio participation by the JCAE.[70] Consequently, it was believed, "the House approach to appropriations in the atomic field [had] . . . suffered." [71]

The views of the two appropriations committees differed with respect to the AEC as well. House committee members were suspicious of the AEC, as illustrated by the remarks of Rep. Francis Case (R., S.D.), who, in 1950, stated:

> No other agency of the Government has been able to get by the Appropriations Committee with the lax presentation of detailed estimates that the Atomic Energy Commission has. No other agency of the Government, so far as I know, has been able to come up and cloak itself with the aura of a scientific subject and get by with such general justifications.[72]

The predominant attitude of the Senate committee, as expressed by Sen. Leverett Saltonstall to an AEC witness, was one of trust:

> I do not know of any expenditure of Government, since I have been sitting on this Appropriations Committee, about which an individual Senator can know less and upon which he must rely more upon you gentlemen to tell us the truth, and keep costs down. . . .[73]

In the period before 1955, therefore, the House committee regularly cut AEC budgets. criticizing the Commission's justifications, and the Senate committee, taking a more lenient attitude, restored about half the funds cut by the House.

• The Period of Conflict

During the first years, the House Appropriations Committee was highly dissatisfied with the AEC's budget presentation. Moreover, it felt that the Commission was operating "on the basis of lavish expenditure" and was taking advantage of its "strategic position" to avoid facing realities on less important parts of its budget.[74] At first, members of the Joint Com-

[70] On April 15, 1953, Cole wrote to Chairman John Taber (R., N.Y.), noting that, since the JCAE lacked authorization powers, "an invitation to have joint committee members join in your deliberations would not set a precedent which other committees might seek to follow." *Cong. Rec.*, 99 (May 19, 1953), 5172.

[71] Jackson, *op. cit.*, p. 81.

[72] "Hearings Before the Independent Offices Subcommittee of the House Appropriations Committee," *Second Supplemental Appropriation Bill for Fiscal Year 1951*, 81st Cong., 2d Sess. (1950), p. 190.

[73] "Hearings Before the Independent Offices Subcommittee of the Senate Appropriations Committee," *Independent Offices Appropriations for Fiscal Year 1952*, 82d Cong., 1st Sess. (1951), p. 78.

[74] *Cong. Rec.*, 93 (June 17, 1947), 7173; 94 (June 9, 1948), 7612; and H.R. Rep. No. 2245, 80th Cong., 2d Sess. (1948).

mittee were quite cautious in dealing with these criticisms, and a few even expressed agreement with the Appropriations Committee.[75] A JCAE member made the first significant effort to defend AEC appropriations in 1948, when, on the floor of the Senate, McMahon sought unsuccessfully to restore a House cut of $48,000,000.[76]

Although still restrained, open involvement of JCAE members increased in 1949. When the House cut the AEC's appropriation request for $1,000,000,000 by $77,000,000, Representative Durham took the floor to criticize the action, but he did not offer an amendment to restore the cut. In the Senate, however, Chairman O'Mahoney of the Independent Offices Subcommittee proposed the "construction rider," which would have prohibited the AEC's starting construction projects not included in its budget (or where the estimated costs exceeded the amount budgeted) unless the projects were specifically approved by the Bureau of the Budget and unless the JCAE and appropriations committees received a detailed explanation. After consultations with O'Mahoney and the AEC, McMahon stated that the construction rider was rewritten so that "we can all live under [it] . . . without impairment of the efficiency of the atomic energy programs." In addition, he noted that the provision would give both the JCAE and appropriations committees "more information than we have heretofore had as a matter of right." [77] Later, McMahon, supported by Hickenlooper and Millikin, obtained enactment of an amendment to the Independent Appropriations Act, making the construction rider inapplicable to certain vital AEC projects.[78]

The first major skirmish between the Joint Committee and the House Appropriations Committee took place in 1950 over a subject which now seems trivial. Despite strenuous objections from the Commission, the House committee reported out the AEC's appropriation bill with a rider drastically limiting the fee which the Commission might pay the cost-plus-fixed-fee contractors who operated its communities at Oak Ridge and Los Alamos. Turning to the JCAE for help, the Commission was assured that an

[75] See remarks of Representatives Cole and Van Zandt, *Cong. Rec.*, 94 (June 9, 1948), 7614.

[76] The Senate Appropriations Committee had restored $20,000,000, and McMahon sought to add the remainder. He was the only JCAE member who spoke against the reduction. *Ibid.* (June 18, 1948), 8769.

[77] *Ibid.*, 95 (April 14, 1949), 4681; (Aug. 2, 1949), 10555. It should be noted that Senator McMahon apparently felt, contrary to the Committee's subsequent attitude as discussed in Chapter III, that the JCAE was not as a matter of right entitled to all information about the Commission's activities.

[78] See S. Rep. No. 1201, 81st Cong., 1st Sess. (1949); 63 Stat. 947 (1949).

attempt would be made to strike the rider from the bill.[79] During debate in the House, Holifield, Van Zandt, Durham, Hinshaw, and Cole spoke in favor of eliminating it, stating that a rider was unnecessary, since the JCAE itself was giving the matter of community management careful consideration. Van Zandt read portions of a letter sent by the AEC stating that the rider "would expose the atomic energy program to unnecessary risks which would adversely affect the early accomplishments of critical projects." Thereupon, Representative Case castigated the Commission for writing such a letter to the JCAE, rather than to the Appropriations Committee, and called it another illustration of "oversights and sloppy management." The outcome of this battle was House rejection of JCAE amendments to delete the rider.[80]

In the meantime, the JCAE tried to persuade the Senate Independent Offices Subcommittee to eliminate the rider. In hearings, McMahon testified that even though community management posed a problem, the rider should be stricken from the appropriation bill.[81] A month later, the Independent Offices Subcommittee still had not reported a bill, and the JCAE held hearings at which McMahon suggested a conference of Bricker, Knowland, and himself with O'Mahoney or, perhaps, all the members of the subcommittee. At the same time, Cole advised AEC Chairman Dean to smooth things over with the House Appropriations Committee, which resented the AEC's constant appeals to the JCAE.[82]

On the recommendation of the Appropriations Subcommittee, the Senate finally struck out the community rider. When the bill went to conference, however, it was restored and then passed by both houses without further debate. After the dust had cleared, the AEC signed new agreements with the same contractors, subject to the fee limitations imposed by the rider, and finally conceded that dire consequences had not material-

---

79 Commissioner Pike suggested that the bill be amended on the House floor, but Holifield said that it would be much easier to eliminate the community-facilities rider on a point of order. However, the California congressman added: "This is no way for this to be handled. It should be handled by a policy committee in a legislative way, rather than by a rider on an appropriation bill. . . ." *Community Policy Hearings* (1950), pt. 1, pp. 17-20.

80 *Cong. Rec.,* 96 (May 5, 1950), 6507-6516. Holifield's amendment deleting the community-management rider was rejected nineteen to eighty-six; Cole's amendment allowing existing community contracts to expire was rejected twenty-seven to eighty-four.

81 McMahon said, "But what I would like to do, if you will bear the analogy, is to keep the burr under the saddle, so that they [AEC] will know that this is something on which they must stay busy." "Hearings Before the Independent Offices Subcommittee of the Senate Committee on Appropriations," *Independent Offices Appropriation Bill for Fiscal Year 1951,* 81st Cong., 2d Sess. (1950), p. 404.

82 *Community Policy Hearings* (1950), pt. 2, pp. 33-35, 40.

ized.[83] This episode was later cited by members of the House committee as evidence that even the JCAE could be wrong.

During 1951, conflict between the JCAE and the House Appropriations Committee subsided.[84] Real difficulty, however, arose in connection with the House-Senate conference committee report on a proposed 10 per-cent cut in personnel. JCAE members Price and Holifield expressed deep concern about the impact of this cut on the AEC's operations, provoking Rep. Albert Thomas, chairman of the Independent Offices Subcommittee, to reply:

> If you listen to that Commission you will find that you cannot change a comma, cross a "t," that they do not come here and "tummy-ache." They are the biggest "tummy-achers" . . . in the whole Government set-up.[85]

In the Senate, McMahon, who had just arrived from a meeting with the Commission on the 10 per-cent cut in personnel, reported on the floor that the Joint Committee had advised the Commission to ignore the personnel provision in the expectation that a supplemental appropriation or deficiency bill would restore the level of man power the AEC desired. The new chairman of the Independent Offices Subcommittee, Sen. Burnet R. Maybank (D., S.C.), was apparently willing to go along with this approach. McMahon's strategy was successful; the first Supplemental Appropriations Act gave the AEC funds for 1,400 new employees.[86]

By 1952, JCAE members were very much aware that the House Committee on Appropriations posed a real threat to the success of the atomic-energy program. Members of the Appropriations Committee, obviously bitter toward the JCAE, felt otherwise. Their attitude was reflected

---

[83] In testimony before the House Appropriations Committee in 1951, Chairman Dean apologized frankly: "I think we ought to say that our face is a little bit red on this, because the contractors in Los Alamos and the contractors in Oak Ridge have come down and met the arbitrary figure which the committee rider carried." "Hearings Before the Independent Offices Subcommittee of the Senate Appropriations Committee," *Independent Offices Appropriations for Fiscal Year 1952,* 82d Cong., 1st Sess. (1951), p. 835.

[84] Although the House committee cut the AEC's $1,200,000,000 request by $70,000,000, there was no objection on the House floor. Indeed, consideration of the bill for fiscal year 1952 featured the Appropriations Committee's defense of the AEC in support of an appropriation of $85,000 for a dog and cat hospital at Los Alamos. *Cong. Rec.,* 97 (May 4, 1951), 4883-4885. On the Senate side, the AEC was plagued once more by riders. One of these, requiring the AEC to notify its architects and engineers that all projects "should be purely utilitarian and without unnecessary refinements," was adopted over the AEC's protests and without opposition from JCAE members. *Ibid.* (June 19, 1951), 6713-6714.

[85] *Ibid.* (July 25, 1951), 8869-8870.

[86] *Ibid.* (Aug. 16, 1951), 10113; (Aug. 20, 1951), 10368. It is revealing that the JCAE and AEC had also seriously discussed the possibility that the AEC circumvent the restriction by arranging to "farm some of its employees to contractors." *Ibid.* (Aug. 16, 1951), 10114.

in a statement by House Appropriations Committee member Albert Gore, who said in 1952:

> I for one have been hoping for some help from the Joint Legislative Committee on Atomic Energy, but . . . this committee has never had one suggestion from the Joint Committee on Atomic Energy as to where we might save $1.

Representative Thomas agreed, adding, on another occasion, that the JCAE always makes "dire predictions" when AEC funds are cut.[87] Thus the House committee cut almost $100,000,000 from the AEC's regular appropriation bill of that year, adding a more stringent construction rider. Despite loud JCAE protest, the House followed the lead of the Appropriations Committee and passed the bill intact.[88]

This battle was only a prelude to a new and more furious fight over a supplemental appropriation bill. The House committee cut the AEC's request for $3,000,000,000 in half and inserted another rider which prohibited the AEC from starting new construction projects unless funds for completion of the projects were available. The cut and the rider threatened to impede the progress of the AEC's major expansion in the production of fissionable material. This was a severe blow, moreover, to a program which the JCAE took credit for initiating.[89] The JCAE unanimously adopted a resolution opposing the rider, but the House nevertheless, by a lopsided margin, rejected Durham's amendment to strike the "funds-to-complete" provision.[90] Although the bill passed the Senate without the rider, which had been eliminated by the Senate Appropriations Committee, it was restored in conference. The conference report was debated vigorously in the Senate, where the JCAE was more influential than it was in the House, and, under Hickenlooper's leadership, two successive conference reports were rejected. Finally, after a protracted night session, held under pressure of a deadline for Congressional adjournment, a third report was accepted. A compromise was reached retaining the rider but increasing the appropriated funds to such a level that the Commission would not be unduly restricted in starting new projects.

---

[87] "Hearings Before the Independent Offices Subcommittee of the House Appropriations Committee," *Independent Offices Appropriations for Fiscal Year 1953,* 82d Cong., 2d Sess. (1952), p. 1095; *Cong. Rec.,* 98 (March 20, 1952), 2614. It should be noted that both Gore and Thomas have since become members of the JCAE.

[88] During debate, one member of the Appropriations Committee said sarcastically that, although the JCAE spent weeks examining AEC programs, never had a JCAE member suggested a single cut to his committee. *Ibid.,* 2615-2616.

[89] See Representative Hinshaw's statement that the expansion program was initiated by the JCAE "through its own processes." *Cong. Rec.,* 98 (June 27, 1952), 8351.

[90] *Ibid.* (June 27, 1952), 8349, 8353. The vote on the Durham amendment was twenty-nine to ninety-two.

• The Period of Normalcy

Since 1952, the Joint Committee has continued to defend appropriations for the atomic-energy program, but, for a number of reasons, the bitterness of the earlier controversies has not recurred. One important reason is that, during 1953 and 1954, a Republican Congress was working with a Republican president and AEC chairman. Second, the relationship between the new JCAE chairman, Sterling Cole, and the new chairman of the House Independent Offices Subcommittee, Rep. John Phillips (R., Calif.), was much closer than that between McMahon and Thomas.[91] Third, the expansion programs of the AEC were well underway, and so there were fewer requests for funds for new, expensive projects. The administration itself, moreover, made cuts in AEC operating expenses, thereby satisfying the House Appropriations Committee. Finally, the Atomic Energy Act of 1954 included authorizing powers for the JCAE permitting Congress to endorse AEC construction programs. The improved JCAE-Appropriations relationship since the Democrats gained control of Congress in 1955 has been largely due to the transfer of jurisdiction for the AEC budget from the Independent Offices Subcommittee to the Public Works Subcommittee. In the Senate, the chairman of the Public Works Appropriations Subcommittee was Allen J. Ellender (D., La.), but a special subgroup headed by Lister Hill, the leader in the fight against Dixon-Yates, considered the AEC and TVA budgets. In the House, the Public Works Appropriations Subcommittee was headed by the chairman of the full committee, Clarence Cannon. Both Hill and Cannon were considered proponents of public power [92] and both shared, or came to share, the civilian reactor views of JCAE Democrats. Also important to a new spirit of harmony, hostility to the AEC chairman, Lewis Strauss, brought Democrats on the House Appropriations Committee and the JCAE closer together.[93]

This new relationship is indicated by the fact that, since 1955, there have been few fights on the floor of the House to restore cuts or eliminate riders inflicted by the Appropriations Committee. In 1959, the Appropria-

---

[91] In 1953, for example, when the AEC requested the appropriations committees to modify prior limitations on the AEC's authority to enter into long-term contracts for electric power, Phillips was willing to have the required authority handled as a legislative item rather than as a provision in an appropriation bill. According to Cole, he and Phillips collaborated on a bill which would meet the Commission's problem. *Long-Term Utility Contracts Hearings* (1953), pp. 39-40, 44.

[92] From 1944 through 1957, Hill voted for public-power legislation on forty-five out of forty-five roll calls. During the same period, Cannon voted for public-power provisions on thirty-seven out of forty roll calls. (Atomic-energy votes are included.)

[93] See H.R. Rep. No. 2849, 84th Cong., 2d Sess. (1956); reprinted in *Strauss Confirmation Hearings* (1959), pp. 915-947, 970ff.

tions Committee cut funds for the AEC's physical-research program; in 1960, it limited the funds that could be spent on ANP. In each instance, however, there was little cause for grave concern by JCAE members. They made only *pro forma* appeals on the House floor, confident that the Senate would restore the cuts and that the conference committee would compromise midway between the Senate and House versions.[94]

By 1960, the House Appropriations Committee had come to think and act more than ever before in terms of encouraging progress in peacetime applications of atomic energy. In fact, like the JCAE, it has, at times, come to the defense of the AEC. The Senate Appropriations Committee has continued its cordial relationship with the JCAE and has given a sympathetic hearing to its recommendations.[95] Thus, the problem of AEC appropriations has been largely resolved.

■ THE COMMITTEE AND CONGRESS

In the early years of the Joint Committee's existence, secrecy, calculated risks, and technological complexity placed atomic-energy policy beyond the active consideration of most congressmen. Because of this, influence on atomic-energy matters flowed primarily from the Joint Committee to Congress, rather than in the opposite direction. With the significant exception of the House Appropriations Committee, which maintained a share of independent authority, it could be stated that "the Committee [JCAE] *is* the Congress when it comes to atomic energy policy." [96] Since 1954, however, the JCAE's exclusive sphere of influence has gradually diminished. Other committees have developed interests competing with those of the JCAE, and even congressmen who are not members of the JCAE have acquired independent views about specific atomic-energy policies. A few, in fact, came to believe that Congress as a whole should play a larger role in atomic-policy-making, but, whenever attempts are made to increase Con-

---

[94] This is cited as the normal appropriations process in Congress. On foreign aid appropriations, for example, out of thirty-five major appropriations studied by Holbert Carroll, *The House of Representatives and Foreign Affairs* (Pittsburgh: University of Pittsburgh Press, 1958), the Senate raised the House-approved sums twenty-four times; of the eleven exceptions, the House and Senate sums were identical in the case of four, and the Senate was below the House in the other seven. For the three categories combined, the Senate-approved appropriations were 6.7 per cent above the House-endorsed totals. In all cases where the Senate was higher than the House, the conference agreement reflected the increases. *Op. cit.*, p. 155.

[95] In 1957, Senator Anderson visited the Senate Appropriations Committee to obtain an additional $9,000,000 for the AEC's Rover project. The committee approved his request. *Cong. Rec.*, 104 (Jan. 16, 1958), 599-603. According to Anderson, the AEC did not get the chance to spend these additional funds because the Bureau of the Budget froze them, but the AEC "didn't have any trouble with the committee and the Congress." *Outer Space Propulsion Hearings* (1958), pp. 6-7, 22.

[96] Dahl and Brown, *op. cit.*, p. 21.

gressional participation, they are resisted by JCAE members, who maintain that it would only "defeat the very theory upon which this Joint Committee was established." [97]

With the exception of the few occasions when legislators have questioned JCAE dominance, Congress has generally looked to the Committee for leadership in the field of atomic energy. Party leaders and the rank and file have taken their cues from the JCAE, which they regard as one of the most successful groups ever established by Congress. They especially recognize the ability of a committee which, at least in its own area, has revitalized the principle of legislative authority and exercised skillful control over the executive branch, particularly over the Atomic Energy Commission.

[97] In 1958, during debate on military-exchange legislation, Rep. Frank Thompson, Jr. (D., N.J.), offered an amendment providing that the JCAE submit a report to Congress on proposed agreements and that, if a resolution of disapproval were filed, the Committee would bring the measure to the floor for disposition. JCAE members resisted the amendment, objecting to any statutory requirement compelling them to report to Congress, but assured the House that they would report as fully as security would permit. *Cong. Rec.*, 104 (June 19, 1958), 11792-11793. The Thompson proposal was easily defeated, and the JCAE retained legislative control of military-exchange agreements.

VII | The JCAE in Action: Military and Civilian Applications

As an important participant in developing the nation's military and civilian atomic-energy programs, the JCAE skillfully employs a variety of devices. Although it has sometimes relied on legislation to push the Executive and lead Congress along paths charted by the Committee, for the most part it has achieved its objectives by surveillance of the atomic-energy establishment, constant pressure on the executive branch, and determined bargaining.

The Committee's techniques are plainly visible in the fields of military applications and civilian power. The appearance of projects having military significance—the hydrogen bomb, the expanded weapons program, the expansion of plutonium production, the aircraft nuclear propulsion program, and the Antarctic reactor—illustrates the manner in which the Committee performs its policy-making role. Two observations should be made about the military-application case studies which follow. First, the JCAE was substantially united in its objectives and approach and confronted the Executive, Congress, and the public with a single voice.[1] Sec-

[1] According to Samuel P. Huntington, ". . . the activities of the Committee were an example of the influential role which congressional committees could assume with respect

ond, these illustrations are not a complete history, since much of the record is classified or otherwise unavailable to the public. In the field of civilian power, however, the Committee often divided along party lines, and the administration usually exercised considerable restraint. But here, too, the Joint Committee effectively used an extensive array of resources, even though it had to settle for less than the Democratic majority desired.

■ MILITARY PROGRAMS

• The Hydrogen Bomb

On January 31, 1950, after several months of intensive debate, President Truman reached his decision to proceed with development of the hydrogen bomb. Forty days later, even before the feasibility of the bomb had been clearly demonstrated, he directed the AEC to embark on a program for quantity production of the weapon.

Prior to this decision, although there had been no public discussion, AEC scientists had been working on the fusion processes underlying the H-bomb concept for some time, but without a sense of urgency. During this period, Joint Committee members apparently showed little interest in the H-bomb, if, indeed, they were even conscious that such work was being done. The situation changed, however, when, on September 23, 1949, President Truman announced that the Soviet Union had detonated an atomic bomb.

Since loss of the A-bomb monopoly provided tremendous impetus for a new program to assure continued U.S. military supremacy, rapid development of the H-bomb seemed logical. On October 5, 1949, Commissioner Strauss called on his AEC colleagues to undertake a "quantum leap" in the development of hydrogen weapons.[2] The Commission responded by calling a special meeting of the General Advisory Committee (GAC) to consider the question of the H-bomb.

Meanwhile, a group of scientists who had been highly sympathetic to Dr. Edward Teller's efforts on fusion at Los Alamos and highly critical of what they regarded as opposition to a vigorous fusion program took their case to the JCAE. On October 10, Dr. Ernest O. Lawrence, and Dr. Luis Alvarez visited Carl Hinshaw of the JCAE and urged him to "get something going" on the thermonuclear program. At about this time, the JCAE met to consider the significance of the Russian A-bomb. The JCAE had not been informed of the evidence which had been the basis

---

to strategic programs." The JCAE's success, Huntington continues, depended on "the unanimity and involvement of its members and the existence of some support for its view among important officials in the Administration." *The Common Defense,* "Strategic Programs in National Politics" (New York: Columbia University Press, 1961), pp. 137-138.

[2] Thomas, *op. cit.,* p. 88.

for the conclusion that the Soviet Union had detonated an A-bomb, and some members were highly skeptical. A good part of the meeting was concerned with this issue, but, by the end of the meeting, Committee members were evidently impressed.[3] A few days later, the JCAE wrote the AEC for more data on the H-bomb program.

By the time the GAC met on October 29, the JCAE clearly favored a crash program to develop the H-bomb. As Dr. J. Robert Oppenheimer wrote at the time: "The Joint Congressional Committee, having tried to find something tangible to chew on ever since September 23, has at last found its answer. We must have a super and we must have it fast." [4] A JCAE subcommittee was dispatched to Los Alamos and Berkeley for consultation with the scientists working on the project.

On October 30, the GAC recommended against an accelerated H-bomb program on the grounds that it would be expensive, of questionable feasibility and military value, and a diversion of resources from more fruitful projects. On November 1, McMahon, having evidently learned of the GAC report, wrote the first of a series of letters to Truman urging a crash program.[5] The AEC, however, after considering the report, voted three-to-two against recommending increased efforts on thermonuclear weapons. Each of the commissioners wrote Truman his individual views, and the President thereupon created a special committee of the National Security Council, consisting of Secretary of State Dean Acheson, Secretary of Defense Louis A. Johnson, and AEC Chairman David E. Lilienthal, to study the problem further and report to him.

While this study was in progress, the two dissenting members of the Commission, Strauss and Dean, joined scientists Teller, Alvarez, and Lawrence and military leaders in carrying the fight to a receptive Joint Committee. McMahon thereupon wrote Truman repeating his views, and JCAE members "marched down to the White House" where they consulted the President personally prior to his decision to proceed with the hydrogen bomb.

The Committee regards its role in the H-bomb controversy as decisive. Whether or not the JCAE's intervention was the most crucial factor, it is significant that the Committee found an issue, aligned itself with certain scientific and executive factions and against others, and exerted pressure as a "special pleader" [6] to produce the desired presidential decision.

---

[3] See U.S. Atomic Energy Commission, *In the Matter of J. Robert Oppenheimer* (1954), pp. 776-777. According to Strauss, the scientists were invited by Chairman McMahon. *Op. cit.*, p. 218.

[4] *Ibid.*, p. 242.

[5] *Strauss Confirmation Hearings* (1959), p. 537.

[6] The phrase is President Truman's. *Memoirs by Harry S. Truman*, v. 2, "Years of Trial and Hope" (Garden City, New York: Doubleday, 1956), p. 307.

• Expansion

In the case of the H-bomb, the JCAE gave its enthusiastic support to a project initiated by others. But no sooner had the H-bomb program been launched than the JCAE independently created a new and even larger expansion program to be sold to the Executive. This program was aimed at the development of an arsenal of smaller nuclear weapons which might be useful for purposes other than massive destruction.

By the spring of 1951, members of the JCAE were already talking about a major expansion, among themselves and with military and AEC officials. On June 7, 1951, McMahon asked the Department of Defense and the AEC to estimate the costs of an expansion program under several alternative assumptions. This information was given to the JCAE about three months later. A few weeks after this report was received, McMahon and Durham, as chairman and vice-chairman of the Committee, introduced a concurrent resolution calling for a vast increase in the portion (then only 3 per cent) of the defense dollar going for atomic weapons. In essence, the resolution proposed that conventional military equipment be replaced by atomic equipment so as to create "an atomic army, and an atomic navy, and an atomic air force." As McMahon put it:

> I, therefore, propose that we now set about the business of building up our atomic bone and muscle and cutting away what will become excess military fat. Specifically, I propose that we make our best and cheapest weapon—the atomic weapon—the real backbone of our peace power.[7]

McMahon went on to describe an army equipped with atomic shells and short-range guided missiles, with weapons of radiological warfare, and supported by atomic-armed light planes; a navy equipped with nuclear-propelled vessels, planes carrying atomic bombs for strategic and tactical use, and guided missiles and torpedoes with nuclear warheads; and an air force armed with hydrogen weapons. All this, he pointed out, could be accomplished at far less cost than arming with conventional weapons; if mass produced, a single atomic bomb would cost less than a single tank.

In order to explore this plan more fully, the Joint Committee commenced a series of executive hearings, in the course of which the development of a "family of atomic weapons" was strongly endorsed by military officials. At the conclusion of these hearings, the JCAE unanimously adopted a resolution calling on the AEC and the Department of Defense to submit by January 3, 1952, "a definite and concrete report on maximizing the role which atomic energy can and should play in the defense of the United

[7] *Cong. Rec.*, 97 (Sept. 18, 1951), 11497.

States." A few days later, the Joint Chiefs of Staff established a formal requirement for production of plutonium, but the Committee was not completely satisfied, and Durham warned that the Joint Chiefs' failure to "ask for all the Atomic Energy Commission is capable of giving them is their solemn decision, one for which they will, of course, be held accountable by the American people and by the judgment of history." [8] Nevertheless, the JCAE was willing to base the expansion program on this statement of need.

The administration proceeded to develop an expansion program to meet the Joint Chiefs' stated requirements. When January 3 came and the Executive still did not have its report ready, the JCAE expressed its impatience. When McMahon emerged from a JCAE meeting on January 11 and remarked that he had been looking at an atomic cannon, this was interpreted as an effort to impress the Congress and prod the Executive. *The New York Times* characterized McMahon's statement as an attempt to persuade Congress that more money was needed for the atomic-energy program and observed that "the Atomic Energy Commission and the Department of Defense are under the necessity of justifying expenditures they cannot explain." [9]

Finally, on January 21, the long-awaited program was submitted to the JCAE, with the information that it had been approved by the Atomic Energy Subcommittee of the National Security Council and by the President. Since no substantive legislation was necessary to implement the program, no JCAE action was required, but the Committee held executive-session hearings on the report and "thoroughly reviewed and weighed" it. Although the report contemplated a $5,000,000,000-to-$6,000,000,000 expansion over a five-year period, it did not include a detailed blueprint. This was being worked on within the executive branch in the form of a request for appropriations, which was finally transmitted to Congress on May 29, four months later. In the interim, according to Durham, an impatient JCAE inquired of the AEC "two and three times a week and sometimes every day or even twice a day" as to when the supplemental budget request would be sent up, and "almost invariably the reply was that the budget request would be received next week." Ultimately, after a delay of three months, the JCAE protested and asked that the appropriations request be submitted "in the immediate future." The delay was apparently attributed to the strenuous efforts of the Executive to cut the costs of the expansion program to a minimum.[10] Although the JCAE enthusiastically supported the budget request and presumably approved the effort to

---

[8] *Cong. Rec.*, 98 (June 27, 1952), 8349-8350.
[9] *N.Y. Times*, Jan. 13, 1952.
[10] *Cong. Rec.*, 98 (June 27, 1952), 8349-8350.

reduce the cost of the program, its spokesmen minced no words in their criticism of the Executive's delay, which they felt to be detrimental to the national security.

The appropriations bill for the expanded program ran into rough sledding in Congress when the House Appropriations Committee slashed the funds requested and affixed a crippling construction rider. The JCAE fought fiercely against these amendments, telling Congress that this was, after all, a program initiated by the JCAE, and it ultimately achieved a satisfactory compromise.

• Plutonium Production

The expanded program resulting from the JCAE's efforts in the early 1950's included expansion of the AEC's production of plutonium. But the JCAE had always had a special interest in plutonium production over and above its interest in expansion of the program generally. As early as 1947, the JCAE was critical of the system employed by the military establishment to determine its requirements for nuclear weapons, claiming that the military requirements were set on the basis of the amount of plutonium to be produced by the AEC. Since the weapons requirements established by the Department of Defense were the basis for determining the quantity of plutonium to be produced by the AEC, the effect of this system was to eliminate military pressure for expanded production. The JCAE took the position that the military should determine its needs independently of AEC production, so that the AEC would produce to meet these needs.[11]

Although it appears that the JCAE's interest in increased plutonium production was continuing, its efforts prior to 1955 are largely hidden in secrecy. Since 1955, however, at least some of the story is a matter of public record. On July 29, 1955, after extensive executive-session hearings on the nation's "atomic preparedness," the JCAE sent a letter to the President, to which was attached a report unanimously adopted by the Military Applications Subcommittee of the JCAE and approved by the full Committee, stating that existing and planned facilities for producing special nuclear materials would, in all probability, be inadequate to meet future requirements. The report recommended that the Joint Chiefs of Staff submit their estimates for future additional requirements and that these estimates be independent of the AEC's planned production rates.[12] There is no public indication of the President's response, if any, but the

---

[11] S. Rep. No. 1793, 85th Cong., 2d Sess. (1958), pp. 24-26. See also S. Rep. No. 1041, 82d Cong., 1st Sess. (1951), and address by James T. Ramey before the 1960 annual meeting of the American Political Science Association.

[12] *Cong. Rec.*, 104 (July 15, 1958), 13807.

repetition of the same type of request each year for the next several years suggests that his reaction was unfavorable.

Ten months later, JCAE Chairman Anderson, Chairman Jackson of the Military Applications Subcommittee, and Chairman Price of the Research and Development Subcommittee jointly wrote the President arguing that there was "little elasticity in the present system of production and allocation" and that, "despite advances in the nuclear art, production quotas remain relatively stable." They proposed as a new and flexible approach the creation of an "Atomic Bank for the stockpiling of uncommitted reserves of fissionable materials." To create the bank, the current rate of production would have to be increased, with all production above that committed for present use to be placed in the bank so that "new and novel military or civilian uses may be quickly exploited as they arise." [13] The proposal was rejected by the President.

The JCAE, however, persisted in advocating an increased supply of plutonium, turning its attention to a dual-purpose reactor capable of producing both plutonium and electric power. Sen. Henry Jackson of Washington had proposed in 1956 the construction of such a reactor at the AEC's Hanford facility, and in 1957 Committee Democrats sought to include this unsolicited project in the Commission's authorization legislation for fiscal year 1958. The AEC contended that such a reactor could produce neither power nor plutonium efficiently and that there was no apparent need for increased plutonium production. Commissioner Vance stressed that the AEC had given considerable thought to "the possibility of increased requirements of plutonium," but "to date we have not been able to obtain from anybody an indication of the necessity of doing it." [14]

The authorization bill, as finally reported by a divided Committee, provided $3,000,000 for an AEC design study of a plutonium production reactor, either single or dual-purpose, and specified that the study be submitted to the JCAE by April 1, 1958. In the Committee report, the majority justified the project primarily by the need for additional plutonium and minimized the reactor's importance as a source of electric power. In support of its contention, the majority cited testimony from Teller, Alvarez, Lawrence, and the directors of the Los Alamos and Livermore weapons laboratories and concluded that "minimum future needs may indicate an increase of production many times the current rate." Republicans did not take issue with the contention that more plutonium was required, but did express strong opposition to the particular project contemplated.[15]

---

[13] *Ibid.*, 102 (July 2, 1956), 11583.
[14] *FY 1958 Authorization Hearings* (1957), p. 658.
[15] H.R. Rep. No. 978, 85th Cong., 1st Sess. (1957), pp. 24-25.

The JCAE Democrats' battle was based on their assertion that a need for more plutonium existed. But neither the AEC nor the Department of Defense supported the JCAE contention. To buttress their position, Anderson and Durham, together with all JCAE subcommittee chairmen, issued a press release on July 30, 1957, calling attention to what they considered a "dangerous situation" in the need for additional plutonium. The authorization bill was finally enacted, with the design-study provision intact. In signing the bill, the President showed his dissatisfaction with some of its provisions, including the study of the plutonium production reactor.

During the next year, JCAE members worked diligently to build a record supporting the need for more plutonium. On November 13, 1957, Chairman Durham and Senator Jackson sent a letter to the new secretary of defense calling his attention to "the inadequate planned production of weapons material and the dangerous methods by which requirements were being determined." Durham and Anderson again wrote to the President on December 3, 1957, expressing JCAE interest in additional weapons material, calling for increased plutonium production, and once more criticizing the manner in which requirements were determined. Then, on January 9, 1958, Durham wrote the secretary of defense, requesting information on the study of the problem which the department purportedly was making.[16]

In addition to direct pressure on the executive branch, JCAE members used other techniques to marshal support for their project. Durham, in a speech on March 19, 1958, criticized the Defense Department "bureaucratic treadmill" on requirements and reargued the need for additional plutonium. Senator Jackson created a special advisory panel to his Military Applications Subcommittee, described as a "nuclear brain trust," including former AEC Chairman Gordon Dean, to study the adequacy of programs for reactor products. The panel, in a classified report in June, was reported to have generally concluded that:

1. Present and planned plutonium production was substantially inadequate to meet future needs.
2. A major expansion in reactor products was economically sound and desirable.
3. The existing system of establishing requirements had shortcomings.[17]

In addition, the Jackson subcommittee held executive-session hear-

[16] S. Rep. No. 1793, 85th Cong., 2d Sess. (1958), pp. 24-26.
[17] JCAE press release, July 3, 1958.

ings on this problem in the spring of 1958. In the course of these hearings, Gen. Nathan Twining, chairman of the Joint Chiefs of Staff, testified that the Joint Chiefs had recommended to the secretary of defense on May 9, 1958, that additional plutonium-producing reactors be built, but that the secretary had sent the recommendation back to the Joint Chiefs "with instructions that it be restudied and resubmitted with a more definitive statement of requirements." The Joint Chiefs had made a similar recommendation at least three times previously, but in each case the secretary had failed to act.[18]

Members of the JCAE used the statements of the military leaders to bolster their demands for more plutonium, but the President continued his firm opposition. On July 10, 1958, he wrote a member of the House Appropriations Committee, pointedly commenting that each military department had given its assessment of plutonium requirements for weapons, but that these assessments were "subject to review by the Joint Chiefs of Staff, the Secretary of Defense, and the President." He further stated that the secretary of defense currently believed that "military needs do not require additional production facilities" and that there was, therefore, "no justifiable basis to proceed." [19]

Despite the opposition of the Eisenhower administration, both Democratic and Republican Committee members joined in supporting the inclusion in the AEC's fiscal year 1959 authorization bill of a provision for the construction of a plutonium-producing reactor. On the floor of Congress, there was some opposition from administration stalwarts, but this opposition could make no headway in the face of the JCAE argument that additional plutonium was required for nuclear weapons. When Eisenhower criticized the project in signing the bill, Senator Anderson replied that the President "has apparently taken the advice of the Bureau of the Budget and members of his staff and overruled the judgment of the Joint Chiefs of Staff; the heads of the Army, Navy and Air Force; the Atomic Energy Commission, every member of which is his appointee; and the Joint Committee on Atomic Energy." [20]

Construction of the plutonium-producing reactor was begun in 1959. In March of that year, Senator Anderson said he had learned that the Defense Department had finally developed a long-term requirement for plutonium, but, he added, "no one should be surprised if this long-

---

[18] *Cong. Rec.*, 104 (July 15, 1958), 13808-13809.

[19] *Loc. cit.* No chronology of the plutonium controversy would be complete without reference to the strange interlude in 1958, when the administration was arguing in favor of increasing the nation's plutonium supply, but by purchasing it abroad rather than by increasing domestic production capacity. See Chapter IV, *supra.*

[20] Press release, Aug. 4, 1958.

term requirement coincides with the production from current AEC facilities . . . and the new Hanford reactor. So round and round they go." [21]

• Aircraft Nuclear Propulsion

The aircraft nuclear propulsion program (ANP) originated in 1946 as an Air Corps project and a year later became a coordinated AEC-Air Force endeavor. Its fifteen-year history shows the JCAE as an active participant in executive policy-making, becoming involved in technological, administrative, and organizational decisions; it reveals uncertainty on the part of the Executive and single-minded effort on the part of the Joint Committee.[22]

At first, the ANP program was largely one of research. In 1951, however, the program was advanced to the research-and-development level with the award of a contract to General Electric for development of a nuclear-propulsion plant. In the same year, the Joint Chiefs of Staff established a requirement for the nuclear-propelled aircraft after JCAE prodding, and the Air Force chief of staff urged that it be given a high priority. Following suggestions by the Joint Committee, a joint Office for Aircraft Nuclear Propulsion was set up a year later to coordinate the AEC-Air Force effort, with an Air Force officer, Maj. Gen. Donald Keirn, as its director.

The new program encountered difficulties almost immediately. With the advent of the Eisenhower administration, an Air Force board recommended a twenty per-cent cutback in the program on the ground that the current effort was not justified by the state of the art. Thereupon, the National Security Council recommended that the program be curtailed. Secretary of Defense Charles E. Wilson gave his views: "The atomic-powered aircraft reminds me of a shite-poke—a great big bird that flies over the marshes, that doesn't have too much body or speed to it, or anything, but can fly." Wilson's comment summed up administration opinion that the project involved an attempt to develop a nuclear-propelled aircraft for the sake of flying it, even though its bulk and inherent safety problems would limit its speed and mobility to the point that it would be militarily useless.

A decision was apparently made by the Department of Defense in the spring of 1953 to cancel the ANP program, but an indignant JCAE met with Deputy Secretary of Defense Roger M. Kyes and Air Force Secretary Harold E. Talbot. These officials explained that the directive

---

[21] Clinton P. Anderson, "The Outlook for the U.S. Atomic Energy Program,"*Nucleonics*, March 1959.

[22] Unless otherwise noted, information in this section is based on *ANP Hearings* (1959) and *Staff Report on ANP* (1959).

was not a cancellation of the program, but merely a reorientation calling for a limited research-and-development effort concentrating on high-temperature and reactor experiments aimed at developing a reactor system for a direct-cycle nuclear-propulsion plant. The new plan did not satisfy the JCAE, and it issued a report in May, 1954, calling for a crash program.

By this time, the ANP program was proceeding along two independent lines. General Electric was working on a direct-cycle propulsion system, while Pratt and Whitney and the Oak Ridge National Laboratory had responsibility for development of an indirect-cycle system. Work on both systems continued from 1954 to 1956 under the program as curtailed in 1953. By 1956, General Keirn was predicting a ground test of the direct-cycle system in 1959 and flight a year or two later. But, in August, 1956, the administration cut the ANP budget, resulting, according to the JCAE, in eighteen months' "slippage." Later that year, the President approved a further cut in the program as an economy measure, with the result that the direct-cycle program was curtailed and the indirect-cycle one almost eliminated.

During JCAE hearings on ANP in February, 1957, JCAE members urged Deputy Secretary Quarles to institute a program which would lead to early flight. Quarles responded that the administration was not interested in early flight as an objective in itself and that it was pointless to contemplate flight until there was a militarily useful plane to be flown. Nevertheless, the JCAE's position had considerable support within the Department of Defense, and, by the fall of 1957, Quarles was being pressed by the Air Force to approve an early flight plan using a modified conventional military plane as a flying test-bed. JCAE members, sensing victory, optimistically predicted early flight of an atomic-powered plane.[23]

At this point, two new factors entered the picture. The loss of prestige suffered by the United States with the launching of the Russian sputnik caused grave concern among JCAE members that the Russians would also be successful in the first nuclear-propelled flight. This concern was reinforced when JCAE member Melvin Price returned in October, 1957, from a trip to the Soviet Union with indications that "the Russians are placing considerable emphasis on their own program to develop a nuclear-propelled aircraft." Second, the Navy Department suddenly developed a keen interest in a nuclear-propelled seaplane and supported the indirect-cycle approach, which it felt was preferable for development of a seaplane. The indirect-cycle system was, of course, far from ready for a flight test, so the effect of the Navy's position was to introduce an element of doubt concerning the early test flight of the direct-cycle system.

Thus, with the Air Force and the AEC pressing for early flight

---

[23] *N.Y. Times,* April 14, 1957.

using the direct cycle, with the Navy in opposition, and Quarles negatively inclined, the problem, characteristically, was referred to still another study committee, headed by Dr. Robert Bacher, one of the original AEC commissioners. Price assailed the Navy's intervention as "senseless interservice rivalry" and deplored the creation of the Bacher committee. Arguing that "what this program needs is action, not another study group," he said:

> This project . . . has almost literally been studied to death over the years of its existence. At last count I think there have been no less than six or seven expert panels and committees who have reviewed the project from time to time, some of them concurrently. The inference naturally arises that some of the study groups, at least, were established not so much for technical reappraisal as a device to permit top officials of the Defense Department to avoid their responsibility for making difficult but necessary decisions.

While the Bacher group was studying the problem, the JCAE maintained relentless pressure on Quarles. On January 27, when Quarles reported to the JCAE that no decision had been reached, Price argued that the three months' delay to that date in approving the Air Force's request for an early test flight "might well be the margin of Russia getting the first atomic plane in the air." [24]

Finally, the Bacher committee recommended against the early flight objective in favor of increased emphasis on development of advanced materials capable of producing higher reactor performances. The President adopted this recommendation, notwithstanding Price's charge that the report was based on "a cursory review of the program . . . and a brief inspection trip to the field" and ignored the psychological importance of winning the race with Russia for nuclear propulsion of aircraft. In replying to Price's bitter criticisms, Eisenhower argued that the objective of "earliest possible achievement of an operational military aircraft" was in direct conflict with the objective of beating the Russians to the first flight and that the former objective was the more important.

By this time, the JCAE was reacting sharply to every report on the subject coming out of Russia. An article in *Aviation Week* on December 1, 1958, stating that the Russians were flight-testing a nuclear bomber, led Price to assail the "bureaucratic snafus" in Washington and to demand again that target dates be set for ground test and the first flight. Eisenhower rejected the Price suggestion again, stating that:

> There is no usefulness that anyone could possibly see for such a plane [the flying test-bed] and, therefore, our own research efforts have been developed toward the production of

[24] *Ibid.,* Jan. 28, 1958.

> an airplane that will have satisfactory performance characteristics either for some peaceful or military purpose, but we do not abandon the basic research on the powerplant . . . which is the basis of the whole thing. And we just merely say that there is no use of going into a field where the whole program would be to get a plane a few hundred feet off the ground.

He added that "there is absolutely no intelligence to back up a report that Russia is flight testing an atomic-powered plane." A month later, in January, 1959, Radio Moscow reported that the Russians planned to fly a nuclear-propelled "civil craft" before the end of 1959. Another executive session hearing was held, and, at the end of this hearing, Anderson, Durham, and Price issued a statement, handed to Quarles on the spot, denouncing "administrative indecision and interservice rivalries." They charged that the modest amounts then being spent on ANP made the program a "holding operation to avoid difficult technical and administrative decisions" and represented "a completely indefensible use of the taxpayers' money."

Quarles responded by issuing a statement the following day restating and defending the administration's position, dismissing the allegations of "administrative indecision" and "interservice rivalries" as having no basis in fact, and suggesting that there was no waste in the present program but that an early flight program would involve such waste. In response to the concern that the Russians might "choose the more spectacular early flight course" and beat the United States in this respect, Quarles concluded that "we can take some satisfaction in the fact that they will have wasted some of their resources."

The JCAE immediately countered with an announcement that its Subcommittee on Research and Development, under the chairmanship of Price, would hold open hearings on the ANP program.[25] Price said:

> If the Department of Defense feels that committee criticism of the conduct of the ANP program is unwarranted, I think the best course for us to follow is to lay the facts out on the table in a public hearing and let the chips fall where they may. For 10 long years the Joint Committee has been pressing the Defense Department and the Atomic Energy Commission to get on with the job of developing a flying prototype of a nuclear-powered aircraft and has urged time and again that difficult technical and administrative decisions be made so that the program can move forward vigorously.

With the hearing scheduled for May 14 and 15, the JCAE maintained its relentless pressure on the Executive and in April arranged for a tour

[25] These hearings were the first public ones scheduled on the ANP program, although thirty-five executive sessions had been held since 1947.

by Quarles and McCone of the General Electric Company's ANP project at Evendale, Ohio. On May 7, AEC officials met with Quarles and his staff, and, according to the Committee, agreement was reached that a recommendation for an early flight be submitted to the President. Quarles died the following day, May 8. His death not only necessitated indefinite postponement of the JCAE's open hearings on ANP, but also left considerable uncertainty as to precisely what decision had been reached on May 7. It apparently is a matter of dispute whether Quarles, on behalf of the Defense Department, actually reversed his position and agreed to support early flight. Conflicting reports over the department's position prompted Price to call an executive session meeting with Dr. Herbert York, director of defense research and engineering, who was now responsible for formulating the Defense Department position on ANP. Although York advised the JCAE that no decision would be forthcoming until June, Price emerged from the meeting with the optimistic report that "we are coming closer to the time when a definite policy and a firm decision will be made." [26]

The Defense Department's final decision was communicated to the Committee on June 7. To the Committee's dismay, the decision was that the ANP program be reoriented toward development of more advanced materials and greater emphasis on the indirect-cycle approach, thereby eliminating any target dates for ground tests and nuclear flight. JCAE members termed this a "backward step," and Price forthwith rescheduled the open hearing for July 23. The hearings were held this time, and subsequently the JCAE issued a report signed by all eighteen members calling for early flight. The eight Republican members, however, filed separate views cautioning that the objective of nuclear flight "as early as possible" did not necessarily "connotate [*sic*] either a 'crash' program or a major step-up in present programming to overcome remaining technical problems." In their view, "as early as possible" meant "to get something in the air flying on nuclear power at the earliest moment technically possible only when technical and non-technical considerations both clearly point to that interpretation."

Nothing was changed by the JCAE hearings and report; the program continued at the level of about $150,000,000 per year—about equally divided between the AEC and the Air Force—with no target dates for flight. Despite the fact that the program was proceeding at a slower pace than demanded by the JCAE, the executive officials in charge of ANP were apparently pleased with its progress. Thus, in the summer of 1960, the AEC told the Senate Appropriations Committee that,

For the first time since the program's inception, we have in

---

[26] *N.Y. Times,* May 22, 1959.

> hand a firm national development objective, a technological position which affords confidence that this objective can be achieved, and carefully planned reactor experiments which will demonstrate feasibility.[27]

But this state of affairs was not to continue.

When President Eisenhower submitted his last budget, that for fiscal year 1962, the ANP program was cut by about 50 per cent. This cut was in contemplation of the abandonment of either the direct-cycle or the indirect-cycle approach, but the decision on which should be eliminated was left to the incoming Kennedy administration. Congressman Price predictably reacted strongly to the Eisenhower cut, terming it "arbitrary" and stating that it would "have the effect, if not the intent, of embarrassing the incoming administration." He criticized the President's decision as involving a choice between the two approaches before a sound factual basis had been developed for making a rational selection.[28]

Price and other JCAE members made a desperate effort to persuade President Kennedy to reverse the Eisenhower decision and to continue work on both the direct-cycle and indirect-cycle methods on at least the same level as in the past. These JCAE members visited President Kennedy early in March, 1961, and emerged believing that he had agreed to continue work on both approaches until a decision could be reached in 1962 as to which was preferable.[29] President Kennedy had other ideas, however. Apparently without any warning to the JCAE proponents of the ANP program, he sent his revised budget to Congress in late March, announcing complete cancellation of the ANP project. The President expressed "concern and amazement" over the fact that over a billion dollars had already been spent on the program and that another billion-dollar expenditure and ten years' time would be necessary before a nuclear-propelled plane could be put into operational use.[30]

Congressman Price, stunned by President Kennedy's decision, expressed gratification that a "forthright decision" had at least been made and, with evident understatement, reflected that "this means indefinite delay for the flight test programs." [31]

• The Antarctic Reactor

The Atomic Energy Commission authorization act for fiscal year 1960 directed the AEC to proceed with design and engineering studies

---

[27] *Forum Memo,* July 1960, p. 22.
[28] *"Sec. 202" Hearings* (1961), pp. 82-83.
[29] *Washington Post and Times Herald,* March 25, 1961.
[30] *N.Y. Times,* March 12, 1961; *Forum Memo,* April 1961, p. 10.
[31] *Loc. cit.*

of a reactor for remote military installations and to submit a report to the JCAE by April 1, 1960. The AEC employed a contractor, Kaiser Engineers, to examine ten possible remote military reactor sites designated by the Department of Defense. The Kaiser report, transmitted by the AEC to the JCAE on March 31, 1960, indicated that a power reactor at McMurdo Sound in Antarctica would be particularly feasible. The AEC informed the JCAE at that time that it had asked Kaiser to study two more Antarctic stations for possible installation of reactors and that the report on these studies would be available by May 1, 1960.[32]

In the meantime, preparation of the AEC budget for fiscal year 1961 had been completed. Included in the budget was an item of $11,600,-000 for a nuclear power plant for a remote military installation on Guam. This sum would pay for the nuclear portion of the Guam reactor, and the Navy Department was expected to budget for the remainder of the cost of the plant. Since the Navy Department was unable to fund its share of the project, the Bureau of the Budget eliminated this item from the AEC's presentation to Congress.

On March 7, 1960, the day before hearings began on the Commission's 1961 authorization legislation, JCAE Executive Director James T. Ramey wrote to the AEC requesting that the Commission be prepared to testify on small, portable reactors for such remote locations as the Antarctic. He noted that such reactors would apparently be economical and therefore "should be very attractive." The next day, Senator Jackson urged Chet Holifield, chairman of the subcommittee responsible for the authorization legislation, to include power reactor plants for the Antarctic bases in the bill. He further requested that the JCAE suggest to both the AEC and the Navy "that design work and procurement be initiated prior to the normal legislative process for the forthcoming year," so that the construction season starting in December could be fully utilized.[33] On March 9, the Navy was asked to testify on reactor applications at remote sites, including Antarctica, and was also asked to defer plans for construction of a conventional power plant on Guam until the JCAE could study the Kaiser report, which was to be submitted to the Committee later that month.

Several days later, Navy Department officials appeared before the JCAE and stated emphatically that, although they wished to install nuclear

---

[32] Unless otherwise noted, information in this section is from *FY 1961 Authorization Hearings* (1960).

[33] Senator Jackson pointed out that the delivered costs of fuel oil at McMurdo Sound were very high because of extremely difficult transportation conditions, that use of reactors for power would save many dollars and lives, and that it would contribute to knowledge of nuclear power and would enhance American prestige. Jackson's strong feelings about the utility of nuclear power in the Antarctic were based on a visit he made to the area in 1959.

power plants at all three Antarctic installations, they were deterred by the high initial cost of such a project. Operating under budgetary ceilings for new construction, the Navy was unwilling to pay a premium price for construction of nuclear power plants, even though operating costs would be substantially less. In view of this difficulty, the Committee was eager that AEC funds be used for such a purpose, and the AEC was apparently willing. Although the Bureau of the Budget recognized the value of nuclear power in remote military installations and agreed that operating costs as well as capital costs should be considered in a choice between nuclear and conventionally fueled power plants, it rejected the use of AEC funds for these reactors. Elmer B. Staats, deputy director of the bureau, told the JCAE:

> For effective management, the responsibility of budgeting for an item should lie with the agency which needs and uses an item. On this basis, we believe that valid power requirements at military sites which can be met to advantage by atomic plants should be funded in full by the Department of Defense. . . . I do not believe that the assumption of capital cost by AEC would have the result intended by the committee, i.e., encouraging the military services to recognize and assess adequately the unique advantages of nuclear power in a number of military situations. On the contrary, it would have the effect of increasing the reliance of the military services on the AEC budget for an indefinite period. . . . Thus the Department of Defense would still have to face the difficult period of "withdrawal" of AEC assistance, or, alternatively, we would have to build into the AEC budget a long-term program of construction subsidy to the military services.

He pointed out that the Department of Defense, responsible for making up its own budget within the ceiling limitations fixed by the president, had not requested funds for Antarctic reactors. If nuclear power plants were not of a sufficiently high relative priority to be included, Staats concluded, the Department of Defense would have to do without the plants even though such plants would be economical over a long period. Despite intensive and occasionally sarcastic interrogation by Committee members and despite lack of support from AEC or Defense officials, Staats stood his ground in refusing to endorse the JCAE's demands.

On April 19, 1960, the JCAE reported the authorization bill, which included $13,000,000 for nuclear power plants for Antarctica. The Committee report stated that three to five plants were needed in the immediate future, but that,

> . . . the actual number and location of reactors to be constructed under this authorization should be left to the determination of the Commission, based upon the technical aspects of the reactor plants selected, procurement economics, and,

> in consultation with the Department of Defense, the requirements schedule. Three reactors are contemplated but more may be possible under the $13 million authorization.

With respect to funding aspects, the report specified that the authorization covered "procurement" of the reactor plants in the United States, but that "it is expected" that all other charges (transportation, erection, procurement, burn-up charges, chemical processing of fuel elements, operation, and maintenance) would be financed from appropriations of the Department of Defense or scientific agencies. But the JCAE was so anxious to have the reactors built that it added the concession that, ". . . if necessary, this authorization would be available for transportation and other incidental costs, but not operating costs." Pointing out that procurement of the plants should start during the early part of 1961, the Committee report stated that this objective could most easily be attained if the AEC were given responsibility. But, for purposes of flexibility, the report continued, "alternative methods of financing may be followed if considered necessary." [34]

Thus, the JCAE in effect directed the expeditious execution of a project which, at the time, was being only preliminarily studied within the executive branch. The project had not yet been subject to the analysis and scrutiny which enters into the normal budgetary processes, and the executive branch had not yet had the opportunity to consider whether it wanted the project as a matter of relative priorities, how much money it was prepared to spend on the project, and how it wished the project to be carried out organizationally. Instead, answers to these questions were thrust on the executive branch by the JCAE's action.

The authorization legislation was speedily passed by both the House and the Senate. Neither the JCAE report nor the floor debate revealed that the inclusion of the authorization for the Antarctic reactors was contrary to the strong views of the Bureau of the Budget, and, so far as can be determined, the attitude of the Bureau of the Budget was not conveyed by the President to Congress or to the majority or minority leadership of either house.

Despite inclusion of the $13,000,000 authorization for the Antarctic reactors in the authorization act, the Commission, in deference to the position taken by the Bureau of the Budget, did not include funds for this project in its appropriations request. During hearings before the House Appropriations Committee, AEC Chairman McCone, in reply to questioning, stated that "the responsibility for installing and for budgeting for installation in the Antarctic is [that of] the Navy" and that the Com-

---

[34] S. Rep. No. 1277, 86th Cong., 2d Sess. (1960), pp. 7-8.

mission was "hopeful that they will be able to find a way to budget for such a reactor." [35] The Appropriations Committee ultimately reported a bill, later passed by the House, which did not include funds for the Antarctic reactors.

During consideration of the AEC budget by the Senate Appropriations Committee, Senator Anderson, as an ex officio member, made a strong plea for inclusion of $13,000,000 for the Antarctic reactors. He also inserted in the Appropriations Committee's record a statement by Senator Jackson characterizing funding for the project as a "classic example of a breakdown of our budgeting process" in that a clearly economic and important project was being delayed, if not killed, "entirely by the budgetary process shortcomings." [36] Subsequently, the Senate Appropriations Committee reported the bill with the $13,000,000 item and a provision permitting transfer of the funds for the Antarctic reactors to the Navy.[37] The Senate passed the bill with these funds intact, but the Senate-House conference committee reduced the Antarctic reactor item to $3,-500,000.[38]

While the appropriations legislation was passing through Congress, the JCAE maintained constant pressure on the Executive. Although the Bureau of the Budget had informed the JCAE in May that it had asked the Department of Defense to review the advantages of nuclear reactors in the Antarctic,[39] the JCAE wrote the bureau on June 17, again urging immediate action. The JCAE had also written the AEC, on June 14, requesting that it immediately solicit proposals for the construction of the Antarctic reactors, subject to availability of appropriations, even though the appropriation had already been refused by the House Appropriations Committee. Six days later, the Commission issued an invitation for proposals, and, on August 10, the very day the Senate was considering the appropriation bill, it announced acceptance of the proposal of the Martin Company.[40]

---

[35] "Hearings Before the Subcommittee on Public Works Appropriations of the House Appropriations Committee," *AEC Appropriation Bill for Fiscal Year 1961*, 86th Cong., 2d Sess. (1960), p. 38.

[36] "Hearings Before a Subcommittee of the Senate Committee on Appropriations," H.R. 12326, 86th Cong., 2d Sess. (1960), pp. 29-33.

[37] S. Rep. No. 1768, 86th Cong., 2d Sess. (1960), pp. 41-42.

[38] In addition to this amount, the Navy Department finally transferred $1,500,000 to the AEC for this purpose.

[39] Senator Anderson regarded this review as unnecessary because of the "very comprehensive review" just completed—presumably a reference to the Kaiser study. The Department of Defense report to the Bureau of the Budget was generally favorable, but not particularly enthusiastic, about the use of nuclear reactors in the Antarctic. *Cong. Rec.*, 107 (Aug. 10, 1960), 16143-16146.

[40] *Loc. cit.*

The JCAE thus brought about the Antarctic reactor project without overt support from any part of the executive branch, largely through pushing, pulling, prodding, and persuading both the Executive and Congress.

■ THE CIVILIAN POWER PROGRAM

Efforts to develop nuclear power began in 1944 when the Manhattan Engineer District initiated a research program in the Argonne National Laboratory and the Clinton Laboratories at Oak Ridge. The Oak Ridge work was discontinued in December, 1947, and all nuclear-power research was centralized in Argonne. In 1948, the AEC announced that an experimental power plant would be built at the Knolls Atomic Power Laboratory near Schenectady, New York. However, cost and other factors led to cancellation of the project in April, 1950, and from 1950 to 1953 no major reactor project with the primary object of producing industrial power was undertaken. Shortly after termination of the Knolls project, the president of Monsanto Chemical Corporation proposed private construction and operation of an atomic-power plant which would generate power and produce plutonium. Supplementing this proposal, the AEC in 1951 instituted an industrial participation program under which industrial groups studied "the practicability of business and industry building and operating reactors for the production of fissionable materials and power." [41]

The JCAE had always had a strong interest in the AEC's reactor program, but principally because of military needs. In 1951, however, the Joint Committee expressed growing interest in nonmilitary uses of reactors and the Commission's industrial participation program. It recommended that the complex factors involved in the construction and operation of dual-purpose reactors by private industry be studied, so that they might be "properly evaluated and judged." [42] Chairman Durham followed this suggestion with a letter to the AEC in August, 1952, indicating his intention to hold hearings in 1953 on industrial participation in the reactor program and requesting a written statement of the Commission's policy.[43] The Commission responded in May, 1953, with a policy statement on nuclear power development, endorsing the attainment of economically competitive nuclear power as a national goal and expressing the conviction that progress toward this goal could be advanced through participation "by qualified and interested groups outside the Commission." Such participation, the statement concluded, could be encouraged by providing certain incentives like private ownership and operation of facilities.[44]

---

[41] *Staff Study of Atomic Power and Private Enterprise* (1952), pp. 174, 199, 216, 7-9.
[42] S. Rep. No. 1041, 82d Cong., 1st Sess. (1951), pp. 4-5.
[43] *Staff Study of Atomic Power and Private Enterprise* (1952), p. iii.
[44] *Atomic Power Development Hearings* (1953), pp. 6-7.

The JCAE held extensive open hearings in June and July on atomic power development and private enterprise. Some spokesmen for industry indicated during these hearings that, with appropriate amendment of the 1946 act, industry could produce competitive atomic power even without governmental assistance.[45] As the hearings drew to an end, Chairman Cole wrote to AEC Chairman Strauss noting, among other things, the references at the hearings to the vagueness of the AEC's plans for research in and development of atomic-power components, pilot plants, and prototypes. He suggested that the AEC develop a "3-to-5-year program—of specific research and development projects," so that interested parties might adjust their plans accordingly.[46]

The AEC responded in February, 1954, proposing a five-year program for research and development on five specific reactor types. The JCAE Subcommittee on Research and Development, under Carl Hinshaw, considered the AEC report and recommended to the full Committee:

> The program as a package should be reviewed at least annually to insure that the approaches being followed are still in proper balance and that every advantage is being taken of new developments.
>
> A meeting should be held with the Commission before any further action on the pressurized water reactor is undertaken in order to insure that both the committee and the Commission are in agreement on its continuation, appreciate its limitations, and have a clear conception of what it can be expected to accomplish.[47]

Thus the Committee served notice that it would thereafter follow the reactor program closely and participate in decisions on specific reactors.

Even before the AEC submitted its five-year plan, the JCAE had acted to encourage the beginning of a civilian reactor program. The first Eisenhower budget had eliminated an AEC request for funds to construct a pilot power plant, but, at the urging of JCAE Chairman Cole and hold-over AEC Chairman Dean, funds for this reactor were restored by the House Appropriations Committee. Shortly thereafter, the AEC announced that Westinghouse Electric Corporation and Duquesne Light Company would build and partially finance the full-scale power plant now known as the Shippingport reactor. Chairman Cole took full credit on behalf of the JCAE and the House Appropriations Committee as "originators of

---

[45] See Walker L. Cisler speech, reprinted in *Staff Study of Atomic Power and Private Enterprise* (1952), pp. 20-21, and Cisler testimony, *Atomic Power Development Hearings* (1953), pp. 134, 156, 161, 169.

[46] *Staff Study of Five-Year Power Reactor Program* (1954), p. 5.

[47] *Ibid.*, p. 4.

this first major step," since funds for the reactor had been authorized and appropriated, he said, "entirely on Congressional initiative."[48]

In 1954, the Atomic Energy Act was rewritten to permit private participation in atomic-power development. The new law allowed private ownership of reactors under AEC licensing, although nuclear fuels would still be owned by the government and leased to private users. The latter provision was of great importance, since it meant that the economics of nuclear-power projects would be closely tied to pricing policies established by the AEC for nuclear fuel. In its report on the 1954 bill, the JCAE explained the basic purpose of opening the nuclear industry to private enterprise:

> It is now evident that greater private participation in power development need not bring with it attendant hazards to the health and safety of the American people. Moreover, the atomic reactor art has already reached the point where atomic power at prices competitive with electricity derived from conventional fuels is on the horizon, though not within our immediate reach.
>
> . . . .
>
> In particular we do not believe that any developmental program carried out solely under governmental auspices, no matter how efficient it may be, can substitute for the cost cutting and other incentives of free and competitive enterprise.[49]

The optimism of the JCAE majority was not shared by Congressmen Holifield and Price. They attacked the revision of the act as premature and criticized the limitation on power production by the AEC, taking the position that:

> The profit making opportunities in atomic enterprise are years distant. Unless the United States Government strikes out boldly in a comprehensive program of reactor development and undertakes to produce and distribute electrical power derived from nuclear fission, we shall find other countries forging rapidly ahead in this field.[50]

The Commission, interpreting the new act as a mandate to rely primarily on private industry for development of nuclear power, proceeded to implement it. In January, 1955, the AEC announced its power-demonstration-reactor program (PDRP),[51] designed "to open the way for American industry to develop, fabricate, construct and operate experimental

[48] Thomas, *op. cit.*, pp. 145, 156.
[49] *Leg. Hist. 1954 Act,* v. 1, p. 999.
[50] *Ibid.*, v. 3, p. 2983.
[51] AEC press release, Jan. 7, 1955.

nuclear power reactors" and offered to consider on a competitive basis proposals for AEC cooperation in privately financed power-reactor projects. Specifically it proposed to waive use charges for materials, to undertake certain mutually agreeable research and development in AEC laboratories, and to enter into fixed-sum research-and-development contracts for buying technical and economic data from the applicant. The fixed-sum commitment placed a ceiling on AEC participation, so that the economic risks of the project would be borne by private enterprise. The PDRP did not specify the types of reactor projects eligible for assistance, but did establish as one criterion the "probable contribution of the proposed project toward achieving economically competitive power."

In a statement on the five-year program submitted to the JCAE Subcommittee on Research and Development on April 29, 1955, the AEC set forth its theory of the roles of private enterprise and government in the atomic-energy field. Development of economically competitive nuclear power for civilian use, said the Commission, would be aided by maximum use of financial incentives and by industry's assumption of technical and economic risks. The Commission saw itself primarily in an auxiliary role, developing advanced technology at government expense and, at the same time, stimulating "outside groups to undertake developmental or demonstration power projects primarily with non-Commission financing." [52]

The first "202" hearings under the new act served as a forum for the AEC to explain its program and industry, labor, and other groups to comment. In general, industry remained optimistic, as did the AEC, but the Joint Committee was less sanguine. JCAE members of both parties questioned whether PDRP violated the no-subsidy provisions of Section 169 of the act.[53] A divided Committee finally adopted the interpretation [54] that the AEC could not enter into such research-and-development contracts until after the reactor had been constructed. Nevertheless, having pressed its view, the JCAE took no action to curb the AEC program, which remained unchanged.

Although Chairman Strauss characterized progress under the first year of the 1954 act as "most gratifying," [55] only four proposals were advanced under the PDRP. Furthermore, there was criticism that municipally owned utilities and rural electrical cooperatives were, in effect, barred from participation under the program, because they lacked access to the

---

[52] *Statement of AEC on Five-Year Reactor Program* (1955), p. 3.

[53] *"Sec. 202" Hearings* (1955), pp. 155-176. Section 169 of the Atomic Energy Act provides: "No funds of the Commission shall be employed in the construction or operation of facilities licensed under Section 103 or 104 except under contract or other arrangement entered into pursuant to Section 31." Section 31 deals with research assistance.

[54] S. Rep. No. 538, 84th Cong., 1st Sess. (1955), p. 7.

[55] *Forum Memo*, September 1955, p. 8.

substantial risk capital needed. Taking cognizance of this criticism, the AEC issued its second-round invitation under the PDRP in September, 1955. This time, it would consider requests for financing power reactors in whole or in part. The AEC would retain title to that portion which it financed. Seven proposals were submitted under the second round.

By early 1956, Democratic members of the JCAE were thoroughly dissatisfied with progress in the development of nuclear power. Their dissatisfaction was compounded by apprehension that the Soviet Union and United Kingdom were outstripping the United States in this field. In January, 1956, the McKinney Panel on the Impact of Peaceful Uses of Atomic Energy, appointed the previous year by Senator Anderson and consisting of prominent nongovernmental people, recommended that, if industry did not take the initiative in constructing full-scale demonstration plants, the AEC should support the program even to the extent of constructing full-scale plants for each major reactor type and size. AEC Commissioner Murray, a holdover from the pre-Eisenhower AEC, disagreed with the Commission's approach and urged a $1,000,000,000 program of reactor construction at home and abroad, with the government bearing the financial burden. He felt strongly that private industry alone, even with limited government assistance, could not meet the challenge.[56]

The Commission continued to insist that adequate progress was being made and denied that a new program was necessary. What was needed, in the Commission's view, was the elimination of certain roadblocks in the path of private development of nuclear power. One such roadblock was the possibility that the combination of utility companies working cooperatively on developing nuclear power might be considered a violation of the Public Utility Holding Company Act; another was the absence of any protection for industry against the potentially catastrophic financial liability which might result from a serious reactor accident—a liability far beyond the capacity of any insurance company to cover. Legislation to eliminate these roadblocks had been introduced and was largely noncontroversial. The JCAE Democrats believed, however, that it was not enough to eliminate obstacles; a vigorous new program was needed. Their apprehension and their desire for an accelerated program of government-financed reactors were reflected in the Gore-Holifield bill, which directed the AEC to construct six large-scale reactors in various parts of the country at a total cost of $400,000,000. The AEC regarded Gore-Holifield as fundamentally incompatible with its theories for developing nuclear power and gave as its reason for supporting private decision-making on reactor types and sizes,

---

[56] *Ibid.*, March 1956, p. 13.

> [the] belief that publicly, cooperatively, and privately owned utilities engaged in the sale of atomic energy and equipment manufacturers are in a much better position than the Commission . . . to assess the economics of particular reactor concepts and to determine which ones are in the stage of development where the construction of a prototype is a logical and appropriate step.[57]

To assist it in its deliberations, the JCAE retained as a special technical consultant Dr. Walter Zinn, a leading reactor specialist who had just resigned as director of the AEC's Argonne Laboratory. JCAE members agreed with Zinn that several reactor types besides those then under development by the AEC had considerable potential and should be developed.[58]

Much of the debate on Gore-Holifield involved differences of public policy and values, but the AEC raised one difficult factual question: could a $400,000,000 civilian power program be conducted without diverting technical personnel from vital national defense work? The AEC maintained that,

> . . . the enforced adoption of arbitrary goals of kilowatt capacity or numbers of full scale reactors for an early date, such as 1960, is unwise because it would divert scarce technical skills from activities which promise greater results in subsequent years.[59]

To meet this argument, the JCAE telegraphed forty-two potential contractors to ask whether, if Gore-Holifield were enacted, they had resources available for participation in the new program. Needless to say, there was overwhelming response from industry that it was well equipped to handle such an expanded program.[60]

The Gore-Holifield bill was ultimately reported by the JCAE without dissent, but it bore little resemblance to the bill originally introduced. In a desperate effort to win the support of the Executive—or at least to still its opposition—and achieve JCAE unanimity, Committee Democrats accepted a substantial weakening of the bill's provisions. Another device used by the JCAE Democrats, aided by the House and Senate majority leaders, was to hold the Public Utility Holding Company Act amendment and the Indemnity Bill as hostages; they would be enacted only if Gore-Holifield were. Their efforts were in vain. Although Gore-Holifield passed in the Senate, it was first watered down, then defeated, in the House.

The struggle was resumed in 1957. The AEC then recognized the

---

[57] *"Gore-Holifield" Civilian Power Hearings* (1956), pt. 1, p. 69.
[58] *Ibid.*, pp. 409, 76-77, 83 ff.
[59] *Ibid.*, p. 27.
[60] *Ibid.*, pp. 524 ff.

need for an accelerated program and issued a third-round invitation under the PDRP for construction of two specific reactors by industry with AEC research-and-development assistance. The AEC's invitation was coupled with the indication that it was prepared to initiate construction of these reactors as federal projects if industry could not do the job within the specified time. JCAE Democrats were still not satisfied, however.[61]

On April 16, 1957, Clarence Cannon, chairman of the House Appropriations Committee, took the House floor to assail the AEC and Chairman Strauss for allegedly illegal action, including the use of funds under the PDRP for civilian power projects which had not been authorized by Congress. Taking their cue from Cannon, JCAE members now discussed with the Commission the dilemma posed by his attitude: AEC appropriation bills would now be subject to Cannon's point of order unless AEC programs were authorized in a manner which he regarded as proper. Faced with this dilemma, the AEC agreed to a Joint Committee proposal for enactment of an amendment to the Cole-Hickenlooper act to bring the entire civilian reactor program within the scope of the authorization requirement. This amendment gave the JCAE great control over the entire civilian power program, especially the AEC's power-demonstration-reactor program. Acting under this new authority, the Joint Committee proceeded to report the AEC's authorizing legislation for fiscal year 1958 and served notice that it would attempt to accomplish in authorizing legislation what it had failed to gain in Gore-Holifield. The 1958 authorization bill, as reported, directed the AEC to construct a gas-cooled reactor and to study a plutonium production reactor and plutonium recycle reactor. These studies were obviously intended by the JCAE as a necessary preliminary to construction of the reactors. The bill also drastically changed the format of the second-round contracts then being negotiated by the AEC and made all forms of AEC assistance to private enterprise subject to JCAE review. In addition, the JCAE report, with sharp Republican dissent, gave the AEC detailed suggestions and instructions on implementing the provisions of the bill. The bill was passed by Congress, but only after it had been diluted by the same coalition that had defeated Gore-Holifield and bitterly opposed by the AEC, President Eisenhower, and Republican JCAE members. It was signed reluctantly by the President.

JCAE Chairman Durham now proposed that the JCAE and the AEC attempt to resolve their differences by agreeing on the objectives of the national atomic-energy program. He suggested informal discussions between representatives of both groups to explore areas of agreement and methods of cooperation.[62] There was a series of discussions and negotia-

---

[61] *"Sec. 202" Hearings* (1957), pp. 118-119, 30-36.

[62] Durham letter of Nov. 27, 1957, in JCAE press release, Dec. 2, 1957.

tions among the Commission, the Committee, and their staffs, and by December it was reported that the JCAE and the AEC, meeting behind closed doors, had agreed on policy objectives.

At the beginning of the 1958 "202" hearings, the scheduled AEC report on civilian power was postponed because of Chairman Durham's hope that the AEC-JCAE negotiations would enable the Commission "to come forward with a more definite atomic-power program, both foreign and domestic." This objective was not realized; the AEC merely filed a status report, "Power Reactor Program in Early 1958." [63] After the conclusion of these hearings, the JCAE showed how it would exercise its new responsibilities for reviewing proposed AEC agreements under the PDRP. It had been evident in the hearings that the JCAE did not envision a passive role for itself. For example, prodding by Senator Anderson had resulted in modification of the patent provisions of a proposed arrangement with one private firm.[64] Still not satisfied, Anderson later introduced a Senate concurrent resolution opposing the proposal, which was eventually withdrawn by the AEC.

The 1958 authorization hearings were, to a large extent, directed against the limitations placed on the AEC's nuclear-power program by the Bureau of the Budget. By this time, it was apparent that the AEC recognized the authority and power of the JCAE and, for its part, was cooperating with the Joint Committee. Thus the JCAE concentrated its attack on the "dominant role assumed by the Bureau of the Budget." Ignoring the limitations imposed by the Budget Bureau, the JCAE reported a bill authorizing all the projects which the AEC had requested and added funds for design studies of four additional reactors, including two that had been turned down by the Bureau of the Budget in the AEC's original request. The major addition was the plutonium production reactor which the Commission had studied in accord with the directive in the 1957 authorization act. On the basis of this study, the AEC had recommended that construction of this reactor be included in the fiscal 1959 budget, but it was eliminated by the Budget Bureau. As reported out by the JCAE, the reactor would be designed so that it also could be easily converted to produce power. With the Joint Committee solidly in support of the authorization bill, it passed the House easily and, in the Senate, survived an attack by the President, who claimed that the plutonium reactor was not needed to meet military needs.

The principal efforts of the JCAE for the next several years were directed toward attaining agreement with the AEC on long-range policy. Prospects for agreement seemed to be heightened in June, 1958, with the

---

[63] *"Sec. 202" Hearings* (1958), pp. 3, 569.

[64] *PDRP Proposal Hearings* (1958), p. 98.

departure of AEC Chairman Strauss. His successor, John McCone, was welcomed by the JCAE with assurances that the past would be forgotten.

The first step in arriving at a mutually acceptable policy was the Commission's presentation, during the fiscal year 1959 authorization hearings, of a long-range reactor program and proposals for specific projects for the next five years. The AEC's objective was the achievement of competitive power in the United States within ten years and in friendly foreign nations within five years. Regarding the AEC's policy statement as a tentative proposal, the JCAE instructed its staff, assisted by unofficial consultants, to prepare a draft long-range program of its own. The JCAE staff called for a program which would demonstrate economic nuclear power in the United States by 1970 and in "high-cost" foreign nations (nations where conventional electricity is expensive) by 1968 and urged more government participation in the form of government construction of advanced prototype plants and "other desirable plants not otherwise proceeding." It also urged an "expanded and modified" PDRP for privately owned "second-generation" plants. The staff program received the personal endorsement of Chairman Durham and Vice-Chairman Anderson, but was not formally reviewed by the full JCAE.[65]

The AEC responded by creating an *ad hoc* advisory committee, chaired by former Commissioner Smyth, who had recently participated in the JCAE staff study. This committee was to reassess the AEC position on the reactor program, taking into consideration the earlier AEC statement and the JCAE staff memorandum. Meanwhile, in late 1958, the AEC took further action to meet JCAE criticism of PDRP by modifying its procedures under the third round so that proposals from industry had to be responsive to the reactor projects which the Commission considered desirable. This modification took cognizance of a policy stated by the Joint Committee in the AEC authorization act for fiscal year 1959 and represented a reversal of AEC's previous policy, which permitted industry to take the initiative in deciding the type and size of reactor to be built under PDRP.[66]

The Smyth committee reported in January, 1959, that its objective was the attainment of competitive nuclear power in some areas of the United States within ten years and in friendly foreign nations in fewer than ten years. It differed from the JCAE staff memorandum in that it placed greater emphasis on prototype plants than on large-scale plants and did not agree that the AEC should construct large-scale plants if private

[65] JCAE press release, Aug. 25, 1958; *Staff Study on Expanded Civilian Power Program* (1958).

[66] *Forum Memo,* December 1958, p. 3; AEC press release, Nov. 17, 1958.

or public utilities failed to make satisfactory proposals. The Smyth committee said,

> The attitude of our committee would be that the absence of a proposal was prima facie evidence that the time had not yet come to build a large-scale plant of the particular type proposed. . . .[67]

As for prototype construction, the panel acknowledged the possibility of AEC construction and ownership, but favored private financing and ownership.

Later that month, Senator Anderson again assumed the chairmanship of the JCAE and continued the conciliatory efforts of the past half year by noting the general areas of agreement between the AEC and the JCAE, despite their differences of opinion as to methods.[68] AEC Chairman McCone was also conciliatory when he presented the AEC's nuclear-power program at the 1959 "202" hearings. He promised vigorous leadership in building experimental reactors on AEC sites. The policy of inviting industry to build specified reactor prototypes would be continued, but the AEC would construct these reactors if it did not receive suitable industry proposals. One innovation in the AEC proposals was McCone's suggestion —evidently a trial balloon—that the AEC might offer assistance of up to 50 per cent of the capital costs of reactor prototypes built by industry. The JCAE showed little enthusiasm for this suggestion and was generally critical of the AEC's progress in the power reactor field since 1954. In general, it seemed that the McCone honeymoon might be nearing its end.[69]

The authorization hearings for fiscal year 1960 commenced with the JCAE in full control. Its role was summarized by Senator Anderson in these terms:

> Now I am sure AEC believes that [the civilian atomic-power] program was a good one for fiscal 1960, especially in view of the general executive budgetary situation. We want to give them credit for good intentions. But it is the job of the Joint Committee and the Congress to see whether it is adequate to meet the objectives of achieving economic power which AEC and the Joint Committee are agreed upon.[70]

In reporting the authorizing bill, the JCAE rejected the AEC's suggestion for a capital-assistance program, saying that it required "further study." On the positive side, it added $16,000,000 to the AEC request for PDRP, supplementing the third round and reinstituting and supplementing the

[67] *"Sec. 202" Hearings* (1959), pp. 510, 533, 535.
[68] JCAE press release, Jan. 30, 1959.
[69] *"Sec. 202" Hearings* (1959), pp. 38 ff., 105 ff., 40-42, 45-47, 100-102.
[70] JCAE press release, Feb. 26, 1959.

second round (which the AEC had wanted to abandon) in order to provide two reactor prototypes. It continued its scrutiny of administrative activities by placing a private industry proposal for a gas-cooled reactor project under third-round ground rules, with detailed provisions on reimbursement in case the project was discontinued.[71] With unanimous JCAE support, the authorization bill sailed easily through Congress.

The AEC's detailed ten-year program was finally unveiled at the 1960 "202" hearings. It called for AEC construction of specified reactor types, including experiments and, possibly, prototypes, but left to industry the primary responsibility for constructing large-scale commercial power plants. The capital-assistance proposal of the previous year was not mentioned. The new program evoked little comment from JCAE members during the "202" hearings, although it was termed a "milestone in Commission planning." Nevertheless, some members showed concern over certain aspects, such as the "big gap in prototype construction with no starts from now until fiscal 1962." Anderson asked, "What is going to happen to our atomic equipment industry during this two and a half year period?" [72]

In reporting the AEC's authorization legislation for fiscal year 1961, the JCAE praised the new ten-year power program, but expressed displeasure at the fact that no new AEC prototype projects were proposed for that fiscal year. Furthermore, it questioned whether the proposed program was adequate for power plants in the small- and medium-sized range and whether the expense and pace of the effort were commensurate with reaching stated goals.[73] The AEC authorization request for PDRP, however, was met in full by the JCAE.

The year 1960 witnessed the re-emergence as a controversial issue of the Hanford reactor, which had been started as a plutonium production reactor, convertible into a dual-purpose reactor. In preparation for a decision on whether the reactor could be converted economically to produce power, a series of studies on its economic feasibility had been undertaken. The first study, made by Stone and Webster Engineering Company in 1958 at the request of the AEC, concluded that the dual-purpose reactor was not economical. Anderson strenuously contested the validity of this study, claiming that:

> They have reversed the assumptions used by the Congress. . . . We squared away for a fight, but I have talked . . . to Mr. McCone and I believe he takes a more reasonable attitude than Stone and Webster did.[74]

---

[71] H.R. Rep. No. 529, 86th Cong., 1st Sess. (1959).
[72] *"Sec. 202" Hearings* (1960), pp. 2 ff.
[73] S. Rep. No. 1277, 86th Cong., 2d Sess. (1960).
[74] *Forum Memo,* April 1959, p. 30.

Then, in February, 1960, the Federal Power Commission submitted a report, which had been requested by the AEC, concluding that, assuming certain costs for plant financing and uranium and plutonium, conversion of the plant would be economical. A third report, made especially for the JCAE by the private firm of R. W. Beck and Associates, indicated that the economic basis on which the Hanford reactor had been authorized was still sound. Finally, in February, 1961, the Federal Power Commission released still another study. With this accumulation of reports, based on varying assumptions, the scene was set for the 1961 debates.

The last Eisenhower atomic-energy budget, which was based on the ten-year power program submitted by the AEC in 1960, was revised by the Kennedy administration to include authorization for converting the Hanford reactor.[75] In May and June, the JCAE held hearings on converting the Hanford reactor, with the AEC fully supporting the proposal. The authorization bill reported by the Joint Committee on June 21 authorized $95,000,000 for the addition of electric generating facilities in excess of the direct power needs at the Hanford installation. Again, however, Committee unanimity was shattered by the public-power issue, and five of the eight Republican members vigorously dissented, attacking the economics and purposes of the project.[76] Essentially the same coalition that had defeated Gore-Holifield eliminated the Hanford reactor from the authorization bill. The Senate, however, accepted the JCAE majority position, and, in a move designed to weaken the opposition of senators and representatives from coal-producing areas, amended the bill to authorize the use of $5,000,000 for study and development of "nuclear processes which have application for improving and utilizing coal and coal products. . . ." The House was not placated. Because the majority of the JCAE favored the Hanford project, House opponents feared it would be restored by a conference committee and presented to the House on a "take-it-or-leave-it" basis. To avoid this dilemma, the House approved, 235 to 164, a motion instructing its conferrees not to agree to the project.[77] Nevertheless, the House conferrees found a way around this obstacle. The conference committee retained the amendment calling for research on coal uses, but

[75] Although the Kennedy budget added an authorization request for the conversion of the Hanford reactor, the administration presented no new policies for the civilian nuclear-power program. AEC Chairman Seaborg informed the Joint Committee that the AEC was studying various types of incentives for encouraging nuclear-power development, but JCAE members pressed the Commission to receive a clear-cut presidential statement on the importance of the program. *FY 1962 Authorization Hearings* (1961), pp. 166-169.

[76] S. Rep. No. 441, 87th Cong., 1st Sess. (1961).

[77] *Cong. Rec.* (daily ed., July 13, 1961), 11583; (daily ed., July 18, 1961), 11058; (daily ed., Aug. 8, 1961), 13896, 13908. In introducing the conference report, Holifield asked unanimous consent for the "Committee on Atomic Energy" rather than for the conference committee. *Ibid.* (daily ed., Aug. 31, 1961), 16728.

reduced the electric generating facilities proposed for the Hanford reactor.[78] Under the new formula, the generating capacity of the reactor would be limited to that used exclusively in operation of the AEC's Hanford facilities. This solution was intended to eliminate the distribution of power as originally contemplated, thereby countering the objections to "public-power favoritism." However, the conferrees' attempt to meet House opposition failed, for the Senate adopted the conference report, but the House once more—by a larger vote—rejected the electric generating facilities for the Hanford reactor.[79]

During the latter months of 1961, the AEC continued to wrestle with the problem of civilian nuclear power and apparently reached the conclusion that no drastic changes in the existing program were warranted. On January 19, 1962, the Commission transmitted to Congress its proposed authorizing legislation for fiscal year 1963. The AEC's authorization request did not include any new starts on prototype nuclear-power plants or additional funds for the power-demonstration-reactor program.

The annual "202" hearings convened in mid-March against a backdrop of JCAE dissatisfaction with the administration's approach to nuclear-power development. This dissatisfaction was heightened by the White House's release, the day before the hearings commenced, of an exchange of letters between President Kennedy and AEC Chairman Seaborg. The President's letter to Dr. Seaborg directed the AEC, in cooperation with the Department of the Interior, the Federal Power Commission, other appropriate agencies, and private industry, to "take a new and hard look at the role of nuclear power in our economy." The purpose of the study requested by the President was to identify the objective, scope, and content of a nuclear-power program in the light of the nation's over-all energy needs and to recommend proper steps to assure correct timing of various phases of the program.

Replying to the President's letter, Dr. Seaborg stated that the Commission accepted the President's assignment "with enthusiasm" and would coordinate its study with concurrent studies which, he understood, were contemplated by the Joint Committee. Democratic members of the JCAE assailed the new study as completely unnecessary, a deliberate tactic to delay confronting the nuclear-power situation. JCAE Chairman Holifield urged consideration of new nuclear-power projects taking into account the possibility of using larger nuclear plants as components of regional interconnections of power systems utilizing higher-voltage lines. He urged the AEC to include in the authorizing legislation, as a minimum, several

---

[78] H.R. Rep. No. 1101, 87th Cong., 1st Sess. (1961), reprinted in *Cong. Rec.* (daily ed., Aug. 31, 1961), 16728-16732.

[79] *Ibid.* (daily ed., Sept. 2, 1961), 16925-16928.

design and development studies on promising prototypes and proposed that the AEC and JCAE staffs meet to outline such a program for consideration by the Commission and the Committee. In addition, adopting a somewhat novel technique of bending the Commission to the JCAE's wishes, Holifield indicated that the AEC's proposed authorizing bill should be amended to include adequate provision for nuclear-power projects prior to its introduction and public consideration. In effect, Holifield served the AEC with an ultimatum that no authorization bill would be introduced by any member of the JCAE until the executive branch itself amended the bill to make it more palatable to the Committee. On May 14, the AEC transmitted the revised bill, which contained more satisfactory civilian nuclear-power provisions. As finally submitted by the AEC, the bill included provision for one prototype reactor and funds for several development and design studies on reactor concepts which might be authorized for 1964. In addition, the Commission proposed that the third-round power-demonstration-reactor program be modified to permit the Commission to provide industry with design assistance as well as research-and-development assistance and waiver of use charges.

The suggestion that the additional incentive of design assistance be offered industry was originally made by Seaborg in his testimony before the Committee at the "202" hearings in March. Initially, the proposal was coolly received by the Committee, which requested the AEC to prepare a study of all subsidies available to industry. By May, 1962, however, JCAE Democrats were apparently won over to design assistance, perhaps as part of a compromise with Committee Republicans. Indeed, the authorizing legislation, as ultimately reported by the Committee and passed by Congress, increased the funds for design-assistance incentive. The Committee, with only one dissent, also supported a new approach to the conversion of energy from the Hanford reactor. After an initial defeat on the House floor of the Hanford provision in the fiscal year 1963 authorization bill, the JCAE in conference formulated a compromise which was finally accepted. Although the Committee did not achieve precisely the civilian power program the Democratic majority wanted in 1962, by persevering it did get more than the administration had originally requested and the House had originally been willing to accept.

VIII | The Integration of Powers

The Joint Committee on Atomic Energy is, in terms of its sustained influence in Congress, its impact and influence on the Executive, and its accomplishments, probably the most powerful Congressional committee in the history of the nation. There can be little doubt that, had Congress chosen to deal with atomic energy through conventional Congressional committees, the history of the atomic-energy program would have been quite different. Almost certainly, the national investment in atomic energy would have been substantially less and the present level of technology considerably lower.

Creation of the JCAE should be considered in the context of the effort made by Congress at about the same time to strengthen its position vis-à-vis the executive branch by enacting the Legislative Reorganization Act of 1946. Although Congress had grown in size since the early nineteenth century as more states were admitted to the Union, it remained relatively stable in its structure and in the way it transacted its business. On the other hand, the complexity of twentieth-century government in the domestic, military, and international spheres had brought about a vast expansion of the personnel, budget, and functions of the executive bureaucracy. To an ever-increasing extent, Congress, in playing its constitutional role, became dependent on executive leadership. National policy was conceived and initiated by the president and his departments and agencies; the Executive proposed, and Congress disposed. Even standing committees, as specialized agents of Congress, found it increasingly difficult, because of limited time and technical competence, to operate independently and effectively. The role of Congress became primarily one of curbing the Executive and modifying its programs. The Legislative Reorganization Act represented an attempt to increase the influence of Congress by streamlining its organization, enlarging its staff, and providing additional resources.

But, even while these reforms were being undertaken, the advent of atomic energy generated new and more difficult problems of government. How could Congress maintain its position and deal effectively with a vital national security program requiring secrecy, involving highly esoteric technical data at the frontiers of scientific knowledge, and necessitating considerable urgency and flexibility? The solution was the creation of the JCAE. Although it was recognized that the JCAE would have to possess unusual powers to accomplish its mission, it is highly doubtful that anyone in 1946 visualized the manner in which the Committee would actually develop.

There can be no doubt that, in establishing the JCAE, Congress devised a powerful counterbalance to executive dominion. In its comparatively brief history, the Committee has developed distinctive techniques for exercising control of the nation's atomic-energy program. Its impact on executive operations has been significant in the following respects:

1. By its skillful employment of statutory powers, the JCAE has made severe and unprecedented inroads on the doctrine of executive privilege. Particularly with respect to the Atomic Energy Commission, the doctrine of executive privilege has come to be almost meaningless. This should not be attributed solely to JCAE encroachment on the executive branch's position; it represents, at least equally, successive abdication by the Executive and deferral to JCAE power.

2. The JCAE's comprehensive access to information and its insistence on obtaining information while matters are pending have given it the opportunity to participate in the Executive's formulation of policies and implementation of programs. The Committee has seldom been reluctant to make recommendations to the Executive and to apply pressure for their adoption. The executive branch, especially the AEC, has in many instances been unusually responsive to such Committee pressures.[1]

---

[1] A recent example is the Commission's decision, resulting from JCAE pressure, to reclassify information concerning the Satellite Nuclear Auxiliary Power program (SNAP), thereby reversing its previous trend toward declassification of this area. *Nucleonics,* XIX (July 1961), 30.

3. The JCAE exerts its influence largely through continuous participation in the Executive's deliberations, rather than by legislating. In this respect, its role appears to have been more administrative than legislative. Indeed, on some occasions when the Committee has involved itself within the executive framework on decisions of national policy, it has operated in a manner analogous to that of the Bureau of the Budget or the president himself.

4. In its support for programs which it deems vital to the national interest, the Committee has steadfastly disregarded the procedures for coordination and control employed by the executive branch. With scant respect for the formal structure of command, the JCAE has encouraged and abetted officials at all levels of the executive branch in order to accomplish Committee objectives.

5. The JCAE has refused to recognize the validity of budgetary ceilings which rule out otherwise desirable programs. Instead, it has made its own determination of essential projects and devoted its energies to bringing them to fruition. In this respect, it is unlike other Congressional committees, which are usually concerned with holding down federal expenditure.

The JCAE is, therefore, not merely a legislative mechanism, but also a coparticipant in executive decision-making. It attempts to shape the organization of the AEC's subordinate divisions, where programs are initiated. It seeks to persuade these divisions, on which the Commission relies for expert advice and recommendations, to propose Committee-sponsored projects. Whether or not these projects are recommended from below, the JCAE tries to convince the Commission, the Bureau of the Budget, and the president that they should be adopted. If a decision is made by executive officials, at whatever level of authority, that the projects are undesirable, the Committee often persists in a campaign to reverse the decision. In some cases where the Executive has postponed or rejected such projects on budgetary or other grounds, the Committee has written them into the AEC's authorization legislation. The result is, according to one JCAE member, that "work the Commission should be doing" (presumably setting policy, among other things) has been allowed "to drift into the hands of higher echelons"—the Joint Committee.[2]

The Committee's approach has had significant procedural consequences for the operation of the executive branch. Over the years, the executive branch, with the encouragement of Congress, has evolved techniques intended to bring about efficient, economic, and effective conduct

[2] Rep. Craig Hosmer, letter to President Kennedy, April 8, 1962, reprinted in *Cong. Rec.* (daily ed., Apr. 12, 1962), 5979.

of the government's affairs. Heads of departments and agencies are appointed by the president. They are in considerable degree subject to his direct control, except perhaps in the case of the independent regulatory commissions, where control is exercised largely in an indirect manner through the budget and appointments. Policies are generally developed under some form of presidential supervision. When two or more agencies have an interest in a matter, procedures exist for coordinating their interests and ironing out differences at a higher level. Agencies are permitted to submit legislative proposals to Congress or to comment on proposed legislation only after review by the Bureau of the Budget to assure that what is done is consistent with the legislative program of the president. Ultimate control rests in the budgetary process, where each agency justifies its requests for funds; and the Bureau of the Budget, on behalf of the president, considers each request within the context of the over-all policy and budget of the administration.

No one could seriously doubt that some such system for discipline and coordination by the president is necessary. On the other hand, the system has imperfections and rigidities. The processes of administration are by no means as orderly as the president might wish. The executive branch, as well as its component parts, is continuously beset by competing points of view, internal conflicts, and informal pressures to influence decisions. It is by no means unprecedented for Congressional committees to take sides with one or another party to these controversies. Yet, the institutionalization of committee intrusion, as in the case of the JCAE, creates additional problems of administrative control. Here, conflict, instead of being subject to hierarchical control, is resolved primarily through outside influences. The fact that a key participant in the internal processes of the executive branch is beyond either formal or informal discipline unsettles bureaucratic routine. Although the Joint Committee's role undoubtedly gives rise to administrative disorder, it also prevents rigidity and complacency and probably generates greater resourcefulness and imagination.

The impact of JCAE involvement in technical decisions must also be considered. It is well recognized that the function of Congress is to establish national policy and to chart the course to be taken by the Executive in implementation of that policy. At the same time, Congress is essentially a political body and possesses little in the way of specialized technical skills which are, today more than ever, necessary for intelligent decisions. In order that the needed technical judgments could be made and the requisite flexibility attained, Congress has found it necessary to delegate increasing responsibility for policy-making to the Executive. Unprecedented responsibility has, therefore, been delegated to the Executive in the atomic-energy field; nevertheless, the JCAE has carved out for itself a substantial policy-making role. Since atomic-energy policy is based on highly technical judgments, the Committee necessarily becomes involved in the details of specific projects. Often, its judgments on highly technical questions have differed from those made by the officials and experts charged with responsibility for the atomic-energy program. Committee review of technical questions is obviously a useful function from the standpoint of sound policy formulation. But the fact that the national interest presumably requires the JCAE, a political body of eighteen men devoting only part time to atomic energy, to substitute its judgment for that of the Executive, with its vast resources, raises considerable doubt about the adequacy of governmental machinery for resolving important technical questions and reaching policy decisions.

Although the JCAE often exercises decisive influence in the formulation of national policy through its involvement in executive processes, it is by no means clear that it bears commensurate responsibility. Obviously, the Committee is not accountable to the president or to any other executive official. To the extent that the Committee influences executive decisions, it brings about decisions for which the executive officials, rather than the Committee, must bear responsibility to their superiors, Congress, the public, and the JCAE itself. If the JCAE is responsible for its activities and its influence to any other governmental body, it must be to Congress.

Although the Committee has been able to systematically participate in and review the operations of the executive branch, its own performance has by no means been subject to comparable Congressional scrutiny. The behavior of the JCAE differs from that of other legislative committees, and the relationship which has developed between the JCAE and Congress is characterized by a number of significant elements:

1. Congress does much of its work through committees and has in fact delegated many of its functions to committees, but the delegation of Congressional power to the JCAE is of a somewhat distinctive quality.

2. Members of Congress are somewhat more inclined to rely on the judgment of the JCAE than on that of other committees.

3. Although comprehension of complicated subjects is usually heavily concentrated in the cognizant committees, other members of Congress frequently have broad knowledge of, and strong interest in, these subjects. However, relatively few other members of Congress appear to have either a high degree of knowledge about, or a strong interest in, the atomic-energy program.

4. The structure of the Joint Committee tends to preclude wide Congressional involvement in atomic-energy affairs. Whereas the typical legislative committees of the Senate and the House have fifteen to seventeen and thirty to thirty-seven members, respectively, the JCAE consists of only nine members of each chamber. Congressional know-how in atomic

energy, therefore, is much more closely held than in the case of other subjects.[3]

5. The use of a joint committee rather than a House and a Senate committee to consider legislation necessarily limits the extent to which important issues are subject to Congressional scrutiny. Instead of two versions of a bill—one from a House committee and one from a Senate committee—only one version of atomic-energy legislation emerges from committee consideration. In addition, there is no second committee to which an appeal may be taken by interested parties who are not satisfied with the legislation as reported. Thus, Congress is presented with less opportunity for choice among alternative ideas.

6. The area and extent of public and Congressional debate on, and examination of, legislative issues are further reduced by the manner in which atomic-energy bills are handled. Becoming involved at an early stage in the formulation of legislative proposals by the Executive, the JCAE makes strenuous efforts to resolve all problems and to achieve consensus within the Committee and between the Committee and the executive branch. The objective is that of presenting a united front to Congress. There is a tendency, therefore, for many important policy questions to be decided in effect by negotiation between the JCAE and the Executive, rather than through the processes of public discussion and Congressional debate. The executive branch has generally acquiesced or participated in this procedure—reluctantly, in some cases, because it recognized the futility of fighting the JCAE on the House and Senate floors; willingly, in other cases, because it recognized the expediency of avoiding expansion of the area of debate.

7. Although the JCAE has had strong views on many policy issues in the atomic-energy program, it has not since the 1954 act sought to gain acceptance of its views through enactment of substantive legislation. To the extent that the JCAE has used legislation to influence the direction of the national atomic-energy program, it has relied on the process of authorizing legislation. Since 1957, the JCAE has made unique use of such legislation to initiate projects which the Executive had opposed. In some instances, basic national policy has been involved, but authorizing legislation does not appear to be the most satisfactory vehicle for the resolution of such policy questions.

8. The extent to which Congress follows the JCAE's leadership

[3] In 1951, Rep. Eugene McCarthy (D., Minn.), who was not a member of the JCAE, introduced a bill calling for rotation of House members of the JCAE. Pointing out that very few members of Congress "have any certain knowledge" of either atomic-energy program or policy, he proposed this new device to provide a means whereby more members of the House "may become responsibly informed." *Ibid.*, 97 (Oct. 19, 1951), 13651-13652.

depends on whether the JCAE in fact provides what Congress regards as leadership. When the Committee is substantially united on a matter (other than jurisdictional disputes or appropriations), Congress almost invariably follows its lead, even when the administration is strongly opposed. When the Committee is divided—which has occurred only on domestic issues involving conflicts of political and economic ideology—it loses its influence, and Congress must decide for itself.

9. When Congress as a whole has been called upon to act on substantive, authorizing, or appropriations legislation, it has been able to act much more knowledgeably and effectively as a result of the JCAE's role. But on most occasions the JCAE has been united, and differences with the executive branch have been resolved prior to floor debate, so that Congress acted without giving much attention to the policy implications. This has facilitated expeditious passage of atomic-energy bills and probably resulted in more efficient Congressional procedures. At the same time, there has been a diminution of Congressional responsibility for atomic-energy legislation.

10. To the extent that the JCAE has relied on means other than legislation to influence policy, it has been largely autonomous, exempt from Congressional control and from direct accountability to Congress.

It must be concluded, therefore, that the JCAE has been functionally independent, although it is structurally an integral part of Congress. Indeed, its effectiveness seems to be based in large part on its semiautonomous, quasiadministrative role. If Congress has, through the JCAE, enhanced its own position, it has done so by creating a legislative-administrative hybrid whose operation has taken away from the Executive far more than it has given Congress.

Congress has generally regarded the Joint Committee on Atomic Energy as a successful legislative mechanism. Nevertheless, it has been little disposed to create similar bodies. Although there have been several recent proposals for creation of joint committees, only two of these have received serious consideration, and neither has been adopted. A resolution for a House-Senate committee to oversee the Central Intelligence Agency was defeated on the Senate floor in 1956, despite the fact that thirty-six senators joined in sponsoring it. Another proposal, to establish a joint committee to oversee the space program, was rejected in 1958, largely because the speaker of the House felt the device to be inconsistent with the bicameral structure of Congress.

Congressional reluctance to adopt the JCAE model in other areas largely reflects an adherence to the tradition of bicameralism. But unicameralism is not the major departure from tradition represented by the JCAE. The essence of the Joint Committee on Atomic Energy is its positive sense of mission. It has a "philosophy" of atomic energy, it has definite objectives, and it has a program. Unlike other Congressional committees, which tend to respond to problems as they arise, the JCAE actively and persistently strives to have its philosophy accepted, its objectives approved, and its program carried out.

It is too early to predict whether this departure from tradition is a passing phenomenon, whether the Joint Committee will act in the future as it has in the past, and whether its form will be adapted for use in other areas of government. Nevertheless, its experience to date provides an intriguing and useful background for the testing and re-evaluation of many long-standing principles of government.

Index

H

I

J

K

L

M

N

T

U

V

W

Y

Z